The Illusion
of History

The Illusion
of History

Time and the Radical Political Imagination

Andrew R. Russ

The Catholic University of America Press
Washington, D.C.

Design and typesetting by Kachergis Book Design.

Library of Congress Cataloging-in-Publication Data
Russ, Andrew R., 1979–
The illusion of history : time and the radical political imagination / Andrew R. Russ.
p. cm.
Includes bibliographical references and index.
ISBN 978-0-8132-2005-5 (cloth : alk. paper)
1. Political science—Europe—History.   2. Rousseau, Jean-Jacques, 1712–1778—
Political and social views.   3. Marx, Karl, 1818–1883—Political and social views.
4. Foucault, Michel, 1926–1984   Political and social views.   I. Title.
JA84.E9R69 2012
320.092′24—dc23   2012023289

Contents

⟊ Introduction

Rousseau, Marx, and Foucault: Three Phases of the Radical Imagination

Radicalism in politics is a perennial presence. A niggling awareness that societal relations must change, that existing affairs are onerous, incompetent, or evidently soul-destroying, has stalked human societies ever since we have become conscious of the need to organize our collective interactions. As the colors of our societies change, so too do the guises of their radical comprehension and transfiguration. The radical imagination dons all apparels; utopians, scientists, aestheticians, historians, realists, and idealists have all transacted in the radical view of political life and used these divergent perceptions of the world to further radical political claims. Each political context through history will unwittingly summon the most appropriate character to shout and push for its downfall, and so the radical political imagination moves multifariously over time, accommodating itself to its particular hour. Not only are its aims squarely concentrated upon a furious need for change, but change itself seems to be its defining attribute. Its very permanence belies its shifting nature. The radical position seems to say, "despite my ubiquity I will not be easily framed and understood with stiff perennial abstractions; no truncated concept will account for my natural desire for change; I am the force that breaks the inertia of time and drives history forward." It is this drive that regularly transforms our social world and that has been responsible for so much of the indisputable political progress and social development of modern Western societies over the last few centuries. As opposed to that other side of the political spectrum, conservatism, with its desire for preservation, stability, resolution, and incontestable order, radicalism at least understands the reality and necessity of change, overthrow, and demolition, does it not? Surely it expects and celebrates the historicity and temporality of social forms? Surely it trumps its political rival with its insistent commitment to change and revolution by thus being closer to the primary spirit of politics as flux?

But what if the reverse were true? That the radical imagination springs from a perpetual and timeless source; that its insistence that the world is unstable and fluctuating only pushes it to ground its worldview more deeply in the eternal. That the outward celebration of change masks a deeper despair of its omniscient presence. What if the radical political imagination's assumed devotion to constant transformation is in fact the surface epiphenomenon of a more amaranthine concern? And what, too, if the increased prevalence, popularity, successes, and general assent given to the radical political perspective in modern Western culture have in fact contributed to the fortifying of its abstract and ahistorical foundations? Today, do radical political desires stem from the contingent, historical needs of a community, or can a timeless, ideological structure be discerned to be the cradle from which these drives are generated? And has an abstract ideological architecture become stronger as the radical's calls for change become more sophisticated? This study is a look at what the radical political imagination is attempting to instill: change for change's sake or the hope for an unchanging reality. Ultimately this book will uncover that the radical mindset's primary desire is for a changeless reality that arrests history and time, but that the illusory and unsustainable nature of this vision forces it into a secondary and contradictory effusiveness for change and unceasing historical succession.

To do this I will interpret a passage of thought spanning the political undertakings of Rousseau, Marx, and Foucault, viewed as representative of three historical phases of the radical political imagination. It is an attempt to uncover the elemental, yet inventive rationale behind their work. Hopefully this will go some way to examine, the power, influence, and inevitability, as much as the dilemmas and intemperance, of their thought. At first glance, their connection is as obvious as it can be tenuous. One can uncomplicatedly note their collective intention of social discontent and longing for social retransformation. But the time frame between these thinkers spans over 230 years, making the assumption of an uncomplicated coherence connecting their projects a risky enterprise. Therefore, the aim of this book is not to simply examine these thinkers from this overly extensive angle of social dissatisfaction and desire for radical alteration of society (an approach far too broad and general to be intellectually useful within such a time frame), but instead to animate this overt intention with reference to an underlying logic that channels it. This common feature can be properly stated as the timelessness of the radical political project.

Timelessness is here understood with regard to a moral and philosophical sense that pervades these thinkers' projects, inasmuch as they all invoke a morality that is philosophically designed to transcend the historico-temporal realm. It is a timelessness that walks hand in hand amid these thinkers' primary concern with freedom. Freedom, for them, is understood primarily to exist in separation from the contingencies of history and time, and yet to be the precondition for a morality that they believe should be imposed upon time and history. Here lies the contradiction that animates these projects' social dissatisfaction.

With these thinkers we have the opportunity to dissect a political consciousness that is captivated by an intellectual cleavage. This cleavage is with differing degrees based around a dualism that separates nature from culture, determinism from freedom, reason from experience, and science from morality. The most formal and sophisticated extrapolation of this problem was supplied by Immanuel Kant, who, taking his cue from Rousseau, upheld an immaterial concept of the free moral will as the transcendent source of moral and political directives. The seat of man's duty and the prescriptions for what he ought to do are to be found within himself and not embedded in the world, history, or society. The transcendence that characterizes this equating of freedom, morality, and the will constitutes the timeless and ahistorical nature that this study will assign to the radical political imagination. This problematic, and its fundamental connection with Kant, will be examined later in this introduction and further in the conclusion.

The adoption (both conscious and unconscious) of this problematic by Rousseau, Marx, and Foucault displays a range of functional peculiarities that will also be explored in depth. Primary among these will be the various ways in which the timeless appropriates history to give temporal form to its dictates. It will be shown that the timelessness in the thought of these thinkers seeks out historical and temporal expression, but in so doing, cultivates illusory visions of, and standards for, history. Furthermore, this need of timeless freedom manifests itself in these thinkers each favoring one direction of time exclusively over the others. Thus it will be shown that Rousseau's philosophy has a predilection for the past, while Marx's preference is for the future, and that Foucault's is predominantly concerned with the present. This will be the contention behind discussions of Rousseau's prehistoric state of Nature, Marx's post-historic postulation of Communism, and Foucault's present-centered modernity. The exclusivity of a past, a present, or a future by these thinkers with regard to time comprises the basis of their respective illusions of history. Paradoxically, it will be demonstrated that these distinctive visions of history are simply various privileged attempts by the timeless mind to transcend or annul history.

The other theoretical peculiarity of the timeless worldview with which this study will engage is the despairing attitude toward institutions by these thinkers. Their abstract desire to go beyond or withdraw from history manifests itself in a corresponding concrete desire to overcome the limitations inherent in institutions, tradition, and custom. As such, all three prescribe solutions to political, economic, and social problems that entail an extreme surmounting of institutions. They all also recommend ways of life and political regimes that emerge, first, as institutionally void, and second, as political recommendations that history cannot realistically establish. This disdain for the necessary limitation that institutions and history impress upon our endeavors is the negative background to their ambiguous and illusory histories.

The converse of this negative attitude to institutions, tradition, and custom is the radical political imagination's positive regard for the individual. In inverse proportion to its low opinion of institutions, there is an inflated belief in the power and possibility of the singular individual abstracted from his social and historical environment. This positive concern of its philosophies is significantly connected to the previously outlined status of institutions in its thought. Concern about the imposition of alienation, brought about by institutions, are vigorously responded to with the postulation of a new goal of wholeness and unity within the individual to combat the extreme division fostered by those institutions. All three thinkers will be shown to have summoned some form of this timeless and a priori conception of the human being as a cornerstone of their political imagination. Rousseau expands the power and rights of the "individual will" into his political conception of the "General Will." He also devises the singular and powerful conception of the "legislator," designed to bring this political state to fruition. Marx greatly expands the power of the individual in order to divine the historical hour of the coming of Communism, allowing his Marxian "scientist" a privileged position with regard to the process of history. It will also be shown that his most idealistic hopes for Communism are based upon an expanded sense of the possibilities contained in the individual. And Foucault's definitive sense of ethics will be seen to presume an individual of unlimited scope for self-invention.

This volume is devoted to studying the effects of timelessness upon these political projects of freedom by discussing the reasons, thrust, and implications of their preference of a past, present, or future in their visions of history, and exploring the connection between institutions, alienation, and the individual in their thought. It will be obvious that within this larger discussion there is an implicit critical assessment of the consequences of the Kantian dualism upon the radical political imagination. The study will conclude with a summary of these Kantian consequences on modernity in order to bring everything into a broader focus.

I acknowledge the imbalance that the figure of Rousseau represents for this study. Preceding Kant chronologically, there is a difficulty in assigning to his thought palpable Kantian procedures. But considering that Kant openly acknowledged the fundamental influence of Rousseau in supplying to him the moral, and hence timeless, dimension of his dualist philosophy, I see no difficulties with his inclusion among radical political theorists animated by timelessness. Furthermore, as a major aim of this study is to show the historical and temporal predilections and distortions that arise from grounding one's thought in moral timelessness, Rousseau's obvious preference for a historical past ensures his membership among those who have utilized the timeless in such a historical fashion. This extended historical trope of thought cannot be readily applied to Kant himself, who did not extend his dualism into a specific mode of time and history, but simply deferred to history in general for the purposes of bridging the dualism. Rousseau may precede Kant chronologically, but with regard to how he deputes to history with moral timelessness he is closer in kin to Marx and Foucault. It should also be acknowledged that coming before the Kantian shift in philosophy, discussion on Rousseau's work has no need to engage with the complexity of Kant's achievement per se, but simply has to be aware of the preexistent association. This understanding accounts for the relative shortness of this study's discussion of Rousseau compared with Marx and Foucault. Consequently, both Marx and Foucault's chronological need to respond to the Kantian dualism as a historical fact trailing their endeavors accounts for the longer length of the discussions on them in this book. The respective lengths are also explained by their rigorous denial of Kant's influence in their work and their dedication to historical and temporal thought. Thus the study needs to delve further in order to explain and uncover their relation to the timeless.

Kant's Timeless Morality: A Look at the Antagonism between Morality, Politics, and History

The importance of Kant for this study lies in his logically formulated construction of a transcendental morality and the sovereignty he gives this faculty in his system. He is certainly not the only one who has removed the moral imperative from the corrupting, incidental machinations of the empirical world, but he is by far the most philosophically gifted and consistent of those ranks. His concept of a transcendental, practical capacity that stands aloof and unchanged by the passage of time is the highly formalistic model of timelessness that this work will attribute to the radical imagination. But as we will see with Kant, and in the bulk of the discussion of our radical political theorists, the existence of such a timeless morality necessarily precipitates a disjunction between that morality and the empirical/social/political world. That disjunction in turn demands a philosophy of history to overcome the gap. Kant is so useful here because this process is so logical. He sets out to secure an independent morality unfettered by the outside phenomenal world and the passage of time, and then tries to bridge the chasm between morality and the world by reintroducing time and history into the equation. The difficulty that Kant reached toward the end of his life's work on the three Critiques is mirrored in varying ways by Rousseau, Marx, and Foucault. The process is very different with each individual thinker, but the general shape of the problematic remains—namely, the difficulty of reconciling timeless morality and freedom allied to the will with a world changing with time.

The driving force behind Kant's philosophy is derived from the tension he creates between science and morality, or the forces of mechanism and freedom. How can we protect humanity's precious moral autonomy from the encroachment of Newtonian necessity? At this time of the Enlightenment no question was in more dire need of a satisfactory philosophical answer. Kant's attempt seems at first glance to be a sound one: to circumscribe the limits of empirical knowledge in order to safeguard our nonempirical knowledge. The bulk of the first Critique is devoted to the task of outlining the operations, laws, and movements of theoretical knowledge, finally and exhaustively to succeed in having "assigned to everything therein its proper place."[1] The aim is to settle the accounts of science so as to explore the "wide and stormy ocean" of the noumenal world—that is, to make a distinction between a world of phenomena, entailing universal determinism and the principle of causality, and the world of noumena, enshrining freedom, the moral conscience, and duty to a self prescribed law.[2] Taking his cue from Rousseau, Kant locates the moral dimension of man in the freedom of his reason. He compartmentalizes all of our endeavors in science to theoretical reason and all of our moral imperatives to practical reason: "For as regards nature, experience presents us with rules and is the source of truth, but in relation to ethical laws experience is the parent of illusion, and it is to the highest degree reprehensible to limit or to deduce the laws which dictate what I ought to do, from what is done."[3]

It must be obvious then that Kant gives ethical laws superiority over the unchangeable limits of nature. Humanity will find its worth and emancipation in our practical reason. Our course is not to be found solely in the progress of an inflexible science, where Descartes had sought

1. Immanuel Kant, *The Critique of Pure Reason* (London: Everyman, 1986), 180.
2. Kant, *Critique of Pure Reason.*
3. Kant, *Critique of Pure Reason,* 221.

our salvation via the mastery of nature, but rather in our morality, as Rousseau had perceived with his admittance of the transcendent free moral will. As I shall show, however, Kant's conception of a reinstated, rejuvenated transcendent morality can prove to be just as inflexible, just as universal, as the dictates of a mechanical naturalism. It would be foolish to deny the radical nature of Kant's morality. In its ideal standing, it is a wholly revolutionary concept that is based on one of the most pure and abstract forms of the law.[4] To say that it is devoid of any specific content and that it scorns the thought of any substantiation or demonstration in the realm of experience is not a farfetched claim. In fact, in all of his ethical tracts it is his expressed aim.

Is it not of the utmost necessity to construct a pure moral philosophy which is completely freed from everything which may be only empirical and thus belong to anthropology?[5]

If a rational being can think of its maxims as practical universal laws, he can do so only by considering them as principles which contain the determining grounds of the will formally and not materially. The object either is the determining grounds of the will or it is not.[6]

Kant's emphasis over other ethical codes is his placing the seat of all morality in the autonomy of the will. The will itself, pure and whole, unfettered by outside objects, is the supreme fount of moral imperatives. Nothing in the phenomenal world can be conceived as good or evil per se, as the only thing that can be confidently called good is a good will. If an outside object gives content to the moral imperative through its relation to the will, its imperative can only be hypothetical, its basis found in heteronomy.[7] Kant demands that the moral imperative be based on far more universal ground than this, and so he asserts that the autonomy of the will be its own content, giving itself its own law. This is the justification behind Kant's critique of happiness as a grounding for morality, as happiness is particular and contingent in nature, pertaining to objects outside the will, and incapable of providing a universal morality. The

---

4. Pierre Hassner, "Immanuel Kant," in *History of Political Philosophy,* edited by Leo Strauss and Joseph Cropsey, 3rd ed. (Chicago: University of Chicago Press, 1987), 583.

5. Kant, *Critique of Practical Reason* (Chicago: University of Chicago Press, 1949), 51–52.

6. Kant, *Critique of Practical Reason,* 138.

7. Kant, *Critique of Practical Reason,* 97.

need for universal unconditional ethical demands leads us to the categorical imperative. Kant states, "The absolutely good will, the principle of which must be a categorical imperative, is thus undetermined with reference to any objects."[8] There is, of course, far more to the Kantian conception of morality. But for the purposes of this study, it suffices to first outline the driving force of that morality, which is the desire to raise itself above experience and empiricism, to remove it from the sensible world, and second to show the timelessness inherent in the universalization of the categorical imperative. It is to here that we now turn.

The dominance and power with which Kant imbues his morality can be plainly seen when examined as the universalization of maxims. The categorical imperative states, "So act that the maxim of your will could always hold at the same time as the principle of a universal legislation."[9] One is being asked to universalize one's motives for action in every given moment. The categorical imperative is also common and binding to all, regardless of their time or place. Having its grounding in the freedom of the will, rather than on material and empirical objects and desires that are subject to change in time and place, the categorical imperative therefore remains atemporal. For Kant the categorical imperative is a guiding principle for a humanity that exists in time, but that is in possession of a reason that is unperturbed and untouched by duration and continuity. Reason in the Kantian system is only capable of giving the universal form, the a priori conditions, the necessary law—never concerned with the variable, the contingent, or the temporal. When Kant moves to the political field, his atemporal morality becomes at once indispensable and untenable.

Kant's political philosophy flows directly from his moral philosophy. The two major tenets upon which Kantian politics hang, namely republican government and international organization and law, are fully deducible from the Kantian morality. It is important to understand the stunning consistency with which Kant moves from moral idealism to political idealism. No one can deny that there is a strong moralistic dimension in modern society and its creeds of liberalism and democracy. In this we are undoubtedly indebted to Kant over other political

8. Kant, *Critique of Practical Reason,* 101.
9. Kant, *Critique of Practical Reason,* 142.

philosophers. It is Kant's great achievement to have proposed a form of international organization that follows so logically from the inner moral law. The achievement is made possible by grounding everything in a universal reason. But while this provides a common ground for all to decide their desired form of political association, this morality does, however, have to overlook or omit other realities necessary for the continuance of political life.

Practical reason is expected to set the standards for political activity in the Kantian system. When this is limited to understanding such goals as republican government, international federation, and respect and duty to law, then the Kantian free moral conscience provides a firm philosophical base for such endeavors. But while practical reason gives these things a noble, overarching rationalization, there are problems reconciling this moral reason with the activities and processes that make politics possible. Kant's politics are on the one hand unthinkable without his morality; on the other hand, that morality relies on conditions that radically transcend the stratagems and contrivances of the dynamic view of politics. It is here that some of Kant's deepest-held convictions about the ethical life, namely that humans are ends in themselves and never to be treated as means, become problematic. In other words, means and actions necessary for the realization of desired political orders are forbidden by a formal and overly rigid morality. In the unpredictable world of politics, the application of an inflexible universal morality can only complicate and make impossible the realization of aims for which such a morality is the philosophical foundation. As much as Kant tries to claim to the contrary,[10] there is an inescapable disjunction between the political and the moral, a disjunc-

---

10. In the two appendices to *Perpetual Peace* Kant treats the perceived opposition and true harmony between morality and politics. The argument here, however, in no way counters our thesis that Kant's timeless morality has trouble being reconciled to politics: "In dealing with the problems of practical reason must we begin from its material principle—the end as the object of free choice—or from its formal principle which is based merely on freedom in its external relation?—from which comes the following law:—'Act so that thou canst will that thy maxim should be a universal law.' Without doubt, the latter determining principle of action must stand first; for, as a principle of right, it carries unconditional necessity with it"; Kant, *Perpectual Peace*, translated with an introduction by M. Campbell Smith (London: Allen and Unwin, 1915), 75.

Kant still maintains his universal and timeless ideal, only mediating it with the phenomenal world by giving the action derived from pure moral intentions an unconditional necessity. In other words, good and right intentions will always be answered

tion that finds its roots in Kant's dualism between the empirical world and an otherworldly reason.

Undoubtedly it is Kant's view of humans as ends in themselves and his respect for the rights of man that save him from the dangerous radicalism of other idealists, who deem it permissible to use nefarious means to achieve improbable ideals. But it is precisely these sentiments that lurk behind such sanguine and naive proposals as the "moral politician." This conception, so opposed to Machiavelli's shrewd and world-wise prince, belies Kant's limited appreciation of the unlettered logic of political life. Kant's grasp of the hidden elements that maintain political and social stability and vitality are hindered greatly by one of the major propellants of his philosophy. Kant's is a philosophy of infinite improvement and eternal striving.[11] It advocates a constant searching inquiry into the constitutive features of a society, in the name of a timeless morality. All social processes and institutions are at all times at its critical mercy. It is hard to deny that this method for social retransformation is a harmful thing. Modernity would be unthinkable without this type of vigilance. However, it does have the tendency to observe the complex and tense relations between institutions and social processes from the dogmatic and abstract perspective of a universal reason. In condemning certain social practices as immoral, it may unravel the very features and procedures that hold that society together. Kant's timeless morality makes it very difficult for him to recognize the existent benefits that lay embedded in a political order. A society adds layers of institutional wisdom to its political order over time, which the timeless mindset has great difficulty in perceiving. Essentially, the timelessness of Kantian morality and the timeliness of political action create a disjunction that corresponds to the dualism between nature and morality. This essentially initiates an ahistorical understanding of political life. As Lewis White Beck observes of Kantian morality, "Each moral act at the time it is done is, as it were, an absolutely new beginning, not determined by history, or by nature. His-

---

with good and right results: "Seek ye first the kingdom of pure practical reason and its righteousness, and the object of your endeavour, the blessing of perpetual peace, will be added unto you"; Kant, *Perpetual Peace*, 177–78. Unfortunately for Kant, history and the world of politics are furnished with examples to the contrary. How Kant solves this problem will be the task of his philosophy of history.

11. Robert Catley and Wayne Cristaudo, *This Great Beast: Progress and the Modern State* (Aldershot, UK, and Sydney: Ashgate, 1997), 147.

tory brings us to each present; but in each future we are on our own."[12]

The Kantian morality consistently asks us to forget the historical passage that brought us to this point when making decisions for the future. This is a wholly negative diagnosis of the Kantian morality, but one that necessarily arises when the question of the process of history becomes entangled in the desire to reconcile politics with that morality. This is precisely what Kant has done, as is evidenced by his occasional historical writings like *Idea For a Universal History From a Cosmopolitan Point of View, Perpetual Peace,* and *Critique of Judgment,* where Kant deals with purpose, history, political destiny, and teleology. But as we shall see, Kant's solutions in these areas are really just architectural additions within the whole system rather than real solutions, and at best simply anticipate problems that will be taken up with more success by other philosophers. Kant's task is not to discover a moral harmony already existent and pre-established within nature, but to impose such a harmony onto its causal chain. It is for this reason that Kant's major stumbling block is practice, or how to make existent in time nonexistent timeless formulations. Kant needs at least the illusion of a philosophy of history to clothe his morality with a necessity in the halls of time. He also requires the valuable unity it affords between morality and politics, morality and nature, duty and self-interest, the universal and the contingent. The problem of history thus becomes Kant's next point of concern.

The purpose of a philosophy of history for Kant is to serve as a guide or guarantee to morality. Reason shows that the impossibility of progress cannot be demonstrated in experience, and thus there is a duty to act as if such progress is attainable. History and teleology are here to be understood as regulative principles, heuristic ideas that promote and give weight to the moral imperatives. It is important to know what Kant means when he muses on the *Idea for a Universal History from the Cosmopolitan Point of View.* "Idea" is to be taken in its wholly Kantian context, as an idea that serves a governing function in the mind and in action, but can never be demonstrated as existing in the phenomenal world. In this respect Kant's attempt to fuse the overwhelming dichotomy of his system between necessity (nature) and freedom (moral auton-

---

12. Lewis White Beck, "Introduction," in *Kant On History,* by Immanuel Kant, edited by Lewis White Beck (Indianapolis: Bobbs Merrill, 1963), xxvi.

omy) is perfectly commensurate with the method of the critical philosophy. But there are problems with this irresolute settlement of the discord between morality and politics. Unlike the postulate of the immortality of the soul as a guarantee for morality, the philosophy of history, or the realization of man's ends in society through time, rests on foundations that are thoroughly empirical and experiential in character. If Kant is unwilling to abandon his ideas of teleology and an organic unity within nature and history as mere regulative principles without real substantiation, then Kant remains a staunch dualist. If the ideas that concern humanity's progressive passage through time are as timeless and abstract as the morality that passage is supposed to bring into being, then these ideas will provide us with no conclusive evidence or encouragement that such progress is authentic. Kant ends his system by intimating the idea of "the cunning of history," an idea that his staunch morality is simply incapable of validating.

Kant's was an awesome articulation and reconciliation of the Enlightenment's inherent tensions, but it bequeathed to the next philosophical generation the problem of an organic unity to culture, history, and society and begged the question of the value of existing institutions and traditions. Kant's contemporaries, Hamann, Jacobi, and Herder, would all pick him up on this unfortunate consequence to his philosophy. They argued that Kant's philosophy itself was part of this organic unity. It was an expression of the needs of a culture requiring a rebirth to its institutions. Rather than being a timeless and transcendental formulation of the way things ought to be for all times and places, it had arisen from the very vital and urgent needs of a particular time and place. But its formalism and abstractness could not recognize its fortuity, and it ended up encapsulating a spirit whose aim was the deracination of any institution and society that did not live up to its rigid benchmark. The individual is given enormous scope in which to prescribe an ethical content for himself. Lacking the guiding power of institutions built in time, this scope is potentially destructive of those institutions that have approval by the very content they give to ethics and morality. It is the Kantian philosophy's legacy to be unable to recognize the fruits of time as they exist in the institutional inheritance of society.

There is an obvious problem with using the Kantian philosophy as a touchstone to clarify the ultimate aims of Marx and Foucault's political and philosophical projects. Rousseau calls his vision of humanity restored as a moral endeavor. However, both Marx and Foucault begin by declaring the Kantian philosophy an idealistic chimera. They defended their projects' efforts to deal with substantial social relations with a real concern for its material conditions. And while Marx's idealism is relatively easy to tease out from his work, there are always those who will defend his work against this charge. With regard to Foucault, the consistency with which he protects his ideas from the hated "idealist" taint is admirable, if somewhat overbearing. However, what connects these thinkers to the Kantian heritage of critique is their attitude to institutional reality, particularly their misunderstanding of the link between institutions, spirit, and time. Their relation to Kant and his timeless moral project exists in their overtly oppositional and anti-hegemonic stance to modern society, as evidenced by their wholly negative readings of the growth of institutions. Their primary concern is with the extension of freedom, and they all give exaggerated license to the will as the constitutive feature of political action. Seen from this angle, one cannot fail to see Rousseau, Marx, and Foucault engaged in the Enlightenment critique of the existing world in the name of freedom. As we have said, the restless spirit of constant and permanent social criticism in these thinkers can only provide us with clues as to their misunderstanding of real social time as it is preserved and sustained in our institutions. The attitude of criticism and the unceasing and abstract need for change make us deaf to the times when society really does require our creative energy for renewal or preservation.

Historical Institutionalists: The Methodology and Model of Social Timeliness

While this book will be examining the feature of timelessness that distinguishes the radical political imagination, an opposing philosophical position will indirectly animate this journey. It is a position that will be here referred to as historical institutionalism, and includes such luminaries as Giambattista Vico, Baron de Montesquieu, Edmund Burke, G. W. F. Hegel, and in the twentieth century the now almost forgotten Eugen Rosenstock-Huessy. What is omitted from the collective thought of these thinkers is the Kantian dualism that affects the radical thinkers that the bulk of this work seeks to explore. The absence of this dualism has ramifications on how these thinkers view time and history and how acutely they are aware of the need for timeliness in the reproduction of social life. We will soon clarify their broad position, listing some of the constitutive features of this attitude to politics, society, and history. But before doing so we will look at how they avoid the contradictions that more radical thinkers inherit from an explicit or unconscious application of Kant's dualism. To do this we need to look at the highly marginal and neglected early criticisms of Kant's project by his contemporaries F. H. Jacobi and J. G. Hamann. While both thinkers did not precisely criticize Kant on the score of the troubling incongruity between morality and history, they were prescient enough to see that this would be the outcome of his analysis of "pure reason." Indeed, both thinkers dove straight into the bowels of Kant's critique of reason and saw that it was precisely the elements of time, institution, and history that were being omitted.

Jacobi was undoubtedly the thorn in the side of the Enlightenment's love affair with rationality and reason. Jacobi saw everywhere about him, in the rational discussions of the day and in the age's mania for reason to baptize all subjects into the bath of universality, the skulking specter of nihilism. And he was not afraid to accuse anyone of such bewitchment. He infamously accused the venerable Lessing of Spinozism, a philosophical position he outlined as perfected rationality that generated nothing more than fatalism, atheism, and nihilism. He viciously haggled with Mendelssohn over Lessing's posthumous reputation to make this point, a point directed more toward the age than the particular participants in the debate. He would later paint Fichte with the same brush of nihilism, describing his philosophy as "inverted Spinozism." He also sparred with Schelling on the same score, and only old age and weariness prevented him from doing likewise with Hegel. But it is his tangle with Immanuel Kant that is instructive to us here.

Even without having seen Kant's *Critique of Practical Reason* or *his Critique of Judgment,* both of which deal with morality and history respectively, Jacobi could see that Kant's conception of reason would do serious violence to these entities. Jacobi felt this premonition keenly when he analyzed *The Critique of Pure Reason.* He struck at the heart of Kant's highly formal understanding of reason and thought, accusing him of having arbitrarily divorced thought from the exigencies of experience. Reason, even Kant's critical reevaluation of it, differed no jot from its other nihilistic Enlightenment conceptions. This was because Kant still conceived it as empty indeterminate concepts hovering above an equally indeterminate manifold of sensory experience, without any proper appreciation of a mediating force or principle. He writes, "Like all the other contemporary philosophers, he called something that is not reason by the name of 'reason'—i.e. the mere faculty of concepts, judgments, and inferences, that hovers above the senses but is unable to reveal anything at all by itself."[13] Jacobi assailed the Kantian project because its thinking subject's whole knowledge of the outside world is forever proven to be only the reflection or manifestation of subjective mental structures and faculties. No true, incontrovertible knowledge of the outside world is really possible here, and reason and thinking are so devoid of experience and material from the senses that they are rendered vacant. The Kantian philosophy led ineluctably to "absolute subjectivity," and thus Jacobi uncompromisingly takes issue with the dualism that lies at the heart of Kant's demarcations between sensibility, understanding, and reason.[14]

We experience the fact that we nowhere experience anything true through the senses; and therefore we do not experience anything true through the understanding either, because (*as the Kantian teaching would have it*) the understanding can only refer to this sensibility and would be entirely empty and destitute of function without the material delivered to it *by the senses alone.*[15]

What divides me from the from the Kantian doctrine is only what divides it from itself too, and makes it incoherent, namely that, as we have shown, it presupposes and denies the existence of two specifically distinct sources of cognition in man's mind.[16]

Jacobi is pointing to the fact that the Kantian dualism had sundered a reality that should never have been separated, and in so doing he was hypostasizing both our empirical experience of the world and our conceptual, intellectual grasp of it. This was the necessary result of all abstraction for Jacobi, "for in abstraction we drop the particular relations

13. Friedrich Heinrich Jacobi, "David Hume on Faith (Preface, 1815)," in *The Main Philosophical Writings and the Novel* "Allwill," translated with an introduction by George di Giovanni (Montreal and Kingston: McGill-Queen's University Press, 1994), 541.

14. Jacobi, "David Hume on Faith," 552.   15. Jacobi, "David Hume on Faith," 544.

16. Jacobi, "David Hume on Faith," 550.

and marks that condition an object of the senses."[17] By effacing these "marks" and "relations" of sensory truth, our knowledge, purged by "pure reason," becomes "pure nothingness."[18] And so Kant falls under Jacobi's charge of "nihilism" like all his *Aufklärung* brethren. By idealizing reason, Kant was disuniting it from its natural embrace of sensual reality, and so it "disappeared from the living reality."[19] And so when we turn to reason thus desiccated of the breath of empirical life, "we then turn to the dead for answers. [...] We open up corpses to discover where life came from."[20]

In much the same way that Kant would isolate our morality away from the warp and woof of social life by ensconcing it in the autonomy of the will, he had also attempted to conceive our reason away from the tainting and cloaking that he imagined it suffered from everyday life and concerns. But reason was much less an isolated faculty to Jacobi than it was an activity, and being an activity it had to have somewhere for its actions to become manifest and seen. Not only this, but reason would not solely direct this realm, but would in large measure be directed by it. As Frederick C. Beiser observed of Jacobi's message to Kant:

The problem is that reason is not a completely self-governing faculty; it is controlled by our needs and functions as living beings. We cannot separate reason from our needs and functions as living beings because its task is to do nothing more than organize and satisfy them. Of course, it is the business of reason to create laws, Jacobi happily concedes to Kant. But he then adds: in doing so, reason is governed by our interests as living beings, which are not in turn subject to rational control and appraisal. Rather, they determine the very criteria of rational appraisal.[21]

Thus Jacobi's whole objection to the tenor of Kant's "revolution" of reason was that it was simply another philosophical hyperbole of that entity. Reason could only be so inflated and sovereign if it was looked at in isolation from history, or the to-and-fro between people in time and space. Reason was always an activity of historically situated people, and thus treating it as a universal faculty distorted considerably reason's scope and capabilities. Ultimately, underneath all the polemic and re-

17. Jacobi, "David Hume on Faith," 571.   18. Jacobi, "David Hume on Faith."
19. Jacobi, "David Hume on Faith," 585.   20. Jacobi, "David Hume on Faith."
21. Frederick C. Beiser, *The Fate of Reason: German Philosophy from Kant to Fichte* (Cambridge, Mass.: Harvard University Press, 1987), 87.

active vitriol that was the stamp of Jacobi's career, he was advancing a more positive vision of philosophy grasped through history. In order to fuse the contingent truths of history with the necessary truths of reason, rationality could not be based on abstractions, but must be centered precisely on the relations between individuals. The understanding of relational reality of humanity was the historical tonic that Jacobi wished to administer to philosophy. And human relations are seen in laws, customs, institutions, dialogue, acts, and events. This is where philosophy should observe its living concepts.

> Just as living philosophy, or a people's mode of thinking, proceeds from a people's history or mode of life, so too this history or mode of life arises from a people's origin, from proceeding institutions and laws. All history leads up to instruction and laws, and the history of all human culture begins from them. Not from *laws of reason* or moving exhortations, but from *instructions, exposition, model, discipline, aid; from counsel and deed, service and command.*[22]

Jacobi's ally and friend in this undertaking, the unorthodox and brilliant J. G. Hamann, also has the distinction of being perhaps the first person to read the *Critique of Pure Reason*. Hamann and Kant were friends, albeit ones who did not see eye to eye intellectually. Despite this, Hamann helped Kant secure a publisher for the work, and then through that contact clandestinely obtained the proof sheets prior to the work's publication.[23] Hamann's impish curiosity to see the outcome of his friend's project was an indication of his awareness that he would have to spar with its outcomes. And Hamann's critique of the work, though ignored and sidelined for many years, would be perhaps one of its deepest and profoundest. Like Jacobi, Hamann had spent years as a vociferous opponent of the rationalist tendencies of his age, and like Jacobi, countered those predispositions with a plea for the awareness of the relational and processional underpinnings of human life, from which modern idealism and naturalism consistently abstracted.

Hamann did not undertake a rigorous survey of the component parts of Kant's project, but instead subjected it to the same critical criteria that Kant subjected to all other things. His reply, the *Metacritique*

---

22. Jacobi, "Concerning the Doctrine of Spinoza (1785)," in *Main Philosophical Writings*, 244.
23. Beiser, *The Fate of Reason*, 38.

on the Purism of Reason, was precisely what its title spells out: a deep questioning of the foundational attempt by Kant to purify reason in the first place. As Hamann was an intensely eccentric Christian thinker, he operated with a conception of Truth as "Incarnation," and as such could not brook any attempt to arrive at truth that did not observe it from its incarnated forms. The attempt to clarify what "pure" reason would look like was for Hamann akin to stripping truth of her clothes. He knew that this was Kant's aim even before the *Critique of Pure Reason* emerged, and wrote as such to Kant in a letter from 1759: "Truth would not let herself be approached to closely by highwaymen; she draws her clothing so tightly about her that reaching her body is doubtful. How terrified they would be if they had their way and actually saw that fearful ghost—the truth."[24]

For Hamann the clothing that truth dons on every single one of its excursions into human life is the apparel of language, and it is on the sword of language that the attempt to transfigure reason into a "permanent and universal" entity, "the same for all intelligent beings at all times and places," must necessarily fall.[25] Kant's great quest was to enshrine reason "to an absolutely autonomous position," but to pull this off "he must entirely eliminate language."[26] It was to expose this absurd and unrecognized problem of rationalism that Hamann sought to achieve in the *Metacritique.* In the style of a good historical thinker he did so by dramatizing the purification of reason in a genealogical fashion.

The first purification of reason consisted in the partly misunderstood, partly failed attempt to make reason independent of all tradition and custom and belief in them. The second is even more transcendent and comes to nothing less than the independence from experience and everyday induction. [...] The third, highest, and, as it were, empirical purism is therefore concerned with language, the only, first, and last organon and criterion of reason, with no credentials but tradition and use.[27]

24. Quoted from W. M. Alexander, *Johann Georg Hamann: Philosophy and Faith* (The Hague: Martinus Nijhoff, 1966), 75.

25. Beiser, *The Fate of Reason,* 40–41.

26. James C. O'Flaherty, *Unity and Language: A Study in the Philosophy of Johann Georg Hamann* (Chapel Hill: University of North Carolina Press, 1952), 74.

27. Johann Georg Hamann, *Hamann: Writings on Philosophy and Language,* translated and edited by Kenneth Haynes (Cambridge: Cambridge University Press, 2007), 207–8.

The first of these "purifications" was enacted by all those rationalists before Kant, the second by Kant himself, and the third is the yet to come, but patently absurd projected outcome of this movement of thought. Demonstrating the absolute impossibility of reason getting around language is also the way for Hamann to reintroduce the abandoned validity of "custom, use, and tradition." For Hamann rails against that great fallacy that undermines all philosophers: that thought precedes language, and that because of this, language is only the system of expendable signs and shrouded ciphers of elementary and original ideas.

If then a chief question still remains—how is the faculty of thought possible? The faculty to think left and right, before and without, with and beyond experience?—then no deduction is needed to demonstrate the genealogical priority of language, and its heraldry, over the seven holy functions of logical propositions and inferences. Not only is the entire faculty of thought founded on language, … but language is also the centerpoint of reason's misunderstanding with itself.[28]

Again, the central target of Hamann's metacritique of Kantian thought is his deployment of ever spiraling, endlessly generating dualisms; between understanding and sensibility, morality and history, theoretical and practical reason, noumena and phenonmena, a priori concepts and empirical intuition. Hamann also struggles to see why this army of dualisms should be deployed to solve problems for which a proper understanding of language provides the unified answer. Words are the soil from which the twin heads of all dualisms rear. As Hamann observes about them, "Words, therefore, have an aesthetic and logical faculty. As visible and audible objects they belong with their elements to the sensibility and intuition; however, by the spirit of their institution and meaning they belong to the understanding and concepts. Consequently, words are pure and empirical intuitions as much as pure and empirical concepts."[29] In other words, language is the singular stuff from which the dualist needlessly abstracts his reified terms, rendering them relationless and divorced from the processes and currents of life registered in language. But perhaps most importantly, language for Hamann is the *Urspring* of human culture and history. Kant had forgotten his membership in the great community

---

28. Hamann, *Writings on Philosophy and Language*, 211.
29. Hamann, *Writings on Philosophy and Language*, 215.

of speakers, for whom the continual use of words makes them participants in history. Kant could no more derive his atemporal and ahistorical autonomous forms from this medium than he could convey his thoughts by being mute. Language is the original human institution and constitution, and is thus the foundation for all attempts to institute and constitute anything in time and history.

What is language but a verbal custom, a cultural tradition embodied in words. It is the repository of all the characteristic ways of thinking of a nation, both shaping its thought and in turn being shaped by it.... What is crucial for the formation of our rationality, Hamann insists, is the internalization of the traditions of a culture: "The stamina and menstrua of our reason are revelation and tradition, which we make into our own property and transform into our powers and vital juices."[30]

But most importantly for this study is how Hamann's understanding of the profundities embedded in history, language, institution, custom, and tradition (all of which go largely unrecognized by philosophy) provide for us a vision of the intimate continuity and connection between the past, present, and future.

What would the most exact and careful knowledge of the present be without a divine renewing of the past, without a presentiment of the future?... What kind of labyrinth would the present be for the spirit of observation without the spirit of prophecy and its guide-lines into the past and future?[31]

Hamann is here pointing us toward that characteristic mistake that will be made by all those who embrace the timeless and ahistorical impulses of the philosopher. For the "guidelines" that connect the past to the present and the present to the future are severed by those who abstract from history. But it is important to now point out that this insight is not isolated to two periphery and peculiar intelligences that were reacting to the great philosophical challenge of their time. The awareness of the great significance and meaning in the temporal halls of history is a commonsense reaction to any overbearing abstraction. It can be easily discerned in many of the great names of modern thought, of which the first sophisticated attempt was made by Giambattista Vico.

30. O'Flaherty, *Unity and Language*, 140.
31. Quoted from Alexander, *Johann Georg Hamann*, 174.

Giambattista Vico is widely considered to be the first such thinker to place history at the center of the human experience. In his great work, *Scienza Nuova,* he argued for a renewal of interest in the historical method. His reaction to the Cartesian methodology of the physical sciences of mathematics and physics, in favor of a living methodology of human endeavor encompassing history, politics, and law, signals the first serious foray into the science of social time. He grasped the evolutionary character of the institutions that we create and saw in them the material by which we can truly measure the worth of human societies. According to Vico, we should be able glean the most valuable and steadfast knowledge from the things we produce ourselves, from our societies and its endowments. Vico postulated evolutionary cycles in the growth and decline of civilizations that coincided with cognitive development. This highly original thesis, which bears such affinity to Hegel's own philosophy of history, is the seed upon which history would be conceived as a storehouse for the wisdom of humanity, and our societies become the parchment upon which we write our journey. Vico's influence is in fact everywhere in the thinkers we discuss.

The other contender for the title of father of modern sociology is the Baron de Montesquieu. Montesquieu was no less concerned with freedom than his more idealistic counterparts, but his greatest singular insight was that freedom's passage into reality was always dependent upon the receptivity of the particular society. Thus Montesquieu's *The Spirit of the Laws* emphasized the relation between the social characteristics of a nation and its people and the political necessities that flow from these considerations. He says of all social innovations and experiments that "they should relate to the degree of liberty which the constitution can sustain, to the religion of the inhabitants, their inclinations, their wealth, their numbers, their commerce, their mores and their manners."[32] Here liberty is predicated on the needs of a culture rather than seeking to redirect the culture from its abstract perspective. Liberty is valued upon the disposition of the people, rather than being the benchmark that shapes their custom. This position holds that any political organization must take into account the social counsel and historical legacies that become sedimented in the lives of a nation's constituents before any proj-

32. Charles de Secondat Montesquieu, *The Spirit of the Laws* (Cambridge: Cambridge University Press, 1999), 9.

ect of freedom is introduced. The circumstances will judge the degree to which political and social power are delegated in the society. This is not, however, to say that social change is something that Montesquieu shies away from; his obvious admiration for the English political achievement as an example of French political, economic, and social progress testifies to that. Montesquieu simply calls for a greater awareness of the complexity of social reality that would show any radical change to the government to be an uprooting of their historical and social ties. To this degree, Montesquieu fashions himself as a historical institutionalist who favors the interpretation of our societies as a tense and complex amalgamation of interests and customs accumulated over time. Montesquieu sees the challenge of freedom's passage from idea to political reality as the balancing and efficient management of these inevitable interests and institutions that have legitimacy simply because of their survival. A keen observer of history and society will know that institutions wither and die, but rarely in one fell swoop. Montesquieu's is a moderate vision of political association and change that is aware of the positive and regulative features of what Edmund Burke would call "prejudice."

Edmund Burke—politician, orator, and consummate purveyor of practical wisdom—defined prejudice as the inherited possession of members born to a social order, which serves to safeguard a nation from regression or degeneration. The conventions and proclivities of a nation, gestated and fostered by time and history, were defenses against "precipitate, rash and doctrinaire reform."[33] Prejudice constituted the character of the state and encouraged a healthy understanding and esteem for the process of history in the formation of our social reality. From the perspective of the group of radical thinkers this study is engaging, Burke, Montesquieu, and others must be seen as guilty of complicity with the repressive social orders they studied and of which they were constituents. This, however, only concerns their lack of an attitude of permanent critique and goes nowhere in dismantling their concern with the need for social change. Burke understood the forces of timely conservation and correction that animated the historical stage. The balance between survival and progress can only be maintained by careful, timely practical analysis and action. Burke qualifies his native conservatism by stating

33. Carl B. Cone, *Burke and the Nature of Politics: The Age of the French Revolution* (Lexington: The University of Kentucky Press, 1964), 333.

that "an irregular, convulsive movement may be necessary to throw off an irregular, convulsive disease,"[34] and that "a state without the means of some change is without the means of its conservation. Without such means it might even risk the loss of that part of the constitution which it wished the most religiously to preserve."[35]

Burke's great adversaries were the philosophers of natural right, exemplified in France by Jean-Jacques Rousseau. The natural-right theorists pitted man against his society by circumscribing a field of abstract rights around the individual. This only cultivated an atmosphere of conflict between the necessary strictures of any civil society and the individual so powerfully conceived as above that society. Burke foresaw the consequences that radical critique could conceivably wreak on society. To secure society from such an infirmity it was necessary to understand the workings and meaning of history. Burke's was an empirical and cumulative concept of history that was uncommitted to any theory, law, or underlying rationality. Society was a distillation of truths that rose from the conflicts and contests of history.

In history a great volume is unrolled for our instruction, drawing the materials for future wisdom from the past errors and infirmities of mankind.[36]

Our political system is placed in a just correspondence and symmetry with the order of the world.... wherein, by the disposition of a stupendous wisdom, molding together the great mysterious incorporation of the human race, the whole, at one time, is never old, or middle-aged, or young, but ... moves through the varied tenor of perpetual decay, fall, renovation, and progression.[37]

Essentially Burke's reflections on the French Revolution and the antecedent natural right–based philosophies that prepared the way advance an organic account of the state. He denies that people could or should prescribe their own moral and ethical content, instead claiming that this very content is embedded with the various societal relations in which individuals engage. This organic view of the state, which entails the balancing of multiple social interests and the variegated institutional structures that give voice to those interests, is one shared by Georg W. F. Hegel.

The greatest idealist metaphysician of the nineteenth century, G. W. F.

34. Edmund Burke, *Reflections on the Revolution in France* (London: Penguin, 1986), 109.
35. Burke, *Reflections on the Revolution*, 106.
36. Burke, *Reflections on the Revolution*, 247.
37. Burke, *Reflections on the Revolution*, 120.

Hegel, seemingly philosophically distant from the life and work of the practically minded Burke, did however share Burke's realistic and pragmatic understanding of politics. Hegel is aligned firmly within the tradition of Rousseau and Kant in establishing the site of freedom within the will, but in keeping with Burke he also calls equally for the establishment of freedom within the substantial relations of the state. This connection between freedom and its institutional reality is one of the major concerns in Hegel's *Philosophy of Right*. These twin needs derive from Hegel's systemic foundation that the rational is actual, that the idea exists in the world, that reason makes itself known in history. The will must receive determinate ethical content from the various societal relations of which it is part, whether they are the family, civil society, or the state itself. To neglect this would be to favor one side of the coin of freedom and fall under the sway of a dangerous and oppressive concept of timeless freedom. Hegel has the excesses of the French Revolution as a firm reminder of the nature of freedom so illegitimately conceived, and he outlined the philosophical rationale behind the terror in his *Phenomenology of Spirit*. With this firmly in mind, Hegel's philosophy of right necessarily had to be a detailed discussion of actual social conditions, a portrayal of the state as it is, rather than as it ought to be. In his famous preface to *The Philosophy of Right*, he writes,

One more word about giving instructions as to what the world ought to be. Philosophy in any case always comes on the scene too late to give it. As the thought of the world, it appears only when actuality is already there cut and dried after its process of formation has been completed. The teaching of the concept, which is also history's inescapable lesson, is that it is only when actuality is mature that the ideal first appears over and against the real and that the ideal apprehends this same real world in its substance and it builds it up for itself into the shape of an intellectual realm. When philosophy paints its grey in grey, then has a shape of life grown old.[38]

Hegel found in history the means of reconciling or synthesizing the competing demands of the substantial and concrete with the abstract. His project can be summed up as a vast philosophical attempt to reconcile the cleavage between the finite and infinite. Thus his idealist position always demands recognition of the unfolding mediations of the concept.

38. G. W. F. Hegel, *The Philosophy of Right* (Oxford: Oxford University Press, 1979), 12–13.

This recognition must take into account the concept's concrete particular existence, its universal self-relating identity, and the ground where these are fused and developed. By taking all of these sides into account, Hegel provides a philosophical, yet historical process of development. So while Hegel is the most absolute of idealists, it however forces him to be a political realist. For Hegel, the process of history is commensurable with the march of freedom, but this freedom can only ever be substantial freedom, institutionally initiated and rising from conflicts of interest. Freedom for Hegel never resides in one area, be it the people, the transcendent will, or a wholly abstract concept. Instead it is actualized in the shifting institutions that are fused in the crucible of history and give expression to the competing and shifting voices of humanity. The insight this study takes from Hegel is that institutions are storehouses for freedoms and knowledge, and that history, the stage of their emergence, should foster an understanding of their endurance, their need for renewal or, indeed, their overthrow. It is in this insight of a strong sense of history and time being needed to judge institutions that the lesser-known modern sociologist and historian Rosenstock-Huessy extended Hegel's example.

But if any modern thinker is the direct heir to the thrust of Jacobi and Hamann's thought, it is Eugen Rosenstock-Huessy. No thinker in the twentieth century has mused so immensely and completely on the great associations between speech, institutions, history, and time. And no thinker has extended the critique of the abstracting and purifying predilections of the philosophers more than Rosenstock-Huessy. Rather than in the figure of Kant, Rosenstock-Huessy saw that the rot had begun to set in from the Parmenides' pre-Socratic example onward. When he created his "omnibus proverb," the concept of Being, he instantly enacted the abstraction from time and history that would be the siren's song for all future philosophy. Rosenstock-Huessy composes a worried but intimate letter written to Parmenides from his opposite number, Heraclitus, the great celebrator of flux and becoming, emergence and passing. Rosenstock-Huessy imagines the letter as a conjuration to aid in curing the great intellectual sickness of his age. That sickness he describes thus: "To reestablish the elementary fact that the human mind cannot think except in the three dimensions of time, is one of the burning scientific needs of our age."[39]

39. Eugen Rosenstock-Huessy, *Lifelines: Quotations from the Work of Eugen Rosenstock-Huessy*, edited by Clinton C. Gardner, 87 (Norwich, Vt.: Argo, 1988), 87.

In the work Heraclitus accuses Parmenides of stultifying the life of the city, or "holon," with his "new generalization," which he calls "Being." It is a concept that smoothes over the ebb and flow of people's individual lives as much as the lives of nations. And it is why Heraclitus feels it necessary to counter with his metaphor of "Fire." Besides the suggestive difference between a metaphor and a concept is the obvious difference between a static, homogenous "Being" and a moving, restless "Fire." He has Heraclitus say, "Fire is uncertain in its central character. It is extinguishable, although it flares up again," and it demonstrates to us palpably that "the act [keeps] its refreshing unexpectedness before, and now, and after."[40] Fire makes us cognizant of the triplicity of temporal existence, whereas "Being" hoodwinks us into standing detached from our rising and falling. Heraclitus proclaims "it was, it is, it shall be," while Parmenides only provides a homogenizing lens for life's spectators to observe things through. Parmenides creates an artificial suspension of the past, present, and future of history in the abstract vessel of "being." And being so suspended, it takes on the appearance of timelessness. In creating this epistolary fantasy Rosenstock-Huessy was pithily, but profoundly restating the mission that had been his life's work. For he had repeatedly counseled, "History is the acknowledgement that we stand facing two fronts: facing backward and facing forward. The man who thinks that he can stand looking into the past without at the same time looking into the future is wrong."[41] And thus the proper attitude to history is one that is reflexively both conservative and progressive.

In his major work, *Out of Revolution*, Rosenstock-Huessy had spoken of the paradox of progress as existing in the institutions of the past: "The paradoxical truth about progress, then, is that it wholly depends on the survival of massive institutions which prevent a relapse from a stage which has once been reached. In general, this is the last thing a progressive is concerned about."[42] Directly after disapproving of the progressive's creed for unceasing newness in his unawareness of the past, he turns on conservatism as equally dangerous to the renewal of social reality, as it cannot graft new branches to the tree of life. What Rosenstock-

40. Rosenstock-Huessy, "Heraclitus to Parmenides," in *I Am an Impure Thinker* (Norwich, Vt.: Argo, 1970), 87.

41. Rosenstock-Huessy, "Lifelines," 56.

42. Rosenstock-Huessy, *Out of Revolution: Autobiography of Western Man* (Providence, R.I.: Berg, 1993), 31.

Huessy's reproach to both radicals and conservatives alike amounts to is a critique of the moralizing mind. The moralist's hard-and-fast principles of good and evil, he cites, "spring from a timeless, static mind which ignores the difference between past and future."[43] If categories of good and evil must be planted in the flux of time, they can only be judged as to their "ripeness" or "immaturity" for the realization of social possibility. Any truly historical vision must recognize the twin categories of necessity and timeliness as the guiding instincts of the human inspiration in its historical passage. Either the circumstances have made institutions and ideas "ripe" for their injection into the social scheme as some remedy to a social ill, or such measures will be "immature," incapable of effecting improvement, and thus abortive. Either way, it is the sense of necessity and timeliness that will determine this status, and to be receptive to these calls, the social sciences must have a more adequate conception of time than the one provided by the mechanical sciences.

Rosenstock-Huessy was a trenchant critic of the conception of time inherited from the natural sciences. This quantifiable, atomistic, a priori impression of time, often saddled to the carriage of space as its "fourth dimension," was a vast mistake when adopted as a model of social time. He wrote in the article "Liturgical Thinking" that time once conceived as mechanical cannot be cured by a recourse to eternity or permanence.[44] Timelessness is no answer to the inadequacies of time conceived as a line of infinitely divisible parts, stretching from the past to the future. Hegel intimated something like this when he observed that the dualism of Kant was dependent on the very mechanistic philosophies to which it was reacting. Rosenstock-Huessy's major aim is to wrestle from the sociologists the error of conceiving "time as being a straight line pointing from the past through the present into the future."[45] And worse still to counter the deficiencies of this matrix of social inquiry with an otherworldly, timeless morality or the permanence of incessant critique. Time, to Rosenstock-Huessy, is no field or matrix upon which social events are plotted; it is instead the very vehicle for social survival and revival, the very furnace in which individuals and societies coalesce.

43. Rosenstock-Huessy, *Out of Revolution*, 719–20.
44. Rosenstock-Huessy, "Liturgical Thinking," in *Rosenstock-Huessy Papers* (Norwich, Vt.: Argo, 1981), 4.
45. Rosenstock-Huessy, *Speech and Reality* (Norwich, Vt.: Argo, 1970), 18.

[A]ny living being, and the social group as well, has to defend a present under the simultaneous stress from past and future. To live means to look backward as well as forward, and to decide, in every moment, between continuity and change.[46]

The new terms are "traject," i.e., he who is forwarded on ways known from the past, and "preject," i.e., he who is thrown out of this rut into an unknown future.... Their interplay is the problem of the social sciences. Traject is the evolutionary; preject is the revolutionary predicate for man.[47]

Rosenstock-Huessy's aim is to reclaim the supremacy of time and its powerful influence on humanity's fortunes, over and against the ascendancy of space as elevated during the scientific revolution and to this day. The methods used to investigate dead matter by physics can give no orientation for the living processes of society. If one looks at society in its complex genesis and development, one would see time as the carrier of human spirit. Time is conceived by Rosenstock-Huessy as a tension between the calls of the past and the future, which requires that we respond in the present. And like the other thinkers we have discussed, our institutions are the vessels of our human spirit. We are constantly under a duty to decide whether our institutions are at any given moment up to the task of carrying us into the future. This requires that we live at once in the past, the present, and the future for the survival of our societies.

In the final estimation, what can be said to constitute the primary insight with which this group of thinkers transacts? The answer is intimately linked with the broader question of what particular illustration of institutions they provide us. Their vision is far more expansive than the mere idea of institutions as some established law, practice, or custom, or even some established association or organization of interests. This prosaic interpretation ignores institution's most fertile and vital aspect as it ignores the nature of their establishment. It removes from the understanding of institutions the drive, spirit, need, or protest that gave birth to the cut-and-dried reality of the institution. The historical institutionalist, by concentrating on the historical nature of institutions, is hence far more attuned to the creative base upon which the institutions

46. Rosenstock-Huessy, *Speech and Reality.*
47. Rosenstock-Huessy, "Heraclitus to Parmenides," 8.

are founded. All institutions that have survived a historical process will mask their vital origins to mere contemporary observers. The energies of the people who fought for their creation and establishment end up being veiled from the sight of those who have no eyes for historical legacies. A theory of institutions should always take into account this hidden aspect, the living human moorings that even the most procrustean law, custom, or association has embedded in its institutional sinews. The sweeping insight of the historical institutionalist is that societies are a constellation of longings. They are a living assemblage of collectively nurtured and articulated appeals for social survival and expansion that echo through time, and hence not necessarily the dead weight of history or the shackles of time.

So while from the radical political perspective the historical institutionalist is nothing more than a conservative, it misses the deeper insight that its conservatism is only seeming and never the prime motivation, even less so the ineluctable conclusion of its thinking. Instead its primary insight is to recognize the vitalism and truth-generating capabilities in history. History is irruption and subsequent development, its insights and truths a constant surprise, embedded, immanent, and changing. History generates indigenous norms indifferent to any norms from an unrelated field, any field that may seek via some frustration with history's seeming perverse operation to redirect and control the warp and woof of its unpredictable movement. And morality is the most foreign norm that history ever encounters. From the timeless moral perspective of the radical, the institution comes to reign over us from some alien, indecipherable impulse. In order to combat the seeming senselessness of history, the radical must deploy a timeless abstract norm to do battle with organically derived types and truths immanent in history, and encapsulated in the institutional scaffolding of society. The inclusion of the historical institutionalist perspective is a non-normative foil to the normative application of morality upon history by radicals throughout modern politics.

Certainly we are all heirs and receivers of historical legacies, gifts both good and bad. But the historical institutionalist's ground for judging the merits or deficiencies of historical inheritances is history itself: history understood as the impulses and powers of individuals and collectives marshaled so as to give continuing life to our efforts and hopes when the individuals and collectives themselves have perished. Institutions are a grasping for social immortality and perseverance in the face of the limitations and powerlessness of the finite human will. And here lies the point of difference with the radical political imagination, whose conception of power is simply too reduced, restrained, and then ultimately inflated within the will. As soon as the will institutes any of its power to live outside itself, the radical imagination will look at this, its very own product, as a new obstacle. The fate of any timeless moral understanding of the will is to be condemned to always devour its children. Ultimately this problem revolves around the radical separation made between the individual and society by radical theorists.

So what separates the historical institutionalists we have briefly surveyed from Rousseau, Marx, and Foucault are their attitudes to, and appraisals of, the institutional makeup of society. It is obvious that Rousseau, Marx, and Foucault are highly critical of the social formations that have developed over time. All three also give effect to serious, if very different, separations between the individual and society. Rather than the individual being expressed through the institutional structures of society, as in the case of the historical institutionalists, the individual is worked upon and coerced by the society. Rather than the examination and study of society helping to comprehend the interests of the individual, the society instead is seen as a formidable barrier or obstacle to his or her satisfaction—hence the importance of Kant's dualism for grasping the workings of the radical political consciousness. The thinkers discussed in this study may not all erect a thorough Kantian dualism in their philosophies, but its residue remains in their attitudes to institutions and critiques of society. If a separation is actively cultivated between individuals and societies, then the institutional architecture of society will always be viewed as being subject to a dehumanizing and alienating effect upon its individual members. The inclusion of the historical institutionalist perspective in this study will help us fathom this tendency to alienation in the radical political imagination. While certainly not attempting to suggest that dehumanization and alienation are not real threats and possibilities in our myriad forms of social interaction, this study reflects on how the radical's erection of a timeless standard may exponentially heighten the possibility that his critical gaze will pathologically detect such dehumanization and alienation, emergent or fully fledged among all things. What is at stake is to what extent the radical political imagination is equipped with the requisite intellectual framework for timely and historically minded social reproduction. And what will be observed is the ways that history is transfigured as solely the past, solely the present, and solely the future by these thinkers. But life is not lived solely.

PART 1

Jean-Jacques Rousseau

1

Rousseau's Convoluted Personal Relation to Time

[t]he child does not explain the man but, perhaps, the man the child.

Eugen Rosenstock-Huessy, *The Origin of Speech*

In studying the timelessness of Rousseau's political scheme, perhaps the most fertile starting point is Rousseau's vast autobiographical project. Not only does it furnish the investigator with many illuminating and disturbing bookmarks in his journey through life, it is also a rich pool of his personal attitudes to time. His desperate need to explain himself to his time, defend his past, to both create and annul his future, has left to history an awesome testament to self-understanding, or indeed self-deception. These works represent the headstone that Rousseau composed for himself. They are the legacy and memory he wished to bequeath to future reading and judging of his life and work. But most importantly, these literary testaments show a mind animated by the timeless while using various temporal measures, with various levels of success, to bring this atemporal state into being.

There are problems and reservations regarding this approach. Why begin with autobiographical works embarked on at the end of Rousseau's literary life, in a work concerned principally with the political and social works formulated earlier? What possible bearing could these later works have on the political, social, and philosophical timelessness already cast? What from the products of a man's later life can be isolated to throw light upon his development? One answer is to follow Rousseau's example and forage through his earliest making for the seed of his life. He himself pointed in this direction when he wrote, "I was almost born dead, and they had little hope of saving me. I brought with me the seed of a disorder which has grown stronger with the years."[1] Certainly one legacy of Rousseau's ideas is the now popular assumption that one's life is shaped and formed in one's childhood. In his *Confessions* Rousseau scoured his life for the key to his woes, discovering the hypersensitive child to be the specter of his adult life. Rousseau considers his supposed uniqueness to be forged in youthful experience. Rousseau's educational novel *Emile* also bears witness to the belief that a child's experiences are the locus of its future path. Rousseau rebuked the thinkers of his day by saying, "We know nothing of childhood.... They are always looking for the man in the child, without considering what he is before he becomes a man."[2] The modern obsession with discovering our nucleus within the explicitness of our infancy is pure Rousseau. Rousseau opened the Pandora's box of childhood, whose spillage seeped not only throughout the rest of his life, but through history itself. Indeed we will see that Rousseau is attempting, politically, nothing less than the rebirth of humanity itself. His philosophy is built on the promise and malleability of a society's regained childhood.

But perhaps for us the reverse is true, a reverse expressed by the quote at the beginning of this chapter. The man explains the child, and not the other way around. Could not the complex array of hopes, prayers, desires, fears, and resignations of adulthood provide richer illumination for a life than the unformed, unelaborated simplicities of the child? If we accept the direction of Rousseau's thinking, then his later work becomes detached from previous work. The three autobiographical writings would have little connection with the discourses or the social contract. There becomes nothing but a succession of events, each one pushing the next further from its origin—works divided by time contributing to the remoteness of their influence on each other, the progress of thought reaching no culmination and hence no ultimate explanation. If we reverse

---

1. Jean-Jacques Rousseau, *Confessions,* selected and translated with an introduction by J. M. Cohen (London: Penguin, 1953), 19.
2. Rousseau, *Emile,* translated by Barbara Foxley (London: J. M. Dent and Sons, 1974), 1.

the investigation, however, we can give all of Rousseau's life and work a richer, stronger unity than the thin, impoverished unity that childhood affords it. The man looking back on his life provides a totality and comprehensiveness to that life, akin to a rebirth, that more profoundly illustrates his movements, motivations, and actions. In other words, in order to study how time and timelessness operate in a body of work, it is best to start from the work that encapsulates and recasts the times that man has lived. We must observe how time has coined this man. With this method there becomes a sense that each work anticipates the next, and that each work in some way completes the last, each text requiring the next. It is for this reason that we must begin with Rousseau's later attempts at autobiography. For only here can we view Rousseau's convoluted personal relationship to time.

Rousseau composed three important autobiographical works: *The Confessions, Rousseau juge de Jean-Jacques—Dialogues,* and *Les Reveries du Promeneur Solitaire.* In one of the more detailed explorations of Rousseau's autobiographical writings, *Memory and Narrative,* James Olney discusses the differing narrative structures of the three autobiographical works with relation to time. If the *Confessions* is a linear account of Rousseau's life, a narration, and the nature of the *Dialogues* is dialectic, or dialogue between Rousseau's perceived and true character, the *Reveries* is a circular work of self-circumscribed tranquility, or a meditation. Olney highlights the trilogistic nature of these three works to show how the whole movement is an attempt to transform the "opposition, conflict and violence of linear time and lived experience" into a timeless appreciation and escape into the eternal.[3] For Olney, one work leads inevitably to the next as each attempt at autobiography is met with failure. The connectedness of the autobiographical project comes from attempting the same thing in three different manners. That same connecting theme is Rousseau's need to justify himself to others and ultimately himself. The autobiographies are hence also connected to his earlier work by being a response to the disdain, censure, spiteful pamphleteering, and burned effigies that work initiated. Olney's trilogistic argument is persuasive and helps us to map Rousseau's relation to time, rather than simply how he wished to portray himself to his audience.

3. James Olney, *Memory and Narrative: The Weave of Lifewriting* (Chicago: University of Chicago Press, 1998), 111.

Each autobiography is principally concerned with one aspect of time. The *Confessions* situates itself within Rousseau's past, while the *Dialogues* is most profoundly concerned with the future. Lastly, the *Reveries* is an exploration of the present of the instant. This approach involves the risk of imposing an overly rigid interpretation upon the texts, since they are all concerned with the triplicity of time. To suggest that each does not touch upon aspects of the past, present, and future of course is not true. But what is clear is that one dominant direction of time applies to each work and changes according to the success or failure of each work.

A Historiography of the Self? and The Solace of the Past

The beginning of the *Confessions,* just as of his lived life, begins with the promise and enthusiasm of a man newly introduced to his history and thereby reborn into time. The expectation and hope are palpable when he states unequivocally, "I have resolved on an enterprise which has no precedent, and which, once complete, will have no imitator. My purpose is to display myself to my kind a portrait in every way true to nature, and the man I shall portray will be myself. Simply myself. I know my heart and understand my fellow man. But I am made unlike any one I have ever met."[4] This buoyantly arrogant opening to an autobiography of unconcealed personal display presents to us the mood of one who wishes to be unfettered by time. The middle-aged man, giving himself the opportunity to live his life again through words, can think of himself as entirely unique to humanity. To be born again in the imagination and memory is to be filled to the brim with possibility and worth. This is an occasion to recast his life and effect a change in the public perception of his character. He is unique not only to his, but to all times. So too is his venture in characterizing his peerless originality. From the outset of the *Confessions,* Rousseau attempts to elevate himself out of time, both his own history by rewriting his life, and history in general by campaigning for his originality. However, by book 12 Rousseau is an empty shell destroyed by his reexperienced biography. The buoyant opening is deflated to a woeful despair.

4. Rousseau, *Confessions,* 17.

Here begins the work of darkness in which I have been entombed for eight years past, without ever having been able, try as I might, to pierce its hideous obscurity. In the abyss of evil in which I am sunk I feel the weight of blows struck at me; I perceive the immediate instrument; but I can neither see the hand which directs it nor the means by which it works.[5]

It is this profound change of attitude, not so startling, since it has taken hundreds of pages to come about, that gives us the clue to Rousseau's personal relation to time. The passage of time, real or reanimated, is a corrupting, destroying force he must escape. Once this is understood as a primary need for Rousseau, much of his work opens up as a myriad of attempts, failed and successful, to understand, harness, or flee time. From the height of the first position to the depths of the last, Rousseau's history is a sustained regression through the agency of time. And this mythical regression has its origin in his childhood.

Rousseau presents his early life as a utopian paradise, immersed in the anaesthetizing haze of the countryside. It is hard not to view it as an idyllic place before time, and forever only a sad but comforting memory for Rousseau. It has been observed that this time at Bossey is similar to the biblical Garden of Eden, where Rousseau's discovery of his taste for masochism corresponds to the Christian doctrine of the Fall.[6] Contact with others dramatically shapes him, making him painfully aware of his lost innocence and virtue. This is the point where temporal descent begins.

It is this regret and remorse that gave rise to Rousseau's need to write his personal history in the first place. He wanted to realign and harness time in a more favorable reenactment. What makes the *Confessions* odd is the fact that Rousseau chose a literary vehicle such as the sequential life narrative, so shackled to a linear historical and temporal trajectory, to attempt an unraveling of its accumulated narrative and emotional weight. We should not underestimate Rousseau's concern and respect for the importance of showing his life as it unfolded in time. Rousseau did apply a historical methodology to the presentation of his life in the *Confessions*.

Commentators, concerned with the overwhelming assumption of

5. Rousseau, *Confessions*, 17, 544.

6. Huntington Williams, *Rousseau and Romantic Autobiography* (Oxford: Oxford University Press, 1983), 136.

Rousseau's lack of concern with time and history, have attempted to demonstrate Rousseau's adoption of some form of historical method. For example, Lionel Gossman writes, "I merely wish to emphasize, by examining his approach to the *Confessions,* that awareness of history is inseparable from Rousseau's thinking, that everything is understood by him in its historical being."[7] Indeed, scholars like Gossman are right to emphasize Rousseau's historical outlook, as it is a method he employs not only in the *Confessions,* but also in the "Second Discourse on Inequality" and the writings on music and language. I do not doubt that Rousseau acknowledges the powerful medium of history in the shaping of not only our individual selves, but also our societies and institutions. But while historicity and temporality are considerable arrows in Rousseau's bow, their overemphasis by commentators tends to drown out a far more central aspect of Rousseau's thinking, an aspect that overturns Rousseau's credentials as a temporal thinker. The aspect that debunks Rousseau's use of the historical method as merely cosmetic and auxiliary is the constant reminder of his unchanging nature, or the constancy of his feelings. It would be more accurate to say, in a way denying neither the historical nor timeless concerns of Rousseau, that in the rush to ground things in a historical development and method he advances unjustifiably the aspects of constancy and eternity in his self, which are hence undisguised as the forefront of Rousseau's concern. The push to historicity advances the timeless.

Rousseau was an ardent believer in the natural goodness of man. It is a doctrine that is abundant in all of his work and shines in all of his most famous statements. The openings to both the *Social Contract* ("Man is born free and everywhere he is in chains"), and *Emile* ("God makes all things good; man meddles with them and they become evil"), convince us that a natural, unsullied goodness is the spring for Rousseau's imagination. It is a sentiment that suggests a sharp opposition between a natural goodness and its enemies, or the outside factors that corrupt its innocent probity. Such a division was not just a theoretical fissure for the purposes of social criticism, but was a manifestation of a deeply felt personal schism. Such was the strength of the conviction

7. Lionel Gossman, "Time and History in Rousseau," *Studies on Voltaire* 30 (1964): 311–49, 313.

that the same creed, under a different guise, is to be found in the *Confessions*. The binary between goodness and corruption mutates into feeling and fact. Observe Rousseau's stated aim when he writes, "But I should not fulfil the aim of this book if I did not at the same time reveal my inner feelings."[8] Rousseau's "inner feelings," or sentiments, are the real characters of his autobiographies. What is miraculous about the *Confessions* is the almost singular concern for divulging the feelings connected with events and facts to the almost complete overturning of those events and facts. Facts are Jean-Jacques's illusion; feelings are his truth. "I had no idea of the facts, but I was already familiar with every feeling. I had grasped nothing; I had sensed everything."[9]

The disturbing machinations of the outside world become of little consequence when contrasted with the natural purity of one's vivid inner emotions, so shamefully neglected of serious account by the mechanistic philosophies of the day. Rousseau would balance this account by writing a confessional history of the unity of his feelings. Despite the disconcerted and contradictory picture we gain of Rousseau from his own actions and those directed toward him from others, all will be revealed and forgiven when Rousseau uncloaks the truth of his passions. In the outside world one's endeavors and actions become dispersed and corrupted, while in the soul the natural goodness of Rousseau's character is retained. By exposing the true feelings behind his actions, Rousseau had found the ultimate redemptive source: literary apologetic abundance. It is indubitable that this is the true narrative feature of the *Confessions*. Unconcerned with logic and reason, this is a subjective observation of the inner life, not an objective observation of outside reality. This powerful romantic drive behind the *Confessions* of course comes at the expense of facts. And while you cannot deny that the facts and events of Rousseau's life are the substance and structure of the *Confessions*, they are nearly always subordinated by the feelings that accompanied, caused, and rose from the ashes of those events.

This was seen clearly by Huntington Williams, who writes, "But the principle for selecting and ordering this material lies elsewhere, in the image of personal identity elaborated in the author's textual world, be-

8. Rousseau, *Confessions*, 88.
9. Rousseau, *Confessions*, 20.

fore the autobiography could begin. Although the image is aesthetic and fictional, it is whole and complete in a way which the actual autobiographer is not."[10] Rousseau's perception of the settings, peoples, events, and actions is always presaged by, or filtered through, the artistic vision of inner harmony he has fashioned of and for himself. Whether it be Rousseau's abandonment of a friend in the throes of an epileptic fit, stealing apples from his master's larder, accusing a young girl of a crime he committed, exposing himself to ladies on the street, his opportunistic religious conversion, or forsaking his five children to the uncertainties of the foundling home, all of these tangible facts are explained away or justified by the nobility of his feelings. At the very least he attempts to garner sympathy from his readers through his gracious contrition and guilt. It is as if confessing these crimes is enough proof of his sterling character to overturn any doubts that the crimes themselves might throw upon the issue. By appealing to the inner core of his experience of events, Rousseau can rein in a life characterized by transition, disjunction, and movement by the stability and unity of his feelings. Of course these emotions can be as tumultuous and violent as the events they are connected to, suggesting that such unity of feeling is as illusory as any unity in real-world relations. But Rousseau views the real world with a distrust and suspicion of its value, while viewing his feelings as inherently good, unarguable, and truthful.

Nowhere is this more conspicuous than in the distinction Rousseau makes between *amour de soi* (love of self) and *amour propre* (self-love). *Amour de soi* is described as the natural condition by which an animal seeks its innocent, but self-centered preservation. It is a concept of the self that is replete with myth, instinct, and solitude, having its foundation and origin within the state of nature. It is an uncontaminated self, unconcerned with the outside world, hence not affected by it or guilty of the injuries it may perpetrate against it in the pursuit of its own survival. It is a state of freedom that allows one to enjoy and love oneself without infection from a fallen society. *Amour propre,* on the other hand, is a concept of the self in its relations and mediations with others. Opposed to the natural absolutism of *amour de soi,* it offers a contrived and relative self that finds its birth in the formation of society. It is a social evil

10. Williams, *Rousseau and Romantic Autobiography,* 126.

brought about simply through contact and awareness of other selves that invade the mental purity of isolation. Such love of the self "leads each individual to make more of himself than of any other," and "causes all the mutual damage men inflict one on another."[11]

This subject rises in much of Jean-Jacques's work, but it isn't until the autobiographical project that its import becomes clear. These two theories of the self become assigned to Rousseau's personal life itself. The *Confessions* shows us that what was once portrayed as mere theory has in fact always been a deeply felt reality. The *Confessions* viewed under this light shows that it is composed of two separate, but interacting narrative threads that correspond to *amour de soi* and *amour propre*. The inexplicable and troubling actions and events of his life are clearly demarcated as occurring under the influence of a varnished and transient *amour propre*, while his true innate nature is contained in the self-circumscribed simplicity and beauty of *amour de soi*. This of course throws Rousseau's status as a historical or temporal thinker into a disquieting relief. The trend of seeing Rousseau as attempting a historiography of the self in the *Confessions* can really only be maintained by applying it to the *amour propre* side of Rousseau's being. And as we shall see, this was precisely what Rousseau was attempting to escape from throughout his life, and through his autobiographical journey. The vague and timeless *amour de soi* state of being is the true hero of this first autobiography and is meant as a foil to the more timely and historical, and thus more concrete, aspects Rousseau is forced to explore. While this work does not deny the position that Rousseau is a historical thinker, it does extend the claim that such historical temporal thinking is designed to further or enhance a timeless understanding of human subjectivity. In this case an autobiographical history is the moving, fluctuating backdrop, better able to contrastingly surround the static and unchanging aspects that Rousseau wishes to impress upon his audience. We will see later how this embrace of the historical tableau helped Rousseau reach and reproduce other timeless entities, not just in his own life, but also in metaphysics, morality, and politics. But there is still further to explore in his vast autobiographic project.

Rousseau ends his *Confessions* by describing the audience reaction to

11. Rousseau, *The Social Contract and Discourses* (London: J. M. Dent and Sons, 1938), 197.

a reading of the completed work. That reading ended with a plea to justice and truth regarding the judgment of his character, and is remembered as follows, "Thus I concluded my reading, and everyone was silent. Mme d'Egmont was the only person who seemed moved. She trembled visibly but quickly controlled herself, and remained quiet, as did the rest of the company."[12] Rousseau's sequential history of his life, his testament to the natural goodness of his soul, is met with resounding silence. A historiography of the self is discovered as a frighteningly poor literary vehicle with which to transcend one's limitations and convince others of a hidden virtue. Can reliving one's past persuade a present or redirect a future? Unfortunately for Rousseau, the audience's silence gave him his answer.

A Tribunal of Selves and a Prayer for the Future

Suffering from persecution mania and a furtively paranoid conspiracy complex, Rousseau undertook to resume his autobiographical project anew. The next autobiographical text is fundamentally entwined in its plot functions with what he perceived to be the suspicious plot of others against him, compounded by the universal silence that had greeted the *Confessions*.[13] In the *Confessions* the two poles of his life had intermingled and coalesced in a way to make them indistinguishable. The timeless graces of Rousseau's *amour de soi* are too closely approximated with the adulterated temporal self wholly the fault of *amour propre*. This outcome is a logical consequence of the narrative structure of the *Confessions*. A historiography of the self must by its nature explore the self in its unfolding. Whatever natural atemporal core exists in a person, it can only be expressed in momentary bursts through the passing evanescence of socially determined existence. Rousseau thus turned to the dialectical, yet emotive possibilities of dialogue.[14]

Rousseau juge de Jean-Jacques—Dialogues, is a dialogue between two characters who represent the two perceptions of Rousseau. They are discussing the reputation of the author, who is referred to only as "J.J.," and

12. Rousseau, *Confessions,* 606.   13. Olney, *Memory and Narrative,* 159.
14. Eugene L. Stelzig, *The Romantic Subject in Autobiography* (Charlottesville: University Press of Virginia, 2000) 117–18: "As a mode of argumentation and rhetoric since the Greeks, the dialogue is a genre both philosophic and literary, and open to the voice of reason as well as that of emotion. The use of the form allows Rousseau to impart a semblance of logical order and dialectical argumentation to his paranoid obsession."

who remains unseen and unheard throughout the dialogues. The defender of his reputation is a native Genevan, receptive to the ideas in his books, named Rousseau. The interlocutor, named the Frenchman, is the public perception of Rousseau, whose opinion of the author is affected and influenced dramatically by the "league" of literary defamers against Rousseau. From this very rudimentary character synopsis, it is obvious that we are dealing with a fractured or broken sense of self. Not only do we have the author himself speaking through all the characters, but we also have his presence as a character named "J.J." Not only this, but his defender is named after him, also. We also have someone representing his public self, the self the author sees as a grossly unfair misrepresentation, and of whom he wishes to be rid. The maddening confusion of this tribunal of selves, whether it is the byproduct of the dialectical structure adopted for the book or the expression of mental derangement, is up for discussion. What is far more interesting for this study is what this separation of the self is a response to, and how it helps Rousseau achieve his ends.

The use of dialogue allows Rousseau to overcome many of the difficulties he encountered in the *Confessions.* The first of these advantages is the ability of dialogue to separate the two senses of his self that he had blurred. Whether or not these two attitudes to self are in any way distinct in actual, linear, and temporal life was severely in doubt after the *Confessions.* By placing the two selves into neatly confined characters that present their differing arguments, Rousseau is not only able to isolate his preferred natural true self from his unjust festering public representation, but is able to kill it off through the workings of the dialectic. His misguided and misunderstood public persona, personified by the highly biased and ignorant Frenchman, is turned onto the road to truth and justice via J.J.'s defense counsel, Rousseau. This brings us to the next major advantage behind the *Dialogues,* namely that Rousseau is free to be his own accuser and justifier. By being in sole control of the characters and their arguments, he has effectively eliminated the outside world from influence in the proceedings of this imaginative literary courtroom. The dialectic is always shielded from interference from other outside voices, and when both sides of the dialectic are in fact one, then complete control is gained. It should, however, be noted at this stage that while it is clear that the *Dialogues* is an attempt to bolster the fortunes of his good, natural self over his constructed social self, Rousseau never fully escapes the ravages of *amour propre*. The whole book still remains a desperate plea for the love of the outside world, the very self-destructive and negative love that crippled Rousseau throughout his life.

The last major benefit to come from the structure of the *Dialogues* concerns the definite abstractions that these characters become when they are no longer situated in an actual continuing life. There is a sense that because Rousseau's contradictory nature has now been clearly divided into differing characters, Rousseau himself no longer exists. Instead of the dynamic and dramatic interplay of his two selves within time in the *Confessions,* this is replaced by two abstract ideas of his self, whose interaction occurs in the atemporal environment of the mind. The self is divided, demarcated, and abstracted in order to resurrect the true Rousseau, who was buried in the unstoppable cascade of time of the *Confessions.* This is one way in which Rousseau was able to escape the confusion and pain of time: not by making his life defensible in every moment, but by making the aggregate of his life a defensible entity. This also meant that he was no longer defending his past to the present, but he was now attempting to defend his life's work to the future.

This becomes patently clear when you consider that the crux of Rousseau's defense of J.J. to the Frenchman rests on the condition that J.J. was actually the author of the writings ascribed to him. The general argument of the *Dialogues* follows the line that this "abominable man" and his heinous actions could not be the same man who wrote such inspiring and exemplary books as the ones associated with his name. Surely then, this man is not the true author of these books. However, if it can be proven that his authorship is valid, then perhaps the conspiratorial rumors and public slander are false.[15] He writes, "Don't even think of the author as you read, and without any bias either in favour or against, let your soul experience the impressions it will receive. You will thus assure yourself of the intention behind the writing of these books and of whether they can be the work of a scoundrel who was harbouring evil designs."[16]

In the third and last dialogue, the Frenchman relays the ideas he

15. For an excellent commentary on the logic behind authorship argument in the *Dialogues,* see James F. Jones, "The Argument as Hermeneutic Quest," in *Rousseau's Dialogues: An Interpretative Essay* (Geneva: Librairie Droz, 1991).

16. Rousseau, *Rousseau, Judge of Jean-Jacques* (Hanover, N.H.: University Press of New England, 1990), 31.

has gleaned from a rigorous and sustained reading of J.J.'s books, and a simple extrapolation of Rousseau's "system" follows. There is an obvious dependence made in the *Dialogues,* which did not exist in the *Confessions,* between Rousseau's character and his system of thought. The two are made to lean for survival upon each other. In other words, Rousseau's entire literary production has become the ultimate defense against the charges brought against him. The man who once thought his honest, innocent life would be his defense has now turned to the most timeless aspect of his life for security: his words. Words that will live beyond his body are where he now rests. The future is now the domain with which he is concerned when he despairingly writes, "The hope that his memory be restored someday to the honour it deserves, and that his books become useful through the esteem owed to their Author is henceforth the only hope that can please him in this world."[17]

All in all, the *Dialogues* are an exhausting last-ditch attempt to control the fate of his work. He is still attached to time in such a way that he cares what becomes of his reputation, but he has all but given up on guaranteeing that to his contemporary world. Rousseau maintains that he is happy and confident to leave his work in the hands of providence: "Oh providence! Oh nature! Treasure of the poor, resource of the unfortunate. The person who feels, knows your holy laws and trusts them, the person whose heart is at peace and whose body does not suffer, thanks to you is not entirely prey to adversity."[18] When the twists and turns of his self reposed within the story of his life, his redemption was always to be sought within the time of his mortality. However, when the self, in all its myriad permutations, has been divested of temporal content and abstracted, resurrection is to be sought in immortality. Throwing your soul to the hands of the future, you no longer have to display it to the present. When your hope resides in the future, you no longer have need of the things or people of this world. The proof of this desire of Rousseau's to transcend time through the instrument of the *Dialogues* is shown by the movements of the manuscript after its completion, which he outlines in a postlude entitled "History of the Proceeding Writing."

On February 24, 1776, Rousseau entered the cathedral of Notre Dame in Paris in order to deposit the manuscript of the *Dialogues* upon the

17. Rousseau, *Rousseau, Judge of Jean-Jacques,* 245.
18. Rousseau, *Rousseau, Judge of Jean-Jacques,* 119.

high altar.[19] However, his objective was thwarted by a locked gate at the entrance to the altar, which Rousseau in his many visits to Notre Dame had never noticed. This was to be Rousseau's literary prayer to the future, and it was being rejected by God. The new audience for this work had been carefully chosen. Rather than his contemporaries, Rousseau was to be judged by God himself. Rather than be judged by the iniquitous minds of men and leave his fortune to the uncertain shifting sands of time, Rousseau would offer himself straight to the ultimate arbiter, he who forgives at all times. Surely God would ensure that Rousseau be received favorably in the future. The locked gates acted the part previously filled by the deafening silence of the *Confessions* audience. Being rejected by the eternal, Rousseau had no choice but to leave the manuscript in the hands of those he wished to shut out. He offered it to Condillac, who duly treated it as a work in need of academic editing, rather than as the soul of a man. Rejected again, he defeatedly left only the first dialogue with a young Englishman, who published it after Rousseau's death.

The Repose of the Self in the Continuous Instant

Having removed himself from a society that does nothing but heap scorn and derision upon him, Rousseau desired to safeguard himself from corruption. Rousseau's desire for divine self-sufficiency had been no great secret among his commentators. He hints at this in the fourth book of *Emile*: "A really happy man is a hermit; God only enjoys absolute happiness."[20] Having been shunned by the God whose approval he coveted, Rousseau now attempts to show the world the wondrous state of Godlike self-sufficiency that he has attained in the absence of that approval. Derided by God, the only answer is to become like him, and the vehicle for this is reverie. Hence Rousseau's last literary work was titled *Reveries of the Solitary Walker*, a work composed of ten meditations outlining his attempts at acquiring and experiencing exquisite reverie. In many ways it is a book typical of Rousseau's conflicted self. Filled with tangled protestations, pitying, doubts, diatribes, and glorifications, it seems to fly in the face of the argument that this is the spontaneous liter-

19. Peter France, "Introduction," in *Reveries of the Solitary Walker*, by Jean-Jacques Rousseau, selected and translated by Peter France (London: Penguin, 1979), 8.
20. Rousseau, *Emile*, 182.

ary meanderings of a happy and dazed nature-worshipper. Under what capacity could this be considered a circular, meditative work conveying tranquility, harmony, and peace? Peter France's close familiarity with the work as one of its translators is instructive here: "My experience as a translator seems to confirm that the language of the *Reveries,* far from being the natural jottings of a dreamer, is the result of careful and elaborate construction."[21] This is all because Rousseau is still engaged in the act of autobiography, is still engaging with an audience and is thus still trying to convince. Rousseau knew full well that writing was a debased activity, making you entirely dependent and needful of gratification. And despite his protestations, he knew he would never be fully free from the hold of a possibly redeeming audience.

But what is interesting is what he is attempting to convince his audience of. What makes the *Reveries* circular is the attempt to convince his audience that he is no longer concerned with them or the world, and to map the times and conditions when he was free from their grip. He dismisses them in this fashion: "So now they are strangers and foreigners to me; they no longer exist for me, since such is their will. But I, detached as I am from them and the whole world, what am I? This must now be the object of my inquiry."[22]

When is Rousseau truly himself, or at least truly self-sufficient and engrossed in *amour de soi?* The answer he arrives at at the end of his autobiographical quest is that his self is left only to repose within a trick of time ... the reverie. The experience of reverie is a trick of time because it couples two contradictory states within the same imaginary apperception. To experience reverie for Rousseau is to fuse the instant with continuity. This implies a strange paradox pointed out to us by Williams: "An instant is discrete and discontinuous with other instants; continuity implies a fused and ongoing process. Rousseau's reveries, however, do not permit this distinction."[23] It can be said that Rousseau's major search in reverie is for a paradoxical state where an instant becomes continuous, or a continuous instant. The instant in this case should be separated from the sharp, unsettling epiphanies experienced by Rousseau, such as the life-changing instant when he read the question for the prize essay of

21. France, "Introduction," in *Reveries of the Solitary Walker,* 14.
22. Rousseau, *Reveries of the Solitary Walker,* 27.
23. Williams, *Rousseau and Romantic Autobiography,* 16.

the Academy of Dijon. Rousseau's reveries couldn't be further removed from such frightening turns. Rousseau's reveries, rather than with a sudden approaching burst, come on calmly and pleasantly with the delicate arrangement of favorable conditions. They take place in quaint rural settings, often precipitated by a rhythmic monotonous hypnotic movement: writing, walking, or the gentle undulation of waves. Its arrival occurs within an instant, is sudden and uncontrolled, but Rousseau slips into them rather than being forcibly and violently pushed. Rousseau captures the joyous instant and holds it in the mind. Reverie is the strange continuation of an instantaneous mood, a momentary escape from time that is endowed with duration in another realm; a continuous instant. It is within this illusory escapism that Rousseau becomes what he was always meant to be. It is here that he can isolate his true self. Mark J. Temper describes it as a state where "action, freedom and goodness are one. Such a trinity renders superfluous any moral and intellectual analysis of past and future, since everything takes place within the confines of an ineffable living present."[24]

Self-sufficiency and *amour de soi,* the common attributes of the good natural man, can only be reached in the social world via isolation and escapism. Action, freedom, and goodness for the natural man become inaction, freedom, and goodness for the social man. Past and future are too painful, and so Rousseau settles for the sterility of a timeless present. In the throes of unmediated experience, all moral and intellectual categories dissipate. In such a state Rousseau can taste the natural life of pre-social man, devoid of the thought processes that inhibit and haunt social man. It is an enduring irony that the most fleeting and unnatural of procedures, the reverie, is the most pure way Rousseau discovered of being natural. Society represents for Rousseau enslavement. Time, as the engine of change and flux that characterizes that enslavement, must be comprehensively escaped. This can only be achieved by retreating into a self attached to nothing but itself. This type of circularity can only come about through reverie. Such thoughts and resignations about society and time have come to the end of their journey in the writing of the *Reveries.* Rousseau expresses it best in one of his most famous and eloquent passages:

24. Mark J. Temper, *Time in Rousseau and Kant* (Geneva: Librarie E. Droz, 1958), 24.

Everything is in constant flux on this earth. Nothing keeps the same unchanging shape, and our affections, being attached to things outside us, necessarily change and pass away as they do. Always out ahead of us or lagging behind, they recall a past which is gone and a future which may never come into being; there is nothing solid there for the heart to attach itself to. Thus our earthly joys are almost without exception creatures of the moment; I doubt whether any of us knows the meaning of lasting happiness ... and how can we give the name of happiness to a fleeting state which leaves our hearts still empty and anxious, either regretting something that is past or desiring something that is yet to come?[25]

Such a crowning personal despair and longing for the eternal and whole have a significant authority over Rousseau's political and social thought. It will be argued that almost all of Rousseau's previous work as a political philosopher, social critic, and author fundamentally presages in other forms all we have learned about his attitude to time in the auto-biographies. This study will now observe how the variable operations of time and timelessness as expressed in Rousseau's autobiographies have antecedent similarities in his more theoretical works. But also, what this examination of the three autobiographies and their relations to the past, future, and present has shown us is how easy it is for a timeless mindset bent on evading the ravages of time to seek an escapist goal by accentuating one of the three dimensions of time over the others. All three radical political thinkers will do this in some way, exaggerating one province of time at the expense of the others. It is this movement of timeless thought into stressing one aspect of time too strenuously that constitutes their respective illusions of history. While Rousseau's autobiographical project runs the whole gamut of these attempts, pushing timeless hopes into all three modes of time, it will be shown that the overwhelming direction behind his theoretical works is to push the eternal into the distant past.

25. Rousseau, *Reveries of the Solitary Walker,* 88.

ᚦ 2

The First Attack and First History

Enlightenment: Rousseau's Enemy and Milieu

How radical was Rousseau's breach with his contemporaries? Exactly how divergent was the prize essay on the Arts and Sciences from the general tenor of eighteenth-century society? To gauge this it is necessary to understand what Rousseau was fortifying himself against. What was the major force of his day to which he objected so forcefully? For Cassirer, the eighteenth century had an "innate thirst for knowledge, an insatiable intellectual curiosity."[1] The amazing advances in the arts and sciences over the previous two centuries and the flowering of an intellectual climate unrivaled in history bequeathed to the eighteenth century not just a desire to continue such disinterested scientific inquiry, but also to declare a very interested crusade to use it for political purposes. A way of thinking had been carefully cultivated, and the eighteenth century saw its mission in the extension, consolidation, and, most importantly, politicizing of that thinking. To use a familiar and popular metaphor of the day, the status of reason had been raised to the "heights of the sun," and was going to illuminate society. Regarded as an original force rediscovered rather than as the inheritance it was, it was to be used to sweep away all other inheritances, customs, traditions, and authorities not living

1. Ernst Cassirer, *Philosophy of the Enlightenment* (Boston: Beacon Press, 1961), 14.

up to its glare. Not only would its rigor dissolve things to their essence for appraisal, but reason could also be used to reconstruct society in its image. In this regard Rousseau is no different from his contemporaries in recognizing the stultifying social structures and the new powers to overcome them. Where he differs is in his opinion of the benefits of art, science, philosophy, and the "community of the enlightened" in society. Rousseau's later, more mature political ideals were in keeping with his times, but the foundation from which they sprang comes from a different world entirely. Such a conflicted position is evidenced by looking at the projected aims of that "weapon" of enlightenment, the *Encyclopaedia*—a work that Rousseau contributed to, but was clearly out of step with. Diderot states in his "Preliminary Discourse" to the *Encyclopaedia* just how important an enlightened society was to the progress of science on nature and Man and on the general advancement of human reason: "The ideas acquired through reading and social contacts are the germs of almost all discoveries. It is the air that we inhale in an unconscious way, and it supplies us with life."[2]

The *Encyclopaedia* spectacularly epitomized its time. Used on the one hand to criticize and evaluate the state and society, it was also to be used as a guide for the reform and education of the society and its people.[3] And in this overt purpose Rousseau is an untroubled member. But the enterprise of the *Encyclopaedia* epitomized something far more profound than the simple critique of society. It was a proud statement of the happy confluence between philosophy and society, condensed in the quote above. Knowledge is first and foremost seen as having a social capacity. Knowledge can only progress with the right social organization, and the right social organization can only be built on a bedrock of rational ideas. Intellectual culture, civilization, progress, society, arts, and science are all collapsed into a vision of future perfected humanity. The *Encyclopaedia* represents a "new play for power by the philosophers."[4] And so "the eighteenth century is a time of the cultural flourishing of

2. Denis Diderot, *The Encyclopedia: Selections,* edited and translated by Stephen J. Gendzier (New York: Harper and Row, 1967), 13.

3. "Diderot himself, originator of the *Encyclopedia*, states that its purpose is not only to supply a certain body of knowledge but also to bring about a change in the mode of thinking"; from Cassirer, *Philosophy of the Enlightenment,* 14.

4. Robert Catley and Wayne Cristaudo, *This Great Beast: Progress and the Modern State* (Aldershot: Ashgate, 1997), 143.

philosophy and the increasing importance that philosophical ideas will play in the political process which was increasingly absorbing the middle class."[5]

But it is here that we locate Rousseau's departure. He simply could not accept such a view of progress on the heels of a general social culture of science. That a work that condemns such a view could be his passport to the very literary world driving such change, and that the essay was written for the Academy of Dijon, undoubtedly a major institutional engine in the surrounding social transformation, goes a long way to show Rousseau's conflicted position in eighteenth-century society. Enlightenment was both his enemy and his milieu. Rousseau's complaint is not so much with wisdom and knowledge in themselves, but with the reality of these things as social prerogatives. The major thesis of the "First Discourse" is to deny that the advance of arts and sciences is in any way connected with the advance of morals and virtue. Not only does he deny the positive connection of the two, which was such a prominent prejudice among the men and women of letters, but he in fact affirms the negative. As knowledge and art gain precedence in a society, morality and virtue are set on an inverse path. A life characterized by urbanity, commerce, literature, ideas, and social engagement is a false and empty existence. Civilization erodes the essential decency of humans. And while this sentiment flew in the face of the cosmopolitan reality of European life, it still struck resonant chords with those being blindly swept away on the wave of the developing nation state. The instant popularity of Rousseau's "Discourse on the Arts and Sciences" was to prove that he had persuasively enunciated a regretful nostalgia latent among the educated classes. While the enlightened populace took part in the complexities of modern social life, they held secret fears of its possible consequences. Should not life be simpler and less anxious, nobler and less fractured? Perhaps Rousseau is right, and a happy ignorance is better than an enlightened mind hamstrung by decrepit morals.

The "First Discourse" is a rigorous moral condemnation of the age, but it becomes a much more complex and abstruse work when it attempts to bolster its moral argument via a comparative reconstruction of earlier historical epochs. Far from the condemnation of his contemporary age

5. Catley and Cristaudo, *This Great Beast*, 142.

being born from the careful analysis of comparable or opposing historical types, it is born primarily from a contemporary moral sentiment that then appeals to arcane historical sources to validate the argument. It is in this relation that we find the locus of time and timelessness in the radical political imagination. Rousseau's appeal to historical examples should not be seen as the motive force behind his dissatisfaction with his present, as his loathing stems from a far more abstract source. It springs from a new sense of freedom that at the stage of the "First Discourse" Rousseau had not fully identified in thought. Commentators such as Bernard Yack deem it necessary to praise Rousseau for both his historical sense and his new understanding of freedom. "Rousseau's longing to get beyond the dehumanising spirit of modern society has two basic elements: his understanding of human freedom and the contrast between the spirit of ancient and modern institutions that he takes from Montesquieu's *The Spirit of the Laws*."[6]

While this is true, I will show later how there is an inherent tension behind these two approaches to the problem of "the dehumanising spirit of modern society." In the "First Discourse" we have a timely appraisal of burgeoning social forces, born from a moral timelessness that will eventually engulf all his work, which is compelled to create an illusion of history into a standard for judgment. The more a radical will defer to history to solve problems or use historical examples to condemn contemporary evils, the more they are in fact advancing their timeless understandings of human subjectivity. History and temporality are invoked precisely to give backing to philosophical belief that demands they be dismissed and impeded. It is this type of tangled temporality and historical levity that is so characteristic in Rousseau's work. Rousseau's negative equation of civilization and morality serves two roles: first to denounce the moral quagmire of his present era, and second to extol the "active and moral virtues" of antiquity. But the question that concerns this examination is,

6. Bernard Yack, *The Longing for Total Revolution* (Princeton, N.J.: Princeton University Press, 1986), 72–73; see the chapter "Rousseau and the Historicity of Modern Institutions." See also previous chapters: "Montesquieu's Appeal to Classical Republicanism" and "Rousseau's Longing for Ancient Virtue." While Montesquieu is appealing to a discernable and approachable form of political governance for the eighteenth century, Rousseau's primary concern is with the morals of ancient peoples. Whatever institutional legacy from antiquity he wishes to instill in modernity is preoccupied with this moral, rather than political, viewpoint.

which of these is the primary focus of Rousseau's thought? Which one precedes the other, and is their connection evidence of Rousseau's historical sense? Is his present disgust manifest in his historical admiration for Sparta, or is his historical longing a product of his present surfeit? The direction of his thought in this discourse is an important precursor for understanding the timelessness that would later become dominant.

Enlightenment: Progress, Morality, and Corruption

From the outset, Rousseau defines himself in opposition. His is an attempt to subvert the self-satisfaction of European intellectual life and raise himself above its polite manners and opinions to a higher calling. "There are in all ages men born to be in bondage to the opinions of the society in which they live…. No author, who has a mind to outlive his own age, should write for such readers."[7] On this account Rousseau separates himself from the politely quarreling, but essentially agreeing, intelligentsia who make up, in his opinion, a habitual orthodoxy. From this position he deems to have knowledge about which they know not that transcends the knowledge of the day. It is not a publicly fashionable, barren knowledge that Rousseau speaks, but knowledge wholly in the service of lost virtue. Rather than "metaphysical subtleties" devoid of natural inclination, Rousseau pleads his readers to accept "a sentiment or feeling of the heart as criterion of truth."[8] From the position of speaking above them, Rousseau immediately begins to diagnose the disease and report the symptoms. "The mind as well as the body, has its needs: those of the body are the basis of society, those of the mind its ornaments."[9]

In a world where government and law provide for the safety and security of their constituents, the arts, literature, and sciences signal an encroaching luxury in them. As the virtue of looking after your fellow man is increasingly encapsulated in the political and economic system, luxuries of art and science offer to a people the appearance of virtue in the place of virtue that has fled their hearts. These things become orna-

7. Jean-Jacques Rousseau, *The Social Contract and Discourses* (London: J. M. Dent and Sons, 1938), 127.
8. Roger D. Masters, *The Political Philosophy of Rousseau* (Princeton, N.J.: Princeton University Press, 1968), 213.
9. Rousseau, *The Social Contract and Discourses,* 130.

ments of the mind, and we begin to speak an "artificial language" under which our natural morals are concealed. In a world such as this there can be no transparency of the human soul, because "we never know with whom we have to deal.... Jealousy, suspicion, fear, coldness, reserve, hate and fraud lie constantly concealed under that uniform and deceitful veil of politeness."[10] When a citizen can no longer discern the true character of his fellow man or gauge his true motivations due to a false modicum of decency and politeness, then the common good of a society is completely out of grasp. No one is held to its standard, because it can no longer be discerned. Where a society proclaims itself freed from the shackles of ignorance, such a freedom has been granted only by a thorough skepticism. And such skepticism engenders a pride as good as ignorance. Rousseau decries this skepticism because it erodes the human heart, which in turn erodes the bonds that held people together. But not only does such a state foster avariciousness, self-interest, duplicity, and hidden desires, it also contributes to a "softening of character" that makes a nation weak. It is an important feature of the "First Discourse" that it opens with what amounts to a psychological appraisal of modern enlightened people. Rousseau is diagnosing their collective souls, or the mind of his time, based upon the deceitful tone of their society and behavior. This is important, because it allows us to understand what exactly Rousseau admired about antiquity. On this subject I will return, but for now it suffices to remember that Rousseau's opening concern is with the character of people, not the character of their institutions.

If Rousseau reacts to the problem of Enlightenment by describing the symptoms of corruption, he then looks for their cause in the arts and sciences. For Rousseau, the arts and sciences must take their fair share of the blame for such a state of affairs. There is no doubt in Rousseau's mind that the European Zeitgeist is a depraved animal, and that this has developed in concurrence with the flowering of our cerebral culture. Such knowledge, liberally disseminated over a culture, serves only to divorce men from their nature. "Astronomy was born from superstition, eloquence of ambition, hatred, falsehood and flattery; geometry of avarice; physics of an idle curiosity; and even moral philosophy of our pride."[11] After isolat-

10. Rousseau, *The Social Contract and Discourses,* 132.
11. Rousseau, *The Social Contract and Discourses,* 140.

ing the vices of his age, Rousseau lists the sciences and philosophies that attend them. Rousseau's passing mention of gods who devised science to make men miserable gives us a clue into his suspicions. Rousseau certainly believes there is a hidden reason behind the pursuit of knowledge. The idea that the sciences, natural and philosophical, are disinterested is false. Just like his descendants Marx and Foucault, there is a desire to uncloak real hidden motivations. He decries them for making morality illusory, dethroning God, denying reality over representation, debasing man as a beast. He regards them as dishonest, misguided thinkers, peddling philosophies to the public that they wouldn't have their children endure. How truthful can a philosophy or science be if it unravels the very threads of the society, or denatures the nobility in man?

The artists fare no better than the pursuers of knowledge. They are portrayed as slaves to applause and the bad taste of their age. Consumed in the fog of a society addicted to theatre, literature, painting, and other artistic production, they do nothing but pander to the artificial needs and wants produced by an "enlightened" society. They show up the luxury of their age, become members themselves in the pursuit of false desires, and perpetuate the obscene obsession. With such a vehement understanding of the artist's purpose in society, is it any wonder that Rousseau invokes that other great artistic defamer against them? Rousseau includes a large quotation from Plato's *Apology,* where the master inveighs against the poets and artists as knowing nothing of the true, the beautiful, or the good. In Rousseau's mind, the fine arts do nothing but create unnecessary needs and destroy freedom by increasing the mutual dependence between people and things.

The most striking aspect of Rousseau's "First Discourse" is the simultaneous feelings one receives that Rousseau was indeed writing for another time, but was also feeding off his contemporary situation. There is much that is relevant and portentous for all eras in the "First Discourse," and Rousseau was admirably able to remove himself from the overwhelming fashions of his day in order to harangue them. But it is also a work roundly situated in its time, burning with a fury that could only have come from the most present and immediate rancour. Unlike C. E. Vaughan, who dismisses the "First Discourse" after the first page of his introduction to Rousseau's political works, I side more with Roger Masters and his favorable appraisal of Rousseau's first literary attempt.

He writes, "Rousseau presents his ideas in a partial way, because he does not as yet commit himself to his ultimate definitions of moral freedom based on natural religion, natural freedom based on man's isolation in the state of nature, and civil freedom based on the formal logic of the general will."[12]

In the "First Discourse" are contained the seeds of Rousseau's mature political and philosophical system. These tenets as yet have not been abstracted from the social context in which they are embedded. They are, however, present to the degree that they give his criticism of civilization an alluring timelessness, a sense that he had uncovered a recurring ailment. You can almost smell the powerful new concept of freedom brewing between the sentences. But this is first and foremost a work that springs from the loins of his society—a stunning judgment of the negative aspects of current social forces. As Masters was able to see, while these social criticisms are paramount to the overall system, they are in another sense detachable, and hence worthy of separate thought.

However, despite this instance of temporal precision and historical foresight, by overstressing the incidence of Enlightenment and corruption, Rousseau had set a course for his new view of history. In his "Second Discourse" Rousseau would greatly extend the idea of history as a process of perpetual decline. What began as a thoughtful, if overly passionate and at times irrational understanding of what people lose through civilization would become a theoretical temporal descent, engendering further dissatisfaction, despair, and timeless measures to overcome the plunge. But before I move to the "Second Discourse," I will examine Rousseau's first historical journey into ancient Sparta.

Utopian Sparta: Lawgivers, Virtue, and Future Demigods

Much of the rhetorical flair of the "First Discourse" is delivered by lengthy and seemingly authoritative historical examples of societies with a high degree of scientific and artistic sophistication who have turned to corruption and eventual military defeat. And while these incidents have been shown to be at times inconsistent, specious, and lacking in

---

12. Masters, *The Political Philosophy of Rousseau*, 439.

historical precision, for the most part they serve the argument admirably.[13] The use of historical examination, while nowhere near echoing the seriousness of someone like Montesquieu, does however give his take on the question of arts and sciences a sustenance that simple vitriol of his age would have lacked. It gives the argument a feeling of emergency to heighten the dire present. What concerns my argument is how far this type of historical approach can be stretched. If history is going to be used rhetorically to suit an argument, is it then not possible that history will be molded to fit the argument? Rousseau's benedictory and hyperbolic introduction of the theme gives us pause for concern: "Can it be forgotten that, in the very heart of Greece, there arose a city as famous for the happy ignorance of its inhabitants, as for the wisdom of its laws; a republic of demigods rather than of men?[14]

Sparta is mentioned rarely in the "First Discourse," but its idea is everywhere. And while Sparta gains minimal wordage, the quote above shows to a great degree where Rousseau's thought lay when he was considering history. Sparta is also a major rallying point in Rousseau's other work. Rousseau received much of his education of Sparta, its virtue, and its heroes from what he had read in Plutarch. He knew nothing of the real city and its inhabitants. Like many of his age, it seems that Rousseau had succumbed to looking backward and imagining utopias that facts could not substantiate. As Frank and Fritzie Manuel note, "Eventually the laws of Solon and Lycurgus assumed a quasi-mythic character, and became an essential ingredient of the European utopian tradition through the age of the French Revolution. Men opted either for the Athenian or Spartan model."[15]

What made Sparta such a helpful ideal was the fact that it actually had existed. Its mythicism and ideality, and the passions projected upon it by others, became mute through the agency of its concrete reality. But what did Rousseau really admire about Sparta? The first of his fixations

13. Masters, *The Political Philosophy of Rousseau*, 218–25. Master's chapter from this work entitled "Historical Evidence of the Coincidence of Enlightenment and Corruption" chronicles Rousseau's use of historical types to garner support for his thesis. It shows that while Rousseau was not entirely accurate or logical with his historical account, there was enough truth and evidence in his account to assist his charges.

14. Rousseau, *The Social Contract and Discourses*, 136.

15. Frank E. Manuel and Fritzie P. Manuel, *Utopian Thought in the Western World* (Cambridge, Mass.: The Belknap Press of Harvard University Press, 1979), 65.

is with the godfather of Spartan fortune, Lycurgus, who is credited with the most substantial reforms ever administered to a body of people. Such legislative reforms were in fact implanted over many years, many governments, and many leaders.[16] Scarcity of adequate historical record makes it difficult to attribute aspects of the Spartan constitution and character to Lycurgus himself or to previous and later reformers. But Rousseau was more than willing to accept uncritically the Greek tradition that such radical transformation of a society could be encapsulated in one man. Lycurgus also seemed to be the perfect historical encapsulation of an idea Rousseau would later develop in *The Social Contract.* That troubling abstract figure of the "lawgiver" in *The Social Contract,* that person of sublime legislative insight, bears striking resemblance to Lycurgus. Troubling it is that such a mythic genius is required to install Rousseau's "social contract." But there is another aspect of the Spartan city state that Rousseau admired. "In the eighteenth century Rousseau could still speak of Sparta as 'this republic of demigods,' but it was the beneficent and constructive legislation of Lykourgus rather than the martial virtuosity of Agesilaos that inspired this view of Sparta and his 'Government de Pologne.'"[17]

It is no mistake that Rousseau saw in Sparta a state with the legislative potential to be a beacon for his age. It is obvious that Rousseau sees Sparta as a model of how institutions can form the individual. This is what he takes from Sparta: the power of law and institutions over people. It is the civic ethos of Sparta that impresses him. From this perspective, Sparta seems to nourish the concept of freedom that Rousseau would later develop. That abstract freedom, Rousseau would later discover, hinges on self-imposed legislation. The concern with Spartan legislation is simply an expression of Rousseau's desire for freedom and morality, and how it must be made manifest through law. Concern with law and institutions goes hand in hand with a burning devotion to freedom, and thus Sparta becomes a loving memory of benevolent legislative dominance over a populace. In summation, Rousseau's turn to the cult of an-

16. P. R. Coleman-Norton, "Socialism at Sparta," in *The Greek Political Experience: Studies in the Honor of William Kelly Prentice* (New York: Russell and Russell, 1969), 63.

17. Paul Cartledge, *Agesilaos and the Crisis of Sparta* (Baltimore: Johns Hopkins University Press, 1987), 420. Agesilaos was a Spartan king who presided over Sparta's most aggressively expansionist imperialism.

tiquity is entirely the fruit of his abstract freedom, and Sparta is seen entirely through its frames. In Rousseau's mind Spartans submit to such repressive institutions as if the principles they were built on were already engraved on their hearts. The truth is, however, that consent to the system was far more autocratic than reciprocal, as "Lycurgus had striven to organise a state fit for heroes, nor did he fail, for none save heroes could have endured his system."[18]

Not only did Sparta and Lycurgus indulge Rousseau's taste in freedom, law, and the virtuous citizen, it also played into his hands as a moral crusader. As we mentioned previously, the "First Discourse" deals predominantly with the moral turpitude of enlightened people of the eighteenth century. Rousseau then condemns institutions based on this moral diagnosis. This concern is first and foremost in Rousseau's mind when thinking on antiquity. He looks back with dewy-eyed affection at the vigorous souls of Spartan men and women, concluding that their institutions are to be thanked for the wonder. The institutions of republican Sparta are, however, obviously not the wonder that Rousseau's reasoning makes them. Being more attuned to extreme martial readiness, familial and societal frugality, and historically exceptional levels of cruelty, all built upon a political bedrock of slavery, it is hard to see Rousseau's praise as anything but romantically tinged.[19] Concerned with a moral state of mind that he admired greatly, Rousseau then twisted historical reality to suit his needs.

His view of the preeminence of the Spartan collective and their psychological and moral superiority to the collective status of the contemporary European world also made him favor forms of political association that were entirely historically inappropriate for the eighteenth century. Lycurgus's division of land of equal lots to form a sort of agrarian communism was a model that Rousseau would favor in his later suggestions for political structure. There are communistic aspects to the *Social Contract* that echo onward to Marx, and in many respects it can be seen as a distillation of the fundamentals of the Spartan utopian chimera. And Rousseau always preferred agricultural communities to

18. Coleman-Norton, "Socialism at Sparta," 71.

19. Manuel and Manuel, *Utopian Thought in the Western World*, 97–99. These pages chronicle the bizarre and harsh nature of many Spartan customs and institutions and the lack of liberty among the Spartan people.

the cosmopolitan cities that were taking grip of modern Europe. One need only look at Rousseau's work regarding Poland and Corsica to see how he wore Sparta on his sleeve, and how misguided such an influence was to modern reality. Rousseau's *Governement de Pologna* opens with a section on the "Spirit of the Ancient Institutions" and then attempts to model Poland in their image, while in the same breath talking of a freedom and equality unknown to ancient peoples. With regard to Corsica he is not just temporally confused, but downright sheltered from time. Corsica is for him a sheltered oasis capable of shunning the complexities of modern social life. "In advising the Corsicans to remain primitive Rousseau was not only protecting them against the evils of civilisation, but against change as such."[20]

For an eighteenth-century society dealing with the expansion of cities, commerce, industry, and all the other hallmarks of modern statehood, Rousseau's advising of nations to turn back the clock is a gross example of an illusionary historical directive. To imitate a historically misapprehended Sparta transfigured by timeless modern preoccupations implanted into its historical character is to have your desire for historical argumentative authority spring from an ahistorical source. And for a society with an increasing taste for freedom, Rousseau's theorizing of political associations designed for moral/political freedom that attempt to mimic a Spartan model devoid of it convinces us both of the timelessness of Rousseau's own concept freedom and how that timeless need constructed a historical Sparta in that spirit. Yack's account of Rousseau's concern for history is instructive by showing how Rousseau used Sparta to demonstrate the historicity of modern institutions.[21] Through this Yack is able to account for the power of Rousseau's assault on modern life and provide a great historical motivation behind Rousseau's desire to transcend the limitations of his time. But his book says nothing of whether Rousseau used that history accurately, appropriately, or serious-

---

20. Judith Shklar, *Men and Citizens* (Cambridge: Cambridge University Press, 1969), 28.

21. The crux of Yack's argument is that Rousseau's rhetorical and highly charged use of ancient examples serves to show the historicity of his contemporary world and hence presumably its ability to change. Thus Rousseau is among the first to proclaim our radical historicity. And while he accepts that Rousseau's vision of Sparta is highly flawed and idealistically blind to the source realities, he can dismiss this because "Sparta is for Rousseau not so much a model for imitation as a proof of his conclusion about the historicity of our limitations"; Yack, *The Longing for Total Revolution*, 77.

ly, and what the falsities of his historical conceptions say about the constructions he developed to overcome our "limitations." Yack appreciates the power of Rousseau's atemporal concepts of freedom and the individual, but does not see their timeless connection to his distorted vision of Sparta or how this connection can erode his credentials as a thinker concerned with history. It seems as if Yack is able to separate Rousseau's new, modern sense of philosophical freedom (a freedom characterized by its ambivalence to time), from any influence it may have on his supposed "historicism" and his appraisals of other historical epochs. I, however, do not see such a separation as being possible. Sparta fuels Rousseau's timeless freedom just as that timeless freedom molds his image of Sparta. The example of Sparta testifies to Rousseau's indifference to history more than to his underlying concern for "historicity." However, what such a historicist reading of Rousseau does allow us to appreciate is the powerful energy Rousseau had tapped into by idealizing Sparta. By looking backward into the past of antiquity, Rousseau had found some historical ballast to at once anchor and further his hopes for his fallen contemporary society. Rousseau may have thought that Sparta was a nation of demigods rather than men, but it was Rousseau's will-based philosophy and atemporal concept of freedom that would do more to make men demigods than Lycurgus ever could. Rousseau would achieve this in part by delving further into the past, beyond the utopian illusions of antiquity and into the prehistoric past of Nature. This deepening of the connection between history and the timeless, of pushing further the use of historical change to arrive at timeless ways of being, would be the topic of his "Second Discourse."

3
The Second Attack and Second History

Rousseau gave intimations of the world of nature he was to open up in the "First Discourse" when he mused, "We cannot reflect on the morality of mankind without contemplating with pleasure the picture of simplicity which prevailed in the earliest times. This image may be justly compared to a beautiful coast, adorned only by the hands of nature; towards which our eyes are constantly turned, and which we see receding with regret."[1]

One can barely imagine a more powerful expression of loss. It is understandable that he could persuade himself to compose the "Second Discourse" from the perspective of this distrait Nature. Through the experimental use of this state of nature, Rousseau brings not only all his imaginative flair to bear on the treatment of inequality in the "Second Discourse," but also a highly rational and scientific approach. The romantic and poetic potency of this quotation may provide us with Rousseau's personal impetus for writing the "Second Discourse," but it is far removed from the philosophic tone and treatment of the material in the work itself. But despite the scientific posturing, the reader never loses sight of

1. Jean-Jacques Rousseau, *The Social Contract and Discourses* (London: J. M. Dent and Sons, 1938), 145.

the mythic, utopian aspects with which Rousseau undoubtedly implants Nature. Nature in the "Second Discourse" is a strange amalgam, treated as a serious and decisive thought experiment, but lurking as an extravagant sentimentality. The two influences are perhaps best evidenced by the famous phrase "to form a true idea of a state which no longer exists, perhaps never did exist, and probably never will exist."[2]

If a state of nature, nostalgic and imaginary, yet in the same breath experimental and scientific, is the theoretical starting point for the "Second Discourse," there can be no doubt that the engine of the work is time. Indeed, the "Second Discourse" is the work most often cited by those who recognize Rousseau's historical sense. Writers such as Lionel Gossman and Bernard Yack, who grant to Rousseau the ability to see historical man and the "extreme malleability of his nature over time,"[3] do so predominantly because of the "Second Discourse." Time is the primary concern of this work, as "Like the statue of Glaucus, which was so disfigured by time ... the human soul, altered in society by a thousand causes perpetually reoccuring ... has, so to speak, changed in appearance, so as to be hardly recognizable."[4] In one sense they are right to emphasize Rousseau's concern for history, but it is too extreme a position to think of Rousseau as having opened the grand vista of history. Such an overstatement can only have come about by underestimating the negative view of time and positive view of nature so fundamental to Rousseau's thought. To reaffirm this it is necessary to appreciate the connection between nature and time in Rousseau. The sheer reach and depth of the historical survey of the "Second Discourse" into the expanse of our history account for the greatly expanded criticism of inequality and property in modern civil society. To evaluate this criticism it is necessary to evaluate the spring of its occurrence: Rousseau's radically new formulation of the problem of nature.

The Time of Nature and the Nature of Time

As observed of the *Confessions*, one of Rousseau's governing beliefs is that the origin of a thing is its most natural state. Not only is this true of

2. Rousseau, *The Social Contract and Discourses*, 169.

3. Arthur M. Melzer, *The Natural Goodness of Man* (Chicago: University of Chicago Press, 1990), 49.

4. Rousseau, *The Social Contract and Discourses*, 168.

the individual, but is also applied to the species. Just like Rousseau's infancy, humanity's infancy is the site of its cardinal goodness. And just like Rousseau's dispersed journey from that moment, humanity's dispersed journey is a history of needless, saddening acquisition of social traits and the slow erosion and burying of natural impulses. If you begin from such a view of nature, then time and history can only be conceived as a story of woe and negative descent. To illustrate the radical temperament of such a conception it helps to look at its opposite. If we assume, as Aristotle did, that a thing is most natural in its finality and not in its origin, then an entirely different conception of time ensues, "for whatever is the end-product of the perfecting process of any object, that we call its nature."[5] Here nature is a process and not a timeless, static, and inert golden age. Time and history are thus understood as pathways to becoming, and thus given positive content and interpretation. If the end is natural, then its passage is desirous and engaged with. If such a view of nature engenders a teleological view of time, we can understand Rousseau's nature as having reversed the teleological order. His is a kind of anti-teleology, where the aim of time is further corruption and movement away from perfection. Time, thus being an amoral agent of needless change, is not engaged with. And if engaged with, it is only to uncover its pernicious fraud. This comparison is done not so much to favor one interpretation of time and nature over another (a teleological view of time and nature is fraught with its own dangers), but instead to show that Rousseau's infamous lionizing of nature has irreparable influence upon how he views time. It also shows us how removed Rousseau was from the thought of the ancients, and also from his many contemporaries who believed in the indefinite perfectibility of the human race. By placing man's destiny at the beginning of his development rather than at the end, strange and radical temporal adjustments are required to set things right.[6]

While Rousseau had devised a bracing new concept of nature, thinking about what might constitute human nature was not new with him.

5. Aristotle, *The Politics* (London: Penguin Books, 1969), book 1, chap. 2, 28.
6. Roger D. Masters also compared Aristotle's concept of nature with Rousseau's to outline the difference between antiquity and modern minds. However, rather than investigating the influence of nature on temporal understanding, he uses Aristotle's example to show Rousseau's ambivalence to the concept of final causes and the prevalence in his thought of the modern and scientific considering of efficient causes when examining nature; Masters, *The Political Philosophy of Rousseau* (Princeton, N.J.: Princeton University Press, 1968), 113.

Any serious political theorist of a philosophical bent was inextricably required to touch the subject. The two leading theorists on nature and contractarian thought preceding Rousseau, Locke and Hobbes, were both important touchstones for Rousseau's musings on nature. Rousseau quite consciously sets up his theory of nature in direct opposition to theirs, which he dismisses as not going far enough backward in time. With regard to Locke, whose nature is filled with duty-bound, peaceful, reasonable inhabitants who possess the murmurings of benevolent civil and social instincts, Rousseau dismisses it as implanting ideas, bonds, and desires wholly outside the capabilities of natural man. To Rousseau, Locke's state of nature is nothing more than "the civil state minus its political machinery."[7] And Hobbes is equally astray when he characterizes the state of nature as a state of war. Again, this conception of calculated force between natural combatants is dismissed because it presupposes a social bond or contract that they wish to destroy for their benefit, and a faculty of reason that enables them to recognize and forge these bonds. Hobbes's take on nature as the right of everyone to everything within his grasp and capability places the social imperatives of property, ownership, power, and might into peoples that as yet know nothing of these concepts. Despite the glaring differences in their speculations of nature, Rousseau sees them both as having described behaviors as natural and that could only have taken root in society. They wrongly determine man's natural features in his relations with others. Nature based on force or mutual goodwill simply confuses true, unspoiled nature with an impure later stage of human evolution. How does Rousseau move past these minimally socialized individuals with the simplest of social imperatives?

Rousseau arrives at his new formulation of nature by blending the features of isolation, solitude, and the resulting goodness that accompanies this state with the application of a scientific method to the nature of man. Rousseau's scientific method consists in requiring any assumption or statement about the nature of man to be subjected to rational proof. In other words, any account of human nature must be contrasted to the bare minimum of what constitutes a human. Humanity must be reduced to an indivisible standard unit for measurement and appraisal of other human types and speculation on their relation to nature. Rousseau

7. C. E. Vaughan, "Introduction," in *The Political Writings of Jean-Jacques Rousseau,* edited and notes by C. E. Vaughan (Cambridge: Cambridge University Press, 1915), 16.

achieves this by subtracting from man all the attributes he has acquired from society. He writes in *Emile*: "The natural man lives for himself; he is the unit, the whole, dependent only on himself and on his like. The citizen is but the numerator of a fraction, whose value depends on its denominator; his value depends on the whole, that is, on the community."[8] The first and most basic constitution of man is to become the first principle for a new science of society. Rousseau even likens his methodology in the "Second Discourse" to the theoretical assumptions made by physicists in their science. But despite the quasi-scientific declarations, the more personal elements of the discourse are not difficult to tease apart. By divulging social man of all his acquired characteristics and layered conventions, Rousseau created a theoretical natural individual betraying remarkable kinship with the vision he had of himself. In following the ironclad logic of a scientific approach to human nature, Rousseau was able to harmonize the endpoint of this process with his admiration for the isolated loner. Rousseau gave voice to his personal need to mitigate the effects of time and change, combined with his desire to place the "Second Discourse" on a scientific footing from the outset of the work's preface. He writes, "And how shall man hope to see himself as nature has made him, across all the changes which the succession of time and place must have produced in his original constitution? How can he distinguish what is fundamental in his nature from the changes and additions which his circumstances and the advances he has made have introduced to modify his primitive condition?"[9]

This desire for scientific authority is also not new with Rousseau. The empirical understanding of nature had taken hold of the social sciences, and an empirical method to politics was utilized by Hobbes, Locke, Hume, and many others. The authority of the scientific method under Newton's discoveries had dazzled the interpreters and theorists on social phenomena to such a degree that to speak authoritatively on a subject such as human nature it was necessary to treat it "scientifically."[10] Rousseau was just appeasing the tendencies of his day by attempting to fuse the gap between natural science and philosophy. Despite the fact that this approach

8. Rousseau, *Emile*, translated by Barbara Foxley (London: J. M. Dent and Sons, 1974), 7.
9. Rousseau, *The Social Contract and Discourses,* 168.
10. David Cameron, *The Social Thought of Rousseau and Burke* (London: Weidenfeld and Nicolson, 1973), 62.

actually sat uncomfortably with Rousseau's eventual claims about natural man, he achieved one of the most diminishing treatments of natural man. The scientific reduction of man executed by Rousseau required that he treat the original inhabitants of nature in purely physical terms. Stripped of sociability, they are transformed into isolated, self-sufficient animals with purely physical needs and the physical hardware to satisfy those needs. Rousseau's natural man is the product of pure egoism.[11] In considering humans as merely instinctual creatures Rousseau is able to push the discussion regarding human nature further and remove himself from the influences of previous theorists on human nature and natural right. But in pushing the natural to its remotest limits he may have overstated his case and betrayed the message he wanted his audience to take from their original nature. The first section of the "Discourse on Inequality" is given over to this discussion of man's physicality. He discusses the natural human with regard to his nourishment and subsistence, sickness and disease, instinct for self-preservation, purely physical desire to propagate the species, and lack of ideas and speech, other than for the bluntest necessity.

Having shed this animal of all its humanity by a process of biological analogy, Rousseau imagined a creature wandering isolated in a land before time. It is in this sense that Vaughan could refer to this creature as the "reductio ad absurdum of his tribe."[12] As a consequence of this scientific approach, Rousseau characterizes the state of nature as an amoral universe. It is a method that if properly followed demands that nature be anterior to both reason and sociability and hence, by association, morality also. Through an empirical process nothing is accepted without a concrete referent in reality. It is because of this that Rousseau has been interpreted as an opponent of natural law theory, which explains his resistance to Locke's natural law suppositions. But this appraisal is faulted because of the troubling role that certain metaphysical ideas play in Rousseau's natural human. Despite the very "low" conception of natural man Rousseau introduces, he is still impelled to furnish this animal with certain endowments contrary to the purely natural. Rousseau

11. Rousseau makes a distinction between the self-interest of natural man and the "egoism" of social man. A purist would take issue with my use of the word "egoism." But in keeping with our interpretation of the disguised personal elements of the discourse, I maintain that Rousseau's "scientific" natural man is the product of his own "egosim."

12. Vaughan, "Introduction," in *The Political Writings of Jean-Jacques Rousseau*, 19.

plants concepts such as compassion or pity, freedom, and perfectibility, which serve to alter his barest nature from its isolation, into his human animal. Rousseau places side by side a mechanistic and empirical concept of man with a rationalist and metaphysical concept, with no uneasiness about the consequences.

I see nothing in any animal but an ingenious machine, to which nature hath given senses to wind itself up, and guard itself, to a certain degree, against anything that might tend to disorder or destroy it. I perceive exactly the same things in the human machine, with this difference, that in the operations of the brute, nature is the sole agent, whereas man has some share in his own operations, in his character as a free agent.[13]

Such a blending of the mechanically inspired metaphor of "man as machine" with the more metaphysical and moral speculations on human free agency are not as contradictory as they may seem. At the time it was common to combine these two contradictory strands of thought because they were both "weapons against the same evil."[14] Such mingling of elements can be seen in Locke's and others' work. But the tensions that would later become prominent between these two schools already display problems in Rousseau's "Second Discourse." They may have been used to combat the same political enemies of inequality, oppression, and absolutism, but they greatly disrupt Rousseau's work regarding time, history, and evolution.

I will first examine the consequences of pity in Rousseau's inert, amoral human foundlings. Pity is supposed to be a companion impulse to the drive for self-preservation, and is meant to mitigate the effects of a thorough egoism. It is described by Rousseau as "an innate repugnance at seeing a fellow creature suffer," and apparently "comes before any reflection."[15] Here he is fortifying himself against any conclusion that could bear resemblance to Hobbes. Belief that natural humans without an idea of goodness are inclined to be the "sole proprietor of the universe" is dispelled by the inclusion of compassion to their instinctual armory.[16] This resolves two problems; first, despite Rousseau characterizing natural

13. Rousseau, *The Social Contract and Discourses*, 184.
14. Cameron, *The Social Thought of Rousseau and Burke*, 62.
15. Rousseau, *The Social Contract and Discourses*, 197.
16. Rousseau, *The Social Contract and Discourses*, 196.

humans as amoral, he really does believe that they are naturally good; second, the scientific approach had conditioned a human devoid of the very impulses that Rousseau wished to awaken in the modern human. Rousseau had to reconstruct that horrifically reduced natural human in terms that betrayed the approach that got him there. By ripping all sociability from his human archetype in an attempt to radically separate the natural from social, Rousseau had to admit at least a particle of social instinct to prove that his vision of natural man was not the vicious, brutish man of Hobbes's imagination. The problem pity produced in Rousseau's system is evident when we observe Rousseau's compromising of its naturalness in his "Essay on the Origin of Languages."

We develop social feeling only as we become enlightened. Although pity is native to the human heart, it would remain eternally quiescent unless it were activated by imagination. How are we moved to pity? By getting outside ourselves and identifying with a being who suffers.... It is not in ourselves, but in him that we suffer. It is clear that such transport supposes a great deal of acquired knowledge.[17]

Although Rousseau maintains pity's naturalness, it becomes obvious that pity cannot be exercised in isolation, but must be expressed through contact with others. This process requires a certain amount of reflective or imaginative thought: a possibility previously denied. It seems perhaps that our nature has within it a drive to socialization via the feeling of empathy we have for others and an idea of suffering that we can imagine them to endure. Perhaps then a part of man's natural being has a social element, throwing into disrepute much of Rousseau's inflexible distinction between the natural and social? As Herder observes in his essay on the origins of language, "So little did nature create us as severed blocks of rock, as egotistic monads. Even the most delicate chords of human feeling ... are aligned in their entire performance for a going out towards other creatures.[18] Perhaps aspects of our socialized selves and world are in fact good? Pity becomes an incurable but essential element in Rousseau's natural world, supplying the small but ample repository of goodness in an amoral world, while at the same time presupposing

17. Jean-Jacques Rousseau and Johann Gottfried Herder, *On the Origin of Language* (Chicago: University of Chicago Press, 1966), 32.
18. Rousseau and Herder, *On the Origin of Language*, 87.

social affectations that are the root of civilized evil. This also throws into serious doubt the distinction he makes between *amour de soi,* the natural and good love of self, and *amour propre*, the unnatural love tainted by its relations to others. These essential ideas to the rhythm of Rousseau's thought are rendered flaccid and unconvincing. This is because of the trouble Rousseau has in harmonizing a scientific appraisal of nature with the belief that nature is constitutionally good. Other troubles arise when Rousseau attempts to further "moralize" nature after having given it scientific validation. These troubles surround the concepts of freedom and perfectibility, which he introduces with "but in the power of willing or rather of choosing, and in the feeling of this power, nothing is to be found but acts which are purely physical and wholly inexplicable by the laws of mechanism."[19]

It is here that Rousseau finally shows his authentic guise by introducing the dualism that pervades his work. Despite the investment Rousseau makes in a scientific understanding of man's origins, man's freedom constitutes his spirituality. An immaterial idea of the soul is introduced that cannot be verified by any amount of scientific analysis. This liberty to stand above instinct is where the natural goodness of humanity resides. But man's freedom cannot be admitted at this point without jeopardizing the hard-fought, isolated natural man that science guarantees, and in turn the opposition between nature and society. It is at this point that Rousseau begins to doubt whether or not natural man is dictated by instinct at all. It follows that the dilemma is solved by making man's sole instinct perfectibility—namely, his instinct for choosing which instincts from other animals most suit his needs. Humans have the unusual animal ability to "invent" themselves. Rousseau would resolve this problem with greater finesse and clarity in the *Social Contract* by differentiating between natural or physical freedom and moral or spiritual freedom. At least by separating these differing but familial freedoms, Rousseau can maintain freedom as man's defining trait, while also maintaining a vast separation between nature and society. But for now the concept of perfectibility must bear the weight of Rousseau's dualism. Perfectibility is there to secure freedom as a reality, but it also becomes a pathway to traverse the oceanic gap between natural man and social man. It is via this

19. Rousseau, *The Social Contract and Discourses,* 184.

anomaly, in the coherence of the "Second Discourse," that many could view the work as proof of Rousseau's evolutionary, temporally, and historically sensitive position. Rousseau describes this perfectibility as "the faculty of self-improvement which, by the help of circumstances, gradually develops all the rest of our faculties, and is inherent in the species as the individual."[20]

With the awkward qualification of our natural freedom (a freedom that is constructed in sharp contrast to the mechanistic view of nature) with the more temporal and historical concept of perfectibility, Rousseau has reached the problem of all such metaphysical dualisms. As outlined in the introduction, if freedom is placed at the seat of humanity's dignity, and as such is placed outside of time to guarantee it as an eternal element, an illusory history must be developed to cover the gap. Rousseau develops this history through the agency of perfectibility. In other words, man's sole unique instinct is his inventiveness and malleability, and, with the aid of circumstances that foster and encourage latent powers, this instinct accounts for his development. The outside world brings man out of himself. The once naturally isolated is actually instinctually programmed to go out in the world and remake the world. Human freedom and its attached movement of perfectibility perfectly account for all human developments, including the birth of civil society. Rousseau's "Second Discourse" is the story of that development, and he traces the phases of social evolution. It is obvious how out of step this is for Rousseau's first principles, and how then Rousseau can be seen as a forerunner for evolutionary anthropology. But despite the unforeseen need to bridge the gap between nature and society via perfectibility, Rousseau seems to use the term as facetiously as possible. Such sentiments are found in despondent flippancies such as, "Why is man alone liable to grow into a dotard?"[21] Why? Because of his freedom to do so, or his perfectibility. Perfectibility becomes just a word for our ability to deceive ourselves and "carries with it the risk of imbecility, error and consequent unhappiness."[22] Despite the fact that humanity's growth into society may be natural after all, Rousseau still refuses to see it as good. Nature was to be the timeless oasis that made no demands on us to leave it, but

20. Rousseau, *The Social Contract and Discourses*, 185.
21. Rousseau, *The Social Contract and Discourses*, 185.
22. J. H. Broome, *Rousseau: A Study of His Thought* (London: Edward Arnold, 1963), 37.

the unintentional and inevitable collapse of the natural and the social occasioned by pity created a vault for human development. This opened history as a world to be explored and time as a force to be condemned. Perfectibility is unwanted but necessary history, uncontrollably formed by dualism and bitterly embraced as an explanation for social inequality.

The Forced Birth of Civil Society and the History of a Mistake

The peculiar aspect of Rousseau's faculty of perfectibility is its passivity. Unlike a dynamic view of perfectibility, which establishes the human animal as a burgeoning species with insatiable drives for exploration and invention, Rousseau's conception is a buried faculty that makes no overt obligation upon its owner. Perfectibility is a faculty and not a force.[23] This means that it is pure latent possibility and not unadulterated actuality. It cannot be a cause in and of itself. Action doesn't necessarily flow from it unprovoked. Its provocation must come from without. In this way Rousseau can pass responsibility for man's movement into society on the outside world. Humanity's passage into society is an induced birth, precipitated by outside circumstances. Nature gives way to history by chance, and man would never have left the womb of nature had he not responded to outward stimuli. Man's history is a mistake, as there is nothing necessary about it, because it is purely contingent upon factors outside of man's control. Despite the fact that natural people had been implanted with an aptitude for malleability, Rousseau does his best to suggest that humanity never really wanted the ability, and it was only coaxed out of us by an unfeeling outside. This is the source of our malevolence. The second section of the "Discourse on Inequality" is a historiography of this mistake.

The existence of perfectibility in the human species sets in train an unstoppable cycle of chance and necessity. The natural world as the agent of chance throws out challenges and intrigues for the innocent individuals to respond to. Once chance has motivated the consciousness of man, his answer to it begins a chain of necessity that follows a deducible logic. Once temptation has been succumbed to, the effects that flow from

23. Dena Goodman, *Criticism in Action: Enlightenment Experiments in Political Writing* (Ithaca: Cornell University Press, 1989), 125.

the decision cannot be escaped. The scarcity of food or the difficultly of attaining it obliged man in the use of weapons and cunning. This new intelligence produced in them a sense of superiority over other animals and hence began the long story of man's dominance over nature. The increased fortunes of the human race led to overpopulation, which made them band together, though they were once separate entities. This led to a certain degree of reflection on their relations that in turn developed conceptions denoted by terms such as "great, small, strong, weak, swift, slow, fearful, bold, and the like."[24] A recognition of their natural inequality ensued. Lightning or a spewing volcano acquainted people with fire, which they slowly learned to harness for their benefit. With communities compelled to live in isolation via floods, earthquakes, or the tectonic shifting of the earth creating islands came the development of speech and language. Communities like these also developed the first ruminations of families and the affections that attend them. Rousseau describes this epoch as the first revolution: "Nevertheless, once the coincidence of overpopulation and natural disasters had its effect on human development, the change they occasioned in man's modus operandi was irreversible by any act of human volition."[25]

The continued working of natural chance on the potentiality of perfectibility effects a second revolution around the arts of metallurgy and agriculture. Metallurgy is again explained by way of the volcano, which ejects "metallic substances already in fusion, (suggesting) to the spectators the idea of imitating the natural operation."[26] The principles of agriculture are derived in the same manner by imitating the observed natural propagation of plants. But the real spread of agriculture is said to be contingent upon metallurgy. As more people take to turning metals and fashioning commodities from them, others are left with the task of feeding mouths other than their own. A rudimentary division of labor occurs that becomes the most powerful impetus for the expansion of agriculture and husbandry. This new understanding of the land, animals, and commodities brings about the idea of property, which in turn precipitates the origin and development of justice and legislation. A me-

24. Rousseau, *The Social Contract and Discourses*, 208.
25. Andrzej Rapaczynski, *Nature and Politics: Liberalism in the Philosophies of Hobbes, Locke and Rousseau* (Ithaca: Cornell University Press, 1987), 269.
26. Rousseau, *The Social Contract and Discourses*, 215.

lange of the idea of property with the reality of natural inequality is then the birthplace of civil society and the evils of social inequality. Thus in the middle of the second part of the "Second Discourse" we reach the point Rousseau described in the first sentence of the section: "The first man who, having enclosed a piece of ground, bethought himself of saying 'This is mine,' and found people simple enough to believe him, was the real founder of civil society."[27]

At this point a sharp change in the operation of time occurs. Whereas previously time was a process inexplicable, needless, and driven by chance, accident, and luck, it now gives way to pure necessity and inevitability. There was no unavoidable reason for man to have left the state of nature. But when he did respond to the chance phenomena of the outside realm, a degree of necessity did compel some inescapable effects. This slow exercise in oscillating chance and necessity took a great time to be played out. This journey could have taken any quality and any direction, as the workings of chance were intertwined with any immanent human rational development. Humans were at their most variable and malleable in these dumb stages within close proximity to nature. But at the point where property is entrenched in law and understood as a right begins a story of human necessity or rational unfolding that cannot be stopped or redirected. From this moment humans are at their pinnacle, and as the parent of inequality they must watch their child turn monstrous. Rousseau sets the scene: "Behold then all the human faculties developed, memory and imagination in full play, egoism interested, reason active, and the mind almost at the highest point of its perfection.... Matters once at this pitch, it is easy to imagine the rest."[28] Thus begins the descent.

Goodman gives special attention to this crux in the "Second Discourse," showing it to be a seminal moment where the temporality of the historical narrative shifts radically. Before the emergence of social inequality, chance is the essential condition of time, but after this lamentable moment is reached, necessity takes over in the operation of history. In essence, Goodman's view is that Rousseau's history of man sways on the fulcrum of inequality—possibility and chance on the one side, inevitability on the other. After uncovering this curious division in the text,

27. Rousseau, *The Social Contract and Discourses*, 207.
28. Rousseau, *The Social Contract and Discourses*, 217.

Goodman unfortunately takes Rousseau's awkward temporal displacements as intended and uses them to overturn traditional criticisms of Rousseau's condemnation of history and his disdain for change.[29] She overly emphasizes the importance of the emergence of inequality as a way of subverting the text's principle dynamic, the dichotomy between nature and society. To doubt this is analytical folly. The abstractions of nature and society are the grander philosophical points of Rousseau's scheme. The "Second Discourse" is simply the involuntary product from these ideas needing a "pseudohistory" to fill in the enormous conceptual time between them. I use the term "pseudohistory" because no capable and historically honest journey can be retold between such obscure and diametrically separated ideas. The portrayal of the origin of inequality also falls victim to this overly broad style and sense of history. The emergence of social inequality is not the sudden, fixed history-altering point that Rousseau and Goodman would have us believe.

The historical time between the state of nature and modern society is a broad canvas upon which to paint, and thus one prone to generalities. The very breadth meant that Rousseau skimmed over eons within paragraphs, dividing history into stages with cartoonish largess. Stages of development become fixed archetypes that betray their evolution and slow gestation. Rousseau himself was well aware of this when in the early examination of human development he said, "I pass over in an instant a multitude of ages; for the slower the events were in their succession, the more rapidly may they be described."[30] When the beginning and end-points of a narrative are so squarely separated, new dimensions in man's nature can only be seen to have "mushroomed" into existence. This is precisely how social inequality emerges in humankind. Whatever process that led to the development has to be focused and made static, because the type of history Rousseau is writing doesn't allow for its characterization as a process. Social inequality seen from this perspective has to be a revolution exploding reality onto a new track, rather than an evolution into new ways of thinking that are connected to past nature. However, the truth is that it is not a sudden protuberance, but a creeping manifestation. The birth of inequality is rhetorically framed between

29. Goodman, *Criticism in Action*, 152–57.
30. Rousseau, *The Social Contract and Discourses*, 211.

nature and society, and hence this birth will always be the product of the temporal difficulties imposed on history by these abstractions.

The second reason Rousseau splits the text into a period of chance before inequality and a period of necessity thereafter concerns the slow collapse of Rousseau's histories that we observed in his *Confessions.* Just as we saw the change in tone from exuberant enthusiasm to defeated despondency over Rousseau's personal history, the same is observable in the "Second Discourse." As Rousseau's history is forced to leave the state of nature, an overwhelming sense of inexplicability pervades the text, as he has to believe that there is no concrete reason to leave such a state. Society has to be born from chance, because there is no such necessity in departing from nature. Seen from this naturally good and timeless state at the beginning of human proceedings, every movement away from the shore of nature is confusing, irrational, and filled with regret. Still within close proximity to nature is the theoretical and imaginative possibility of detouring from our fate, or at least of arresting its forward march. The problem is, of course, that Rousseau already knows humankind's unfortunate destiny, and at some point in the text he must acknowledge it. This point comes with the origin of inequality. By this stage humanity is sufficiently evolved away from nature, both mentally and temporally, for there to be no hope of redemption. Eighteenth-century French monarchical absolutism and the *ancien regime* are now within sight, and a situation of necessity takes over from chance. Before, Rousseau was thinking forward from the point of nature, but now he is thinking backward from his own present. Thinking forward from prehistory is open to prospects and opportunities, while thinking backward from the present must follow a predetermined line. The origin of inequality can in one sense represent the point in Rousseau's mind where the direction of his thought switches from forward thinking through time to backward thinking through time. This greatly contributes to the impression of inequality in the text as a moment changing all, rather than an evolution fusing time periods. This *forward = chance, backward = necessity* equation is of course simply a temporal displacement that is solely the product of the illusion of history that the "Second Discourse" represents. History is at all times a dance between chance and necessity, and there is no singular point in history upon which the two processes are divided from each other.

The realization of inequality in the social realm is the hinge of Rousseau's hope and despair. Once inequality has a foothold in the affairs of men, it follows a necessary path downward to arbitrary power. Rousseau outlines the pathway: "If we follow the progress of inequality in these various revolutions, we shall find that the establishment of laws and of the right of property was the first term, the institution of magistracy the second, and the conversion of legitimate into arbitrary power the third and last."[31] These phases of inequality authorize certain formidable relations between people: the first a relation of rich and poor, the second of strong and weak, and the third of master and slave. The last is his final damning indictment on the French monarchy, which "wherever it prevails, admits no other master; it no sooner speaks than probity and duty lose their weight and blind obedience is the only virtue which slaves can still practice."[32] The necessity conditioned by the emergence of inequality sends the doom-ridden mind into the arms of absolute monarchy. The present situation is unavoidable and unbearable. The sheer volume of time passed through, and the beautiful simplicity of where it began, makes the end point of the narrative both heartbreakingly inevitable and demanding of future. What is required is a cleansing of the civic body that is tainted by the violence of its birth. The demands of the future would be met in Rousseau's *The Social Contract*, which I will deal with in the next chapter. But before I examine this new aspect of Rousseau's political history of man, I will end my discussion on the "Second Discourse" by discussing the inevitability of inequality's passage, better described as the irreversibility of time.

The inability of the social man to return to nature, or indeed to recapture any previous stage of development once it has been instituted, amounts to an irreversible concept of time. On one level this is a consequence of the massive history of the species that Rousseau is attempting, as any gauged change in the human lot is as much mental and psychological as it is social and institutional. Mental stages of development are of course virtually impossible to erase. But this irreversibility of faculty development is extended to institutional development also, and when coupled with Rousseau's "anti-teleology" that we examined earlier, this

31. Rousseau, *The Social Contract and Discourses*, 231.
32. Rousseau, *The Social Contract and Discourses*, 235.

creates a highly destructive view of the purpose and benefit of institutions. Take, for example, Rousseau's own words on the formation and abuse of institutions: "for the flaws that make social institutions necessary are the same as make the abuse of them unavoidable."[33]

Institutions for Rousseau are the testaments to our flaws and vices, and simply become areas around which they can continue to thrive. As stated before, institutions are the signposts of our downfall, and they are constructed as impenetrable barriers fixed behind us to prevent us regressing (or paradoxically progressing) to a better time in the past. Our mental development and its attending institutional face are like a flowing river with a system of locks and dams. Institutions prevent backflow by substantiating an undesirable aspect of our characters: a constant and inerasable aspect of ourselves made concrete, pushing us further to our doom. The flow of time cannot be reversed. And when the flow of time is a teleology of sinking fortunes, a bleak view of institutions follows. Institutions are seen as agents imprisoning our natural liberties or as tombstones commemorating the death of our freedoms. Such a view of institutions does much to diminish any claims Rousseau has to being an evolutionary thinker. Evolutionary politics implies a belief in progress. It implies that there are no arbitrary, valueless decisions made in history. It implies that what has survived has survived for some reason, and what dies is no longer needed. Unfortunately, Rousseau overwhelmingly sees any reason and progress in history to be a malignancy. Because this history seems so callous and indifferent to Rousseau's timeless beliefs, he could only ever prescribe a revolutionary political apparatus that has no investment with that history. And by delving so far into an imaginary past, Rousseau had to envisage a totally new imaginary future based solely upon the timeless will rather than with any historical legacy. This would be the rationale behind his development of the General Will, and its standpoint is the exact opposite of that evolutionary pathology that can be observed in that constellation of thinkers labeled the historical institutionalists.

As our human nature is being developed, invented, and discovered, institutions are formed to safeguard its passage, for there is the real understanding of the threat to its continuance. If we look at the formation

33. Rousseau, *The Social Contract and Discourses,* 231.

of institutions from the historical point of their emergence without the weight of an oppressive past or future to distort our view, we can see that they are formed precisely to protect new-found freedoms. Rather than chaining us to our vices, they emancipate our virtues. Seen from this angle, where the future is unknown, institutions are attempts to move time onward, when time's natural tendency is toward inertia and regression. Institutions are signs of human belief in the possibility for time and progress to reverse, and also of our slow fight to avert this. Rather than monolithic monuments to the forward onslaught of time, institutions are the living apparatuses that we use to harness and control it. Institutions seen this way are the true engines of evolutionary history, and to miss this vital point, as Rousseau has done, is to miss the true import of our evolutionary natures. "The paradoxical truth then about progress, then, is that it wholly depends on the survival of massive institutions which prevent a relapse from a stage that has once been reached."[34]

34. Eugen Rosenstock-Huessy, *Out of Revolution: Autobiography of Western Man* (Providence, R.I.: Berg, 1993), 31.

4

The Social Contract

The *Social Contract* is Rousseau's crowning work of political influence. Its preeminence comes not only from its influence in the realm of political theory, but also its moment of influential grace during one of European history's most intemperate events. It is an incongruous phenomenon that one of political theory's most timeless constructions could have had such a momentous and timely moment of prestige in the French Revolution. The forlorn histories, the temporal despairing, the search for origins, and the raging against the present that I have discussed so far have their final moment of transcendence in the theoretical purity of the *Social Contract*. In this work time and history are hypothetically conquered, resolved, escaped, and lifted; but then almost ironically, in the incredible historical hour of French Revolution, the timeless ideas of this work energized the revolutionary zeal of its major participants. Ideas of this nature can only have the most fleeting moment of historical grace. Its revolutionary content must inevitably be used by history in a blinding flash by minds turned toward the eternal hopes of humankind; but rarely can these ideas be utilized in the evolutionary cycle of politics. Nor can it explain the reality of historical legacies. This chapter will outline the converging timeless threads that make up the historical surpassing of the *Social Contract*.

Spinozian Elements of the *Social Contract*

At first glance to talk of the influence of Spinoza's thought on Rousseau's social contract seems an absurdity. The thinker who railed so vehemently against the materialist tendencies of his day cannot be thought to have fraternized with the devil incarnate of European materialism. There is nothing so diametrically opposed as Spinoza's necessity and Rousseau's freedom. But as I have observed in the "Second Discourse," Rousseau was not uncommon in his age for mixing elements of materialist and scientific thought into his grander project of freedom stemming from the immaterial. However, what is illuminating is how the adoption of certain Spinozist themes lends to the *Social Contract* a degree of timelessness, purity, circularity, and theoretical certainty that is so endemic to Rousseau's thought. It is not so far-fetched that two of the most adamant modern democrats would share similar tendencies in thought.

In his work *Radical Enlightenment*, Jonathon I. Israel ends his study of the rise of philosophical radicalism and Spinoza's conspicuous role in that rise, with a short section dealing with how Rousseau fed on that radical tradition. He also alludes to Rousseau's "Janus-headed mixing" of material and immaterial elements, and in so doing highlights many of the similarities that Rousseau and Spinoza shared. This common heritage is characterized by the "sweeping rejection of tradition and authority, its delegitimizing of the social and political structures of the day, its egalitarianism, underlying pantheism and, above all, in the doctrine of the 'general will,' it is aligned unmistakably with a radical philosophical tradition reaching back to the mid-seventeenth century."[1] Israel makes the link between Spinoza and Rousseau through Rousseau's one-time good friend but eventual loathsome enemy, Diderot. Rousseau's *Social Contract* was dependant for much of its influence upon Diderot's own work on the "volonté genéralé" in the *Encyclopedia*. That Diderot was an exponent of the theory of necessity and among the new Spinozists goes some way to confirming the link, as if the philosophical freight of Spinozian necessity was always residual when discussing the general will. However, what is incontestable about the Rousseau and Spinoza connec-

---

1. Jonathon I. Israel, *Radical Enlightenment: Philosophy and the Making of Modernity 1650–1750* (Oxford and New York: Oxford University Press, 2001), 720.

tion is that their philosophies both summon a deracinating power that radically puts into doubt all existing institutions. This type of radicalism makes them the oddest of political brothers.

In much the same manner as Hobbes's position in the realm of political thought, Spinoza looms as a philosophical specter whose influence is denied and decried, but is obliquely and obscurely prevalent in much Enlightenment thinking. Friedrich Heinrich Jacobi, the German thinker most noted for divining the encroaching Spinozism within the Enlightenment, spent most of his career accusing philosophical luminaries of Spinozist- related atheism. To Fichte's "self positing self" philosophy he sarcastically posed the question, "Strange that the thought never occurred to Spinoza of inverting his philosophical cube."[2] He was, in other words, saying that Fichte's all-inclusive "I" is nothing more than the inversion of Spinoza's all-inclusive "Nature." Spinoza's cube has many faces: the face of the totality of nature, the face of the totality of the self, and perhaps in Rousseau's case, the totality of the people and the state.

When reading the *Social Contract* for the first time one is struck by the circularity of argumentation and the necessity that drives the general will. In the first two books of the *Social Contract,* which deal exclusively with the abstract aspects of political right (as opposed to the latter two books, which are concerned with more practical political considerations), the picture contained therein of "sovereignty" corresponds in many respects with that of Spinoza's "substance." Sovereignty is inalienable and indivisible, and the general will is indestructible and infallible. The vision given of the *Social Contract* is of a totality of wills, bound together by inviolable laws of belonging, impossible to consciously disregard once the contract is enacted. The binding of individual wills into an immanent, all-pervasive, all–powerful, and intangible common will has the effect of artificially creating what could be called a "political substance" or a "social nature," running by the same laws that would govern any totality constructed along the lines of an overwhelming generality. Just as the totality of mechanism enabled Spinoza to conceive nature as a general mass containing everything, paradoxically, Rousseau's totality of freedom enabled him to conceive the social contract as an equally

2. Friedrich Heinrich Jacobi, *The Main Philosophical Writings and the Novel* "Allwill," translated by George di Giovanni (Montreal and Kingston: McGill-Queens University Press, 1994), 502.

general will, or mass of individual wills. Nowhere is this strange affinity more prevalent when we consider how and why Spinoza's substance and Rousseau's sovereignty operate. "The Sovereign, merely by virtue of what it is, is always what it should be."[3] Notice the circularity of purpose behind the Rousseauian state and the Spinozian conception of God: "Things could have been produced by God in no other way, and in no other order than they have been produced."[4]

Just like Spinoza's God, the state acts from the laws of its nature alone. Once the primary act of social contract occurs, all following actions and laws flow legitimately and explicably from this original source. The Rousseauian state under the eternal guidance of the social contract is a perfectly synchronous entity that, once established, has its citizens participate with a suspicious degree of necessity in the unfolding of its legal nature. Being so incontestably certain and legitimate (a natural consequence of most entities based on such a circularity), what it is and how it behaves ends up being what it must necessarily be. We have already seen, in my discussion of his last autobiographical work, The *Reveries of a Solitary Walker,* that this penchant for circularity is a common, or at least sought-after, trait in Rousseau's thinking. In that work the sense of circularity gave his fragile self an imperviousness to the outside world. The same imperviousness is given to the social contract. The problem with views of the world (or institutions) based on such circular argumentation is the impossibility of placing limits on the derived circular being. While citizens must limit themselves in order to form the general will, once their surrender is complete, an unfettered and unlimited general will can act according to its now infallible greater will with assurance, authority, and impunity. We are now in a position to understand how many commentators have seen totalitarian origins in Rousseau's thought. The general will only errs when it errs against itself, which, like Spinoza's substance, is impossible, because not obeying its own laws implies its nonexistence. Rousseau writes, "But the body politic or the Sovereign, drawing its being wholly from the sanctity of the contract, can never bind itself ... to do anything derogatory to the original act, for instance, to alienate any part of itself, or to submit to

3. Jean-Jacques Rousseau, *The Social Contract and Discourses* (London: J. M. Dent and Sons, 1938), 17.

4. Benedict de Spinoza, *Ethics* (London: Penguin, 1996), 22.

another Sovereign. Violation of the act by which it exists would be self-annihilation; and that which is itself nothing can create nothing."[5] Notice the allusion to the well-known principle behind Spinoza's philosophy, "gigni de nihilo nihil, in nihilum nil potest reverti."[6] We can also notice other parallels with Spinoza. Just like the quote above, Spinoza also shows the purity with which his substance maintains itself; how it cannot be conceived in any meaningful sense if it is mediated by an outside influence; and how it must be understood through itself. Spinoza says that "God acts from the laws of his nature alone, and is compelled by no one,"[7] and "What cannot be conceived through another, must be conceived through itself."[8]

The social contract is a theoretical/political manifestation of the *amour se soi* selfhood that Rousseau saw as the only pure mode of being. As humans are essentially driven by self-interest in a contaminated social environment and hence incapable of conceiving themselves through themselves, the social contract becomes the ultimate voluntarist institution capable of such self-reflexivity. Just as Spinoza's philosophy is the most perfect and complete of philosophical demonstrations of the world, Rousseau's social contract is the perfect political abstraction through which all politics must be judged and all right must be demonstrated. Spinoza's substance cannot be divided against itself or bound by the outside. The same can be said of Rousseau's general will.

An illuminating, if somewhat oblique recognition of the correlation between Spinoza and Rousseau comes from one of his most gifted and stringent commentators, Roger D. Masters. In truth, Masters never explicitly confirms the reciprocity, even though he was highly receptive to the scientific pretensions of Rousseau's thought. In his authoritative work *The Political Philosophy of Rousseau* is included a curious section entitled "The Geometric Formula for Legitimate Government."[9] The parallel is immediately obvious when you muse on Spinoza's own desire

5. Rousseau, *The Social Contract and Discourses,* 17.

6. "From nothing, nothing is generated; into nothing, nothing returns." This fundamental tenet of Western metaphysics was stated by Jacobi to be the primary axiom upon which Spinoza's philosophy rested.

7. Spinoza, *Ethics,* 13.

8. *Spinoza, Ethics,* 2.

9. Roger D. Masters, *The Political Philosophy of Rousseau* (Princeton, N.J.: Princeton University Press, 1968), 340–48.

to demonstrate the world "in geometric order."[10] Masters takes Rousseau's claim of an equilibrium or "continuous proportion" between sovereign, government, and people and the possibility of expressing the relationship mathematically seriously enough to devise such an equation. I will not go into this argument, but only observe that Masters follows the mathematical argumentative line, discussing the algebraic permutations of Rousseau's formulation in great detail. What is important is to assert that no such reading of Rousseau's *Social Contract* could take place unless there were very real and serious allusions to Spinoza's scientific synchronicity, stability, and purity. The belief in a mathematical reality to the mechanisms of politics is one of Rousseau's burning desires, as it eliminates any unwanted complexity and irrationality and makes his social contract a paragon of explanation. As Masters concludes his thought-provoking section, "Rousseau's conception of a continuous proportion between the sovereign, the government, and the subjects is thus a mathematical formulation of his principles of political right which, like a frictionless surface, is of explanatory value only."[11]

Another way to view the affinity between Rousseau and Spinoza is to look at it through the lens of the "common good." This of course comes down to the fact that they were both democrats. Spinoza is afforded the title of the first modern democrat because he deduced such political principles from the new scientific understanding of natural man. If humans have no recourse to an external natural right, or their right is coextensive with their means to self-preservation, then the only political system that can approximate this beginning is a democracy. Only a democracy can preserve the right to self-preservation of individuals in a legitimately political way. Democracy essentially approximates the state of nature.[12] Rousseau shared many of the same views regarding man's primary urge to self-preservation, and saw the fatal flaw of natural-right theory. In this he was essentially in agreement with Hobbes, and hence also Spinoza. Both Spinoza and Rousseau agree that there is no extrinsic standard to determine the good, but that instead good is to be found immanently within the commonwealth. Both are in agreement that when revelation,

10. Spinoza, *Ethics*, 1.

11. Masters, *The Political Philosophy of Rousseau*, 348.

12. Leo Strauss, *Natural Right and History* (Chicago: University of Chicago Press, 1963), 286.

tradition, and existing political and religious authority have been neu-tered by right reason, the only criterion left to judge the worth of a thing is the common good.[13] When all past historical guidance and testimony have been eliminated from speaking to the present or future, and the common good is touted as the only measure for determining the just, that common good always tends to a certain inchoate and formless character, which we can see in both Spinoza and Rousseau. In both cases the indi-vidual will, which can either be good or bad, is subsumed under a general or common will. Because of being a composite of all wills, its simplicity and all-inclusiveness secure its supposed rightness. This amorphous gen-erality in Spinoza's case flows directly from the state of nature that is the fountainhead of his metaphysics and politics. With all having individual power and right granted by nature, the natural tendency is toward de-mocracy, where such power is banded together, and where security and free cultivation can be ensured. Spinoza writes, "In it no one transfers his natural right so absolutely that he has no further voice in affairs, he only hands it over to the majority of a society, whereof he is a unit. Thus all men remain, as they were in the state of nature, equals."[14]

Of course Rousseau's general will and the common good that it guarantees are also influenced from another very different source than an indifferent nature. The modern incarnation of democracy rests far more upon the legal and moral tradition of rights than on Spinoza's radi-cal naturalism. In *The Rebel,* Albert Camus referred to Rousseau's *Social Contract* as the "New Gospel." Camus says that Rousseau had formulated a new religion where "the will of the people (is) substituted for God Him-self."[15] What Rousseau had achieved was the deification of the people and their will, derived from a strong sense of natural freedom. What Spinoza achieved was the deification of science, derived from a strong sense of determinism and natural necessity. Both were radical democrats and be-lieved in the common good, but only one provided the necessary spring for motivated political action. Rousseau imbibed political philosophy with a radical rousing spirit that uplifted the people to take active control over their destiny. Spinoza's philosophy was in a practical sense unable to

13. Israel, "Epilogue," in *Radical Enlightenment,* 720.

14. Benedict de Spinoza, *Works of Spinoza,* translated by R. H. M. Elwes (New York: Dover, 1951), 207.

15. Albert Camus, *The Rebel* (Harmondsworth: Penguin, 1971), 85.

do this, but in some measure Rousseau was only able to achieve this by turning to another face of Spinoza's cube and adopt some of the method of his thinking. While Rousseau denied adamantly that humanity would ever be able to return to nature, he certainly wanted his social contract to have the natural simplicity that someone like Spinoza saw in it. Perhaps the peculiar similarity between Spinoza's monist natural whole and Rousseau's political whole, obtained from one side of his metaphysical dualism, is that Rousseau wanted his social contract to be a "second nature." It is in this sense that we can understand what J. L. Talmon meant when he remarked in his *The Origins of Totalitarian Democracy,* "Ultimately the general will is to Rousseau something like a mathematical truth or a Platonic idea."[16] These two concepts, mathematical proof and Platonic ideal, while seemingly incompatible, do coalesce comfortably within the social contract. The "mathematical" content of the social contract is derived from the Spinozist elements that are present in the manner and method of its composition. The *Social Contract'*s sense of certainty, generality, totality, and circularity are all accounted for by this Spinoza-tinged quasi-scientific purity. Just like any balanced equation, it is constructed so that there can be no remainder. The pantheistic metaphysics of Spinoza can be felt in the all-inclusive necessity behind the social contract. The "Platonic" content of the *Social Contract* is, however, derived from the very aspect of Rousseau's system that flies in Spinoza's face: its freedom. This is the aspect to which we will now turn. To conclude, the Platonic and the mathematical are able to live harmoniously together because they are both eternal and timeless, and hence impenetrable.

Freedom and Morality: The Artificial State of Nature

The problematic aspect of the *Social Contract* is the relation between what Rousseau wants to say on abstract right and what he wants to say on sociological reality. There is always present the intractable problem of theory versus practice. Roger Masters does not see such a radical division as problematic, feeling that Rousseau provides a bridge between the claims of ideality and the claims of reality.[17] Albert Camus, however,

16. J. L. Talmon, *The Origins of Totalitarian Democracy* (London: Mercury, 1966), 41.
17. Masters, *The Political Philosophy of Rousseau,* 306.

adamantly states that it is a book oriented in its entire message toward rights and not facts, entirely unconcerned with the sociological observation of its time.[18] Vaughan also labored over what he saw as the fatal contradiction of the *Social Contract:* "Few things have caused more perplexity ... than Rousseau's failure to distinguish between the abstract and the concrete elements of his theory.... How is the 'empire of climate' to be reconciled with the assertion that 'all men are born free'? Is the Contract, which ex hypothesi lies at the root of the whole system, a historical fact? or is it no more than a 'tacit understanding'?"[19] Vaughan comes close to solving the dilemma of this contradiction when he asks about the historical nature of the compact. Thrown against the backdrop of time and history, there is nothing to defend Rousseau from accusations of a doomed abstraction incapable of organic articulation. To doubt the wholly philosophical nature of the social contract and entertain the more concrete sociological considerations as more than just fancies is to fatally disregard the atemporal temper of Rousseau's thinking. As Vaughan notes, "He was wrong in assuming that either the civil state, or the sense of duty, could ever have sprung to birth in a single moment; that it was possible for them to be anything but the slow growth of time. Time, however, is just what he is not willing to give."[20]

But what makes Rousseau's social contract so temporally disrupting is the violent demands that his theory makes upon the practice of politics and the structures of society. If the division between his philosophizing mind and the tangible requirements of his age were clearly demarcated, then Rousseau would have avoided the dangerous revolutionary urges inherent in unbridled political idealism. But the urgent timelessness instinctual in the radical political imagination occasions a type of "temporal moral gravity" that requires moral constructions to fall to the earth and make eternal demands on the living. "It was not merely the fact that someone reflected philosophically upon the nature of the state that made a theory idealist, but the extent to which the philosophising consciousness sets itself up as the benchmark of value."[21]

18. Camus, *The Rebel,* 84.

19. C. E. Vaughan, "Introduction," in *The Political Writings of Jean-Jacques Rousseau.* Edited, with notes by C. E. Vaughan (Cambridge: Cambridge University Press), 1915, 436.

20. Vaughan, *The Political Writings of Jean-Jacques Rousseau,* 44.

21. Robert Catley and Wayne Cristaudo, *This Great Beast: Progress and the Modern State* (Aldershot: Ashgate, 1997), 126.

If we contrast this type of thinking with the methodology of the historical institutionalist, we can see that even though they do philosophize about the nature of the state, they never subject political and historical processes to the unlimited workings of a philosophical idea devoid of content. With the historical institutionalist there is a tacit understanding of the composite relationship between social dynamics and philosophic statics, neither being swamped by the other. Rousseau's *Social Contract* is the study of a mind whose metaphysical dualism shapes a radicalism incapable of this subtle comprehension. With this understanding we have come full circle, where we are finally able to examine the extreme translation of Rousseau's concept of free will into political vocabulary.

The three major streams of Rousseau's thought—nature, morality, and politics—are in many senses separate entities that jostle for priority. Nature can have no strictly moral elements. Individual morality (that sight of societal goodness that Rousseau secures and defends in *Emile*) cannot be fostered by the general will, but only by a civic virtue that may at times be contrary to individual morality. The more these three streams are subjected to philosophical treatment, the more they separate and must have differing spheres of influence and differing modes of understanding. But this fact does nothing to detract from our appreciation of Rousseau's belief that all three are one, or at least that these three motifs rhyme harmoniously within the entirety of man's individual and collective being and current and past experience. This desire is behind our assertion that Rousseau conceived of the general will as a way of deploying a new social "second nature," whereby nature and politics can forge a meaningful new impetus for the future. It is also the reason Rousseau felt compelled to magnify the individual's site for moral feeling, the free will, into the general will, thus making politics commensurate with morality, politicizing every aspect of personal life, and politically energizing the whole community. The vehicle through which all three streams of Rousseau's system become conceptual siblings is freedom. Freedom is the umbrella that gives these concepts a commonality and the scaffolding upon which their legitimacy hang.

Among the vagaries of Rousseau's state of nature emerges its one concrete characteristic: that the free will is the source of the goodness in our nature. We have already seen that this creates problems. In the "Second Discourse," Rousseau melds the free will into the concept of perfectibility as an *ad hoc* explanation behind the pessimistic anthropology that he is dictating. In the *Social Contract* free will is given a different treatment, whereby it becomes the immaterial source of constitutionality and hence the foundation of the state and civic virtue. It is not a force working through history by some strange form of necessity. Free will is no longer a confused natural faculty because of its urge to take part in the temporal flux of the world. It is now removed from nature, no longer attempting to bridge the gap of the dualism, because the political is now a work of a convention or human artifice born from our atemporal ability to moralize our actions. Thus, this freedom should also be coupled with the moral freedom of the individual outlined most emphatically in *Emile*. Here the free will, or conscience, is used to become sovereign over one's natural or childlike freedom, which is a slave to the passions. This, in essence, is self-legislation for the individual, and its emergence or possibility is a prerequisite for the more general self-legislation of the state. In *Emile*, Rousseau characterizes these three streams as separate, but parallel factors: "Now after he has considered himself in his physical relations to other creatures, in his moral relations with other men, there remains to be considered his civil relations with his fellow citizens."[22]

The three working terms of Rousseau's mature philosophy—nature, morality, and politics—are thus intimately connected. The governing principle behind these three sides of human experience is always the immaterial free will, the confirmation of our spirituality. It just has differing expression through the separate modes: nature and the *amour de soi* dreamer; morality and the good individual of *Emile;* and politics and the virtuous citizen. They are all separate realities with a familiar kinship through the natural goodness of man. And by making the distinction between natural freedom, moral freedom, and political freedom, Rousseau no longer has to rely on perfectibility as a defining trait of humanity. Perfectibility reeks too much of necessity and historical death. The timeless free will, finally distinct from natural necessity in every respect, can now be used to determine legitimacy in the social realm and provide a new meaning to humanity. Moral and political perfection can be sought after and achieved at any time, and not be contingent upon his-

22. Rousseau, *Emile,* translated by Barbara Foxley (London: J. M. Dent and Sons, 1974), 419.

torical circumstance. Free will can descend from our lofty selves on our choosing. However, some theorists maintain that the *Social Contract* is determined in its possibility by history. Situated as it is after the "Second Discourse," commentators like Asher Horowitz assume that the *Social Contract* is a practical antidote to eighteenth-century monarchical and aristocratic abuses.

> But if the second Discourse is understood as the foundation of a historical and social ontology according to which nature is unfolded inside the matrix of human historical activity, then there are strong reasons for presuming that the starting point of the Social Contract is just that historical predicament analysed in the Discourse and that this predicament is what delimits the boundaries to the solution proposed in the Contract.[23]

This is obviously true on the level that any work of political philosophy is situated in the needs of its time, even if it doesn't present itself as such. The historical freight that is carried throughout the "Second Discourse" and that transfers onto the *Social Contract* also adds weight to this perception. But what this assumption ignores is Rousseau's complete inability to face up honestly to the problems of his day, which in turn leads to his morose view of social affairs and history. The "solution proposed in the Contract" has to be an act of pure historical transcendence for it to be legitimate in the time-tainted eyes of the revolutionary. What this also ignores is that the source of the "solution" is timeless freedom conceived abstractly and not socially. A historically orientated thinker can see the intimate connection between the "Second Discourse" and the *Social Contract*. The "Second Discourse" as a work of philosophy is like a temporal canon projecting Rousseau's subsequent considerations into the future realm. I showed how a despairing historiography tends to the possibilities of future when I discussed Rousseau's *Confessions* leading to his *Dialogues*. The "Second Discourse" prepares the historical ground for the ahistorical *Social Contract*. So the problem of political legitimacy is undoubtedly framed historically, but there is no evidence to suggest that it is solved historically. The issue here revolves around framing and solving. Rousseau frames his timeless hopes in historical grab, but the hope is simply too timeless to be solved by the vision of history he summons.

---

23. Asher Horowitz, *Rousseau, Nature, and History* (Toronto: University of Toronto Press, 1987), 177.

The key to understanding the rationale behind the *Social Contract* is that its formal source must come from humanity's most natural possession, its free will. Free will is the only human capacity that existed in the state of nature and that all human beings collectively share today. Hence the *Social Contract* represents a collective person imbibed with will and reason. It is a moral incorporation that shares, in common with its individual members, the possession of a will that informs its morality and secures its freedom. Moral agency is conferred on any being, individual or collective, that contains the possibility of freely willing the good. The general will of the social contract is in many regards the political magnification of the individual will and the magnification of the individual's good into the community's good. This is important to remember so as to avoid the terminal problem of Rousseau's supposedly contradictory individualism and collectivism. This does not constitute an unworkable reversal in Rousseau's thought or mean that Rousseau was inconsistent on the primary message of his "system." Rosenstock-Huessy showed how the individual human atom of naturalistic philosophy always tends toward massive generalization: "Whoever starts with the individual must end with the universe. Once the standard unit of power is conceived as one man, enterprising, free, well-equipped, no barrier can be found to his activities. His field is the world. The naturalistic viewpoint of an Adam is valid for all mankind without any difference of creed, faith, church, denomination."[24] The leap from one to all is the easiest of leaps to make when you inflate the individual's site for freedom and morality beyond all national, religious, social, age, and economic barriers. There is no social incoherency in this thought movement. Ernst Cassirer was one of the first commentators to take Rousseau's pleas to read his works as a coherent totality seriously. By doing a Kantian reading of Rousseau he was able to isolate the aspect of his thought that Kant admired most, and that happens to be the aspect that gives the project meaning and stability. This study concurs with the idea that Kant continued and expanded Rousseau's project by focusing on the overwhelming concern for freedom that figures in all Rousseau's books. This was its revolutionary content, and in the annals of philosophical history was the gift he had

24. Eugen Rosenstock-Huessy, *Out of Revolution: Autobiography of Western Man* (Providence, R.I.: Berg, 1993), 184–85.

passed onto other thinkers. The principle of political right must be the will and the attendant new concept of freedom grounded in its operation.

Freedom is the birthright of mankind and thus not a commodity to be traded. It cannot be renounced or invested in another, lest the accompanying political order be unbearable slavery. Rousseau is the first to make freedom the supreme human desire and demand its complete realization into the political reality. The individual can only ever consent to govern him or herself, and thus the only laws we can legitimately obey are ones that are self-legislated. Obligation to anything else is false. This indeed becomes Rousseau's definition of freedom. Freedom is obedience to a law that you give yourself. In order to create the free society, one must collectivize this sentiment and surrender one's will to the will of people. The social body of this operation is the law. Law is simply the expression of the demand that one tune his private will to the public will, that he understand his interest to be the enlightened interest of all citizens. Law must be binding on all equally and benefit all equally for this to be legitimate. In this way Rousseau was able to make the general will the embodiment of the natural drives for self-preservation and compassion. The law at one and the same time satisfies both your own interest and recognizes the interests of others; in other words, one's self-interest becomes coextensive with the interests of others. The right to self-preservation as the material foundation of nature becomes moralized into the duty to self-legislation. This duty is then "generalized," or, a Kantian term, "universalized."

The actualization of this ideal then becomes the greatest challenge to this concept of modernity. This leads us in two directions: the practical realization, which is left to the character of the legislator, and the theoretical realization, which is left to the general will itself. I will deal with the "legislator" later, but first I will deal with the general will's relation to history. It is no mistake that Rousseau is the intellectual forebear of German idealistic philosophy. That tradition is most concerned with the philosophy of history because of the problems Rousseau articulated, problems that demanded the agency of history for their realization. Perhaps then it is easier to understand why there is the attempt to find within his work, the "history" that Rousseau consciously or unconsciously presupposes. I do not deny that Rousseau left many allusions and clues in that direction. *Emile* certainly belongs to this desire. Education becomes a huge theme and necessary project when you are concerned with actualizing an ideal. But in the final appraisal, Rousseau's utter loathing of time and the timelessness he brought to the consideration of his age forces him to leave the business of politics entirely in the hands of the general will. The general will must be the complete transcendence of a history that has been so vicious to our nature.

Leo Strauss attempts to show that Rousseau's rejection of the teachings of natural law means that he attempts to realize the ideal of freedom in a radically new way—one that doesn't find its sanction from a transcendental source, but finds it emanating from within the community of citizens. Rather than our knowledge of the good descending from a higher principle, it is developed immanently within the general will. The general will is like a mechanism for determining the good, or for subsuming the lofty natural law into the grounded positive law. Positive law will be just if it emanates from a society perfectly constructed on what is naturally good—namely, our wills. Strauss uses a vertical/horizontal image to describe the movement.

These men acknowledged a limitation of license which comes from above, a vertical limitation. On the basis of Rousseau, the limitation of license is effected horizontally by the license of other men. I am just if I grant to every other man the same rights which I claim for myself, regardless of what these rights might be. The horizontal limitation is preferred to the vertical limitation because it seems to be more realistic: the horizontal limitation, the limitation of my claim by the claims of others is self enforcing.[25]

This is essentially what was meant by the assertion that the general will is constructed to realize the ideal theoretically. The general will is a masterstroke of theoretical realization and grounding. And one is tempted to imagine the theoretical purity of the move as a persuasive argument in favor of its actual realization. But this is an illusion in the mind, as it can only remain theoretical. In the eyes of time and history this must remain an ideal or vision for the future. It has no real historical realization. But this is no statement on the historical relativity of all things, or a denial of the presence and power of ideals. This is simply to assert that the reality and working of ideals can only be proven histori-

25. Leo Strauss, *What Is Political Philosophy?* (Glencoe, Ill.: Free Press, 1959), 51–52.

cally. History is the field where ideals are tested. Time is the force that chooses to accept or deny the ideals' demand for passage. The general will is no historical reality that serves as the gatekeeper between the ideal and the real. It remains a vertical limitation, while time is left waiting. While time is left out of Rousseau's political equation, the theoretical will never become the practical. And as we have seen, "Time, however, is just what he is not willing to give."[26] Time is not willingly given, because the concept of freedom at the base of this philosophy is existent and sacred before time. As Rosenstock-Huessy points out, "'The God who gave us life, gave us liberty at the same time,' said Jefferson. The words 'at the same time' are the essence and the Achilles heel of this naturalistic philosophy, for they mean that man is to be considered a priori as a free being."[27] Nothing could be further from the truth if freedom is looked upon in its social contingencies and existential articulations. Instead, Rousseau can only look upon freedom in its philosophical and reasonable guise; and thus time and history are not admitted to give freedom any content.

The Taste for the Legislator

The legislator, or lawgiver, is perhaps the strangest of additions to Rousseau's political thinking. Many have struggled to reconcile it with the general will. It seems to be an unresolved annex to the theoretical purity of the *Social Contract*. If the general will is so theoretically sound, why does it need to be taught to a people? The legislator's genesis comes from two sources: Rousseau's need for a practical realization of the general will and Rousseau's admiration for the utopian classical political ideal. Rousseau understood that his general will was in one sense just the machinery that generated law. As any law emanating from it is legitimate, the general will doesn't direct its members toward a certain inescapable form of community or dictate inexorable laws. If it were left up to the general will alone, the state would remain inchoate and formless. Hence someone or something has to give the general will and its law content and context. This is the practical necessity for having a legislator. But as always, the legislator also fulfills a romantic need for Rousseau.

26. Vaughan, "Introduction," in *The Political Writings of Jean-Jacques Rousseau*, 44.
27. Rosenstock-Huessy, *Out of Revolution*, 181.

His love of such mythic figures as Moses, Lycurgus, and Numa gave him his taste for the legislator. There is a sense that great and transcendent politics rest on quasi-religious foundations. The people are molded by the general will and the legislator, but the legislator is molded by some more mysterious morality; he is a superior intelligence who gives the state its divine code. Strangely, he does not interfere with or have any authority in the general workings of the polity, as he is vested with no executive power. As Rousseau observes, "When Lycurgus gave laws to his country, he began by resigning the throne."[28] He is outside the state, but of the state. Not concerned with the mundanity of governance, his position is perched more in the mind of a nation. He is, as J. H. Broome describes him, an expression of the "subconscious" of the people.[29] This makes him a very improbable and vague presence upon which to legitimize the state. But he certainly fulfills Rousseau's desire for a political hero in a time when all he saw were political managers and economists. "The Lawgiver is thus a theoretical necessity, invoked by Rousseau to make the transition from abstract principles to the concrete realities of the lawful society; and his appearance brings to a somewhat unsatisfactory end the main theory of legitimacy."[30]

It is generally appreciated that the two ways of bridging the dualism between morality and nature are history and education. For the most part the concern with history was left to later generations of thinkers. Rousseau consistently ignored it. What he was far more interested in exploring was how education or cultivation could be used to make the ideal real. *Emile* is the ultimate expression of this. A child taken in its infancy can be protected, redirected, and sculpted into the ideal before time has had its opportunity to fashion him or her. The legislator plays the role of a political tutor to a people who do not know their common good. The general will doesn't involuntarily turn to its good; it must be directed toward it by the miraculous actions of the legislator. This "educator of a nation" highlights many of the troubling attitudes in Rousseau's work. This is because of his privileged and intimate connection with the very spirit of the nation … its customs and institutions. His role as a protector, maintainer, destroyer, and creator of institutions and

28. Rousseau, *The Social Contract and Discourses*, 36.
29. J. H. Broome, *Rousseau: A Study of His Thought* (London: Edward Arnold, 1963), 72.
30. Broome, *Rousseau*, 58–59.

customs means that many of the problems with Rousseau's politics co-agulate around his person.

For a thinker so fundamentally concerned with uncovering the basis of society, for plumbing the depths of the origins of things, it seems strange that in the final instance, the practical existence of a nation would have to rely on a confidence trick, needing a figure who leads the nation to its common good like a horse to water, and does so by garbing his mission in robes of spiritual authority. The work of a legislator as mythic guide with a sublime, almost religious, wisdom would certainly not stand up to a rigorous exploration of the origins of his handiwork. The superhuman origin of his code for social spirit would have to be rejected by any enlightened thinker not given over to superstition. Why then does Rousseau rest his final formulation of the social contract in the legislator's hands? There is unfortunately no adequate answer to the question, other than the assertion that politics rest on religious platforms that the questioning philosophical consciousness must reject as illegitimate. Leo Strauss saw this when he wrote, "The problem posed by political philosophy must be forgotten if the solution to which political philosophy leads is to work."[31] The legislator is the strange concept in Rousseau's thought that bears witness to this understanding. He embodies the realization that a massive program such as the authorship of a nation's laws cannot possibly be conceived within the nation itself. For such a task the people would require the very divine wisdom that the legislation itself provides. Thus they require this wisdom from another source. So after having said that the general will itself is enough to provide the law, Rousseau presents the legislator as its real source.

The purpose of the legislator is to socialize the wills of individuals. Hence civil religion, custom, tradition, and early institutions become the means by which he appeals to the heart of a nation. After Montesquieu's sociological understanding of the peculiarity of nations, it was impossible for Rousseau to disregard the things that gave nations their uniqueness and peculiarity. Custom, tradition, and institutions, ideas that feature so strongly in the work of Montesquieu, Burke, and others, are shamefully lacking in Rousseau's social contract until we arrive at the legislator. Rousseau does not see their veracity in modern civil society, as

---

31. Strauss, *Natural Right and History*, 288.

the general will and social contract usurp their purpose after they have formed the nation. These things, rather than being the ongoing, evolving bedrock of a nation, are relegated in their supposed utility to a nation's birth. Working secretly with this substance of the nation, the legislator is expected to mold this tangled mess of influences and present it back to its members as a "social contract." As Ronald Grimsley states, "The unwritten law consists of 'manners (moeurs), customs and especially opinion'—intangible elements which are ignored by most political theorists but which are indispensible to the survival of the state. It is with this elusive but vital factor that the legislator must secretly concern himself."[32]

Dare we ask why the lifeblood of a nation needs such an improbable figurehead to inject its lessons and wisdom into the void of political right and social contract? Surely this is a symptom of the inability of Rousseau and his timeless creation to recognize bodies of institutional time. The *Social Contract* and the general will are generally blind to manners, customs, and institutions, but when forced to discuss how these constructs find reality, Rousseau ushers in a character that deals with these vital factors. There is no talk of these "elusive" elements in the theoretical construct of the *Social Contract,* because its nature cannot recognize them. These things speak to a nation at all times, and a political vision deaf to their demands can only be a vision deaf to time. Rousseau knows his political vision is ignorant to these elements, and that is why he needs to invent a character who can be conversant with them. Ironically for this study, it is precisely the moment that the legislator enters the stage that timeliness becomes the essence of political action for Rousseau. "Timing is the all-important factor, the essential prerequisite of a nation ... in its childhood, the nation has not the necessary judgment, while in its old age, its bad habits are too deeply engrained for them to be altered."[33]

The legislator is a character endowed with some sort of civic clock, able to divine the right moment when a nation can be delivered. Timeliness is his essence, and a nation has but a fleeting moment where it can benefit from his productive, associative, and institutional insights. It is a troubling coincidence that a matter of the gravest importance, such as the birth of a nation, its freedom, law, and unity, depends entirely on

32. Ronald Grimsley, "Introduction," in *Du Contrat Social* [The Social Contract] (Oxford: Oxford University Press, 1972), 33.

33. Grimsley, "Introduction," in *Du Contrat Social,* 31.

the lottery of one exceptional figure. When timeliness is finally admitted into the Rousseauian political rationale, it is given a miraculous opening, dependant on an unsure, unstable, and unreal confluence of elements, and spearheaded by a figure of which history has presented to us only a few charmed individuals. In many ways the precariousness and dire responsibility of political timeliness are demonstrated by this balancing act. But a philosophy that makes timeliness so rare and critical can never be a stabilizing element in the political state. Timeliness is required in every political situation and at every time. A philosophy in which time is only valuable when an allusive relation of variables exists is really just a philosophy of a timeless imagination. All the improbable legislator ends up convincing us of is the absolute timelessness of the social contract. The lawgiver shows us just how unreasonable and extreme are the demands that Rousseau's theory makes on practice. If the ideal's real world guardian is an unfathomable genius bringing impossibility into being, surely this should convince us of the improbability of the ideal. The general will can only be as possible as its progenitor. In the last instance, Rousseau's social contract is an eternal (that is, timeless) reality, a realm unaffected by the vicissitudes of change and decay. Its passage into time is the intrusive work of an improbable legislator, as he is the face of the state that can effect meaningful lasting change. One is left only to ask the question, why are the general will and social contract not political entities endowed with the institutional ability to respond through time on their own? Where is their connection to time that emanates from themselves, and not from their equally timeless legislator?

The figure of the legislator also points us back in the direction of the implicit view of the individual in Rousseau's general will. I have already shown that the collectivity of the general will in no way contradicts Rousseau's individualism, as the individual conceived naturalistically as an atomic unit endowed a priori with freedom simply expands out in social expression as the general will. The individual thus conceived has as his natural right a corresponding social field to be constructed purely from himself and his will. While there is no philosophical contradiction here, there is the feeling that having thus been expanded socially beyond himself, the individual does become consumed and lost in its generality. While the legislator initially is devised only to help bring about such a miraculous generality of wills, there is also a sense that his emergence represents the individual re-reflected back from generality. The powerful and miraculous legislator is an endpoint expression and reminder of how the individual was conceived at the beginning of the enterprise.

Being reminded in the first and final instances of the expanded place of the individual in this political venture of Rousseau's, one is also directed to remember the past from which it derives its impetus. As in all moments of the *Social Contract*'s argument, one should never forget that it is designed to provide scope for the expression of the individual's naturally good and innate freedom, and that thus the individual is the cornerstone of the edifice. One should also always keep close to mind that the enterprise receives its historical ballast from the past. Having our goodness and nature within us before time, Rousseau provided philosophically and imaginatively for this view by assembling a scientific and mythic sense of our prehistoric Nature. He devised for us a distant past that sought to lend authority and legitimacy to our timeless attempts to radically reform our historically contingent societies. Such attempts to circumvent history, of which the timeless general will is Rousseau's preeminent political attempt, are made possible by depositing the requisite timelessness back into the past.

In summary, as Rousseau's assaults and censures against his society and against the world in general become more insistent, more overarching, more theorized, and more universal, one can observe a corresponding deepening of his concern for history. The more he succumbs to the siren call of transcendent ahistorical freedom, the more he misleadingly demands from history a reinforcement and encouragement for his timeless principles. Eventually this tandem relationship between his increasing timeless abstraction and his corresponding entreaties for historical ballast runs aground onto a wholly timeless and ahistorical model: the social contract. As his timeless freedom becomes more austere and detached from reality, so his historical consciousness recedes further into the insensible hypothesizing of the past. The "First Discourse" is exceedingly well situated in its contemporary day and reaches modestly, but hopefully to ancient Sparta as a springboard for criticism. The "Second Discourse" is an attempt at a more general criticism of his age, and of civilization generally, and hence goes further into a theoretical state of nature for its argumentative weight. This growing tension of increasing abstraction and belief in atemporally conceived freedom, needing still further and deeper visions of history, pushes history into such an illusory state that it is eventually dispensed with altogether in the social contract.

The contentious issue of Rousseau's legacy as a thinker concerned with history is best described as a master/slave relationship between timelessness and history. One cannot deny that he is very interested in the historically contingent nature of humanity, and much of his revolutionary zeal comes from the promise of historically intervening into societies by remaking and reinstructing human character. But such a promise seems more a historical consolation prize for the man who looks primarily at history as decay and devolution; in other words, at least history allows its adversary to use its own parchment and nature to expunge perceived mistakes. This, however, is not the same thing as understanding history's operations and lessons, or seeking within time our political deliverance. Instead, this is the attempt to refashion history in such a way that it will bring about its own dissolution or transcendence, an operation that we will observe in an even more promethean dimension under Karl Marx, to whom we now turn.

PART 2

Karl Marx

5

Eternity and Constant Transformation

Marx's Redirection of the Problem of Time

What must first be acknowledged when turning to Karl Marx and his project's relation to time and history is that he was a thinker avowedly committed to temporality, and that his corpus is built directly on the agency of history for its fruition. Compared with Rousseau, Marx unflinchingly faces, even embraces, the pernicious reality of time. And unlike Rousseau, a firm argument can be made that he is a theorist who thought seriously on the problems of history. Thus it becomes difficult to attempt to align Marx's thought with a timelessness that creates an illusory historical picture of reality. We seem to be moving from Rousseau, the despairing sociologist of time and utopian historical fantasist of Nature, to Marx, the revolutionary firebrand unafraid of time and scientifically prophesizing the historical future of Communism. And yet their positions are not as conflicting as one may initially think. Rousseau's past "Nature" and Marx's future "Communism" resemble each other so much in their obscure depiction—uncertainty toward institutions of any kind and fervent conviction in the power of the individual—that one is prompted to find the obscured governing principle behind these important aspects of their philosophies. This chapter will attempt to demonstrate the timeless basis behind Marx's Communism, and that Communism, and its predicted passage into reality by Marx, are the illusory history based on such timelessness. However, the significant argumentative difference between this approach and the approach to Rousseau will be to show that Marx's favoring of the future over the past means that his timeless vision does utilize to a far more sophisticated degree temporal and historical methods. This methodological incongruity will be shown to be a consequence of Marx's increased obligation to bring about his timeless vision in the future, a concern not so pressing for Rousseau.

There seems nothing more diametrically opposed than the sensitive countenance of a Rousseau and the stiff scientific deliberation of a Marx. Yet in both Marx's and Engels' early years we find literary experiments in poetry and prose. Marx looked back on these attempts with uncertainty and embarrassment, while at the same time admiring their youthful warmth and sincerity of feeling. The insipid and the monstrous shine simultaneously in Marx's earliest pieces of poetical writing as apocalyptic visions and grandiose pronouncements stand side by side with sweet love poems and glib witticisms. Such an early romantic persuasion, so difficult to reconcile with the later cold and hard construction of scientific and philosophic systems, should not be dismissed as a premature and forgettable peculiarity. It has been shown that Marx moved from adolescent romantic, to Kantian Idealist, to critical Hegelian.[1] This should certainly not be viewed in a linear way in which each movement leaves the past moment behind, thus doing away with the romantic and idealistic. Instead this should be seen as a burgeoning of possibilities, expanding and retaining their motivations. Marx's poetic side should not be relegated to the label of "early," but should be seen as "formative." Rousseau's romantic "man of feeling" can very easily be perceived as the pilot light of Marx's Communistic bonfire. Indeed, some commentators have described Marx's vision of Communism as a society of artists, freely creating and finding inspiration in all aspects of their lives.[2] Such a favorable and romantic interpretation of Communism can only be sustained with reference to the romantic, utopian echoes in Marx's thought. In Marx's unfinished poetic tragedy, *Oulanem*, the hero, in the middle of

1. Warren Breckman, *Marx, the Young Hegelians, and the Origins of Radical Social Theory* (Cambridge: Cambridge University Press, 1999), 261.
2. Eugene Kamenka noted this in his *Marxism and Ethics* (London: Macmillan, 1970), 18.

a bout of furious writing and with papers strewn around him, delivers an impassioned soliloquy.

> All lost! The hour is now expired, and time
> Stands still. This pigmy universe collapses.
> Soon I shall clasp Eternity and howl
> Humanity's giant curse into its ear.

Later he continues,

> To be the calendar-fools of Time; to be,
> Only that something thus at least might happen;
> And to decay, that there might be decay!
> The worlds must have had need of one more thing

And finally,

> And in Eternity's ring I'll dance my frenzy!
> If aught besides that frenzy could devour,
> I'd leap therein, though I must smash a world
> That towered high between myself and it!
> It would be shattered by my long drawn curse.[3]

The Promethean ethic that one can sense in all of Marx's work, whether philosophic, scientific, economic, or revolutionary, lies before us here in naked poetic form. Equal measures of destructive urge and creative zeal vibrate in the young Marx's psyche. Here, too, we find a striving sense of a coming eternity, and humanity's message that will reverberate forever in it. We also see the desire to "smash" the world anew, and to bring about its "decay." We are seen as the "calendar-fools of Time," and when time's majesty is arrested and stands still, we will have collapsed this "pigmy universe." The dramatic itch is never far from any of Marx's projects, as has been imaginatively shown by Louis J. Halle in his work *The Ideological Imagination;* "Marx was a philosopher only secondarily, and a revolutionist only secondarily. Primarily he was a dramatist, like Aeschylus. He composed his drama of the revolution on the mythic framework of Hegel's philosophy as Aeschylus had composed the drama of Prometheus on the framework of Greek myth."[4]

---

3. Karl Marx and Friedrich Engels, *Collected Works,* vol.1 (London: Lawrence and Wishart, 1975), 599.

4. Louis J. Halle, *The Ideological Imagination* (London: Chatto and Windus, 1972), 57.

In this early work can be found a shifting and conflicted relation to time as the longing for eternity dances alongside an exuberant willingness to submerge into the world of time and decay. This position holds sway in all of Marx's work. This temporal willingness amounts to a kind of acceptance of time's all-pervasiveness, which will border on dogmatic irrationality in much of Marx's later polemical writings. And yet the specter of eternity embodied in the form of Communism and the classless society can never be omitted from the equation when reading these radically temporal pronouncements. I will discuss the logic of this conflicted relation between eternity and constant transformation further on, but first let me illustrate Marx's temporal methodology and its application to his opponents.

The radical temporality of Marx's praxis has its origins in the influence of Ludwig Feuerbach's work on the Young Hegelians, Marx's early compatriots. Feuerbach strongly objected to any thought, whether philosophic or religious, that catapulted humans from their time-based earthly moorings. A healthy respect for time was also the governing attitude for practice, where the timeless was the province of theory. He writes, "A timeless sensation, a timeless will, a timeless thought, a timeless essence—are figments. Space and time are the primary criteria of practice. A people which excludes time from its metaphysics and hypostatises external, i.e., abstract existence sundered from time, necessarily excludes time from its politics, too, and hypostatises the unjust, irrational and anti-historical principle of stability."[5] Marx certainly ran with these sentiments in his philosophy, and it would be impossible to deny that he was in many respects a committed temporal thinker. Sidney Hook, in his study of Marx and Hegel, also emphasized the temporal nature of Marx's Feuerbachian twist.

What Marx is protesting against is Hegel's attempt to deduce the historical succession of things in time from the immanent development of ideas out of time. From logic we can never get to existence.[6]

In Marx's eyes, to refer to the development of categories as ontologically independent of the development of existential subject matter was metaphysical ex-

5. Ludwig Feuerbach, quoted in Sidney Hook's *From Hegel to Marx: Studies in the Intellectual Development of Karl Marx* (Ann Arbor: University of Michigan Press, 1968), 256–57.
6. Hook, *From Hegel to Marx*, 31.

travaganza. It could only be done by first dissociating development from time and then reducing development to a purely formal attribute of the absolute.[7]

For Marx, however, there was no distinction between development and time. Development is immanent, rather than set in motion externally from human activity. This is a view of man as constantly transformed by his ceaseless activity and labor. For Marx, the impossibility of timelessness rests on the primacy that he places on labor in the human question. What constitutes humanity is its labor or its productive powers. Thus, that which constitutes history is the unfolding of these powers. This unfolding comes from humanity's labor itself, not from timeless ideas outside it, and thus not from anything outside of time. The human species is in the process of constant transformation, constant development. To view something as changeless or ever present is to have alienated some production from our pursuit and remove it from the temporal theatre of our endeavors. Time is the methodological starting point of all Marx's thought, and he would indiscriminately apply its omnipotence and ravages to all his opponents. In *The Poverty of Philosophy* he gives a sarcastic polemical account of what he describes as the atemporal "metaphysics" of political economy.

We shall concede that economic relations, viewed as immutable laws, eternal principles, ideal categories, existed before active and energetic men did; we shall concede further that these laws, principles and categories had, since the beginning of time, slumbered "in the impersonal reason of humanity." We have already seen that, with all these changeless and motionless eternities, there is no history left; there is at most history in the idea, that is, history reflected in the dialectic movement of pure reason.[8]

In *The German Ideology*, that tome to the materialist conception of history, Marx and Engels sow Kant's timeless moral will so deeply into time that it reemerges as the weed of German middle-class interests. They write, "The characteristic form which French liberalism, based on real class interests, assumed in Germany we find again in Kant. Neither he, nor the German middle class, whose whitewashing spokesman he was, noticed that these theoretical ideas of the bourgeoisie have as their

---

7. Hook, *From Hegel to Marx*, 33.
8. Marx, *The Poverty of Philosophy* (New York: International Publishers, 1969), 115–16.

basis material interest and a will that was conditioned and determined by the material relations of production."[9] Marx's dogmatic commitment to the temporal foundations of everything even extended to things that hadn't yet seen their time. Thus he disciplined his communistic colleagues for searching for their ideal in the imagination rather than seeing Communism's ominous outline emanating from the capitalist economic structure of their time. They were duly branded utopian: "The significance of Critical-Utopian Socialism and Communism bears an inverse relation to historical development. In proportion as the modern class struggle develops and takes a definite shape, these fantastic attacks on it, lose all practical value and theoretical justification."[10]

My point of chronicling some of Marx's approaches to various social philosophies is to show his unswerving commitment to temporal awareness. Its adoption serves three crucial purposes for Marx. First, it is the methodological premise upon which historical or dialectical materialism is based. Second, it furthers Marx's credentials as a scientific thinker. And last, it is the source of Marx's subterfuge on the question of morality. But can this mean that Marx sets sail on the shifting murky waters of uncontrollable, unfathomable time? Can this mean that Marx is nothing more than a relativistic historicist, unable to affirm an overriding position? Plainly this is not the case, as Marx is not only a moralist, but a rationalist, a believer in scientific laws, a teleologist, and even more importantly a prophet. This chapter is devoted precisely to revealing the various levels where Marx's radical imagination divulges the timelessness behind his assertive temporality.

Before one can uncover the timelessness of Marx's project, one must grasp Marx's psychology of time. Marx's reappraisal of the problem of time differs from Rousseau's in many respects. It looks very much like he turns the whole problem on its head, approaching the problem from the opposite historical direction, giving its machinations a definite social scenery, and embracing it as a force you would rather have working for you than against you. And while this amounts to a real advance beyond Rousseau's despairing psychology of time, the ultimate aim remains the same, which is the suspension of the destructive and alienating affects of

9. Marx and Engels, *The German Ideology* (Moscow: Progress, 1976), 210.
10. Marx and Engels, *The Communist Manifesto* (Harmondsworth: Penguin, 1967), 117.

time on human relations, housed within an ahistorical era. In order to illustrate this, it is necessary to return to Rousseau's last definitive statement on time.

Everything is in constant flux on this earth. Nothing keeps the same unchanging shape, and our affections, being attached to things outside us, necessarily change and pass away as they do. Always out ahead of us or lagging behind, they recall a past which is gone and a future which may never come into being; there is nothing solid there for the heart to attach itself to. Thus our earthly joys are almost without exception creatures of the moment.[11]

One is hard-pressed to find a similar statement in Marx's corpus, especially one as despairing and poetic. But if we flag the basic elements of what Rousseau is saying about how we experience the effects of time, we are able to discern a similar characterization in Marx, albeit with some very important distinctions. Marx wrote enigmatically about the bourgeois epoch and its frantic need for the acceleration of time and change in the *Communist Manifesto.*

The bourgeoisie cannot exist without constantly revolutionizing the instruments of production, and thereby the relations of production, and with them the whole relations of society. Conservation of the old modes of production in unaltered form, was, on the contrary, the first condition of existence for all earlier industrial classes. Constant revolutionizing of production, uninterrupted disturbance of all social conditions, everlasting uncertainty and agitation distinguish the bourgeois epoch from all earlier ones. All fixed, fast-frozen relations, with their train of ancient and venerable prejudices and opinions are swept away, all new formed ones become antiquated before they can ossify. All that is solid melts into air, all that is holy is profaned, and man is at last compelled to face with sober senses, his real conditions and life, and his relations with his kind.[12]

Like Rousseau, Marx and Engels understand that the experience of time and history is felt via one's relations. The unending genesis, development, degradation, and passing of relations, either personal, economic, or political, are the observed working of temporal flux. Where Rousseau feels time most keenly in his personal relations, Marx and Engels' appreciation of time is concentrated on the observation of class

11. Jean-Jacques Rousseau, *Reveries of the Solitary Walker,* selected and translated with an introduction by Peter France (London: Penguin, 1979), 88.
12. Marx and Engels, *The Communist Manifesto,* 83.

relations. Hence Rousseau's most striking passages on time are personal testimonies, while Marx's and Engels', as shown from the passage above, illustrate the functions of time in the forces, instruments, and relations of production engendering and engendered by various classes. Despite these differences in where it is observed, time and its maneuvers are ostensibly the same in both Marx and Rousseau. Time is the assassin of stability, refusing to allow things to "ossify," "sweeping away" ideas, "disturbing" relations, constantly "revolutionizing," "profaning," and "melting" all that is fixed and consecrated. And just as Rousseau's later life was consumed with increasingly complex and violent relations undermining any peace or permanence, Marx sees the last antagonistic form of social organization, the bourgeois epoch, as an all-consuming frenzy of shifting relations and temporal disorder. Indeed the capitalist actively fuels this temporal velocity and abandon, and Marx observes it with a peculiar relish.

The difficulty that one has in distinguishing Marx and Engels' exact attitude to the era accounts for the enigmatic nature of the above passage. Does Marx approve of this working of time, or does he wish it to cease? His interpretation would read as both a condemnation and an encouragement. With intrepid bravado Marx and Engels beckon an impending fight, encouraging the necessary preparations before a future conflict, but unable to hide their disdain for what they are witnessing. From the perspective of this study, Marx and Engels delight in the acceleration of time in increasingly violent class relations from the secret perspective of an upcoming time of classlessness. The abolition of classes and antagonistic social relations is, according to Marx, tantamount to the abolition of time itself; and yet such a future state can only be carried forwarded by time. Time is enlisted in the fight against itself. It is in the dimensions of the future that we are given the clue to Marx's altered psychology of time.

If we deem that Rousseau diagnosed a weary society in its noon, longing for the past innocence of its infancy, we can consider Marx as examining what he saw as a society kept in a state of childishness, able to see and preparing for the fruits of its maturity in the future. This helps us to appreciate the differing forces to which these similar figures subjected history. Where Rousseau turned to the past for solace and orientation, Marx sought his goal by turning his temporal telescope to the future. Rousseau's preoccupation was with the beginning of history, where Marx concentrates on its end. The forces of past and future, beginning and end, youth and maturity are two directions for minds animated by a sense of the timeless to take. In historical terms there is no great difference between the distant past and a distant future. In both Rousseau and Marx's cases history is the thing to be overcome. But how a thinker situates his attitude to time is radically determined by the historical direction that dominates his mind. We have seen how a preoccupation with the past created in Rousseau a despairing attitude to time and an unabashed need to condemn it. There is no guarantee that the past can be regained or its benefits artificially recreated, so for Rousseau, time's overwhelming effect is to sweep you away from your goal. But the future is an open realm, where time is just the atmosphere of positive anticipation, and it was within this temporal expectation that Marx composed his philosophy. And as Marx's whole philosophy is foreshadowed by the future, time is favorably looked upon as pregnant with possibility. Thus this is the difficulty one has in finding despairing comments by Marx on time. Time is as much his friend as his enemy. Time and history are the vehicles needed for the transport to humanity's new destination, wherefrom they are expected to dissipate in favor of the fixity of economic relations and the establishment of an equality and dignity previously denied by history. And while Marx's overall purpose with regard to time is no different than Rousseau's, the belief in the future dispersal of time's pernicious effects makes Marx a far more complex and supple historical thinker.

But first a clarifying word on the differing status of the timeless as understood by Marx and as understood by the standpoint of this book. Marx's repugnance to sciences advocating timeless abstractions was predicated on what he perceived such timelessness fostering in society. Marx sees timelessness not as an energized and progressive fount of change, but rather as a reactionary force, stultifying change and calcifying dynamic economic relations. Maintenance of the status quo, passive acceptance of changeable forms as fixed, denial of the malleability of people and their social products; these are the things Marx combats with his temporal method. Timeless and static ideas reify the constant transformation of man and thus preclude the possibility of the future resolution of Marx's problems, problems themselves that ignore time. This is the role assigned to the timeless, and thus to adopt timeless abstractions in the service of change, which many of Marx's socialist brethren attempted, was equally anathema to Marx. Timelessness as social passivity is Marx's anxiety. However, I am concerned with the active aspects of the timeless. Timelessness as understood by this work is less connected with forces of justification and apology than with operations of will, decision, and action. I will explore timelessness as the source of the very changes that Marx wished so earnestly to bring about.

In a nutshell, we are concerned with the ominous statement Marx makes against timeless thought in *The Poverty of Philosophy.* "One would have set oneself the absurd problem of eliminating history."[13] In so many ways it is this "absurd problem" that is the gravitational center of Marx's system.

13. Karl Marx, Friedrich Engels, and Vladimir Lenin, *Marx, Engels, Lenin: On Historical Materialism* (Moscow: Progress, 1972), 78.

6

Marx's Early Years

The Young Hegelians and Futurity

My discussion of Rousseau began with the works of his later life in order to strip back a philosophy that attempts to push society into a regained childhood. Contrarily, Marx's youthful life can give us the direction to discuss his mission of dragging the human species into adulthood. Where for Rousseau society had lost the enthusiasm and simplicity of its youth, for Marx society had been kept in an enforced state of immaturity, unable to grow up from its alienated supervision. This is not a flippant analogy when one considers that Rousseau found his philosophical feet late in life, where Marx discovered them early. Philosophy found these men in different periods of their life and hence had differing ramifications. The philosophical making of Marx in his early life gave him the peculiar, yet recognizable taste for future that guided his other youthful intellectual peers, the young or left Hegelians. Karl Lowith classifies these "young" Hegelians (somewhat unconventionally, but essentially justly) when he connects their endeavors with the social aspects of youth.

The elders, unlike the youths, do not live in a relationship of unsatisfied tension to a world which they find inappropriate, with "antipathy toward reality." … In contrast, the young adhere to the particular and are attracted to the future, seek to alter the world…. To the young, the realisation of the universal seems apostasy to duty ... the Young Hegelians represented the party of youth, not because they were themselves real youths, but in order to overcome the consciousness of being epigones. Recognising the fugacity of all that exists, they turned from the "universal" and the past in order to anticipate the future, to promote the "particular" and "individual," and negate that which exists.[1]

Having moved to Berlin to study philosophy after abandoning his legal studies, Marx defended this seemingly unconsidered move in a letter to his father. In this letter Marx remarked that the overriding problem that plagued his mind was the antagonism between the "is" and the "ought," a problem he recognized as constitutive of German Idealism.[2] In the study of philosophy, especially the Hegelian philosophy, Marx believed he had found the key to the realization of freedom within natural necessity, of idealism in reality. And yet along with the Young Hegelians, Marx saw the Hegelian philosophy not so much as a grand monolithic synthesis for the contemplation of this freedom/nature fusion, but as a project in need of completion, as a methodology for radical change. The call for the realization of philosophy became the mutated cry that the realization of freedom had once been for the radical generation after Kant.[3] This displaced demand would have lasting and confused consequences on the nature/freedom dichotomy, as the Young Hegelians combined Hegel's determinant historical metaphysics with Kant's self-motivated ahistorical judgments. The region of time where these contradictory powers were to be played out was the future.

It is important to situate and acknowledge the radical temperaments of these young thinkers properly into any textual analyses of their work. Marx was born and raised in the pools of Napoleonic influence left over after the wave of the French Revolution had subsided. Marx was hence a member of the youthful, precocious, and cosmopolitan descendants of the French Revolution. The French Revolution created men as well as

1. Karl Lowith, *From Hegel to Nietzsche,* translated by David E. Green (London: Constable, 1965), 66.

2. Schlomo Avineri, *The Social and Political Thought of Karl Marx* (Cambridge: Cambridge University Press, 1970), 8.

3. For a discussion on the similarities between the radical generations after both Kant and Hegel and the difficulties that this spawned, see Bernard Yack's chapter "Left Kantian Echoes in Left Hegelian Social Criticism," from his *The Longing for Total Revolution* (Princeton: Princeton University Press, 1986), 238.

political conditions, and most of all it created a generation buoyed by visions of new freedom and possibility. The French Revolution's destruction of tradition historicized the generations that came after it, giving its progeny previously unseen perspectives on the role of time. The present became baptized with the future, the course of history turning from the anchored appreciation of the past into an awareness of its imminent destiny. Is it any wonder that Marx would be attracted to the Young Hegelians and the heady mood of *Sturm und Drang* that accompanied their endeavors? William J. Brazil's book on the Young Hegelians evocatively described the exciting scandalous spirit of the times and characterized the membership of the "Freien" as "many rootless radicals, hapless intellectuals and bored dilettantes."[4] Scholars with a spirit of rabblerousing, they picked over the bones of Hegel's enormous philosophical carcass for any sign of revolutionary intent and direction. Rather than a dense comprehension of the world, Hegel's achievement became a vast sounding board for the censure and revolution against existing society. Marx described their impudent and imprudent agenda in a letter to Arnold Ruge: "If we have no business with the construction of the future or with organising it for all time there can still be no doubt about the task confronting us at the present: the ruthless criticism of the existing order, ruthless in that it will shrink neither from its own discoveries nor from conflict with the powers that be."[5]

And yet any comprehensive assault upon a present state is in the same breath to marshal the powers of some past or future shape of life. Change, innovation, and novelty were the rousing tempers of these young radicals, who looked to expand their universal vision for a new time and place. Marx breathed the atmosphere of social and political dissatisfaction nurtured by Rousseau's example. And if the Young Hegelian's programmatic and pamphleteering endeavors seem frivolous and insipid to modern dispositions, we cannot disparage their willingness to suffer for their resolve. Many Young Hegelians materially removed themselves from the social order they had spurned in thought. Feuerbach, Ruge, and Bruno Bauer were forced to step down from their teaching positions for their radical views. They set up and contributed to jour-

4. William J. Brazil, *The Young Hegelians* (London: Yale University Press, 1970), 79.
5. Karl Marx, *Early Writings,* translated by Rodney Livingstone and Gregor Benton (New York: Vintage, 1975), 207.

nals in dangerous and hostile opposition to ruling powers; many were pursued by authorities for their activities and fled around Europe from imprisonment, while many others left themselves financially diminished their whole lives for their causes. Marx's life also shows us this characteristic willingness to endure all of the personal indignities that attend any revolutionary commitment to the future dignity of all. This compulsion to dignity is everywhere in Marx's work, but actually acknowledged rarely. In an often retold story from his later life, when asked the vice he most hated, Marx replied that anything that is an affront to the natural dignity of man was the most loathsome sin. This private admission is conspicuous because of the saddening lack of such principled and personal statements of compulsion in Marx's work. It is here that we find something akin to the atemporal form of judgment that governs moral legitimacy—that judgment so thoroughly realized in Kant's philosophy. Such moral claims are consistently depreciated in the bulk of Marx's work because of his obligation to a radical temporality, and hence to all morality and ethics being historically and socially bound. And yet such judgments based upon the moral will, the free "I," cannot be eliminated from an understanding of Marx's project. The problem is ably illustrated when Marx proclaimed in the "Introduction" to the critique of Hegel's *Philosophy of Right* that "The criticism of religion ends with the doctrine that for man the supreme being is man, and thus with the categorical imperative to overthrow all conditions in which man is a debased, enslaved, neglected and contemptible being."[6]

Following in the wake of Feuerbach's "transformation" of theology into anthropology, which was based on the reflection that God is nothing more than the specie's mind torn from its living human moorings, Marx gives this insight a social and political vocation.[7] Once man has recognized his essential dignity concealed from him in alienated forms such as religion, he is compelled to overcome any alienation of himself in the social, political, and economic realm. Marx even uses the loaded term "categorical imperative" to describe this campaign. The influence

6. Marx, *Early Writings,* 251.

7. "Religion is the disuniting of man from himself; he sets God before him as the antithesis of himself.... But in religion man contemplates his own latent nature. Hence it must be shown that this antithesis, this differencing of God and man, with which religion begins, is a differencing of man with his own nature"; see Ludwig Feuerbach, *The Essence of Christianity,* translated by George Eliot (New York: Harper and Brothers, 1957), 33.

of Kant's ahistorical will is palpable from this passage, and yet it has been transplanted into historically determined society. It is not Feuerbach's new concept of man that has been given a political imperative; it is Kant's vision of man's freedom. Kant's categorical imperative in Marx's hands should properly be called the social categorical imperative. Bernard Yack describes this shifting of emphasis from Kant's regulated operations of free will blind to time and Marx's compelled operations of will beckoned to change time: "If Kant demands that we overcome heteronomy in the will, Marx demands that we overcome heteronomy in the world."[8]

The primary difference here is not one of kind, but of time. Overcoming heteronomy in the world is still dependent upon overcoming heteronomy in the will. In other words, it still relies on the timeless operations of freewill and is still concerned with the imposition of our noumenal freedom upon the phenomena of nature. The difference lies in Marx's occupation with the demands that the timeless will makes on the world of time; what is the future secured by our a priori freedom? This problem was not central to Kant's philosophy, but became central to the philosophies that came in its stead. So while in the first instance Marx's initial problematic of discerning the future guaranteed by Kant's securing of the timeless does not presumably change their approaches in kind, in the last instance this problem plays itself out by significantly diverging the types of claims these two thinkers were making. Marx delves further into the future in order to affirm the realities of timeless dignity. Yet as he does so he is forced to depreciate the timeless thought and ideals that are the foundation of his project. It is the future dimension of the timeless that was the unwitting drive of Marx and the Young Hegelians.

The most typical formulation of the Young Hegelian amalgamation of will and future came from the man who coined their creed of praxis, Count August von Cieszkowski. Cieszkowski's main aim was to graft upon the Hegelian speculative philosophy a call for social action. In Cieszkowski are found the two combined urges of the Young Hegelians; the teleological, organic account of history, or the future predicted on the arrangements of the past; and the volitional view of history, where the atemporal will imposes its power on history. In both accounts, ex-

8. Yack, *The Longing for Total Revolution*, 256.

istence and essence, the fusion of which had eluded history, are finally combined.[9] In the former, the future is deduced a posteriori, in the latter it is deduced a priori. The summoning of both these constructed futures was to become the stock and trade of all Young Hegelian politics. Angry that Hegel had stopped the voyage of the absolute spirit in his contemporary political situation, they lashed out. Hegel had made a personal compromise with the Prussian government, and arbitrarily halted the irrepressibly active principle of his philosophy, the dialectical logic in history. Hegel had left no work for his descendants to do. Such a position was unbearable to progressives, and the future was the weak spot of Hegel's philosophical prison. Cieszkowski formulated two paths to the future available to the Young Hegelians. Cieszkowski explores the first, the Hegelian path, in his amendment to the three historical epochs outlined by Hegel. Rather than the three epochs of Oriental, Greek, and Christian-German extending from the past to the present, Cieszkowski projects the schematization into the future. Cieszkowski's three periods were now the epoch of antiquity, the epoch from Christ to Hegel, and a future period whose emergence was to come. The Young Hegelians were sitting on the fault line between the second and third periods. This approach to the future maintains the historicist bent of Hegelian thinking. And yet, when it comes to how this future period will be characterized, Cieszkowski returns to a formulation that unravels the complex architecture of Hegel's historical philosophy. The third era of "praxis" will be carried forth not through subjective emotion or objective thought, but through active, practical will. Human freedom and action resolve to steer the historical course.

But Warren Breckman observes the contradiction that is involved

9. Both interpretations are equally valid. Schlomo Avineri concentrates on the teleological organic account with reference to Cieszkowski's "tooth of an ancient fossil" being used to infer the form of the whole organism. How can the future not be organically conceived from the processes of the past? This is done to show that Cieszkowski didn't stray too far from his master, Hegel; Avineri, *The Social and Political Thought of Karl Marx* (Cambridge: Cambridge University Press, 1970), 126–27. David McClellan, on the other hand, concentrates on the volitional elements of Cieszkowski's "historiosophy." Cieszkowski burst out of the Hegelian framework and into the future via the will. This interpretation maintains that Cieszkowski escaped the difficulties imposed by the Hegelian present by returning to Fichte: "future history would be one of acts and not facts. Here Cieszkowski, like the Young Hegelians after him, is nearer to Fichte than Hegel"; David McClellan, *The Young Hegelians and Karl Marx* (London: Macmillan, 1969), 10.

here: "Commentators have rightly emphasised the contradiction in this conception of humanity's participation in the divine telos: If the philosopher can know the course and end of history as the fulfilment of an immanent divine teleology, then it seems odd that Cieszkowski should make history dependent upon voluntary human action."[10] In their utter discomfort with prevailing institutions and their pathological need for future, the Young Hegelians and Marx enlisted two contradictory visions of history. One vision denied the separation between nature and freedom, while the other affirmed it. One made man a historical being, while the other lifted him above history's contingencies by making his essence a priori. This had strange consequences upon the demands they made on Hegel's thought. Where Hegel had believed that he had reconciled the finite with the infinite and illuminated the path of the rational in the real, the Young Hegelians startled this belief by demanding that now philosophy itself must enter the real. Flying directly in the face of Hegel's sage belief that philosophy only enters the scene when a shape of life has "grown old," the Young Hegelians now charged philosophy with the responsibility of determining the new shape of life. The freedom so comprehensively thought out by Hegel was for the Young Hegelians now ripe for its transfusion into the bloodstreams of history. From Hegel's perspective this is, of course, a complete misreading of his meaning, whereby freedom is by its very nature coursing through time. The Young Hegelians are asking for freedom to become real, but demanding it from a system of thought devoted precisely to that end. The path that led to the reconciliation of human freedom with natural necessity in Hegel had been bulldozed and forgotten by the Young Hegelians, while still unconsciously retaining some of its residues. They demanded that Hegel come back down to earth from his abstraction, while at the same time wished to retain the reconciliation that can only be maintained by that abstraction. They wanted to reverse the logic that led to their ideal so as to make it real, while believing that the ideal will stay unharmed when its elaborate philosophical foundation had been unraveled or even disregarded. The major premise of German Idealism, namely the dichotomy between freedom and necessity, is also the problematic that they severely distort-

10. Warren Breckman, *Marx, The Young Hegelians, and the Origins of Radical Social Theory* (Cambridge: Cambridge University Press, 1999), 185.

ed. In the end, much of this confusion accounts for the schizophrenic relation of realism and idealism that was to haunt Marx all his life. In the interests of concreteness, they deny that man can extract himself from his natural contingency; indeed they celebrate it, but, in the interests of overcoming the limitations of the present, they must affirm man's sovereign ability to command and guide his external environment via a power outside that environment. The only way that these contradictory approaches can jostle productively in the Young Hegelian's programs is for their aims to be suspended into the future. Both understandings of history serve the same future purpose. Later I will demonstrate as an incorrect assumption the belief that Marx removed himself from this Young Hegelian problematic by ascending the rungs of praxis so completely that he did away with all utopian residues in his thought. These two contradictory processes working in a temporal fashion can be seen within the mechanism of history that Marx perceives. The philosophical tension of the Young Hegelians, which resolves itself in an imagined future, is transformed in Marx's work into a temporal historical tension that is resolved in Communism.

And yet this infiltration of the timeless into the future is not new with the Young Hegelians, but is the peculiar theoretical shift of utopian thought in general in the nineteenth century. Krishan Kumar in *Utopia and Anti-Utopia in Modern Times* outlines the radical and problematic swing that utopian thought made from the static and timeless to the dynamic, historical, and changing future.

The utopias—if we may call them that—of Rousseau and Saint-Just, of Morelly and Babeuf, were made in the Morean mould. They were timeless static entities. Little attention was paid to how the new order would be brought into being.... But from another quarter of Enlightenment thought the new feature, the dynamic element, of the nineteenth century utopia was developing powerfully. Stimulated by developments in geology and biology, European thought was increasingly penetrated by concepts of change, evolution and progress.[11]

A humanity of indomitable will, of incontrovertible freedom, must have an attendant social order. It is demanded by the timeless individual's very existence and it flows from his very power. Just as Rousseau had

---

11. Krishan Kumar, *Utopia and Anti-Utopia in Modern Times* (Oxford: Basil Blackwell, 1987), 42.

to construct the social contract to house the free individual he had fashioned, so the even more powerfully conceived and theoretically developed individual that Kant christened, in homage to Rousseau's example, had to have his political setting. But where Rousseau could largely ignore the historical dimensions of his vision, the Young Hegelians did not have this luxury. Indeed their whole output is directed to the historical dimensions of their new individual. When the unlimited immediacy of an autonomous will, able to deploy its power at any present, is given social shape in the imaginations of its admirers, that imagination can only realize itself in the future. There is a certain radicalism or immoderateness to the belief that the present is pregnant with the future, and hence the Young Hegelians cannot be omitted from this utopian tradition. And yet the introduction of time into thought, animated by the timeless, exposes utopias to a great many logical difficulties.

If there is one thing that students of utopia agree upon, it is that utopias are perfected social orders. They are societies, that is, which have more or less satisfactorily solved all known human problems. Change is, almost by definition, not only unnecessary but a distinct threat. It can only signal degeneration and decay of the good society.[12]

And so the formal utopia gave way to science and socialism; the contemplation of perfection succumbs to the contemplation of passage. Rather than construct their own utopia, future thinkers latched onto the ready-made utopia of socialism and concentrated on how time would deliver its assumed graces. In Marx, this tension is seen at its most tensile. In the "Economic and Philosophic Manuscripts" Marx waxes utopian on Communism. "Communism is the positive supersession of private property as human self-estrangement, and hence the true appropriation of the human essence through and for man; it is the complete restoration of man to himself as a social, i.e. human, being, a restoration which has become conscious and which takes place within the entire wealth of previous periods of development."[13]

And so Communism is the completion of both "humanism" and "naturalism," the resolution of man and nature, of freedom and necessity. Such Hegelian vocabulary, as Marx later denigrates it, is later done

12. Kumar, *Utopia and Anti-Utopia*, 48.
13. Marx, *Early Writings*, 348.

away with to expunge the rest of his life's production of any imaginative future. The rest of his life is taken up with scientifically divining the dissolution of existing conditions, constantly avoiding pronouncements on the future society, and ridding his philosophy of any expressions of longing. Marxism is scientific because it pictures the journey, while other socialisms/communisms are utopian because they picture the destination. Because of the logical difficulties of nineteenth-century utopianism, Marx's project remains clouded by a constantly unfulfilled sense of expectation and anticipation, ever attempting to divine when the time is "ripe," like a scientific mystic with a cumbersome utopian hangover. This is the consequence of a future that remains unstable because it is sold out to the temporal mechanisms that are constructed in order to bring that future into being. In Marx, the utopian radical imagination cautiously retreats from the future and puts its considerable aptitudes to work on various historical and temporal methods and models that will carry the future to us. Hence "future" is the God of Marxism; indeed it is its very imaginative substance, but it is also the realm that cannot be imagined upon. Future is the God, and Marx dares not speak its name.

Alienation and Institutions: Hegel's Philosophy of Right

The best way to loosen the paradox of time as it resounded in Marx's project is to observe how Hegel reconciled its antagonism. In doing this I will also show that Marx was unable and unwilling to resolve the unceasing conflict of alienated humanity because of his hostility to the present, and hence also demonstrate his resistance to institutions of all kinds. The difference between Hegel and Marx collapses down to the mediations of reality made by Hegel on the one hand and the unraveling of those mediations by Marx on the other. For Marx the thorn of Hegel's "rose" of the present is the assertion that "What is rational is actual and what is actual is rational," for "Once that is granted, the great thing is to apprehend in the show of the temporal and transient the substance which is immanent and the eternal which is present."[14]

For all Hegel's credentials as the historical thinker par excellence,

14. G. W. F. Hegel, *The Philosophy of Right* (Oxford: Oxford University Press, 1979), 10.

Hegel achieves his historical method only by endowing the present with eternity. Hegel's reconciliation of nature and freedom depends on transfiguring time from a series of moments, or the process of succession, to an immanent whole or totality of times. The absolute does not express itself gradually in time, but time itself must be conceived as absolute. The simplest way to understand this vision of time is in the mathematical analogy frequently used by Hegel to explain the absolute infinite. Cristaudo explained it thus: "Series such as 0.285714 ... or $1 + 1 + a + a2 + a3$ ... are both infinite, yet each can be expressed in a finite or holistic manner, i.e. as $2/7$ or $1/(1 - a)$. In the case of the fraction all possibilities are brought under one overarching principle. We know the series conforms to a pattern."[15]

With time traditionally understood as a series of distinguishable moments, one misunderstands the fullness or completeness of time. For Hegel nothing can be outside the absolute infinite. Everything being intrinsic to it, it necessarily contains its past, present, and future within itself, and hence so does time. Time is not simply an unceasing infinite sequence, but an enclosed and completed infinite, comprehending its own possibilities all the time. Thus real understanding is the appreciation of eternity at every present moment, because the present no longer represents just the partial and finite.

For Hegel the eternity that grasps its lifespan is gained only through the complete interchangeability of reason and reality, of ideas and history. Ideas are by nature dynamic. The separation of these permanently conjugal entities amounts to a dangerous, one-sided, and partial understanding of the world and time. The favoring of one over the other amounts to the favoring of serial time or timelessness. For instance, to favor reason or the ideal as the source of truth, one is forced to depreciate the claims of time so as to oblige the claims of reason upon it. Reality and time are counterfeits of truth, which must be directed by timeless thought. A totalitarianism of thought destructive to the glacial forming of societies and institutions is the dangerous result of reason's opposition to reality. On the other hand, to favor the real, the contingent, and the historical implies that truth resides solely in the often irrational

15. Wayne Cristaudo, "Hegel, Marx and the Absolute Infinite," *International Studies in Philosophy* 24, no. 1 (1992): 1.

maneuverings of the world unmediated by thought. To take the world as one immediately finds it, unadorned with the structuring power of "stored" mediations, is to have to accept its indifference. The old dictum of "might equals right" is the equally dangerous result of reality's hostility to reason.

However, Marx's opposition to the present meant that the real could not at every moment be reconciled with reason. Eternalizing the present poses grave problems for any philosophy attempting to characterize that present as schismatically alienated and irrational. Thus, in order to characterize the world as divided and contradictory and work toward its resolution, Marx was forced to divide and contradict Hegel's sense of absolute time. Marx sunders the two opposing types of temporality that had been fused in Hegel, appealing to both a naturalistic sense of temporal sequence and an abstract timeless standard opposed to the world. This development was made conceptually possible by the work of Ludwig Feuerbach, whose influence held particular sway over Marx's engagement with Hegel's philosophy of right.

Essentially, Feuerbach's criticism revolves around the fact that Hegel's system strove for eternity from the finite. But where Hegel's *Logic* presents itself as a development from pure being to the absolute idea, Feuerbach contends that Hegel's real beginning is his end.[16] His argument was that Hegel had his organic and circular totality in mind from the outset, and that reality must be made to fit within this preexisting model. Or in his own words, "Everything is required either to present (prove) itself or to flow into, and be dissolved in, the presentation. The presentation ignores that which was known before the presentation."[17]

Everything is preordained from the outset, and so the concrete is coarsely and inappropriately crammed into the theory, while the theory is furnished with grabbed pieces and shards of reality. Connected with this critique, Feuerbach also took issue with Hegel's claim that his philosophy held a privileged position in history, undetermined by its historical moment and all-encompassing, even when only the product of a

---

16. Ludwig Feuerbach, "The Beginning of Philosophy," in *The Fiery Brook: Selected Writings of Ludwig Feuerbach*, translated by Zawar Hanfi, 138 (New York: Anchor, Doubleday, 1972); see: "The spirit follows upon the senses, not the senses upon the spirit; spirit is the end and not the beginning of things."

17. Feuerbach, "The Beginning of Philosophy," 69.

finite mind. He used the historicism of the Hegelian philosophy against itself in order to depreciate its claims to absolute truth. But the major bone of contention boiled down to the fact that Hegel's method involves resolving the tensions between essence and existence, the ideal and the real, one-sidedly in thought. Reality is forced to traverse the creases and furrows of Hegel's logic, rather than Hegel's logic being channeled by the creases and furrows of reality. All this amounted to Hegel distorting the truth of sensory experience. Hegel was inverting the order of subject and predicate by making "thought" the subject and "being" the predicate.

To abstract means to posit the essence of nature outside nature, the essence of man outside man, the essence of thought outside the act of thinking. The Hegelian philosophy has alienated man from himself in so far as its whole system is based on these acts of abstraction. Although it again identifies what it separates, it does so only in a separate and mediated way. The Hegelian philosophy lacks immediate unity, immediate certainty, immediate truth.[18]

The problem with the Hegelian philosophy is that it creates an obdurate division, like an hourglass in which the empirical and the speculative constantly slosh from one side to the other, and where neither realm retains its sovereignty. Hegel is a circular thinker, uncritically idealist while at the same time uncritically positivist.[19] The only way to fuse this cleft for Feuerbach was to return to the immediate certainty of sensory perception.

In keeping with his mission to tunnel the deepest mines of praxis, Marx was not concerned with disclosing the nature of Hegel's entire metaphysics, instead limiting himself only to Hegel's social and political thought. Marx accepts Feuerbach's reading of Hegel's philosophical whole and gives it a new application in Hegel's reading of politics.

The truth is that Hegel has done no more than dissolve the "political constitution" into the general, abstract idea of the "organism." In appearance and in his own opinion, however, he has derived the particular from the "universal idea." He has converted into a product, a predicate of the Idea, what was properly its subject. He does not develop his thought from the object, but instead the object

18. Feuerbach, "The Beginning of Philosophy," 157.
19. The terms "uncritical idealism" and "uncritical positivism" were used by Marx in his "Economic and Philosophical Manuscripts" when he reformulated his original critique of Hegel. I use it here when talking on Feuerbach to demonstrate how indebted Marx was to his critique of Hegel; Marx, *Early Writings*, 385.

is constructed according to a system of thought perfected in the abstract sphere of logic. His task is not to elaborate the definite idea of the political constitution, but to provide the political constitution with a relationship to the abstract Idea and to establish it as a link in the life history of the Idea—an obvious mystification.[20]

Marx was in the habit of describing Hegel's use of reason as "mysticism," a leaf he took from the book of Feuerbach. Marx was able to label modern philosophy's greatest rationalist as a mystic because he felt that in Hegel's view of the world, the movement of reason is coextensive with the movement of his logic. Marx knew logic could balloon irrationally in the realm of fantasy if left unbridled and unchecked. Reason thus conceived is really only a way of thinking that ignores its ground and generates wispy superstitions. The especially irrational and superstitious results of Hegel's total philosophy were disclosed to Marx in the *Philosophy of Right,* because here he could clearly observe the irrationalities and mysteries in a political order that Hegel's logic attempts to rationalize.

Hegel's true interest is not the philosophy of right but logic. The task of philosophy is not to understand how thought can be embodied in political determinations but to dissolve the existing political determinations into abstract ideas. The concern of philosophy is not the logic of the subject-matter but the subject-matter of logic. Logic does not provide a proof of the state but the state provides a proof of logic.[21]

Hegel has it all upside-down. Hegel first establishes the abstract state as an embodied moment of the Idea. Hegel is then forced to endow the house of his abstraction with the institutional furniture he finds in reality. The upside-down character of Hegel's operation is shown by how he appropriates the family and civil society as determinations of the state. Under Hegel, things such as the family and civil society, which are both temporally and foundationally prior to the state, are converted from true subjects into mystical objects in the state's field of operation. They derive their meaning from the state rather than the state deriving its meaning from their combination.[22] If Hegel could be so completely backward

20. Marx, *Early Writings,* 69–70.
21. Marx, *Early Writings,* 73.
22. Marx, *Early Writings,* 62–63: "The family and civil society are real parts of the state, real spiritual manifestations of the will, they are the state's forms of existence; the family and civil society make themselves into the state. They are the driving force. According to

with regard to his logic of the state's formation, then surely his more detailed rationalization of state machinery is also backward and irrational. After critiquing the first movement of Hegel's double inversion, namely the construction of the abstract state, Marx moves on to the second inversion, the reintroduction of eschewed empirical reality to give shape to the abstraction.

Where the Young Hegelians accused Hegel of making a personal compromise with the Prussian state, Marx on the other hand attempts to show that it is Hegel's wrong method that makes him rationalize the Prussian state. Hegel is not attempting to find the truth in a preexistent observed reality, but is instead attempting to find the reality of a preexistent truth, and thus he views whatever is at hand as the self-realization of the truth, that being the Prussian state and its institutions. There are three points of contention in this eschewed institutional makeup with which Marx takes issue. These are the hereditary monarch, the universal class or bureaucracy, and the landed property owner and his right of primogeniture. Marx wishes to strip these entities of their Hegelian idealized veneer.

Where Hegel saw the constitutional monarch as a bulwark against the atomistic self-interest and the creed of unconstrained clashing of the bourgeoisie, Marx saw his person as an arbitrary, capricious will, with no other legitimacy than an accident of birth, because "The body of the monarch determines his dignity. At the apex of the state, mere physicality, and not reason, is the deciding factor. Birth determines the quality of the monarch as it determines the quality of cattle."[23]

Where Hegel talks of the bureaucracy as a universal class comprising the virtues of merit, opportunity, and dutiful service to the state, Marx characterizes them as a careerist and secretive priesthood that protects and attends to the false and illusory condition of universal political freedom. He writes, "As this 'state formalism' constitutes itself as a real power and thus becomes its own material content, it follows inevitably that the 'bureaucracy' is a network of practical illusions or the 'illusion of the state.' The bureaucrats are the Jesuits and theologians of the state. The

---

Hegel, however, they are produced by the real Idea; it is not the course of their own life that joins them together to comprise the state, but the life of the Idea which has distinguished them from itself."

23. Marx, *Early Writings*, 91.

bureaucracy is the religious republic."[24] Or more bluntly he states, "The universal spirit of the bureaucracy is secrecy."[25]

Where Hegel saw the necessity of an upper house of landed property owners to balance the popularly elected lower house, Marx saw it as simply instituted self-interest and privilege. And where Hegel wished to revive the guilds and estates to give concrete voice to various layers of society and to bind and reconcile particular interests into more public-minded assemblies, Marx saw this as just feudal resuscitation, out of step with the tenor of modern demands for freedom, and a misreading of the emergence of modern socio-economic classes. In all of these cases, Marx is lamenting that politics and sovereignty are being hijacked from its rightful possessors, the people.

What Hegel and Marx are arguing over is the role assigned to estrangement and alienation as social prerogatives. This is shown amply by their differing views on democracy. Hegel achieves his reconciliation with the world only by accepting the estrangement inherent in institutions. Institutions become the very social mediation between time and the timeless. As Karl Lowith observes, institutions are the ground where humanity and its projections seek conjugal holism: "But such an alienation between subject and object cannot seek to remain as it is, according to Hegel. By its very nature it is an alienation between what was originally one and seeks to become one again. Man must be able to act as a native in what is other and strange, in order not to be a stranger to himself in the otherness of the world outside."[26]

To avoid these two directions, it is our responsibility to make our home in our institutions or see the rationality of their existence. This operation carries the stigma of division and estrangement from our purity as sovereign individuals or our harmony as "the people," yet it solves the disparity between unresponsive, unsympathetic time and our power as beings thinking beyond time. An institution for Hegel is a self-negating alienation common to the human enterprise. For Hegel, it is impossible to try to return to the "original one" in any way that disqualifies the possibility for institutions to confer this state upon us in an alienated and qualified way. For Hegel, politics is the process over time and history whereby

24. Marx, *Early Writings*, 107.
25. Marx, *Early Writings*, 108.
26. Lowith, *From Hegel to Nietzsche*, 172.

conflicting interests and forces are given institutional currency and then balanced and played off against each other. The reality of various institutional actors that litter the political stage simply proves the need to institute interest in order to make the eternal conflict of time and timelessness work for a people's benefit. A people's benefit is gained through giving its interests a rich variety of expression, rather than harmonizing or idealizing its common interest. This is the real development of civilization: the harnessing of this conflict in institutions rather than its elimination. On this basis Hegel dismisses democracy, as it derives its power from the abstract and unsubstantial concept of "the people." For Hegel, to base sovereignty on an entity with no political reality simply expresses an "empty ought" of wishing to eliminate conflict from politics by willing unity.

Marx, on the other hand, is reproaching Hegel's varied and complicated understanding of the state precisely because he fails to understand the ultimate sovereignty of the people. Marx's uneasiness with the present and lionizing of the future make him unable to make this institutional compromise on the question of alienation. A human can be native only within himself and in his humanity, not in institutions that divide him from these indigenous concepts. A radically democratic constitution is the only guarantee for Marx that the interests of the people will not be alienated away from them. He says,

Democracy is the solution to the riddle of every constitution. In it we find the constitution founded on its true ground: real human beings and the real people: not merely implicitly and in essence, but in existence and in reality.[27]

In democracy the formal principle is identical with the substantial principle. For this reason it is the first true unity of the particular and the universal.[28]

In Marx's early conception of democracy can be seen all the hallmarks of Communism, and one can very well say that in the process of writing the critique of the *Philosophy of Right*, Marx had gropingly formulated the politics that would sit with him all his life. Marx's vision of democracy revolves around a critique of representative democracy, or of a state of separation between the governors and the governed. Parliamentary democracy is in Marx's crosshairs simply because this is another case of the people being alienated from themselves. Representation

27. Marx, *Early Writings*, 87.
28. Marx, *Early Writings*, 88.

implies a separation, where Marx yearns for an "organism of solidary and homogenous interests."[29] Instead of representative democracy Marx proposes a type of popular delegation, and with these two positions seems to be implying the disappearance of the state altogether. "In all forms of the state other than democracy the state, the law, the constitution is dominant, but without really dominating, i.e. without materially penetrating the content of all the non-political spheres. In a democracy the constitution, the law i.e. the political state, is itself only a self determination of the people and a determinate content of the people."[30]

In other words, in a democracy as Marx envisages it, the law, the constitution, indeed anything that makes up the state, is such a pure and radiant emanation from the people that the state and its institutions as such do not exist. All that is needed to complete this communistic picture is Marx's economics, which adds private property to the list of denunciations. This aligns beautifully with the willed unity of Rousseau's general will. Indeed Lucio Colletti is correct in showing that Marx added nothing politically new to Rousseau's powerful example of a homogenous society purged of conflict and rupture. "It is Rousseau to whom the critique of parliamentarism, the theory of popular delegacy and even the idea of the state's disappearance can all be traced."[31]

Marx's interpretation of institutions as alienated encrustations of living human beings that function only to obstruct their natural activity is something that shows us how Marx split Hegel's absolute time into its objective temporality and its subjective timelessness. Because Marx understands that much of the world is in the process of dissolution, there is by necessity a contrast between essence and existence. Hegel's eternalizing of the present means that this difference is suspended. Marx's eternalizing of the future means that he must navigate essence and existence as two separate fronts on the way to their reconciliation. Hence, in Feuerbachian parlance, "the species," "the people," or "real living human beings" are Marx's existential material. Hence, also, Marx claims to examine the institutions that Hegel idealizes as they "really" are. This is the front of the "real," where it is shown to have not yet attained the "rational." It is

---

29. Lucio Colletti, "Introduction," in *Early Writings*, translated by Rodney Livingstone and Gregor Benton (New York: Vintage, 1975), 44.

30. Marx, *Early Writings*, 89.

31. Colletti, "Introduction," in *Early Writings*, 46.

to here that we must turn to avoid the methodological absurdities of the real being rational, but it is equally here that we must seek to find the rational of our future. Yet Marx must also have his rational front squarely separated from his real front. Radical democracy, the communal state of unalienated man, must be the rational benchmark that is not yet real.

I have concentrated heavily on Marx's appropriation of Feuerbach in his attempt to transcend Hegel's absolute idealism, only in the final instance for him to have retreated into an unconscious Kantian dualistic position. In other words, the example of Feuerbach's naturalistic materialist criticisms of Hegel showed Marx the way to a materialist philosophy, but the materialist subject promoted by this move was in fact simply a naturalized version of the timeless critical subject of the Kantian philosophy. By demanding a future of Hegel's present-centered synthesis between history and freedom, Marx tore apart history and freedom once again until such time as they could be reconciled again in the future. So while Marx thought his embryonic materialism was a move forward, he did not in fact fully realize it was a regression to Kant, to a timeless idealism that was still screaming for historical expression.

But of course Marx's relation with Feuerbach does not end with his intellectual movement toward materialism, but also a movement beyond Feuerbach through the criticism of his "contemplative and inconsistent materialism." In the famous *Theses on Feuerbach* and *The German Ideology,* Feuerbach is ultimately criticized for omitting from the materialist picture of reality its most important feature, its historical nature. Marx now moves on from the static naturalist/sensualist materialism of Feuerbach to the historical materialism that he is most famous for. Feuerbach had failed to see that human nature is not static, but develops as it moves through time; that the conditions by which we reproduce our material lives in turn change and reproduce our nature.

He does not see that the sensuous world around him is not a thing given direct from all eternity, remaining ever the same, but the product of industry and of the state of society; and, indeed, a product in the sense that it is a historical product, the result of the activity of a whole succession of generations, each standing on the shoulders of the preceding one, developing its industry and its intercourse and modifying its social system according to its changed needs.[32]

32. Marx and Friedrich Engels, *The German Ideology* (Moscow: Progress, 1976), 45.

This is indeed a valid criticism of what can only be described as the partial materialism of Feuerbach, and on the surface seems so very much to count in Marx's favor as a historical thinker of high standing, but what makes this new move forward interesting is that it cannot in all honesty be viewed as the deepening or widening of the materialist position that Marx views it as. This is because the assumed materialist transcending of Hegel was in fact a retreat into an earlier Kantian form of transcendental idealism. History and freedom are not reconciled in historical materialism; they are reconciled in future Communism, which is in fact the end of history. So historical materialism will be the illusion of history that Marx will develop in order to reach the prophecy of a Communism that will arrest history and bring freedom to all. This returned reemphasis upon history and temporality is Marx's way of making historically actual the Kantian timeless will and critical subject. In other words, Marx's historical materialism, which is in reality a masked idealism, is really a means of transcending history in the future. Marx will now set about examining the historical driving force that he believes will eventually bring about history's own dissolution.

So to conclude, it seems from this reading that all Marx was doing was retreating to the Kantian dualism, which neglects many of the Hegelian features so prominent in Marx's mature philosophy. In fact, just as Marx moved backward from Hegel to Kant, so when it comes time to show historically how the future ideal of Communism will come about, Marx would again return to some of Hegel's logical operations to achieve it. Marx's project bears the unmistakable marks of teleology, a deployment of the dialectic determinism, and a sense of social totality that can only be accounted for by reference to Hegel. In a sense then, it is important to remember that the return to Kant was not done completely retrogressively, but to get beyond Hegel. In an ironic mirroring of the way he understood history as simultaneously moving forward and backward, the philosophical bedrock of Marxism rests on this to and fro, backward and forward oscillation between Kant and Hegel. In the next chapter we will observe how the necessity of probing the two fronts of the real and rational, existence and essence, time and the timeless, a manifestation of the Young Hegelian predilection for futurity in its dealings with Hegel, plays its tensions out in the opposing temporalities of Marx's methodological powerhouse, the mode of production.

7

The Mode of Production

Marx's Engine of History as Simultaneous Forward and Backward Movement

In a speech delivered at the anniversary of the "People's Paper," Marx outlined the rupture of history, which had produced such a lamentable state of wealth and inequality, progress and deepening failure.

There is one great fact, characteristic of this our nineteenth century, a fact which no party dares deny. On the one hand, there have started into life industrial and scientific processes which no epoch of former human history had ever suspected. On the other hand, there exist symptoms of decay, far surpassing the horrors recorded of the later times of the Roman empire. In our days everything seems pregnant with its contrary.... This antagonism between modern industry and science on the one hand, modern misery and dissolution on the other hand; this antagonism between the productive powers and the social relations of our epoch is a fact, palpable, overwhelming, and not to be controverted.[1]

Humanity is divided against itself because history is divided against itself. People being wholly the products of history, history

1. Karl Marx, *Surveys From Exile: Political Writings* (London: Allen Lane, 1973), 2:299–300.

itself must be set right in order to accomplish ourselves. Labor being humanity's prime want and need, history is hence for Marx the working of the mode of production. And yet as Marx sees it, the mode of production has reached its point of sharpest conflict. Productive powers and social relations are tort in opposition. Marx is hence explicit in his reading of the separated nature of productive forces and social relations. Yet when he talks of the causal mechanism of history, the mode of production, he seems less understanding of it as a conflicted entity. Taken from the famous preface to *A Contribution to the Critique of Political Economy,* it is obvious that there exist two distinct motive powers within the mode of production, at times cooperating in harmony, at other times conflicting.

In the social production of their life, men enter into definite relations that are indispensable and independent of their will, relations of production which correspond to a definite stage of development of their material productive forces.... At a certain stage of their development, the material productive forces of society come in conflict with the existing relations of production, or—what is but a legal expression for the same thing—with the property relations within which they have been at work hitherto. From forms of development of the productive forces these relations turn into their fetters. Then begins an epoch of social revolution.[2]

The mode of production then comprises both the relations of production and the forces of production. Their proper relation to one another has been a contentious issue among commentators on historical materialism. Steven Best, in his work *The Politics of Historical Vision,* has surveyed the two opposing positions in an attempt to fuse the forces and relations of production into a homogenous mode of historical causality. In doing so he wishes to counter and balance out the conflicting claims of the technological determinist and class-conflict readings of Marx's work. He shows us that the "key problem relates to the issue of whether or not Marx was a technological determinist, whether he privileged forces of production (technology, knowledge, work relations) over relations of production (social classes) as the fundamental causal dynamic of history."[3] Of the technological determinist school, G. A. Cohen and W. H.

2. Marx, Friedrich Engels, and Vladimir Lenin, *Marx, Engels, Lenin: On Historical Materialism* (Moscow: Progress, 1972), 137–38.
3. Steven Best, *The Politics of Historical Vision* (New York: Guilford, 1995), 54.

Shaw are cited as the most lucid in the field. Shaw opines that "from the 'Preface' itself, it should be clear that Marx saw the key to human history in the development of man's productive forces. They are 'the material basis of all social organization'; their improvement explains the advance of society."[4] This position holds that forces determine relations, and this arrangement of the mode of production is allied to a particular view of history. A perusal of key words in this passage, such as "development," "improvement," and "advance," gives us the background tone to this approach to Marx. Technological determinism is the narrative of progress in the human species. Cohen outlines the dynamic in his "development thesis."

The primacy thesis, as we find it in Marx, is associated with a second thesis, which will be called the development thesis. We shall, accordingly, be concerned with the following pair of claims:

(a) The productive forces tend to develop throughout history (the Development Thesis).

(b) The nature of the production relations of a society is explained by the level of development of its productive forces (the Primacy Thesis proper).[5]

Later he adds another claim:

(e) Men possess intelligence of a kind and degree which enables them to improve their situation.[6]

This is the story of the burgeoning potentialities of humankind, who act upon nature for their benefit. The ways in which we act upon nature through technology and knowledge determine the relations we enter into and the type of people we become. This position is famously stated in Marx's comment that "the hand-mill gives you society with the feudal lord; the steam-mill, society with the industrial capitalist."[7] This is very often an approach favored by those who wish to amplify the scientific dimensions of Marx's thought, and as such it often devolves into a dogmatic determinism more in keeping with positivism than with the emancipa-

4. William S. Shaw, *Marx's Theory of History* (London: Hutchinson, 1978), 55.

5. G. A. Cohen, *Karl Marx's Theory of History: A Defence* (Oxford: Clarendon Press, 2000), 134.

6. Cohen, *Karl Marx's Theory of History*, 152.

7. Marx, Engels, and Lenin, *On Historical Materialism*, 77.

tory foundations of Marxism. Important for the current examination is the observation that this approach embraces the forward march of history and the optimistic vision of time. It looks upon the material progress and advances in knowledge of the species, with an evolutionary and progressive understanding of time and history. Also important for this examination are the affinities that this shares with Rousseau's concept of "perfectibility" in "The Second Discourse." This will be discussed further on.

On the other hand, Best isolates B. Hindess and P. Hirst as the most forceful carriers of the relations of production thesis. Here the relations of production are seen as the governing ground of the overall mode of production. "Mode of production must be replaced by a distinct type of object, namely, determinate sets of relations of production, conceived as determinate forms of economic class relations, their conditions of existence and the forms in which those conditions are provided. Mode of production, in other words, is displaced by social formation as an object of analysis."[8]

The emphasis on relations of production over forces of productions takes its lead from the more emancipatory dimensions of Marx's project. Rather than an indifferent escalation of technological progress where humanity and nature are forged in a meaningful unity of purpose, the privilege given to relations of production emphasizes class struggle, class-consciousness, and conflict as the causal force of history. Forces of production are provoked and plundered by the wills and interests of humans, rather than will and volition gaining their substance and structure from the forces abounding. Seen from this angle nature and humanity are not so much in accord, but humanity retains a degree of sovereignty over nature and blind force through its agency. This is a position favored by followers who see Marxism as principally an activist science, a position famously paved by Marx's statement, "The philosophers have only interpreted the world in various ways; the point is to change it."[9] For these theorists, social formations are favored as explanatory models because if the causal primacy of economic class conflict is denied, the ultimate aims of Marxism evaporate; the ends of human existence are out of our control.

Social formation and its varying conflicting interests are the matrix

8. B. Hindess and P. Hirst, *Mode of Production and Social Formation* (London: Macmillan, 1977), 55.

9. Marx and Engels, *The German Ideology* (Moscow: Progress, 1976), 617.

upon which we understand the productive forces that emanate from a society. This, rather than productive forces, gives to a society the interests that color its activities. Relational views of history (as we have seen previously) transact with an opposing view of time than does history conceived as forces. Interactions such as class relations, property relations, and various divisions of labor presuppose that time is a struggle. Will and volition are required to overcome the violence and increasing misery that ever grinding and more complex relations and divisions yield. Again, the pessimistic role assigned by Rousseau to history helps us envisage this. Rather than history being a journey of ever-empowering forces, history is a journey of increasingly crippling and inequitable relations. The species devolves and decays by enacting private property, dividing labor into more disenfranchised, meaningless, and humiliating roles, and sharpening the power relations between the dominating and the dominated. The appeal to the primacy of relations of production is a testimony to the need for history to be rectified or set anew, and thus also of time being a backward march through history until that fated day. Relations of production assume that there is a power that can be summoned within classes and societies that can bring about change, where productive forces make people subject to the changes arising from these forces' development.

So essentially the choice between these two components in the mode of production reduces down to which mechanism one favors for social change. Does social change inevitably loom when the relations people enter into hinder the onslaught of continuing technological forces? Or can classes and social actors bring about change by consciously accepting, rejecting, retarding, accelerating, socializing, or capitalizing on productive forces? Can classes change their position and relations on their own accord, or are their wills and desires entirely delivered and authorized by material forces beyond them? Steven Best believes that adhering to one position over the other means you only entertain half the message Marx was assembling about the mode of production. "Neither position grasps the tensions and ambiguities in Marx's analyses. The one-sidedness of the readings of Cohen and Shaw and Hindess and Hirst need to be rejected in favour of a more nuanced, contextualist approach."[10]

His aim is to broaden the mode of production into a more pliable and

10. Best, *The Politics of Historical Vision*, 56.

context-driven method for chronicling social and economic change. This involves a "nonreductionist" reading of the two branches of the mode of production. I agree with Best that reducing the mode of production to one of its two constituent parts as the primary cause of change involves the commentator in a dogmatism that is not to be found in Marx. However, ignoring the radically opposing temporalities in the mode of production is the only way he can do this. By attempting to homogenize forces and relations in a more open and receptive method, Best obliterates the tension of Marx's temporal and historical imagination. Best has rightly seen that Marx never fundamentally favored one approach over the other, but this does not mean that they were designed to cooperate together. The mode of production is not a nuanced and assuaging impression; it is a torn and antagonistic entity, where any fine distinction is the epiphenomenon of a deeply oppositional structure.

The mode of production as the engine of history is a mirror image of Marx's conflicted relation to time. Just as Marx's mind operated with a deep loathing of time saddled to an appreciation of its supremacy and usefulness, so too does his engine of change make history move simultaneously forward and backward, progressing and decaying. Forces of production improve our lot through time, while our relations are simultaneously characterized as devolving. This peculiar dynamic in Marx's histories will now be explored through a connection with Rousseau's major history in the "Second Discourse."

Production, Progress, and Perfectibility: The Forward March of History

Marx and Engels teased out the premises of the materialist conception of history most methodically in their work *The German Ideology*. In it they comprehensively discussed the workings of their "mode of production," and so it is here that we find ample treatment of the dynamic interplay of the forces and relations of history. Rarely is one mentioned without the other, suggesting that when Marx and Engels mused on grand history they were convinced of the united working of forces and relations. And yet the marriage of forces and relations is more an uneasy truce for scholarly purposes, which inevitably and unintentionally displays the signs of its gagged antagonism. In *The Poverty of Philosophy*,

Marx quickly reins in any movement one way or the other. "Of all the instruments of production, the greatest productive power is the revolutionary class itself. The organization of revolutionary elements as a class supposes the existence of all the productive forces which could be engendered in the bosom of the old society."[11] And again in *The German Ideology*: "Thus things have now come to such a pass that the individuals must appropriate the existing totality of productive forces.... This appropriation is first determined by the object to be appropriated, the productive forces."[12]

Any mention of the relations of production engendering a consciousness whereby they themselves become a force of production, indeed a force of revolution, is tempered by Marx's quick insistence that this process is determined by the historical stage of the totality of productive forces. Forces and relations walk awkwardly hand in hand through Marx's imagined history of the species, and in the name of remaining on the methodologically firm and polemically displacing ground of temporality, relations of production are often sold out as the poor handmaidens to material forces. Marx seems to need to constantly remind himself of humanity's fortunes being shackled to the progress of our expertise and equipment. Marx overtly states that any real social change or "liberation" must be predicated on such material forces. "Slavery cannot be abolished without the mule jenny, serfdom cannot be abolished without improved agriculture ... people cannot be liberated as long as they are unable to obtain food and drink, housing and clothing in adequate quality and quantity. 'Liberation' is a historical and not mental act, and it is brought about by historical conditions."[13]

If our freedom is unwaveringly a historical occurrence, this presupposes the confluence of the natural and the social. In much the same way as Rousseau saw his belligerent division between the natural and social drives of man evaporate in his confused concept of perfectibility, Marx's use of productive forces as the causal thread of history contains many of the hallmarks of the concept of perfectibility. For Rousseau, perfectibility was the notion that allowed him to explore the canvas of history that he had stretched between nature and his fallen society. It enabled

11. Marx, *The Poverty of Philosophy* (New York: International Publishers, 1963), 174.
12. Marx and Engels, *The German Ideology*, 96.
13. Marx and Engels, *The German Ideology*, 44.

that devolving history to be presented at the expense of the abstractions of society and nature, abstractions that usually disallow the possibility of doing history, and abstractions that sustained Rousseau's vision of atemporal human powers and ahistorical societal constructs. Marx, however, begins from the premise that nature and society are reciprocal and united rather than exclusive and divided, a sentiment expressed in the assertion that "the human being is in the most literal sense a *zoon politikon*."[14]

Where Rousseau begrudgingly admitted the naturalness of human sociality with the pessimistic disclaimer that it simply made us "liable to grow into a dotard," Marx has no uneasiness with our natural sociability. As such, perfectibility sat far more comfortably within Marx's understanding of our history than it did for Rousseau. And yet this assuredness does not attend Marx's philosophy, because he had solved the problem of the nature/society dualism. Nature and society are simply housed in Marx's history in differing regions and in a differing arrangement to that of Rousseau. Rousseau attempted his history of the species, his evolutionary anthropology, upon the framework of a strict linear narrative. As such, the abstractions of nature and society are placed as points at the beginning and end of the narrative, which goes some way to conceal their abstract character by giving to them an imaginary historical being. As a consequence, the two perceived modes of our history, namely our perfectibility and our innate and instituted inequality, are placed with awkward temporalities within the history framed by nature and society. We remember that the birth of inequality was an arbitrary point in the narrative where time shifts from a forward to a backward movement, dividing chance and necessity. We also remember that perfectibility is a precarious and unstable tightrope suspended suspiciously between nature and society—a bewildering concept for Rousseau, as it accounts for the progress that he knows is endemic to history, but that he can't reconcile with the inequality that is the conceptual product of his abstract division between nature and society.

Marx, however, is relatively unconcerned with dictating a chronological history of human fortunes. Such histories do occur throughout

---

14. Marx, *Grundrisse: Foundations of the Critique of Political Economy,* translated by Martin Nicolaus (Harmondsworth: Penguin, 1973), 84.

Marx's work, but this is more a consequential emanation from his primary concern … the development and dictation of a viable model of historical causation. In Marx and Rousseau the orders are reversed. In Rousseau the story is first written and a mélange of causalities jostle and bend within its space, while for Marx there is an attempt to homogenize a mélange of causalities with the purpose of then telling history's story. In Marx's mode of production all the causal foment of Rousseau's history can be found in a structured state of suspension. Rather than the causal foment being stretched across the historical landscape, it is concentrated like a hurricane that is occurring at every moment of the historical sequence. Rather than nature and society being assigned as beginning and end points, in Marx they are vertically arranged within the mode of production corresponding to forces and relations.

The production of life, both of one's own in labour and of fresh life in procreation, now appears as a twofold relation: on the one hand as a natural, on the other as a social relation—social in the sense that it denotes the cooperation of several individuals, no matter under what conditions, in what manner and to what end. It follows from this that a certain mode of production, or industrial stage, is always combined with a certain mode of cooperation, or social stage, and this mode of cooperation is itself a "productive force."[15]

And hence the story of our production, progress, and perfectibility is told in the forces of the mode of production, while the story of our enslavement to property and the social division of labor is told in the relations of the mode of production. In this way the abstractions of nature and society do not frame history, but constitute it as its constant forward and backward movement. History's evolution and devolution do not swing suddenly from one to the other at some particular point in time like they do for Rousseau. Instead they are two opposing processes that are occurring continuously throughout all history and at every moment. The opposing temporalities of our naturally felt forces and socially conditioned relations tell a tale of divided and alienated humanity.

15. Marx, *The German Ideology*, 48–49. Notice here again Marx's incessant need to fold any "social stage," "mode of cooperation," or "relation of production" back into a force of production. This process of constantly dissolving relations into forces would make us ask the question of why a division needs to be made at all. Such dissolving is the natural unifying movement of a mind and philosophy plagued by a divided allegiance to time and a causal mode of history that hence utilizes opposing temporalities.

Nature and society are not so much solved as pitted against each other in an eternal conflict. I will return to discuss the historical dynamic of the mode of production, but I will begin by exploring its determinist half. Marx's often stubborn perseverance with the primacy of productive forces suggests that this is where we should begin our look at Marx's historical vision: in the realm of our material production, our natural perfectibility, and our historical progress.

The first similarity between Marx and Rousseau's concept of perfectibility concerns the role population plays in its provocation. In both cases the birth of labor and production find their axis upon the movement of population. Observe the parallel between Rousseau's "In proportion as the human race grew more numerous, men's cares increased"[16] and Marx's "what individuals are depends on the material conditions of their production. This production only makes its appearance with the increase of population."[17] What seems a rather innocuous observation between Rousseau and Marx is rather the identification of indispensable signposts in the triumvirate of progressive economic thought. Both Rousseau and Marx are outlining the constellation of population, need, and labor that makes up the working elements of perfectibility. This is the conceptual equation of all economic thought that aligns itself to the positive analysis of history, the ideas that frame the process that is perfectibility. Any such talk of the technical mastery of our external world must begin and end in a theoretical reckoning with the meaning of these terms. As life becomes more burdened by the incidence of an increasing population, so must we increase the intensity of our labor and tools and confront the corresponding expansion of our needs. This is the basic premise of the school of economic progress. Perfectibility is that passive instinct lying in wait for population to transform it from a mere slumbering faculty into an inexorable force. Perfectibility in Rousseau is nothing more than productive force in Marx. Overpopulation's deployment of productive forces in order to satisfy needs is not only the primary causal thread of history, but constitutes the first of historical acts. For Marx, life is foremost the existence of material needs, and so the first historical act is the development of means to satisfy them. Simultaneous

16. Jean-Jacques Rousseau, *The Social Contract and Discourses* (London: J. M. Dent and Sons, 1938), 208.
17. Marx, *The German Ideology*, 37.

with this instrumental act of satisfaction is the creation of new needs. Instruments of satisfaction introduce further need, which constitutes a cycle of perfectibility. It is no mistake that Marx has one foot of his philosophy in the economic collective of population, need, and productive force, because it is this syndicate that keeps guard of history's forward progress. But it is equally no mistake that from the other angle of his thought he is one of the harshest critics of theories on overpopulation.

Man's perpetual mediation between his abundant wants and the dearth of his surroundings via his escalating labor power was thrown into its most striking relief in the population theories of Malthus, one of Marx's frequent polemical targets. Malthus's particular arrangement of the perfectibility equation attracted the ire of Marx, and it is his peculiar response to his economic influence that helps us tease out Marx's even more peculiar economic footing. In Malthus's work, the three terms of perfectibility are off-balance as he depreciates the power of our labor in favor of the power of population over the scarcity of the earth.

The power of population is indefinitely greater than the power in the earth to produce subsistence for man.

This natural inequality of the two powers of population, and of production in the earth, and the great law of our nature which must constantly keep their effects equal, form the great difficulty that to me appears insurmountable in the way to the perfectibility of society.[18]

Malthus's thesis that population expands geometrically, while the production of the earth only expands arithmetically, creates the need to constantly span the imbalance. The assigning of differing rates of progression to population and to the material goods that meet the needs of that population is a disjointed, yet logical imbalance that occurs because Malthus leaves out of the equation the expanding power of our labor force. The plane of history that is our perfectibility is disrupted in Malthus's work because of his overemphasis on the role of population in the equation of our forward progress through history. In Malthus, our labor power, our perfectibility, our technical prowess, our ability to extract from the earth are taken as a fixed, constant, and limited force. Thus a

18. Marx and Engels, *Marx and Engels on Malthus: Selections from the Writings of Marx and Engels Dealing with the Theories of Thomas Robert Malthus,* edited with an introduction by R. L. Meek; translated by Dorothea L. Meek and Ronald L. Meek (London: Lawrence and Wishart, 1953), 12.

disproportionate ratio between population and material is required to balance the equation. This creates a crisis that, while possibly containing elements of truth at certain times, is ridiculously heightened. Marx and Engels saw this flaw in Malthus's argument: "there still remains a third element … namely, science, the progress of which is just as limitless and at least as rapid as that of population."[19]

However, Marx sustains another critique of Malthus that comes from a very different place than from within the tradition of perfectibility, progress, and productive force. If Marx were purely an economist in this positive and progressive mode of history, he would have contented himself with reestablishing the claims of human productive forces within our natural progress. But Marx's major criticism comes from an altogether different plane of history.

The whole of human history can be brought under a single great natural law. This natural law is the phrase … "the struggle for existence," and the content of this phrase is the Malthusian law of population, or rather, over-population. So instead of analysing the struggle for existence as represented historically in varying and definite forms of society, all that has to be done is to translate every concrete struggle into the phrase, "struggle for existence," and this phrase itself into the Malthusian population fantasy. One must admit that this is a very impressive method—for swaggering, sham-scientific, bombastic ignorance and intellectual laziness.[20]

This critique comes from the reverse angle that views with scorn any attempt to formulate general laws of economic motion that are valid for all times and places. Such attempts are completely natural to the tradition of perfectibility, for perfectibility is simply the dispersal of "the struggle for existence," or our converse with nature throughout all human history. And since Marx admits that this process is at all times primary, the question arises as to where he finds the traction to criticize endeavors that unify this process with inexorable laws. This very process of perfectibility and swelling productive forces is indispensable to Marx's edifice of the future, yet he finds himself demolishing the legitimate claims made by his fellow proponents of this forward-moving history. All this suggests the existence of another distinct history taking place

19. Marx and Engels, *Marx and Engels on Malthus*, 63.
20. Marx's letter to Kugelmann, 1870, in *Marx and Engels on Malthus*, 174.

in Marx's method, a history working in the opposite direction from perfectibility, one that traces its development backward, while fragmenting the unified record of production. This is the history of relations, relations that grate against the acceleration of forces, disrupting its elegant uniform laws into distinct epochs, "definite forms of society" and "concrete struggles" that cannot be ordered by perfectibility. This is how Marx can maintain a critical distance from his progressive economic brothers, Malthus, the classical economists, and others, because he has one foot in another history.

If the first important similarity between Marx and Rousseau concerns the origin of perfectibility in its relation to population and need, then the next major similarity concerns the causal character of perfectibility. Thus we move from the origin to that origin's dispersal through time, or the manner in which perfectibility functions. We recall that perfectibility in Rousseau, or the instinct of our natural self-improvement, was divided between a period of chance and a period of necessity that switched upon the moment of inequality. Seen as the awkward temporal displacements that attended Rousseau's separation between nature and society at the opposing ends of history, we can now see in Marx, where no such historical parting exists, that chance and necessity are the twin causalities of our nature as perfectible beings. Rather than perfectibility being a passive impulse activated by dumb chance, which then mutates into a steely necessity, perfectibility is characterized by the dual operation of chance and necessity. And yet this shift is problematic.

For Rousseau humanity lurched from one technological and scientific advancement to the next, triggered by the outside world callously acting upon our latent potentiality in spite of our overall neutrality. For Marx, our technological achievements are our very own doing. Rather than a passive perfectibility, we are dealing with productive forces that are active and seemingly free. How then can we say that Marx's view of perfectibility retains the causal seals of chance and necessity? The way through this problem is to observe it at its first point, nature, and its last, society. First, considerations of what we were before we began to "produce the means of our subsistence" are not required by Marx, because he never mused on that theoretical starting point of all previous political philosophy ... the "state of nature." The question is left hanging, because to Marx our nature is self-explanatory; hence he disposes of that first moment that differentiated us from the animal kingdom. This has ramifications for how Marx would view our aptitude for developing productive forces and powers. Second, in Marx the promenade of chance and necessity in productive forces is not seen as constitutive of productive force as such, but as its outward expression. Where for Rousseau the violent necessity and chance of nature puppeteer our perfectibility, for Marx that violent necessity and chance foist themselves from our productive forces onto the other side of our history: our productive relations or our society. But let me begin with the first of these concerns. Marx from the beginning to the end of his philosophy sidesteps the issue of our transformation from animals to humans. In *The German Ideology* he writes, "Man can be distinguished from animals by consciousness, by religion or anything else you like. They themselves begin to distinguish themselves from the animals as soon as they begin to produce their means of subsistence, a step that is conditioned by their physical organization. By producing their means of subsistence men are indirectly producing their material life."[21] And again in *Capital,* "What distinguishes the worst architect from the best bee is this, that the architect raises his structure in imagination before he erects it in reality."[22] In both cases a separation is enacted between the animal and the human without having chronicled the transformation. Man is simply asserted as possessing a sovereignty over nature that is at the same time a force of nature.

Labour is, in the first place, a process in which both man and nature participate, and in which man of his own accord starts, regulates, and controls the material re-actions between himself and nature. He opposes himself to nature as one of her own forces.... By thus acting on the external world and changing it, he at the same time changes his own nature. He develops his slumbering powers and compels them to act in obedience to his sway.[23]

Because Marx "presuppose(s) labour in a form that stamps it as exclusively human," he never has to confront the starting point of the process of our perfectibility or our "slumbering powers." Marx presupposes a stage of humanity that is several historical strides beyond the theoretically reduced "human foundling" of Rousseau's state of nature, and as such has

21. Marx, *The German Ideology,* 37.
22. Karl Marx, *Capital* (Moscow: Foreign Languages Publishing House, 1954), 1:178.
23. Marx, *Capital,* 1:177.

a fundamentally different view of how that human operates within his productive force. With Rousseau's instinctless and depleted conception of man, this barely perceptible human is set on his course by the natural operations of chance and necessity. He is so theoretically limp that he becomes the plaything of the forces of nature. This why his "slumbering power" of perfectibility must be a passive, empty vessel determined by the whims of fortuity and indifference. Marx's theoretical starting point, however, is not the human solitary empty vessel or "robinsonade," but a human at least partially set in motion, at least partially empowered by something that Marx gives no consideration. As such he can be viewed as somewhat free, reasonably in control, and actively regulating his material life. Marx can have it both ways, where the human is at once a natural force subject to necessity and a force opposed to nature, willing itself freely and acting rather than reacting. Man's "slumbering powers" are compelled and determined by man. From this perspective it is impossible to seek an exact similarity of causation in Rousseau's and Marx's versions of perfectibility and productive force, as Marx's concept of productive forces contains some of the necessary freedom, not unlike Spinozian substance, that is contrarily played out upon Rousseau's concept of perfectibility by nature. Where we will find the similarity is from the opposite perspective, by asking the question: upon what do productive forces play out their necessary freedom? What is the realm that is subjected to the arbitrary indifference of our productive forces? The answer as always comes from the opposite side of the mode of production, that side that has its own reverse history, the relations of production. "The worker exists as a worker only when he exists for himself as capital, and he exists as capital only when capital exists for him. The existence of capital is his existence, his life, for it determines the content of his life in a manner indifferent to him."[24]

Here we are now in a position to appreciate why for Marx productive force was such a primary concern—why everything was continually sold out to it as "necessary," and why we cannot escape its formation of our social relations. Where Rousseau tipped the scales in favor of nature over perfectibility, Marx armed productive force with a grave power over nature. In the first case, perfectibility is an inert and receptive aptitude

---

24. Marx, "Economic and Philosophic Manuscripts," in *Early Writings,* translated by Rodney Livingstone and Gregor Bention (New York: Vintage, 1975), 335.

given content and form by nature. In the second, productive force is an active principle giving content and form to an inert and receptive nature. Thus in Marx, nature is no longer a starting point in the history of the species, but is transferred from out of history to become a process, an extracted and conceptual history of its own. Marx cares very little about nature as an entity indifferent from our aims, because he has endorsed the history of our productive forces as nature. Perfectibility is baptized as nature, and as such nature's attributes are conferred upon it. Thus perfectibility becomes indifferent to our humanity, and productive forces are seen as the realm making our relations of production dance to the hypnotic tune of chance and necessity. Marx writes, "How does it happen that their relations assume an independent existence over against them? And that the forces of their own life become superior to them? In short: division of labour, the level of which depends on the development of the productive power at any particular time."[25]

Because Marx has dissolved the old abstraction of nature into the forward history of productive forces, he can collude with that old concept of nature in convincing himself that he has solved the dichotomy of necessity and freedom. However, a close examination of this operation shows us that rather than solving it, he has simply relocated nature and society vertically instead of horizontally and reassigned the terms of the debate to correspond with productive forces and productive relations. We have seen how nature becomes compatible with our productive forces, conferring progress and perfectibility upon the human exercise. We will now turn to the societal aspect of the equation, embodied in our productive relations, our divisions of labor, and our divided associations over property, or class conflict. This is the story of our backward passage through time, the history of our descent.

Relations, Division and Property: The Backward March of History

Marx presents the divided nature of our history as the consequence of our own productive forces being encountered by us as a nature not of our authorship. Somehow or other process is occurring in animosity

25. Marx, *The German Ideology*, 102.

to our very nature. It is the believed eventual concurrence of these processes that presents itself as the solution to history.

Thus two facts are here revealed. First the productive forces appear as a world for themselves, quite independent of and divorced from individuals, alongside the individuals; the reason for this is that the individuals, whose forces they are, exist split up and in opposition to one another, whilst, on the other hand, these forces are only real forces in the intercourse and association of these individuals.[26]

I have discussed how the Young Hegelians' infectious enthusiasm for the future meant that a dualism was required to divide a present they saw as inadequate. This equally implied a monism or reconciliation that reigned in their imaginary future. In *The German Ideology* we can see Marx's own variant of this temporal procedure. Forces of production are an alien prerogative felt pressing against the divided relations that these forces create. And yet, these forces are of our own doing, and will only work for our fullest benefit when our "intercourse" and "association" are arranged such that they can harness the force's benefits for the whole of humanity. The question at all times is, why do forces require the submission of great swathes of humanity into relations that demean those on one side and corrupt those on the other? This is the question constantly asked of the present. The question for the future is how and when this situation will be remedied. I will examine these two moments of Marxism, the schismatic dualism of any present (and by implication the past), and the resolution of the future as the hypothetical answer to that eternally present question.

Despite Marxism's overt stance on the unity of nature and society, of naturally conditioned ends and humanly willed aims, *The German Ideology* contains quite explicit statements on the antagonism between what nature implores from us and what we ourselves wish for. This revolves squarely upon the division of labor and hence the class conflict that arises from it.

And finally, the division of labour offers us the first example of the fact that, as long as man remains in naturally evolved society, that is, as long as a cleavage exists between the particular and the common interest, as long, therefore, as activity is not voluntarily, but naturally, divided, man's own deed become a

26. Marx, *The German Ideology*, 95.

alien power opposed to him, which enslaves him instead of being controlled by him.[27]

And again,

The social power, i.e., the multiplied productive force, which arises through the co-operation of different individuals as it is caused by the division of labour, appears to these individuals, since their co-operation is not voluntary but has come about naturally, not as their own united power, but as an alien force existing outside them ... which they thus are no longer able to control, which on the contrary passes through a peculiar series of phases and stages independent of the will and action of man.[28]

There is an obvious difference between "naturally evolved society" and a cooperation that is "voluntary." We have seen that for Marx nature becomes our own possession in productive forces, and yet somehow it aggravates within us a passion for orienting our societies in the most unnatural fashion. Productive force is not just a senseless nature blind to our aspirations, but it actively fuels a demented fervor for inequality and enslavement. What exactly this aberrant passion, or this wayward course, is, is very much the province of both Marx's and Rousseau's thought. Almost exclusively their lives were devoted to the uncovering of the retrograde history that was taking place beneath the nose of progress. John Plamenatz is one of the few commentators to have taken seriously the two major themes of Rousseau's second discourse—not only how they anticipate the two major movements that comprised Marx's dialectic, but also how the primary concern was always the theme of corruption and alienation. "Perfectibility, in the non-moral sense, is one of the two main themes of perhaps the most imaginative and original of Rousseau's essays in social theory, his *Discourse on the Origins of Inequality Among Men*. The other is the corruption of man by society."[29]

Marx's backward passage of history, in much the same manner as Rousseau's anti-teleology of societal corruption, is founded upon the effect that private property has on the fortunes of men. When forces of production inculcate themselves in private property, a vast inverse of history takes place. "We have seen what significance of the wealth of hu-

27. Marx, *The German Ideology*, 53.
28. Marx, *The German Ideology*, 53–54.
29. John Plamenatz, *Karl Marx's Philosophy of Man* (Oxford: Clarendon Press, 1975), 55.

man needs has, on the presupposition of socialism, and consequently what significance a new mode of production and a new object of production have. A fresh confirmation of human powers and a fresh enrichment of human nature. Under the system of private property their significance is reversed."[30] Rousseau, in one of his most famous phrases, covers the same ground that Marx treads some ninety years later. "The first man who, having enclosed a piece of ground, bethought himself of saying *This is mine,* and found people simple enough to believe him, was the real founder of civil society.... Beware of listening to this impostor; you are undone if you once forget that the fruits of the earth belong to us all, and the earth itself to nobody."[31]

Private property is responsible for the ills of the world and grows upon our productive nature as a leech to our moral progress. As we materially master our world, escalating our needs and products, establishing property relations to expand our ability to produce our subsistence, a "new potentiality for mutual fraud and mutual pillage" presents itself for our temptation.[32] Two processes occur in tandem, the growth of our "production and needs" and a dominion of "inhuman, refined, unnatural and imaginary appetites."[33] The realm of unnatural appetites accounts for the "mephitic and pestilential breath of civilisation" and the "pollution and putrefaction of man."[34] Notice here that in Marx's more acerbic and colorful moments, he most clearly resembles the Rousseau of the first and second discourses. It is in those moments when he waxes spiteful on our inhumanity that we detect his indebtedness to Rousseau's original invective against a backward society moving away from its fulfillment. It almost seems as if private property is the newel upon which the two histories of progress and decline twirl. They play each other off through the insoluble medium of private property that "does not know how to transform crude need into human need."[35] It is the intermediary between our two histories until that time when our discordant natures can be unified and history as we know it suspended. Our confused binary history will be arrested when private property is abolished. Marx writes, "It is precisely in the fact that the division of labour and exchange are configu-

---

30. Marx, "Economic and Philosophic Manuscripts," in *Early Writings,* 358.
31. Rousseau, *The Social Contract and Discourses,* 207.
32. Marx, *Early Writings,* 358.   33. Marx, *Early Writings,* 359.
34. Marx, *Early Writings,* 359.   35. Marx, *Early Writings,* 359.

rations of private property that we find proof, both that human life need-ed private property for its realisation and that it now needs the abolition of private property."[36] As can be seen from this quote, Marx is far more able to recognize the value of private property as a necessary component of humanity's realization than Rousseau, for he more clearly demarcated the histories of productive forces and productive relations in his historical imagination. Rousseau's historical imagination is of the same species as Marx, yet his perfectibility and anti-teleology melt into one another upon the vista of a unified history. With history seen as one singular, yet con-flicted course, rather than two differentiated, yet interacting histories, it is harder for Rousseau to see any historical value in private property. Despite this, both Marx and Rousseau are in agreement as to the ultimate des-tination of private property: complete eradication. Also from this quote we can see how Marx viewed the division of labor as a "configuration" of private property. In this understanding of the tandem concepts of private property and the division of labor, we again see the kinship between Marx and Rousseau. Both these concepts are part of the necessary constitution of the "relational" history that they are both tracing.

While Rousseau rarely uses the direct term "division of labor," his history of our mistake, the birth of our inequality, is as much premised upon our reflective recognition of naturally inequitable relations as it is upon the establishment of private property. We recall that Rousseau pres-ents the consideration of our relations, "great, small, strong, weak, swift, slow, fearful, bold and the like," as a moment in our burgeoning nature, as the announcement of our natural inequalities, and as the natural divi-sion of labor. Seen in this natural sense, or within the morally neutral story of perfectibility, these relations seem innocuous and relatively in-consequential. But the discourse on inequality breathes with the social reality of this natural division of labor. The division of labor unnaturally allies itself with private property in an unholy bond generating our de-volving moral universe, our anti-teleology. Marx describes this process as "the transformation, through the division of labour, of personal powers (relations) into material powers."[37] In other words, the division of labor makes our own social freedom seem naturally conditioned, and not our

36. Marx, *Early Writings*, 374.
37. Marx, *The German Ideology*, 86.

freedom at all. Marx's moral reading of private property and its insidious tendency to utilize the division of labor in its historical mission to march us backward through time, dividing us into ever greater class conflict, is thoroughly anticipated in Rousseau's "Second Discourse." It is this correlation between Marx's backward history of our productive relations and Rousseau's anti-teleology of inequality that makes it possible for Robert Wokler to compare them both as revolutionary class-conflict theorists. "We have only to juxtapose their respective philosophies of history in which class conflict is the vehicle of revolutionary change, and the substitution of egalitarian for inegalitarian property relations the condition of society to which men should aspire."[38]

Under the despotic reign of private property, the natural division of talents becomes the social division of labor, a condition "fomenting everything that might sow in it the seeds of actual division, while it gave society the air of harmony."[39] This state described by Rousseau is precisely Marx's brief against the last antagonistic phase of society, the capitalist mode of production. Our sliding history of society, in both Rousseau and Marx, ends in the most deplorable relish for increased division for exploitation, taking place under the legitimizing illusory auspices of legal and governmental harmony. Both thinkers have sketched the "progress of our inequality" as it has played itself out in various "restricted revolutionary appropriations." This leads to such a tense historical standoff between our nature as production and our society as extreme relational division that an all-consuming revolution must be released to remove the "muck of ages." And this mission knew that its escape could only be found in the "voluntary." In essence the history of our demise, chronicled by both Marx and Rousseau, is always allied to an awakening of the will. Rousseau formulated this theoretical awakening in his *Social Contract,* where for Marx the extreme reshaping of men and society was to take place not theoretically, but actually in scientific Communism.

Both for the production on a mass scale of this communist consciousness, and for the success of the cause itself, the alteration of men on a mass scale is necessary, an alteration which can only take place in a practical movement, a revolu-

---

38. Robert Wokler, "Rousseau and Marx," in *The Nature of Political Theory,* edited by David Miller and Larry Siedentop (Oxford: Clarendon Press, 1983), 226–27.
39. Rousseau, *The Social Contract and Discourses,* 235.

tion; the revolution is necessary, therefore, not only because the ruling class cannot be overthrown in any other way, but also because the class overthrowing it can only in a revolution succeed in ridding itself of all the muck of ages and become fitted to found society anew.[40]

And so Marx, following in Rousseau's footsteps, is forced to resolve history, transform men and "consciousness," and set society "anew." Yet for Rousseau this was always going to be a theoretical endeavor, an event never guaranteed. For Marx it is a certainty, scientific in its actuality. We saw how Rousseau adopted a scientific footing for his "Second Discourse," which translated itself into the amoral history of perfectibility, and yet this scientific pretension never invaded any of Rousseau's more speculative pronouncements. Marx's belief in the ironclad necessity of productive force, his sense of the scientific bedrock upon which his ideas sat, was so strong that this timeless state of transformation and historical overcoming was a reality. "Communism is for us not a state of affairs which is to be established, an ideal to which reality will have to adjust itself. We call communism the real movement which abolishes the present state of things. The conditions of this movement result from the now existing premise."[41]

Communism can be a definite scientific reality for Marx while in the same breath being dependent upon the revolutionary will and the consciousness of the proletariat. This is because Marx has two histories: productive forces that can keep promises with an inevitability like nature and productive relations that demand the mushrooming of the atemporal will from the hard earth of history. Communism as scientific reality gains all of its sustenance from the natural working of productive forces. But Communism is also certainty for Marx because of the dictates of the future, that historical expanse from which Marxism flows. Rousseau's only certainty in his life was the past, a realm of nature whose veracity nothing could dislodge. Thus future society was an open question, and forever only the province of the theoretical and speculative. The opposite is true of Marx, where the future of Communism is at all times a given. Thus the past is a hazy landscape fit for only idealists and romantics to ponder. This is why Marx never inquired about our nature before society. The future killed his appreciation for origins and overinflated his sense of destination.

40. Marx, *The German Ideology*, 60.   41. Marx, *The German Ideology*, 57.

Conclusion: Inevitable Circumvolution

The similarity between Rousseau and Marx that I have been chroni-cling is at its initial level a very simple assertion made by the two think-ers. Both are saying that our material, technological, and mental prog-ress can in no way be seen as conferring that moral progress that makes us virtuous and equitable in our relations with others. I have shown that this simple assertion manifests itself in very compound and intricate historical and temporal arrangements, arrangements that can be suc-cinctly expressed in an illustrative form outlined in appendixes 1 and 2.

If we survey some of the striking features of their visions of history, we see that overall the shape of history remains the same in both. Both histories are comprised of twin processes at odds with one another. Both deal with our amoral progress upon nature and with our moral alien-ation among our own kind. One of course is able to notice in Rousseau's concept of perfectibility, the same dialectical spirit that Hegel bestowed on Marx, as Engels did when rereading Rousseau in later life.[42] And the dialecticism of their approaches draws them into outlining similar po-litical projections, although Marx's becomes more radicalized.

What in Rousseau was a limited suggestion, although an emphatic one, came to be the dogmatic core of a confident prognosis, a strident propaganda, a rev-olutionary incitation in Marx: the state or political order will wholly wither away, and homogeneous mankind will live socially under the rule of benevo-lence—from each according to his ability, to each according to his needs.[43]

And yet this is just a general similarity that does not move on to an-swer the question of why this dialectical movement is arrested in the futures of both these thinkers. Why does the *Social Contract* and Com-munism bring this estranged situation to a close? The Young Hegelians may have lamented Hegel's disbanding of the dialectic, yet Hegel only achieved this through an institutional mediation of the two opposing his-

---

42. Wokler describes how after having read the *Discourse on Inequality,* Engels was struck by how similar in dialectical makeup and material it was to Marx's *Capital.* It is almost certain Engels passed on these observations to Marx, thus making it even more puz-zling that Marx never reevaluated the misguided critique of Rousseau's static social con-tract made in his youth; Wokler, "Rousseau and Marx," 220.

43. Joseph Cropsey, "Karl Marx," in *History of Political Philosophy,* edited by Leo Strauss and Joseph Cropsey, 3rd ed. (Chicago: University of Chicago Press, 1987), 824–25.

tories and a degree of acceptance of alienation. Marx remobilized the dialectic and freshly detached the opposing histories with an assault upon all present institutions in order to bring those histories to a more satisfactory closure in the future. Thus, as I have said before, it is not enough to say that Marx was a purely historical thinker wielding the dialectic like a newly sharpened knife, because that knife was sharpened by a timelessness that can only be understood with reference to Kant's atemporal will, or at least that atemporal will given its proper social house in the future. Thus with both Rousseau and Marx, we are not simply observing the operation of dialectics in history, we are also witnessing the groundwork for the timeless and ahistorical. The clue to this type of historical imagination has always been given by a strong ignorance and loathing of the present, always directed at its institutional face, a type of "unhappy consciousness" or tormented countenance toward the institutional present. This strange historical imagination is surprisingly enough akin to the temporal limitations inflicted upon the damned in Dante's *Inferno*. As Dante reaches the City of Dis, he discovers that the inhabitants of Hell have no knowledge of the present, only visions of the past and future.

> It seems you can foresee and prophesy
> Events that time will bring, if I hear right,
> But with things present, you deal differently.

> "We see" said he, "like men who are dim of sight,
> Things that are distant from us; just so far
> We still have gleams of the All-Guider's light.

> But when these things draw near, or when they are,
> Our intellect is void, and your world's state
> Unknown, save someone bring us news from there.

> Hence thou wilt see that all we can await
> Is the stark death of knowledge in us, then
> When time's last hour shall shut the future's gate.[44]

Dante discovers that Hell is a state of awareness of the past and the imprecise and hazy cognition of the future, but where knowledge of the present is completely surrendered. Hell comprises a population of "lost

---

44. Dante Alighieri, *The Divine Comedy,* part 1, "Hell," translated by Dorothy L. Sayers (Harmondsworth: Penguin, 1975), 130–31.

souls" who "are ignorant of the present" and who "shall know only what can torment them."[45] Here we have a literary expression of the historical imaginations of Rousseau and Marx. Instead of being the spiritually tormented in Hell, they are the institutionally tormented in a social hell. Because of their inability to consider the present of institutionally embodied time, they are forced to live their lives in the past and future, since they approach the present in a timeless fashion that pleads ignorance at time's tribunal. And in an ill-fated irony for Marx, Dante discovers this knowledge from the mouth of a man consigned to Hell for his belief that when the body dies, so too does the soul. In other words, the City of Dis is littered with the burning opened tombs of materialists, left in torment with their eternal souls aflame. The timelessness so much a part of their life, yet denied by them in life, is their sardonic punishment. For Marx, the timelessness so much a part of his philosophy, yet denied by his philosophy, is also the source of his eternal chastisement of, and agony with, the present.

The two diagrams of Marx and Rousseau do not just outline the similarities between the two thinkers, but also their differences, many of which I have already discussed. Of the major differences, the most obvious is the arrangement of the histories. Rousseau's history is portrayed in a traditionally linear, horizontal fashion framing a variety of historical causalities between a beginning and an end. Marx's is arranged vertically as a mode of conflicted causality occurring at every moment in history. Hence history is told not as a story by Marx; instead he attempts to contain the story of history in a comprehensive explanatory model. By treating the plateau of times that is history as a spatial entity rather than a temporal one, Marx involves himself in another game of timelessness. The timeless game is that of the scientist included with the timeless game of the metaphysician that I have already examined. We will look into the scientific timelessness of Marxism in the next chapter.

The problem of arrangement is also attached to the problem of nature and society, and brings us close to answering the question we set out at the beginning of this chapter. Because Rousseau was giving a narrative of history, nature and society, just as inequality, were to be consigned

---

45. C. H. Grandgent, *Companion to The Divine Comedy*, edited by Charles S. Singleton (Cambridge, Mass.: Harvard University Press, 1975), 53–54.

to resembling points upon the terrain of history. Nature was anchored at the beginning, with society projected toward the end, and inequality flagged somewhere between. This of course is not strictly how Rousseau would have conceived of them, nor how they are always represented in the "Second Discourse," but we have already seen how the type of history that was written forced his hand at transforming them into abstractions that had to be demarcated from each other. However, it at first seems that Marx, with his vertical organization of historical explanation, has resolved the problem by bringing nature and society down from their immobile abstractions and making them into cooperating processes. This, however, must be severely qualified by the discovery that the vertical arrangement revolves around two diametrically opposed causalities and directions of movement. If nature and society are not abstractions and not divergent entities in Marx, why have they been animated as separate processes at odds with one another? Marx has in reality gone to much greater lengths than Rousseau to separate nature and society, and in the execution has cleaved and divided the history that Rousseau merely saw as hopelessly tangled. And thus we are now in a position to answer those critics such as Steven Best who wish to tame the mode of production as a cooperating and obliging engine of history. Sitting on the fence between the technological determinist and class-conflict schools of Marxism cannot be a passive exercise. It is not a matter of having it both ways, but of understanding the violence and incompatibility of the two ways Marx views history. Steven Best's great ally in this passive appropriation of the mode of production is Alfred Schmidt and his view of Marx's concept of nature: "Natural and human history together constitute for Marx a differentiated unity. Thus human history is not merged in pure natural history; natural history is not merged in human history."[46]

Such fence-sitting does not do justice to the fact that Marxism is not only a revolutionary science, but also a science of revolution. Natural and human history are proven not to be the feeble and indecisive realms as viewed by Best and Schmidt, because the only time they do interact is in a moment of violence, or a revolution. The word itself describes the process that is occurring. Two histories moving in opposite directions create a revolving movement between them, like a wave building up

46. Alfred Schmidt, *The Concept of Nature in Marx* (London: NLB, 1973), 45.

momentum until that wave must crash in a vast, rotating force. Marx's idea of revolution is one of the most physicalist of notions, seen simply as the unavoidable circular consequence of two great forces rubbing against one another. The inevitability of Marx hewing history into two is circumvolution. The problem for Marx becomes how to deduce that this process of periodic circumvolution is not eternal, but temporary, and that the two contrary forces that bring about cyclic revolution will soon be truly unified. Thus Marx colored previous movements before his own: "All earlier revolutionary appropriations were restricted; individuals whose self-activity was restricted by a crude instrument of production and a limited intercourse, appropriated this crude instrument of production, and hence merely achieved a new state of limitation. Their instrument of production became their property, but they themselves remained subordinate to the division of labour and their own instrument of production."[47]

Marxism is based on the assumption that the mode of production of capitalism is no such "limited appropriation." It relies on the belief that capitalism is worldwide in its scope and ambition, that the proletariat is universal in its suffering, and that the two histories are moving at such velocity that a revolution of gargantuan proportions is looming to deliver history into a state of constant circularity. Marx devoted the rest of his life to the study of circular movement in capitalism. Capitalism is the great maelstrom of forces, the destructive whirlwind of money and labor, the tornado age of reproduction and appropriation for reproduction and appropriation's sake. In Marx's masterwork, *Capital,* time is viewed as a circular phenomenon, which the abundance of circular processes verifies. The examination of the universality of history, the inevitable circumvolution occurring in *Capital,* and the peculiarity of the proletariat is where I will now turn.

47. Marx, *The German Ideology,* 97.

ʕ 8

Science, Capital, Proles

Objectivity, Universality, and History: The Privileged Individual and His Privileged Science

Despite Marx's supposed position on the radical temporality of all individuals and ideas, Marx himself and the type of science he was forging were not subjected to such a limitation. In typical nineteenth-century style, Marx made his social scientist stand outside time and history. From this perspective much of Marx's insistence on everything being embedded in time and history seems to be a way of depreciating the claims of his opponents. Timelessness is a branding iron used like a weapon to protect Marx and his claims from similar accusations. This begs the important question of where precisely the Marxist scientist, and the Marxian science itself, sit in relation to history. The best way to begin this quest is to look at Marx's criticism of the *Robinsonade* and the theoretical purity of isolation. Albert Camus has noticed that the infeasibility of isolation as an adequate category for the scientific evaluation of man was a distinctively nineteenth-century discovery. "To put economic determinations at the root of all human action is to sum man up in terms of his social relations. There is no such thing as a solitary man, that is the indisputable discovery of the nineteenth century."[1] He arrives at

1. Albert Camus, *The Rebel*, translated by Anthony Bower (Harmondsworth: Penguin, 1971), 167.

this after an allusion to Comte and the century's urge for positivism, a stream in which he places Marx because of the similar theme of anti-transcendence that they shared. With transcendence denied, the hopes of humanity spill horizontally across the social landscape. As we have seen, collapsing transcendence means embracing temporality, and this operation has two contradictory consequences. First, it prevents the possibility of that nexus point devoid of relations, the isolated man, the theoretical man, or as Marx described him, the *Robinsonade.* Isolation is that category that has led the human sciences down fruitless avenues and the category rejected by positivist and historical thinking. Second, the space occupied between time and eternity, the mythic vertical space denoted by the upward movement of transcendence, must be laid equally across the horizontal plane of society and time. In other words, these inverters of transcendence did not want to relinquish the universality that lay inherent in transcendence. The enlargement of the scope of Marx's project and science is directly proportional to the universality of transcendence, and the more things that are dragged from the transcendent, the more they help to widen the worldwide ambitions of Marxism.

This is the peculiar dynamic of Marxism, and to a degree the nineteenth century. The enlightening and redemptive powers of science unhinge the transcendent proclivities of metaphysics and its accompanying timelessness. In this climate, the isolated, relationless man as the touchstone of social, political, and economic thought dissipates. But the totalizing contour and universal form of metaphysics remain in the outlines of nineteenth-century human sciences. In the case of Marxism, the isolated man does not so much disappear as the object of the human sciences as he crosses the barricades of these sciences. The isolated man is no longer the observed entity of Marxist science; he is the protagonist. Disinterested awareness of historical necessity is his defining asset, because he is now the man sundered from time and history. While everything else sways to time and history's push and pull, his mind remains untouched; retaining the objectivity, his science denies others and their ideas. Where the universality of social and economic laws was once guaranteed by observing a reduced, isolated, timeless, and relationless individual, it is now the province of the timeless and isolated mind of the Marxist scientist to observe universality. Marxism cannot relinquish the timelessness of the all-knowing mind. As Rosenstock-Huessy has pointed out, Marxism demands that the individual has a knowledge, foresight, and wisdom granted only to the whole of humanity. He writes, "Marxism tries to give to the knowing individual the power within society which united mankind has over external nature. That campaign is of worldwide significance. If it should be victorious, it would change the aspect of things. No country in the world could fail to adopt the government of the knowing."[2] To rephrase this insight by Rosenstock-Huessy in the terms of this study, Marxism is a movement that attempts to contract the totality of history into a form that can be utilized by the "knowing individual." The wisdom of the world and its history are surrendered, usurped by the intelligence of the isolated scientist sitting outside history. I have already touched upon how this campaign operates. At the same time as transcendence is splayed across history, history is compressed from the sheer breadth of its comprehension to the mere concentration of an explanation. The story and lessons of history are rotated, so that rather than being draped over time, they are stacked upon each other for utilization in all times. The wisdom of history is squeezed into a method easily integrated with the individual, who before that breakthrough could only be a partial carrier of history. The individual Marxist scientist can now be the deliverer of total history, the personification of timelessness. The status conferred by Marxism upon the all-knowing eye of historical reason gives us some indication of the vision he had for the future.

In Rosenstock-Huessy's formulation of Marxism above, we can isolate the four elements of Marx's constellation of objectivity, universality, and history. First we have the privileged individual. Second, this individual's position is opposed, and in contradistinction to the wisdom of the world, not so much because it deliberately sets out to be, but because, in confidently and condescendingly trying to usurp the wisdom of history, it automatically counters itself to it. Third, this individual's right and his campaign are "worldwide" or universal. And last, if successful, his reign will be a "government of the knowing." Let us begin by looking at the last of these in order to place the previous three in relation. This "government of the knowing," a natural consequence of this type of anti-transcendent nineteenth-century thinking, is recognized by both Camus and Rosenstock-Huessy. Camus describes Comte's scientific utopia, which runs parallel to the type of society Marx's project would also yield: "a society whose scien-

2. Eugen Rosenstock-Huessy, *Out of Revolution: Autobiography of Western Man* (Providence R. I.: Berg, 1993), 69.

tists would be priests, two thousand bankers and technicians ruling over a Europe of one hundred and twenty million inhabitants where private life would be absolutely identified with public life."[3] Rosenstock-Huessy toyed with the same idea when he considered the legacy of Marxist speech: "The vocabulary of modern political success is the mystic speech of figures. Each age has its specific political melody: ours in the music of numbers … wages and taxes, battleships and armaments, unemployed and figures before us which seem to show a necessity for it."[4]

The speech of the scientist and a priesthood of the bureaucratic technician all allude to this "government of the knowing." Both of these thinkers have noticed that Marx is doing nothing significantly different from Plato when he espoused the Philosopher King as the only rational archetype of governance. However, Marx's socialist scientist is a very different creature from Plato's Philosopher King, although both conceptions are born from the same myth. That myth is that the mind is divine and that it establishes nonnegotiable and fixed standards. Marxism is based solely upon the privileged individual, his privileged science, and the absolutes it creates. In the last analysis this "government of the knowing" is the reflection of the philosopher's mind. Thus the idea of the "government of the knowing" contains within it the understanding of the three other elements of objectivity, universality, and history. A "government of the knowing" is the political establishment of the objectivity of the Marxian science, the universality of his creed, and his distinctive temporally transcended historical prescience. In other words, Marxism as a science transcends time and history in order to be devastatingly aware of the historical temperament at any given moment. "The consciousness of the historical hour is the core of Marxian theory."[5]

The question that arises is whether the consciousness of the historical hour can be achieved from the outer peripheries of its natural environment of time. Could it be that a historical consciousness as remote from time as Marxism accounts for its more immoderate and audacious claims and aims? It would be this question of universality and objectivity with regard to history and time, and the attendant grandeur of the ventures that emanate from this attitude, that would be observed with

3. Camus, *The Rebel*, 164.
4. Rosenstock-Huessy, *Out of Revolution*, 70.
5. Rosenstock-Huessy, *Out of Revolution*, 68.

suspicion by the generation of twentieth-century radical thinkers led by Foucault. Objectivity and universality would be decimated by such thinkers as they attempted to dissolve the privileged individual, or in their parlance the centered subject of knowledge, within time and history. Regardless of the answer, the majority of Marx's life was spent as one of those privileged individuals in that scientific, timeless stratosphere surrounding capitalism, deducing its dissolution.

The Unraveled Circuit of Capital? Time, Hieroglyphs, Vampires, and the Children of Esau

It was inevitable that, after navigating the warring temporalities of history to arrive at his contemporary world, Marx would see that world as a maelstrom of destructive time. Marx views bourgeois economics not simply as the indifferent maneuvers of time, but as the active application of its ceaseless powers of separation, division, and acceleration. It is not simply the opening of the economic system to time's unhindered movement, but the offensive imposition of time regimes into the lives of individuals in order to better serve an alien master of capital. Time is seen as a tool in the hands of mankind, used perplexingly to enslave rather than emancipate us. It is this diagnostic aspect of Marxism and its assault on capitalism that sustains its force as an important philosophy. Marx is at his most acute and earnest when describing the degradation capitalism imposes upon our sense of time and space.

In periods of crisis the progressive bourgeoisie radically transforms concepts of time and space to speed up the turnover time of capital. Accelerating production, exchange, and consumption raises profits and gives a comparative (or survival) advantage over competitors. The annihilation of spatial boundaries and the movement into new territories are particularly emphasized in crises, when the rate of change increases. In this "annihilation of space and time" capitalism globalizes further and aggressively socializes new and existing workers into new time disciplines, while imposing novel conceptions of space. Styles of living and an extensive array of physical assets constructed around previous systems of space and time are creatively destroyed. The progressive bourgeoisie imposes new forms of time and space on global capitalism to interrelate the world.[6]

6. Anthony van Fossen, "Globalisation," in *Everlasting Uncertainty: Interrogating the Communist Manifesto 1848–1998*, edited by Geoff Dow and George Lafferty (Annandale, NSW: Pluto Press, 1998), 66–67.

Not only is time conceived and applied in the daily life of individuals in a novel way to maximize profit, but time becomes the very substance of capitalism—the standard upon which it hitches its value. Capitalism is a vast system of time farming. The life cycles, seasons, and daily routines of men, women, and children alike, are all mutilated by time management in order to extract any remaining time embodied as money.

The very principle of a market economy, abstract labour is what creates exchange value, what imposes the law of equivalences without any other relation to use-values qualitatively defined and suited to needs. The most aberrant movement has become the everyday itself, the daily mastery of time. Here is found the old curse: money is time. "Remember that time is money," signs Benjamin Franklin. He is the founder of political economy.[7]

The reign of capital is nothing more than the process whereby time is wrung from our custody and control to hover above us as capital perpetuating itself in an endless cycle. This is the mastery of time for the benefit of capital, rather than the mastery of time for our own human promotion. The commodification of such a universal element as time by the system of capitalism is the essential ingredient behind the Marxist postulate of capitalist universality. The idea of the universality of capitalism's methods and ambitions is an essential prerequisite for the realization of a planetary socialist order. Thus, in the idea of time, Marx had found the most basic universal element that could be commodified by capitalists, and the merest, yet dearest of appropriable birthrights from the sons and daughters of Esau. Time is the inheritance of all, and in identifying this singular belonging of humanity, capitalism is able to circulate its tendrils across the world and across all times. It matters not where it finds itself geographically or what stages of economic development it meets in its path, for everything bows to the revolutionary pressure of capitalist production. Capitalism is as much the consummation of time's talents as it is of time's annihilation. It is the culmination of economic stages and the leveler of historical times. It sweeps the "muck of ages" away, destroying old life cycles, consuming our creative time rapaciously, transforming it into scientifically calculated time and leaving it unresponsively circulating out of our reach. Marx's exhaustive study of the capitalist mode of production is devoted precisely to finding out ex-

7. Eric Alliez, *Capital Times,* translated by Georges Van Den Abbeele (Minneapolis: University of Minnesota Press, 1996), xvi.

actly how and when this stored time will be returned to its rightful owners. According to Marx's two rival histories, this process of draining surplus time from society can be seen in two lights. First it is seen morally, as the simple theft of workers' labor time by the avaricious and powerful: a kleptocratic system. Second, it is seen pragmatically as the extraction of surplus time, converted into profit, which is used to massively expand our productive capacities and infrastructure. This radically altered and powerful economic state of affairs will eventually be reunited with its progenitors, who will organize a new society on its effective basis. The question for this study is how Marx sees the alien circuit of capital unraveling. How is this rapidly accelerating circular time of capitalism, which was produced by the two contrarily animated histories discussed in the previous chapter, arrested? We will see that far from having unraveled the circuit of capital, or having fused the forward and backward histories of his mode of production, Marx in fact has two answers to the problem of capitalism's degradation of human time: one that corresponds to the history of our social relations and the other to the opposite history of our productive progress. These two answers contradict one another, and as such this signals Marx's inability to fuse the radical cleft of society. In examining these two contrasting answers, answers that hang like protuberances upon the ends of his two historical questions, we are able to place Communism and the proletariat in their respective lights. The proletarians are the historical deliverers of the temporal leveling of capitalism and the unravelers of the circuit of capital, while Communism is the state of affairs after the temporal abandon; as such they presuppose the fusion of Marx's histories. If it can be shown that Marx is unable to fuse these histories in a satisfying way, then we are able to present Marx's hopes for the proletariat and his vision of Communism in another light: in the light of his romantic youth, the light of his Promethean ethic and prophecy, and in the light of the timeless.

While Marx was writing his extensive notebooks of 1857–1858, later to be known as the *Grundrisse,* he was fortunate to peruse a copy of Hegel's *Logic.* Marx reported to Engels that this reintroduction with his old master had yielded some significant developments.[8] The *Grundrisse*

8. Martin Nicolaus, "Foreword," in *Grundrisse: Foundations of the Critique of Political Economy,* by Karl Marx, translated by Martin Nicolaus (London: Allen Lane, 1973), 25–26.

in many respects defines the major outlines of Marx's mature system, and *Capital,* purged of the Hegelian language found in the notebooks, is animated by many of its procedures, expansions, and dialectical oppositions. This revisiting of Hegel in the preparation of his advanced economic thought would have a lasting effect upon the degree to which that thought imitated his earlier philosophical making.

Marx's appropriation of dialectical method, albeit revolutionary and condensed to being grounded solely in economic relations, does mean that his work in *Capital* follows the "Hegelism contour" of metaphysical totality and teleology.[9] As with Hegel, Marx's object of analysis, capitalism, is taken as a social totality in which given components of the whole are dialectically and dynamically related to one another. Marxism is a holistic doctrine that prioritizes the whole over its parts, where the network of relationships within a totality is all that can be attested to. Within a totality a number of dialectical laws operate: the transformation of quantity into quality, the resolution of interpenetrating oppositions, and the negation of negations.[10] In other words, capitalism progresses via its inherent oppositions and crises, negating the proletariat, who in turn will eventually negate capital, while the expanding quantitative of capitalism transforms into the higher qualitative of socialism. These relational laws guarantee the omnipresent unity of economic and social systems, an overarching principle that configures all the motley possibilities of a social order. These types of dialectics give Marx his predictive and prophetic powers, where nothing can affect the model. Thus these laws also give Marxism its teleological form. Marx was convinced that Communism was the "real movement" springing from the loins of capitalism, not some ideal that will have to fashion and "adjust" reality. Such statements can only be maintained with the use of a dialectical thinking that posits a social end toward which history is moving by necessity. While both Feuerbach and Marx criticized Hegel for having the end of his process in mind before that process was adequately traced, Marx also has his historical process work toward its end, and all previous moments

9. Wayne Cristaudo, "Hegel, Marx and the Absolute Infinite," *International Studies in Philosophy* 24, no. 1 (1992): 7.

10. These Hegelian laws were formulated in this manner by Engels in his *Dialectics of Nature,* a work devoted in far greater measure than anything Marx wrote to demonstrate the material rather than logical basis of dialectics.

evaluated in its light. This is the hallmark of teleological thinking, and Marx, like Hegel, is unable to avoid its metaphysical outline because of his methodological implementation of determinist dialectics. In summary, *Capital* is loaded with the use of the dialectical method, a methodology Marx testified to in its preface, but with one important distinction. It is this distinction that enables Marx to deny that he suffers from the abstracting tendencies of Hegel's conservative and mystical logic: "To Hegel, the life-process of the human brain ... is the demiurgos of the real world, and the real world is only the external, phenomenal form of 'the Idea.' With me on the contrary, the ideal is nothing else than the material world reflected by the human mind, and translated into forms of thought."[11]

Marx inverts the Hegelian dialectic by making it a material function rather than a logical one. As we have seen previously, Marx believed that by this Feuerbachian inversion he was able to remove the mystical and metaphysical elements of Hegelian dialectics. Marx deals with how dialectics swerve within the realm of production as an empirical dialectic, rather than within the realm of thought as a logical dialectic. But as we have seen, Marx does have to bear the stigma of confusing an unreal abstraction with a contingent truth. Previously we have also seen how this error of Marx's empirical estimation of Communism is connected with his preoccupation with the future. Marx is unable to crown himself as any type of empiricist or scientist if he talks of the future in such an a priori manner. Capitalism cannot be seen scientifically as the last antagonistic form of society, nor Communism and the abolition of classes as the future set of social relations, nor the proletarians as the carriers of historical necessity, because, as the suppositions are based on the future, there can be no definitive empirical evidence to prove them. As soon as Marx's empirical dialectic of production traipses across the line in the sand of time into the future, it too undergoes a qualitative change, as it returns to being a logical dialectic in the metaphysical domain of thought. We have already seen how this projection into the future by Marx and his youthful Young Hegelians caused this schizophrenic splitting of Hegel's absolute infinite. After having now discussed Marx's commitment to the empiricisms of human labor and production, we are

11. Karl Marx, *Capital* (Moscow: Foreign Languages Publishing House, 1954), 1:19.

able to see the drastic reduction Marx made of Hegel's dialectic, a reduction that made it inevitable that his philosophy would unconsciously sway to the nonempirical to redress the balance.

As well as appropriating the metaphysical features of the absolute infinite, Marx's philosophy is peculiar because it is animated by the cleaved ways of thinking that the absolute infinite was designed to unify. By expunging dialectics of their logical and epistemological foundations, Marx had reduced it to a material process, but in so doing his philosophy balanced itself out with a ballast of immaterial content. By making everything measurable in empirical terms, he surreptitiously allowed immeasurable terms and ideas to symbolize the empirical facts that he found irrational as perverted, and with this move allowed those empirical facts in an economic order to be subverted by the immaterial. In other words, as well as working with the wholes, totalities, and unities of the absolute infinite, Marx also transacts in the splits, oppositions, and chasms of the Phenomena/Noumena dualism. This is no new ground—I have already discussed Marx's joint affiliation with Hegel and Kant in his early years. But this philosophic schizophrenia is integral to the makeup of *Capital*, despite the difficulty in prising apart dialectic from pure dualism. The internal logic of *Capital* is unthinkable without the renowned pairs of *use value/exchange value and labor/labor power*. It is these starting points of *Capital* that I will examine to see whether these terms are fluid dialectical oppositions, or whether they are more hardened dualisms that allow no blending.

It is no coincidence that *Capital* opens with a discussion of the twofold character of commodities. Commodities are at the same time a use value and an exchange value. They take on one life in the process of being used, a life irrelevant to price. They take on another life in the process of being exchanged, a separate life as a transferable, relational entity where price is the governing factor. Marx writes, "While, therefore, with reference to use-value, the labour contained in a commodity counts only qualitatively, with reference to value it counts only quantitatively, and must first be reduced to human labour pure and simple. In the former case, it is a question of How and What, in the latter of How much? How long a time?"[12] Marx hence separates commodities into their substance

---

12. Marx, *Capital*, 1:45.

and their magnitude. Use value describes that which is intrinsic and essential to an object, while exchange value describes that which is relative, extrinsic, and accidental to objects. So while the worth of all commodities is determined by labor, use value refers to the very substance, quality, or essence of labor, while exchange value refers to the mere quantitative amount of labor, or the simple scientifically calculated time of labor. This double existence of commodities, rather than being two dialectically related moments leading to an elevated synthesis, in fact betrays the existence of the irreconcilable realms of the natural and the human in Marx's thought. The production of commodities for their use value is a dignified and purely human activity, whereas production for the purposes of expanding exchange value is an inhuman and indifferent activity. This is the new Marxian variant of the Nature/Freedom dichotomy. Capitalism as an economic system devoted to the exponential and boundless increase of exchange value simply means for Marx that we are subsidiaries to an alien, inhuman rationale that we are unable to incorporate as our own product.

But the variants on the Kantian Nature/Freedom dualism do not end at "use" and "exchange" value in *Capital*. Marx's other great conceptual dualism in his assault upon classical political economy concerns the difference between *labor* and *labor power*. Marx had perceived that with the adoption of the labor theory of value by classical economics, an insoluble contradiction had clogged the continuance of the science. A tautological impasse is reached when one confers all value upon labor and then poses the question of the value of labor itself. With any inquiry into the value of labor, a discrepancy looms between the value of labor and the wages of the worker. Two options open themselves up to this discrepancy. On the one hand, labor can be perceived as not having been paid its full value, as there is no equivalence between the wages of the worker and the output of production; on the other side of the spectrum, it is concluded that labor is not the sole source of value, but only a component of worth that also includes the values bestowed by capital, land, and the like. Marx sees these as the two oppositions in which bourgeois economics have entangled themselves. In true dialectical style, Marx's resolution of the dilemma revolves around splitting the erroneous bourgeois conception of the commodity form in order to grasp a higher plane of comprehension. This process is intimately linked with the *use value/exchange value* doublet, as these concepts are applied to the "commodity" of labor. Traditional economics viewed labor as simply another commodity that services a need, and it is in this characterization that the theory of labor value becomes absurd, for labor cannot be conceived simply as a commodity. Engels, in his introduction to the 1891 edition of *Wage Labour and Capital,* gave the most concise and lucid explanation of the special nature of labor as a commodity under capitalism. "In our present-day capitalist society, labour power is a commodity, a commodity like any other, and yet quite a peculiar commodity. It has, namely, the peculiar property of being a value creating power, a source of value and, indeed, with suitable treatment, a source of more value than it itself possesses."[13]

So Marx makes a distinction between labor and labor/power in order to avoid the difficulties of viewing labor as a simple, inanimate commodity. With this move Marx believes he has explained the internal dynamic of capitalism. Labor power is a pure fount of value, the use/value par excellence, which under capitalist production is treated as an exchange value. Labor is that commodity perceived by capitalists as being an exchangeable entity, where in fact its true nature is as a use/value, more accurately described as *labor power.* How can a science and its society relegate the source of value, labor, to being made of the same stuff that it gives value to?

What the economists had regarded as the cost of production of "labour" was the cost of production not of labour but of the living worker himself. And what this worker sold to the capitalist was not his labour ... he does not sell labour, but puts his labour power at the disposal of the capitalist for a definite time.... But this labor power is intergrown with his person and is inseparable from it.[14]

Again we are able to see the outlines of the human and nonhuman in this distinction. Labor power is no commodity that the laborer can relinquish from himself, as it is his very creative core. What is perceived as the transfer of the detachable commodity of labor for a wage is in fact the residency of an innate power outside in an alien environment. In other words, an autonomous capacity is subjected to a heteronomous world. With this move, labor is no longer worldly, but part of our supersensible

13. Engels, *Karl Marx and Friedrich Engels Collected Works,* vol. 27, *Engels: 1890–95* (London: Lawrence and Wishart, 1990), 200.

14. Engels, *Collected Works,* vol. 27, 198–99.

arsenal against the earth. It is as if all Marx's early humanist musings on labor being "life's prime want" and the very essence of our humanity are contracted and intensified into the concept of labor power. Just because Marx's early idealism is codified into a two-word phrase that then jostles within more "realistic" economic deliberations, this in no way supports Marx's claim that he had done away with the idealistic aspects of his youth. The very fact that *Capital* turns upon this most important concept convinces us of the romantic mission behind that work. Our very humanity is displaced into the heterogenous realm of exchange, and this route guarantees the expansion of this realm over and above us, as our limitless humanity feeds the inhuman. The aim is to return this human limitlessness, this human dignity, or this human autonomy to the people. The drama of freedom and nature is simply played in the theatre of economics.

The Kantian nature of these dualisms is obvious when they are seen as a means of answering the very Kantian question *How are profits possible?*[15] The system of exchange is a system of equivalence. Based on laws of supply and demand, commodities are exchanged in equal quantities. The equal quantities are determined by the amount of socially necessary labor embodied in each commodity. This is a closed circular system, made possible by the conceptual achievement of the labor theory of value, in which there is no remainder leftover. The accumulation of profits is thus the anomaly of this circulation. To explain the existence of profits, one has to resort to some other process occurring beneath the cyclical exchanging of equally valued quantities of commodities. According to Marx, this is the very essence of his "scientific" evaluation of society. Simply looking at the astrology of prices and the fluctuations of supply and demand, distanced from the concept of value, is for Marx to simply observe the surface phenomena glistening upon a mode of production, or to describe the hieroglyphs of reality without translating them.

Marx, however, following the methods of physical science, occupies himself with the necessity of finding the essence behind these appearances, or the laws that determine these surface effects. Marx finds this essence within a separate cycle, the cycle of capital. Unlike the system of exchange, which is a cycle of equivalence, the cycle of capital is a cycle of

15. N. Scott Arnold has also noted the "Kantian" nature of this question in his book *Marx's Radical Critique of Capitalist Society* (New York: Oxford University Press, 1990), 68.

accumulation. Each cycle of capital produces some new capital, which is then introduced to the next cycle. This is an expanding system that has somehow come upon a limitless entity that can be mined. We already know this entity to be the metaphysically loaded idea of ... "labor power." We also know that this cycle mines labor power by treating it as an exchange value rather than as the use value that it naturally is. And so Marx's two dualisms coincide to explain the phenomena of profit and accumulation. This forced excavating cycle of accumulation is the true operation of capitalist society, where the equalized and free cycle of exchange is the appearance that masks its true operation. This is not simply an economic interpretation of reality, but a pointed interpretation of the political/ideological mystification common to the bourgeois epoch.

It must be acknowledged that our labourer comes out of the process of production other than he entered. In the market he stood as owner of the commodity "labour-power" face to face with other owners of commodities, dealer against dealer ... (disposing) of himself freely. The bargain concluded, it is discovered that he was no "free agent," that the time for which he is free to sell his labour-power is the time for which he is forced to sell it, that in fact the vampire will not lose its hold on him "so long as there is a muscle, a nerve, a drop of blood to be exploited."[16]

It is in the best interests of the capitalist class to present the economic system as a trading of equal values, where all things are allowed free movement within the system. If this is presented as the nature of commodities, then that wrongfully christened commodity "labor" is also made to feel that it exists as equal and free within the system. Labour's true nature as the benchmark of value is masked from it by the false incentives of its freedom and equality within the economic realm. Labor is free to sell its power on the market to the highest bidder, and in this exchange it is seemingly on equal footing to the purchaser of said labor. The bourgeois political ideals of equality and freedom are from this perspective seen as ideological halos that hover above this economic appearance, politically servicing the illusion of free and equal economic rights. It is with this interpretation that Marx most closely mimics the religious criticism of his youthful influences and cohorts, which he redirected politically in his *On the Jewish Question*. The political ideals of the

16. Marx, *Capital,* 1:301–2.

bourgeois era are nothing more than a heavenly emanation of an under-lying economic confidence trick. He writes, "In order, therefore, to find an analogy, we must have recourse to the mist-enveloped regions of the religious world. In that world the productions of the human brain ap-pear as independent beings endowed with life, and entering into relation both with one another and the human race."[17] Marx clothes not only the political superstructure of the bourgeois in sarcastic religious anal-ogy, but also the world of commodities. Religious motifs enable Marx to characterize money and exchange as the modern divinities, while also indulging his fondness for cataloguing the vicious cycles of capitalism.

In the second part of *Capital,* Marx introduces into the discussion of commodities two cycles that describe clearly the perverse preoccu-pation of capitalized humankind: "The circuit C-M-C starts with one commodity, and finishes with another, which falls out of circulation and into consumption. Consumption, the satisfaction of wants, in one word, use-value, is its end and aim. The circuit of M-C-M, on the contrary, commences with money and ends with money. It leading motive, and the goal that attracts it, is therefore mere exchange-value."[18] Capitalism is not concerned with the commodity cycle that services our needs, but instead with its inversion, an inverted cycle that thus projects its energy away from our needs and wants. The first cycle, corresponding to "uses," is not a self-reflexive, aimless, and everlasting cycle, for each revolution ends by satisfying some human urge. This is a system of appropriation of usefulness and as such not strictly circulatory, for each revolution is "cut," so to speak, by the human, and redirected by our freedom and will. The second cycle corresponding to "exchange" is precisely a self-reflexive, aimless, and everlasting venture, for rather than a system of human appropriation it is a system of monetary expansion for its own sake. M-C-M is the formulation for the astronomical movement of in-dustrial capital, circulations of "buying in order to sell dearer," which make money and exchange the deities of the order, which then replace truly human relationships.[19]

This discussion of the idol of exchange turns Marx to what was recognized by many as his single greatest achievement in examining modern economics and class relations, the idea of a "surplus," often

17. Marx, *Capital,* 1:72.   18. Marx, *Capital,* 1:149.
19. Marx, *Capital,* 1:155.

understood in the variegated terms of surplus value, surplus labor, and surplus time. He writes, "It is, however, clear that in any given economic formation of society, where not the exchange-value but the use-value of the product predominates, surplus-labour will be limited by a given set of wants which may be greater or less, and that here no boundless thirst for surplus-labour arises from the nature of the production itself."[20] This is obviously not the case with the exchange-obsessed capitalist order, and thus to fully understand the swindle of capital one has to delve into the ambit of "surplus." Quite simply, surplus value is the difference between the value of the commodities produced by labor and the cost of keeping labor power sustained. More simply still, it is the difference between the price of commodities and the price of wages. To explain this discrepancy, time, labor, and value are split into two distinct domains, the necessary and the surplus. Necessary time, labor, and value are simply those parts of the working day that produce the value of commodities. The second domain of time, labor, and value produces profits.

During the second period of the labour-process, that in which his labour is no longer necessary labour, the workman … expends labour-power; but his labour being no longer necessary labour, he creates no value for himself. He creates surplus-value which, for the capitalist, has all the charms of a creation out of nothing.… It is every bit as important, for a correct understanding of surplus-value, to conceive it as a mere congelation of surplus labour-time, as nothing but materialised surplus-labour.[21]

It is this surplus that the vampires of capitalism feed upon, the prize for which the whole of capitalist machinery is arranged and set to work. The concept of surplus value is the true heart of *Capital,* the core upon which the drama of exploiters and exploited battle. As well as being the heart of capitalism, the inequalities implied by surplus value are also the roads of capitalistic unraveling that Marx follows for the rest of his masterwork. The first half of *Capital* ends thus: The Marxian connection between the dignified circuit of use value, the humanity of labor power, and the fullness of that humanity implied by surplus value, meet the capitalistic alien circuit of exchange, the commodification of labor power into mere "labor," and the vampiric appropriation of humanity's

20. Marx, *Capital,* 1:235.
21. Marx, *Capital,* 1:217.

innate "surplus." The rest of *Capital* flows from the gaping mouth of this dualistic interpretation of the world, the hateful fraying twins of the autonomous and the heterogenous realms.

It is from these conceptual foundations that Marx begins to plot the downfall of capitalism. Among the major reasons Marx posits for the unraveling of the circuit of capital, the lowering of wages to a level of relative subsistence, labor displacement by machinery and other technology, the reality of deepening economic crises endemic to the system, the eventual lowering of the rate of profit, the absorption of all fractured middle classes into the proletariat, and the emergence of an industrial reserve army all figure prominently. The general form of Marx's argument runs thus: independent producers succumb to the almighty forces of the means of production being concentrated in a few hands, thereby being absorbed by a growing proletariat. This polarizes class conflict and contributes to the emergence of class consciousness. This movement also hastens the equalization of wages to a relative subsistence level and thus impoverishes vast swathes of workers. An industrial reserve army of unemployed workers to service the market is also seen by Marx as a corollary (Marx even calls it the "absolute general law") of capitalist accumulation and the reality of crises. The siphoning of wealth from labor power (capitalist accumulation) has as its antithesis the formation of "Lazarus layers" of "pauperism."[22] This official and necessary unemployment creates competition among workers, which also contributes to the depression of workers' wages, sustaining profits. The introduction of machinery to make the labor process more efficient and increase production has a depressing effect upon the rate of profit. As labor power is the only true source of expanding value, diminishing labor time through technology lowers the rate of profit (based upon the dubious variable/constant capital division), adding to the restless uncertainty of capital. Capital thus digs its own grave in the attempt to alleviate its own tensions, and, while excavating its imposing mortality, awakens the outraged consciousness of the "Lazarus layers" of society. Impending crisis and the establishment of a future hegemony is inborn to capitalism. This, in very broad strokes, is the way Marx envisaged the circuit of capital unraveling.

This prophecy is very contentious, with many points, tendencies, and

22. Marx, *Capital*, 1:644.

appraisals proven to be false with time. Reality has not been the friend to Marxist prophecy, a fact in itself that demonstrates the timeless dimensions of Marx's thought. However, I am not concerned with retracing the historical downfall of Marxist thought and its implausible economic predictions and reconstructing the debates of Marxism's receptivity with reality. It has always been maintained that timelessness animated Marx's thought from its inception, and as such it was always going to clash with the world. Rather than demonstrating Marxism's timeless course outwardly by looking at its destructive path through time, I seek to isolate the embedded timelessness from its source in the theoretical.

I have surveyed the trajectory that Marx felt capitalism would take in its unraveling into Communism. While events have shown that this perceived trajectory was deeply flawed, capitalism's supposed demise is problematic in the first instance when one examines Marx's vision of Communism. If capitalism is characterized by the conflicted nature of labor (humanity), what becomes of our labor under Communism? One would presume that Marx was in no doubt as to the unified, free, and unalienated nature of human labor. From the outset of his career it was this idealized vision of human endeavor that sustained the lifelong critique of estranged labor.

For as soon as the division of labour comes into being, each man has a particular, exclusive sphere of activity, which is forced upon him and from which he cannot escape. He is a hunter, a fisherman, a shepherd, or a critical critic, and must remain so if he does not want to lose his means of livelihood; whereas in communist society, where nobody has one exclusive sphere of activity but each can become accomplished in any branch he wishes, society regulates the general production and thus makes it possible for me to do one thing today and another tomorrow, to hunt in the morning, fish in the afternoon, rear cattle in the evening, criticise after dinner, just as I have a mind, without ever becoming hunter, fisherman, shepherd or critic.[23]

In some respects this is one of the most idyllic, fanciful, and laughable passages you will find in Marx, but in another more important sense Marx has here underlined the difficulties he faced when confronted with Communism. No amount of denying that he wrote "recipes for the cookshops of the future" can remove these unresolved difficulties

23. Marx and Engels, *The German Ideology* (Moscow: Progress, 1976), 53.

from his responsibility. And coming full circle, having in the beginning viewed capitalism as the commodification of time, the problem of Communism also revolves around the role of time in the production of society and individuals. What is telling from the above passage is the difficulty in reconciling the idea of the emancipated socialized human type with the concept of free time. Is the expansion of a society's free leisure time commensurate with the idea of an elevated and unalienated human? Is Communism a realm of free and nurturing labor or freedom from the necessity of labor; the humanization of work or the broadening of leisure time? Hannah Arendt observed the "mechanistic illusion" that generates these questions:

> The hope that inspired Marx and the best men of the various workers' movements—that free time eventually will emancipate men from necessity and make the "animal laborans" productive—rests on the illusion of a mechanistic philosophy which assumes that labour power, like any other energy, can never be lost, so that if it is not spent and exhausted in the drudgery of life it will automatically nourish other, "higher," activities.[24]

What Marx perceives to be one of the major historical missions of capitalism, the enlarged formation of fixed or constant capital, throws this problem of human time into sharp relief. As fixed capital develops in more complex and superior arrangements, this isolates variable capital (labor) further and further from the activity of production. This gradual productive independence from burdened laboring for the world's subsistence, presents itself as the promise of Communism. The stored time of humanity is released back to the world as a technological apparatus to save us from the "drudgery" of maintaining our physical and socially conditioned wants. This delivers us from our naturally and socially imposed necessity into a position of "free time." Two options present themselves to Marx at this point. Free time can appear as that "modest Magna Carta" of limited working hours or the relative freedom from necessary labor. Marx can leave the project at this stage and be consistent. But this seems like unfinished business, as there is an overwhelming temptation to transform this moderate achievement of time into a feat of timelessness. This "modest" quantitative of time transforms qualitatively into a new realm of free labor, adding value not to commodities, but to each

24. Hannah Arendt, *The Human Condition* (Chicago: University of Chicago Press, 1969), 133.

human individual. One option attempts to release mankind from labor that is unbecoming to truly human existence; the other still lionizes labor as our dignifying and valued activity, which will enrich us unlimitedly. These two options are indistinct enough to resemble each other to the degree that Marx never fully accounted for their differences. There is no reason the realm of free time cannot be the time that humans will use to disalienate and develop themselves to establish a post-history unconnected to the past. But, on the other hand, there is no concrete reason proposed for why the expansion of free time signals the demise of capitalism, or that free time will be used for the higher purposes of man. At best the emergence of free time in Marx's story of history is little more than a precarious and partial victory that murmurs grander possibilities, and at worst it is a depleted betrayal of the promise of socialized mankind and the humanization of labor. Marx seems to perceive the troubled notion that free time represents for Communism, and as such leaves the issue hanging, an issue that would perturb later Marxist theorists. Ernst Mandel grappled with the "Dialectics of Labour Time and Free Time":

The transformation of the quantitative ratio between work and leisure (say from 1:1 to 1:2 or 1:3, which implies a week of 32 or 24 hours, or more precisely, half a day's work instead of a full day's) will give rise to a qualitative revolution, on the condition that it be integrated into a process of progressive disalienation of labour, consumption, and man himself, through the progressive withering away of commodity production, classes, the state and the social division of labour.[25]

In this passage two processes are discussed with the assumption that these must be conjoined courses, but with the knowledge that one does not guarantee the passage of the other and vice versa. The innocuous phrase "on the condition that" mediates two differing visions of history. The Marxian thought process does not allow the total blending of these two ideas of future. If we examine this irresolute end point of the system in the light of Marx's previous historical imagination, it becomes more fruitful to wholly separate these two options of the future. It seems more likely that Marx's "futures" are mismatched, and that this problematic of future human time is actually carrying on the drama of dualistic human

25. Ernst Mandel, *The Formation of Economic Thought of Karl Marx* (London: Unwin Brothers, 1971), 113.

existence. Marx and his followers downplay the differences and even try to smooth over the fractured nature of their solution, because, if allowed to fester, this "Communism" will eventually dissolve into past antagonisms and reignite the history they wished to arrest. The incompatibility of free time and dealienated humankind is directly a result of the incompatibility of Marx's forward and backward histories, those warring temporalities that make up the mode of production. Free time is the future seen from the perspective of historically grounded and progressing productive forces, while the absolute dictate of dealienated humanity is a future that can only be seen from the more timeless and will-based history of our social relations. Marx simply cannot fuse these two contrary views of history and time, and, by dint of this fact, his overwhelming vision of future human relations, the total transcendence of human self-alienation, appears as being born from the timeless side of his dualistic worldview. This therefore suggests that Marx's dialecticism in *Capital* is a costume to persuade the synthesis of his warring histories. Thus, as Communism can be shown theoretically not to be the synthesis of capitalism's tensions, Marx's philosophy becomes a totally dualist philosophy (although superficially deviating dialectically). In this light, Communism cannot be viewed as the necessary historical and dialectical unraveling of the circuit of capital, but instead as the future imposition of a post-history sustained by the powerful timelessness of the human will. Yet Marx's genius lies in the strange sympathetic knowledge he has for the plight of the modern worker. He seems to sense the temporal disruption of modern production and the deep need to find a new future for the mechanized *Unmensch*.

The modern variety of time which we call working time is explored territory. It is anticipated time, the time necessary for production, reckoned backwards from a certain fixed point in the future. He who is caught in its schedule belongs to a framework of thought which was arranged in the past. The framework of an industrialised world leaves the cog in the machine in the precincts or antechamber of real life, in a pre-arranged world without future. The question arises: where is he going to find his future?[26]

This was largely the general scope of Marx's project: the search for the future of a humankind that had been radically altered by its power-

26. Rosenstock-Huessy, *The Multiformity of Man* (Norwich, Vt.: Argo, 1973), 21–22.

ful productive forces and debilitating productive arrangements. Unfortunately for Marx, the idealism, utopianism, and timelessness that trail his philosophy from beginning to end serve to derail the historical reality of his prophecies, not to mention the very theoretical instability of the future he envisaged. Robert C. Tucker observes the ultimate goal: "To Marx communism did not mean a new economic system. It meant the end of economics in a society where man, liberated from labour, would realize his creative nature in a life of leisure."[27] But if we have estranged ourselves in all the productive endeavors of our previous history, is a "life of leisure" going to suffice as the savior of our future labor, the transcendence of alienation? It is this volatile and ambivalent conception of leisure/labor that suggests that Communism is not the historically necessary answer to the vital social question Marx had asked himself all his life.

Conclusion: Circularity of a Revolving Sun/Man

Marx's main problem revolves around the currency that he gives labor. Rather than under Kant and Hegel, where reason and thought were the peculiarly human attributes, for Marx labor provided the human with its uniqueness. Labor creates man rather than reason. This is all part and parcel of Marx's major mission of reformulating the hieroglyphs of ideality into a material interpretation. Idealizing labor was the preeminent and most human avenue for this agenda. And yet the only blueprint, the only theoretical configuration of the "human" at Marx's disposal, was the human reflected in reason and thought. Thus Marx sculpts the laboring animal in the light of the thinking human. As Hannah Arendt notes, the "glorification of labour as the source of all values" is accompanied by the "elevation of the *animal laborans* to the position traditionally held by the *animal rationale*."[28] With this shift the two tend to merge. The ideational constructs that sustain human thought, that nourish its endeavors and give it its mental framework and boundaries, are by necessity of this labor shift implanted into reality by Marx. Communism, or the community of homogenous interests, or the reinstallation of unalienated humanity, is a necessary, timeless, mental

27. Robert C. Tucker, *The Marxian Revolutionary Idea* (London: Allen and Unwin, 1970), 217.
28. Arendt, *The Human Condition*, 85.

figment that gives our thought on the political, social, and economic its breadth and depth. Like a Kantian regulatory idea, it is a bordering presence of thought without demanding a concrete reality. However, Marx's move to labor instead of reason attempts to make this timeless regulatory idea burst into the scene of the real and the temporal. Karl Marx did not introduce the Communistic idea, as this is the idealistic firmament and foundation of all modern economic and political thought. Marx simply took this hypothetical gravitational of thought as a gravitational of reality. Marx's philosophy gains its bearings from the timeless, and Promethean-like, it storms the gates of time. That economists have run roughshod over the labor theory of value has helped us see the economic errors to which Marx's thought is prone. It shows us that the placement of labor as all-encompassing value is nothing more than the philosophical move of making our labor our humanity in order to have our timeless thought seep through our temporal world of action. This is a philosophically awesome move that unfortunately crashes headfirst in its contact with reality, as the development of economics has shown.

The truly timeless core of Marx's thought is found in the concept of alienation. If one constant can be said of his life's work, it is his insistence on the alienated status of man throughout history. Behind this insistence is the timeless-tinged hope that man would one day "revolve about himself as his own true sun."[29] Alienation as one of the major thrusts of Marxism wasn't fully appreciated by his followers and detractors until the emergence of his early works, such as the "Economic and Philosophic Manuscripts." For his detractors, this discovery convinced them of the obvious, yet concealed moral purpose of his project. They duly charged him with hypocritical inconsistency, much to the ire of his followers, who subsequently scrambled to safeguard the realist and determinist dimensions of his work. Others saw no real contradiction between the idealist and realist positions of Marx and gladly mediated between them. Still other Marxists embraced alienation and its attendant critique of society wholeheartedly as the true legacy of Marxism and served to reorient the tradition. This complex story has largely been the battleground upon which Marx's name has been pitched and flown

---

29. Marx, quoted in John Plamenatz, *Karl Marx's Philosophy of Man* (Oxford: Clarendon Press, 1975), 322.

throughout the twentieth century, thus obscuring from scholarship proper discussion on the scopes and meanings of alienation. Its centrality to the radical imagination is undeniable; yet as a process seen by that imagination as so pervasive to society, it becomes so morally loaded that it is rendered unintelligible. The question of why individuals in a society allow themselves so unconsciously to estrange or alienate themselves is rarely, if ever, discussed.

Alienation and estrangement are phenomena whose only field of incidence is within the world of institutions, or even more emphatically within the manmade world itself. The artifice of political, religious, economic, and social forms, an arena of wholly human genesis, is the first and only condition by which alienation and estrangement can rear their heads. Their existence is predicated on and determined by this realm. And yet alienation is seldom viewed as an inherent or inevitable human phenomenon, but is almost exclusively seen as an inexplicable, unneeded, imposed, and unwanted aberration emanating from the institutional landscape. Our estrangement within our institutions is viewed suspiciously as the very work of those institutions. It is as if, in our covetousness, we demand back from our societies the energy, sacrifice, genius, and spirit expended by us in their making. Never is alienation seen as the accompanying feeling of personal loss when one of our lasting creations begins the work we designed for it, work initially planned to unburden and free ourselves. Nor is it seen as the confused pangs of forgetfulness when confronted with the institutionalized work of the past, no longer understanding the kinship with the past spirit that brought our present state to bear. It is always viewed not from within us, but from outside us, as a force working upon the individual by the world we created and that we unknowingly maintain. Alienation is to be rectified by the correction, adjustment, and even wholesale destruction of our guilty institutions, rather than via the correct consciousness of our own strange place in the world we constantly craft. Alienation is viewed as a foreign, inhuman experience, rather than the confirmation of our anxious and difficult humanity. How is this one-sided understanding of alienation sustained?

If the world of institutions is the only environment where alienation can reside and survive, it is sustained in the opposite direction by a highly idealized conception of man. If the uneasiness with institutional reality represents the social dimensions of alienation, the idealized human is the psychological source and origin of alienation. A human being of incalculable power, capacity, and largesse is the foundation upon which the perceived process of alienation embarks out into the manmade world. Essentially, the true nature of man's inner life is reflected in the richness of the outside world. It is believed that the imposing strength and variety of the institutional architecture of reality are simply signs of the betrayed strength and variety of the human subject. Alienation's arena is the structures induced by human association, yet its peculiar sense of indignation toward the surroundings of that association is based solely upon the abstract ideal human of which it has such a high opinion. This human is a being of superhuman will, capacity, and potential, a product of an imagination that must ignore questions of action and deed. This timeless human archetype must of necessity be thus colorless and abstract, for the experience of alienation is not capable of facing the issue of the potential deeds of this human. To animate this human with action and deed already presupposes the fact that whatever his productions, they will inevitably be alienated away from him. According to the strictures of alienation, this human must be of himself and for himself; he must revolve around himself "as his own true sun," for if anything else were to exist beside him, it would be a source of estrangement. Alienation must sustain itself by inflating the philosophically timeless concept of man, while also neutering his activity in the world and time. There is only one way to animate this unalienated powerhouse of potential: by housing him in an environ that takes nothing away from him, by providing him with surroundings that can in no way diminish the plenitude of his being. This is the perennial connection between the negative interpretation of alienation and Communism.

What else is Communism but the denunciation of the world in the hope of guaranteeing an undivided mankind? Communism is that nebulous social state that promises to individuals the empty space needed for filling with their limitless activity and creation. A classless state, devoid of money, commodity production, religion, legal and political apparatus, social and economic institutions, and professional and personal associations, is the wasted bare, social landscape left after the wave of the sovereign human will recedes back into the individual. Communism is the barren background of the metaphysically adorned man.

What the negative sense of alienation steadfastly ignores is the natural osmosis between human capacities and the world. A man endowed with the power, imagination, and freedom to give reality to his creative constructs, to solve the problems he sets himself, and to improve himself seemingly unlimitedly, cannot remain in this state of being both a man and sun to himself. There is a powerful urge to go out into the world and produce. What makes Marx such a conflicted thinker is his Promethean understanding of this human drive and the shackling of this drive by the timelessness inherent to the concept of alienation. Alienation in the first instance begins by empowering the human intimidated by the pressures of the outside world, but ends by preserving this human in a social vacuum of institutionless reality.

A positive understanding of alienation, however, does not suffer from this either/or ultimatum with regard to the internal individual and the outside world, but preserves the osmotic relationship between the two. When one views alienation as an external force, one is forced into the cul-de-sacs of the eternal individual and the transitory and fallen institutional world. This is what Marx does through the labor shift; he makes alienation a material force requiring a material solution. The positive sense of alienation, on the other hand, views it not as a material force, but a mental experience requiring a shift in consciousness for its rectification. What we create does not rear up to enslave us, but the very act of creation has an accompanying inner experience of alienation. It is this understanding of alienation that was important to Hegel's project, where the created world had to be reconciled with its author in thought. To repeat Karl Lowith's observation,

But such an alienation between subject and object cannot seek to remain as it is, according to Hegel. By its very nature it is an alienation between what was originally one and seeks to become one again. Man must be able to act as a native in what is other and strange, in order not to be a stranger to himself in the otherness of the world outside.[30]

This does not sanctify the legitimacy of the outside world wholesale, or even dismiss the need for institutional change. What it does provide is a psychological foundation for balancing the rights of the sovereign

30. Karl Lowith, *From Hegel to Nietzsche,* translated by David E. Green (London: Constable, 1965), 172.

individual with the control and conscious mastery of the house that humans are constantly furnishing. This avenue reintegrates man and the world, without resorting to the extremes of postulating the world as an unlivable prison and without postulating a timeless human being that could not possibly exist in concord with the world. In essence, alienation properly understood does not sentence us to a life of circularity, revolving mindlessly around ourselves as our "own true sun." For humankind's lot is to have our alienated societies revolve precariously around us, while we constantly keep their orbits in check.

PART 3

Michel Foucault

9

The Timeless Will Attacks Itself

Kant's timeless will, the foundation of all modern emancipatory political projects, was such a powerfully endowed conception of human thought and judgment that it was inevitable that that activity would seek itself out and subject itself to the treatment that it inflicts upon the world. Critique allows nothing to remain solid and unquestioned, as it is obedient to nothing but itself. When such activity solidifies its initially variable and flexible nature into a rigid constellation of thought over the course of time, it is inevitable that its original impulse will rise above its institutionalized pretense and question its capabilities for radical critical thought. Much of Michel Foucault's thought represents this self-reflexivity of the critical tradition. In Foucault's entry in the *Dictionnaire des philosophes,* signed pseudonymously by *Maurice Florence,* but almost certainly written by Foucault himself, the opening sentence clearly states his allegiance to the critical project: "To the extent that Foucault fits into the philosophical tradition, it is the critical tradition of Kant, and his project could be called a Critical History of Thought."[1]

This sentence sums up the contradiction at the center of Foucault's enterprise: a critical project that will eventually survey the

1. Michel Foucault, *Foucault: Aesthetics, Method, and Epistemology,* edited by James D. Faubion (New York: New Press, 1998), 459.

thought that nourishes it—modern thought devouring its tail. Within the twentieth century this particular curve of thought is not isolated to Foucault, as one could easily find more radical proponents of this school. Yet Foucault does represent one of the more popularly received variants of this modern tendency, and more importantly he is the one theorist who met with a definite reckoning of this impasse and who began to dialogue with himself on this subject in his later work.

This suspicion with the endless litany of truth claims and ethical values that are perceived as being constitutive of the "Enlightenment" by Foucault and others in the postmodern enterprise is represented quite differently within the angle adopted by this study. What has traditionally been seen as the skepticism of reason, an exhaustion of metanarratives, the death of "Man," or the decentered subject, can alternatively be understood as indicators or symptoms of this project's forced closure of two directions of time. The past and the future dimensions of critical thought are negated so as to affirm the limited and nominal, yet historically unpolluted dimensions of the present. This idea needs justification and explication.

What is undeniable is Foucault's affiliation with the critical spirit, a modern incantation that flourishes only in the wake of Kant's thought. What is in question is only the aspect of time that Foucault invokes within this slipstream. Many have affirmed that Kant represents a rupture within the philosophical tradition, and yet the Rousseauean inspiration for this epistemic break is also its one anchor of continuity with the past. Rousseau imbibes the past (of nature and antiquity) as his stimulus for the future. As his example of the free will was bequeathed to Kant, his philosophy represents the nostalgic pangs of loss within Kant's commanding conception of the timeless morality. In many ways it creates a bond for Kant's timelessness with the virtues of the past, or more accurately, favors the illusions of the past reflecting upon the surface of timelessness's abstract expanse. The social contract is like an intellectual/political structural antenna for the reception of an imagined past. With the timeless will and a universal morality as its sponsors, the social contract is a future mechanism for the faint reminding of a previous innocence, a memorial of past dignity for heartening moral use in the future.

On the other side of the spectrum is Marx's philosophy. In the same vein as Rousseau, his philosophy is a particular type of historical imagining upon the endless ocean of timelessness. In Marx's case, timelessness is projected into the future. Rather than bearing the marks of reminiscence, melancholy, defeated nostalgia, and future artificial communion with the past, Marx's future represents the hopeful, cataclysmic promise of new historical life, an as yet unfulfilled future pledged to history by Kantian morality's timeless break with history. Marx views philosophy as having closed the doors of the past behind him, giving him only one directive ... the future. Rousseau's yearning preoccupation with the past saw him create a theoretical future state similar to Communism. Correspondingly, Marx's rampant fury for the future made his stark vision of Communism (a vision of progressive denunciation, simplification, and depletion of society's institutional complexity) appear very much in accord with Rousseau's depleted and unadorned state of nature. Marx is the vague and distant, yet boisterous horizon of timelessness, whereas Rousseau is the guilt-ridden reflections of history's once chaste precedents. Both thinkers allowed timelessness to spill from its lofty heights, directing it in a privileged temporal direction. Let us imagine Kant's ethical mountain with two rivers cascading down its sides. One river flowed both literally and imaginatively to the past, whereas the other flowed to the future. As such, there was bound to be an inevitable and unintended temporal backflow when dealing with thoughts descending from this height. This is certainly part of the reason these two thinkers so closely resemble each other, as their imaginings of past and future are capable of becoming secondary waves of each other. Foucault seems to vaguely recognize the kinship of these waves: "writing was caught in a fundamental curve which was that of the Homeric return, but which was at the same time that of the fulfilment of the Jewish prophet."[2] Less cryptically in *The Archaeology of Knowledge,* he explicitly attributes these twin directions as descending from Kant's transcendentalism. He describes this state of affairs as "a crisis that concerns that transcendental reflexion with which philosophy since Kant has identified itself; which concerns the theme of the origin, that promise of the return, by which we avoid the difference of the present."[3]

Foucault is rehearsing the anxious historical vertigo felt by his pro-

2. Foucault, "The Language of Space," in *Geography, History and the Social Sciences,* edited by Georges B. Benko and Ulf Strohmayer (Dordrecht and Boston: Kluwer, 1995), 51.

3. Foucault, *The Archaeology of Knowledge* (New York: Pantheon, 1972), 204.

to-pagan predecessor, Albert Camus, who recognized that the modern rebellious mind had exhausted and outlived the apocalyptic future and the arcane past. Camus knew that "in a universe suddenly divested of illusions and lights, man feels an alien, a stranger. His exile is without remedy since he is deprived of the memory of a lost home or the hope of promised land."[4] In a way this is the starting point for Foucault's exploration of the possibilities of the present. Foucault deals in a very different fashion with the historical powers of the critical tradition. With historical hindsight, he knows the weakness of critical thought for mammoth temporal projection. This predilection he interprets in two ways: a burning desire for universalization and, as a necessary corollary to that urge, a need to anchor such outlandish temporal adventures with stiff, arbitrary, and needless conceptions that hinder the continuation of the pure act of criticism. What is seen as Foucault's controversial "death of man" thesis is nothing more than his attempt to dissolve these unnecessary epistemic "bricks." In an operation similar to Marx's attack on the eternal laws of classical economics, Foucault assaults these historically stagnant conceptions, these "scientific" strongholds, by describing them with the aptly contradictory "historical apriori." Evolution, teleology, and progress are dissipated and compartmentalized within a process of historical dislocation. For Foucault, historical dislocation, or discontinuity, is the remnant of possibility for critical thought that has as its unblinking focus the pure present, the sterilized contemporary. This seems odd for a thinker whose resume clearly labels him a historian.

Undoubtedly Foucault was a temporal thinker like Marx, and certainly he was a historian, even if at odds with historians of a more traditional composure. Yet what sets him apart from a temporality that embraces the differing dimensions of time and from the historian's eye for the past is his avowal that he was conducting a "history of the present," or an "ontology of the present," or even further "mapping the present." The extreme limitation that Foucault foisted upon the surface of history is the necessary operation of this concern for the present. It is the aim of this chapter to demonstrate how this singularity is the temporal thread of Foucault's various "periods," archaeological, genealogical, and problematical, and how this singularity is channeled throughout the project

4. Albert Camus, *The Myth of Sisyphus* (London: Penguin, 1975), 13.

within the critical spirit. As opposed to timelessness as Foucault was, ironically his critical labor is devoted to safeguarding the timelessness of societal criticism by imprisoning it in the historical singularity of the present. Only by limiting the grander historical breadths of timeless forays into the past and future with an unflinching philosophical appreciation of the transitory can Foucault resharpen the timeless critical saber and its delicate operative incisions of the present. The atemporality of the politico-moral act is thus rejuvenated by the very criticism of the static theoretical products of that atemporality.

ᘐ 10

Archaeology

History as Autistic Savant: Foucault's Restructure of Kant's Critical Philosophy

By way of introduction, it is helpful to observe the grander historical elements of Foucault's early archaeological project before delving into its more nuanced architecture. This will provide a framework for a later discussion of the inner workings of Foucauldian history. If we accept that Foucault's is no less a project of freedom and critique than Kant's, then, by comparing their differing positioning of the major themes of epistemology and morality, we are able very quickly to discern Foucault's early understanding of history. What is beyond doubt is that knowledge and freedom are the major concerns of these thinkers. Foucault chose to concentrate his epistemological labors on those unstable human sciences of life, labor, language, medicine, and madness, where Kant gave pride of place to the "noble and rigorous" sciences of mathematics and physics.

The other disciplines, however—those, for example, that concern living beings, languages, or economic facts—are considered too tinged with empirical thought, too exposed to the vagaries of chance and imagery ... for it to be supposed that their history could be anything other than irregular.... But what if empirical knowledge, at a given time and in a given culture, did possess a well-defined regularity?[1]

1. Michel Foucault, *The Order of Things* (London: Tavistock and Routledge, 1989), ix.

Thus, while the domains are worlds apart, the kindred fascination with the limits and illegitimate extensions of knowledge are at the heart of both Kant and Foucault. Faced with the stunning continuity, progress, and seeming necessity of the mathematical sciences, Kant felt compelled to ground that body of objective knowledge in the human subject and map its use of pure reason. Faced with the vagaries and irregularities of the human sciences, Foucault felt himself compelled to categorize and regulate these seemingly subjective and intuitive scientific distensions far away from the human subjects that formulated them, in anonymous bodies of hovering discourse. Certainly they are differing outlooks, yet they share a common desire to expose the limits of knowledge. Their understandings of the rightful places and operations of knowledge and the purpose of its limits is, however, up for discussion. With regard to freedom, a word from John Rajchman sheds light on Foucault's investment in its modern project: "Foucault's freedom is not liberation, a process with an end. It is not liberty, a possession of each individual person. It is the motor and principle of his scepticism: the endless questioning of constituted experience."[2] When understood this way, Foucault seems to be closest to the immediate spirit of Kantian critique. He does not view it as a possession we have always owned and must guard or regain, nor does he view it as a process with a definable end in the future. Instead, it is an engine of the present, the freedom of questioning limited simply to its initial impulse and scorning any outlandish prescription based upon it. If as a result of Hume's skepticism Kant is seen to have become skeptical of unjustifiable metaphysical claims, the constant questioning of Kantian critique can be seen to be the source of a Foucauldian idea of freedom, boiled down to a skepticism of moral claims. Foucault transfers the skepticism of knowledge into the moral world.

A clue to untangling Foucault's redirection of Kantian themes is supplied by Gilles Deleuze's discussion of the "poetical" dimensions of the Kantian legacy. In the preface to *Kant's Critical Philosophy: The Doctrine of the Faculties,* Deleuze presupposes four poetic formulae that explain the Kantian inversion of our understanding of the world. Of those four, two concern us here. The first inversion is between time and movement, as encapsulated by the Shakespearean "Time is out of joint." The sec-

2. John Rajchman, *Foucault: The Freedom of Philosophy* (New York: Columbia University Press, 1985), 7.

ond, an inversion between the good and the law, is encapsulated by the Kafkaesque "The Good is what the Law says." I will now explore these inversions.

The unending growth, decay, emergence, and passing of the empirical world have traditionally been the precedents for an understanding of the temporal. The existence of time is only revealed to the world via the world's movement. Movement precedes time; time is dependent on change. Kant reverses this age-old truism with the transcendental ideality of time. Time resolves in our inner sense or internal state and is in no way supplied by outward appearances. It is an empty form awaiting fulfillment. He writes, "Here I shall add that the concept of change, and with it the concept of motion, as change of place, is possible only through and in the representation of time."[3] And again, "Time passes not, but in it passes the existence of the changeable."[4] By this move Kant shifts time from being distinguished by change, fleetingness, transition, and movement to being unchangeable and permanent. It becomes a pure unadulterated inner form, which makes possible our comprehension of the adulteration of outer empirical forms. Such a reversal is also seen in the relation between the good and the law.

Traditionally the assumption is made that the law mimics the good, or is a secondary and worldly emanation upon the good. Law is primarily understood as a codification, or an agent. Viewed as a partial and derivative securing of the demanding, intangible purity of goodness, the law is thus an adulterated form. Kant, however, reverses this view. In his view, law is that utmost of purities, the universal entity, the empty form. It is law that directs the good, its emptiness provoking its advocates to enact it or act it out with all manner of secondhand "goods." Law is primary, while goodness corresponding to the law is secondary. But most importantly, the reversal is in every respect analogous to the time/movement reversal.

The law does not tell us which object the will must pursue in order to be good, but the form which it must take in order to be moral. The law as empty form in the *Critique of Practical Reason* corresponds to time as the pure form in *The*

3. Immanuel Kant, *The Critique of Pure Reason,* translated by J. M. D. Meiklejohn (London: Dent, 1986), 48–49.

4. Kant, *Critique of Pure Reason,* 120.

Critique of Pure Reason. The law does not tell us what we must do, it merely tells us "you must!," leaving us to deduce from it the Good, that is, the object of this pure imperative.[5]

According to Deleuze, Kant uses the same reversing formula for both his epistemological and his moral concerns. But how does this insight help us to appreciate the Kantian dimensions of Foucault's historical project? First, this helps us to reappraise what has been seen as Foucault's uneven philosophy, where his early work on anonymous and determinist realms of knowledge suddenly swings to a later concern for ethical and moral fashioning. What more could be said of Foucault than that his epistemological outlook is governed by the caesuralist and agonistic dictum that "time is out of joint"? Further, Foucault's project is a search for a methodology, rule, or law that would direct one toward the good, but would not dogmatically confine one within its dehydrated grasp; instead it looks for a fluid and accommodating idea of the good life. Foucault's philosophy is a consistent whole in the precise sense that the issue of epistemology is always entwined with the problem of morality, politics, and ethics. Kant's two inversions remain intact.

Where Kant uses the same operating procedure for empirical reality and ethical reality, this similar *modus operandi* in no way confers on these two realms familial relation. The noumenal world retains an enshrined independence from the phenomenal. Foucault's project, however, is built upon the kinship or crossover of these domains in his conceptual universe. Their separate sovereignty, a Kantian mainstay, is no longer felt to be a protected prerequisite for the project of freedom. Obstacles to freedom are no longer to be found in nature and the encroaching understanding of it achieved by natural science, but in the natures we ascribe to ourselves as speaking, producing, and living beings. Thus Foucault's masterwork of archaeology, *The Order of Things,* pursues the constraints of freedom in the confused episto/ethical landscape of the "moral" and "humane" sciences. As such this unaccustomed union, this curiously conjoined twin becomes the backbone of Foucault's often contradictory intentions. People's freedom is intimately tied to how they constitute themselves as objects of knowledge. Of course, with re-

5. Gilles Deleuze, *Kant's Critical Philosophy: The Doctrine of the Faculties* (Minneapolis: University of Minnesota Press, 1984), x.

gard to epistemology, Kant is not concerned with people as objects of knowledge, but is primarily interested with the conceptual armory that governs our apprehension of the world. Foucault, however, is concerned with those realms of knowledge that arose after Kant's achievement, where man became the center of knowledge. Seeing the social scientific blasphemies that grew in the name of "man" after he was crowned the ordering principle of knowledge, Foucault undertakes to unpack the mystifications that have befogged the work of critique. Critique must once again be limited to its purest role as moral skepticism. Foucault is in both respects a trenchant critic of Kant and the newly appointed protector of his legacy. Perhaps he is the protector of a legacy whose inherent tensions between ethics and knowledge he will constantly re-formulate throughout his career. This project is necessarily historical in nature.

While the two Kantian procedures remain intact, Foucault melds these two inversions upon the expanse of history. This conflation involves two versions of history. In the first, universalist morality melts in the contingency of history. In the second, epistemology or knowledge (a realm more often seen as progressing toward a completed logic or accord) is an uncooperative contingency playing within the universal vacuum of history. History becomes both morality's and time's empty form. These two newly conditional realities fuse together in the unconditional, yet vacant reality of history. Foucault's illusion of history is one where it guarantees contingency, but also one where this contingency is secured by history taking on the characteristics of a universal, pure, and empty form. Like Kant's understanding of the transcendental ideality of time as the crux and starting point of the critical philosophy, history is Foucault's transcendental ideality, the absolute empty form that displays the contingency and finiteness of all knowledge and morality. Foucault treats history in the manner with which Kant treats time, and this involves him in an intractable paradox and tension, for he wants to eradicate history while also making it the universal cornerstone of archaeology.

This is an extraordinarily compacted philosophical move, which can be unpacked in a number of ways. Essentially Foucault compressed knowledge (whose Kantian starting point is time) and morality (whose Kantian starting point is timelessness) into a conceptual nightmare. Both are seen as timely and timeless. Where Kant's look at knowledge focused on the individual subject, limited but universal, Foucault no longer sees knowledge as disinterested subjective apprehension, comprehension, and inference, but as allied to social realms of morality and ethics. He thus begins to see knowledge as a nightmarish eternal encumbrance upon human freedom, but also like tectonic plates subject to the shifting of time. This is a vision of eternal change. Similarly, whereas morality entered the Kantian scene when the limits of knowledge had been secured, closing the empirical gates behind it before it soared into the timeless, for Foucault morality is knowledge's partner in crime. It is the ineluctable desire of knowledge to mutate itself into an ethical configuration.

Foucault wants to awaken the world from its "history drunkenness." This amounts to nothing more than removing the ingrained teleology, the progressions and continuities, and most drastically the multitude of meanings that have accrued on the sheen of its surface. As such he desiccates history and drags the shore of history's sea to the barren clarity of its slimmest perimeter, the present. This tide withdraws from both sides. The past is treated as an excavation site for the present, never allowing critique to succumb to the past's own more moderate terms, while the future is never spoken of as it constantly dissipates and recedes the further one pushes into it. Hence history—its fruitfulness, its breadth, and its meaning—evaporates as it takes on the arid and absolute characteristics of time's empty vessel. We cannot perceive history in itself—only those things that take place within it. Hence history becomes the idiot savant of a priori conditions. It is an autistic entity lacking in the recognition, reflection, or consciousness of what takes place in its name, but also brilliant and astounding in the complexity and unpredictable nature of its effects.

In a strange inverted form of Marxism, a history that was once the cause of alienation is now the subject of a vast alienation of its own import. What better way to combat a history whose sole effect on human relations is estrangement than to estrange history itself from its overbearing influence on human affairs? To make it an aloof, indifferent, and primary condition of all events and thoughts, and yet confer no real significance upon those events or thoughts? History is out of joint. Doing away with the Kantian dualism, Foucault establishes the first of his monadologies in the name of history, a history all-pervasive, yet powerless to comprehend itself, dumb in its categorization of the manifold of raw, meaningless historical facts, works, and events. Categorization of history is to take the fecundity from it and render it spatial. Foucault both knows he is doing this, and yet doesn't recognize the Kantian problems that are the inspiration for this historical vision. Later Foucault would establish a new monadology of power to coincide with his new genealogical work, yet power would remain a very similar entity to the vision of history we receive from Foucault's archaeological period.

The Historical A Priori and the Spatialization of History

Under the stoic gaze of the archeologist, history hardens into an iceberg covered with the crystalline forms of arbitrary formations of discourse.[6]

There is a plethora of literature subscribing to Foucault's spatial rendering of history and to the recent intellectual fascination for space as a renewed and primary category of social inquiry. Key Foucauldian terms such as *archive, discursive formation, limit, threshold, positivity, episteme,* and the important historical a priori all point to Foucault's early interest in compartmentalizing the historical flow of human knowledge. Seen purely as a project of spatialization, this course can look meaningless and facile, nothing more than a sway of the pendulum. Yet Foucault's favoring of space over time is more than a swing of emphasis, or some concerted and calculated use of a category unsuited to historical thought in order to subvert history itself. At its basis is a method of analysis that necessarily produces an image of history favorable to spatialization. Spatial history is implicit and consequential to the Foucauldian procedure, and not simply a conscious choice. This assertion, however, is not to suggest that there is no polemical or oppositional stance inherent to Foucault's archaeological method. Many commentators have been partially correct when they emphasized this important directive in his thought. As Thomas Flynn has correctly observed, "His shift from time to space as the paradigm guiding his approach to historical topics counters the totalising, teleological method favoured by standard histories of ideas,

---

6. Jurgen Habermas, *The Philosophical Discourse of Modernity* (Cambridge, Mass.: MIT Press, 1987), 253.

with their appeal to individual and collective consciousness and to a "tangled network of influences."[7]

Foucault, in a published conversation with the editors of a geography journal, also attested to the resistant impetus behind his adoption of historical space. He seemed to view his archaeological method as a conscious positioning against the old methods and mistakes of historical thinking.

Space was treated as the dead, the fixed, the undialectical, the immobile. Time on the contrary, was richness, fecundity, life, dialectic. For all those who confuse history with the old schemas of evolution, living continuity, organic development, the progress of consciousness or the project of existence, the use of spatial terms seems to have the air of an anti-history.... It meant, as the fools say, that one "denied history," that one was a "technocrat."[8]

As statements like this demonstrate, Foucault recognizes his polemical mission and often portrays his histories as fulfilling the need to redress the teleological and evolutionary preference of garden-variety historians and philosophers. The imbalance of traditional historical thought certainly lies in Foucault's crosshairs. But there is a less oppositional, more subtle and embedded reason for Foucault's spatial preoccupation. It is a reason that is obliquely connected with and can be interestingly made apparent by the Kantian project of demarcating the limits of reason. This fruitful kinship has not so much to do with a deliberate appropriation and use of the Kantian program, but more to do with a kind of unconscious intellectual mimicry that graces similar projects conducted in different historical periods. In simple terms, it is a matter of the similarities between two projects that attempt to circumscribe the limits of knowledge. What knowledge they are examining and their motives for doing it may differ, but a methodological similarity still resides within the initial attempt. However, how one can christen Kant and Foucault as historical brothers, and how the connection can explain Foucault's spatial histories are certainly ideas that need considerable clarification.

The most determined efforts to link Foucault and Kant in some sympathetic relationship have tended to concentrate upon Foucault's later en-

---

7. Thomas Flynn, "Foucault's Mapping of History," in *The Cambridge Companion to Foucault*, edited by Gary Gutting (Cambridge: Cambridge University Press, 1994), 41.

8. Michel Foucault, *Power/Knowledge: Selected Interviews and Other Writings, 1972–1977*, edited by Colin Gordon, translated by Colin Gordon, et al. (Brighton, Sussex: Harvester Press, 1980), 70.

gagement with Kant's famous essay *What Is Enlightenment* and his later preoccupation with the agency of the self in the last volumes of *The History of Sexuality*. This interpretation focuses upon what is perceived as Foucault's reversal or reappraisal of the role of freedom and the will within the world—a factor that is seen as implicit to the purpose of his histories, but categorically denied by the methodology adopted within—and their philosophical results. Very few, if any, concerted attempts have been made to search for Kantian residues or connections in his earlier archaeological work, taking Foucault on his word about Kant as an insentient herald of a dogmatic and passing episteme. This seems a rather odd and generous approach to a thinker who so often subsumed other thinkers' intentions within larger unconscious frameworks of thoughts and words beyond their control. There is, however, an unconscious Kantianism in Foucault's archaeology that directly relates to his spatialization of history.

While there has been no systematic look at the affinities between Kant's aims in the *Critique of Pure Reason* and the aims of Foucault's archaeological method, some commentators have made passing associations between the two projects, some general and abstractly sweeping, others more limited and acutely focused. Gary Gutting makes a slight and vague intimation of the methodological affinity between Kant and Foucault in his evaluation of Foucault as a historian. Gutting believes that Foucault provokes the ire of historians primarily because of his "idealist" approach. His imaginative historical constructions, in which indifferent random facts, statements, and events are subsumed and made intelligible, are ideally rendered configurations that thumb their noses at a discipline with resolutely empiricist foundations. That Gutting can conceive of Foucault as an "idealist" of any stripe vaguely suggests that there may exist some correspondence between his histories and Kant's idealist project.

Foucault's penchant for using facts as illustration rather than support does not mean that ... he is "simply indulging in a whim for arbitrary and witty assertions." It is rather a sign of what I will call his idealist (as opposed to empiricist) approach to history.... What he wants is a comprehensive, unifying interpretation that will give intelligible order to an otherwise meaningless jumble of individual historical facts.[9]

9. Gary Gutting, "Foucault and the History of Madness," in *The Cambridge Companion to Foucault*, edited by Gary Gutting (Cambridge: Cambridge University Press, 1994), 63–64.

This quote displays the ambiguity of the Kantian/Foucauldian relation. A reading of Foucault's archaeologies of madness, medicine, and the human sciences give one the impression that ideal schemas of categorization are certainly employed, often with the feeling that this historical categorizing procedure is perversely akin to the Kantian categorization of empirical reality in the ahistorical natural sciences. But the word "perversely" is the rub, for while Foucault is in an important sense a historical idealist in his method, he does treat himself to the intellectually perverse caprice for "arbitrary and witty assertions." This divergence is significantly explained by the role that the imagination plays in their respective worldviews.

While for Kant the imagination was an integral mental capacity for the apprehension of reality, he was always a staunch rationalist where the imagination was concerned. Relegated to being a faculty in the architectonic of our mental armory, it rarely, if ever, is left to impinge upon Kant's own intellectual constructions. Imagination is sandwiched between the appearances and the categories of the understanding and dismissed as "an art, hidden in the depths of the human soul," where it is left to flounder in mystery. For Foucault, however, the imagination is his main historical asset. Unleashed as it is from its cognitive compliance, it is empowered and autonomous. It is paralleled in its Foucauldian rendering with the importance and creative power given to it by Blake. Note the reverence of which Foucault speaks on the imagination's integral role in intellectual endeavor in "Fantasia of the Library."

The imaginary now resides between the book and the lamp. The fantastic is no longer a property of the heart, nor is it found in the incongruities of nature; it evolves from the accuracy of knowledge, and its treasures lie dormant in documents. Dreams are no longer summoned with closed eye, but in reading; and a true image is now a product of learning.... The imaginary is not formed in opposition to reality as its denial or compensation; it grows amongst signs, from book to book, in the interstice of repetitions and commentaries; it is born and takes shape in the interval between books.[10]

---

10. Foucault, *Language, Counter Memory and Practice* (Ithaca, N.Y.: Cornell University Press, 1992), 90–91. While "Fantasia of the Library" is a meditation on Flaubert, it is clear that these ideas are held by Foucault himself and, further, that this is an astute and accurate self-understanding of his intellectual labors.

This Blakean view of the imagination as a place where art, thought, and the fantastic coalesce could not be further removed from the Kantian, where art not so much weaves within thought, but is in every respect an "afterthought" (one need only remember that Kant only took up the subject of art and the sublime in his last critique). Rather than a rationally shackled faculty, the imagination is an expectant, intrusive, and prerational force that Foucault allows to shape his historical idealities, which often leads to his methodological "witticism." Based simply on these deviating understandings of the role of the imagination, Foucault and Kant would be distant and aloof stars in any idealist universe. Yet, as this chapter will show, much of Foucault's imaginative historical force bursts from Kant's restricted understanding of the role of the imagination. This will be disclosed later in the chapter.

One of the more obscure connections is the thought put forward in the foreword to *Power/Knowledge,* by Colin Gordon: that the operation of Kant's concept of the "schema" in the *Critique of Pure Reason* is reminiscent of the way Foucault views the operation of programmatic knowledge. Foucault's project is seen as the detailed elaboration of the success or failure of "strategies, technologies and programmes of power." Programs for knowledge and power assume or create an aspect of historical reality that must come under its sway; a program of thought must engineer a social object upon which it will mold and maneuver:

The common axiom of programmes is that an effective power is and must be a power which knows the objects upon which it is exercised. Further, the condition that programmatic knowledge must satisfy is that it renders reality in the form of an object which is programmable. This operation is reminiscent of the function Kant attributes in the *Critique of Pure Reason* to the concept of the schema which, as Deleuze puts it, "does not answer the question, how are phenomena made subject to the understanding, but the question, how does the understanding apply itself to the phenomena which are subject to it?"[11]

The immediate worry that arises from this comparison is the fact that Kant was chiefly concerned with tracing the a priori structures and postulates of the mind and the categories of a subjective, yet collective and universal understanding. Foucault, however, was more concerned with the relative and historical categories of troubled universalistic at-

11. Colin Gordon, "Afterword," in *Power/Knowledge*, by Michel Foucault, 248.

tempts at scientific thought. Both of their projects inhabit epistemological domains that would ordinarily glare at each other with malice aforethought. And yet there is persistence among the literature of a vague correspondence between Kant's universalist and Foucault's historicist methods. Foucault is understood to have imbued the structures of history with the same operative functions as Kant's categories.

An episteme, therefore, may be called a paradigm, providing it is not conceived of as an exemplar, a model of cognitive work. It is a basement *(sous-sol)* of thought, a mental infrastructure underlying all strands of the knowledge (on man) at a given age, a conceptual grid (grille, in Foucault's Levi-Straussian wording) that amounts to a historical a priori—almost a historicized form of Kant's categories.[12]

This thematic of "historicizing the Kantian question" is one taken up by Stuart Elden in *Mapping the Present,* a work that not only explores this remote and unfamiliar connection, but traces its descent from Kant through Nietzsche and Heidegger to Foucault, while also framing it within the "project of a spatial history": "Synthetic a priori knowledge is possible on the basis of the original synthetic unity of the pure productive power of imagination, on the basis of temporality.... In Kant, as in *Being and Time,* this is a radically ahistorical question. In Nietzsche and the later Heidegger this question, the problem of metaphysics, or the question of being, is posed historically."[13] Foucault is believed to be enacting a Kantian critique via Nietzsche's and Heidegger's historicism, not upon the realm of ahistorical and indispensable judgments, but upon the realm of historical and hence dispensable statements. Not only is this part of the historicist twist knowledge has taken in defiance of universalism and transcendentalism, but it also shows Foucault's allegiance to the linguistic turn of twentieth-century thought: "Foucault is, like Nietzsche and the later Heidegger, historicizing the Kantian question. Foucault's understanding of the historical a priori does not function as 'a condition of validity for judgements, but a condition of reality for *énonces.*'"[14] By situating these discussions within the framework of Foucault's project of spatial history and his concern with "mapping the

12. J. G. Merquior, *Foucault* (Los Angeles: University of California Press, 1985), 38.
13. Stuart Elden, *Mapping the Present* (London: Continuum, 2001), 23.
14. Elden, *Mapping the Present,* 96.

present," Elden seems to intimate that by recasting Kantian questions on reason historically, it necessarily involves a certain spatialization of history. Unfortunately Elden, who seems more interested in Foucault's analyses of space as a fundamental political apparatus rather than the actual archaeological premise of history being spatially conceived, does not exhaustively explore the exact reasons for this tendency.

From this short survey a confusing mélange of affinities and points of difference emerge between Kant and Foucault, ranging from idealist configurations, the role of the imagination, the operation of schematism, and the radical temporality of our life to categories of understanding, historicism, linguistics, and spatialization. The question becomes how to make sense of these elements to connect these thinkers and thus bring Foucault's early archaeological project to a better understanding. The most interesting and undeveloped of these insights is the assertion that Foucault's historical studies resemble in their method the operational role Kant assigns to the schema. If it is taken as granted that Foucault's primary historical assumption is that people are "made" the objects of the sciences and practices they themselves choose to employ, that humans are forever "objectified" by their own knowledge, then the connection to schematism becomes clear. Let us explore Kant's idea of schematism further, for many of the other elements of this comparison fall into place with an in-depth look at its essential features.

The short chapter Kant devotes to schematism is designed to explain how the categories of the atemporal understanding apply themselves to the temporal world of intuitions. How does the timeless temporalize itself? Its whole gist lies in the possibility of synthesis, or how two separate realms that cannot be experienced meaningfully on their own terms can coalesce within the same singular experience, and in what medium this meaningful connection takes place. Kant describes it thus: "The schema of substance is the permanence of the real in time; that is, the representation of it as a substratum of the empirical determination of time; a substratum therefore remains, whilst all else changes."[15] And so, "Hence the schema is properly only the phenomenon, or the sensuous conception of an object in harmony with a category."[16]

---

15. Kant, *Critique of Pure Reason*, 120.
16. Kant, *Critique of Pure Reason*, 122.

Within the analytical tradition of Kantian scholarship, this problem is often considered a "pseudo-problem," where asking about the applicability of concepts to the world unravels the work of the transcendental deduction.[17] From the standpoint of schematism, the objective validity of concepts of the understanding, an objectivity that should have been proven in the deduction, is rendered problematic. Kant either failed in his purpose and schematism further confuses the issue, or he succeeded and schematism is unnecessary. The very paradoxical language used by Kant in his elaboration of schematism does support this dismissing attitude.

The procedure of schematization, for example, is variously ascribed to sensibility, to understanding, to empirical, reproductive imagination, and to a priori productive imagination. Schemata are distinguished from concepts, and then identified with them; they are said to be determinate, and also indeterminate; and it is one place implied that empirical concepts do not require schemata, but in another that they do.... Kant calls schemata "sensible concepts"—though from the critical standpoint such things ought to be as irrelevant to us as "intellectual intuitions."[18]

From these observations it is obvious that if the schematism chapter holds any weight it is to be found in the unresolved areas between the relentless oscillations of Kant's dualisms. If concepts cannot be adequately applied to intuitions, where is judgment to find any kind of grounding? This is where the analytical tradition leaves the problem, unable to navigate in this intellectual fog or simply discharging the problem as erroneous. Those more concerned with the cultural import of the Kantian philosophy, however, have found in schematism a fruitful boulevard of possibility, none better described than by Kant's first culturally concerned critic, Jacobi, who gushed of schematism, "the most wonderful and most mysterious of all unfathomable mysteries and wonders."[19] Here they find less of a cul-de-sac of impenetrable knowledge and more of a crack in the armor of Kantian critique, a crack that allows much light to flood into the dark corridors of his philosophy.

Let us explore Jacobi's seminal, yet forgotten critique of Kant. Jaco-

17. Sarah L. Gibbons, *Kant's Theory of Imagination* (Oxford: Clarendon Press, 1994), 54.

18. David Bell, "The Art of Judgement," *Mind* 96, no. 382 (1987): 229.

19. Quoted from Eva Schaper, "Kant's Schematism Revisted," *Review of Metaphysics* 18, no. 2 (1964): 267–92; here 270.

bi, one of Kant's first serious commentators, initiated the question that is still asked of Kant to this day. How can the separate and indeterminate realms of reflective, empty thought, and unprocessed, meaningless sensation team together to produce a determinate object of experience? An unexplained synthesis of thought and sensation lies at the interior of Kant's philosophy. The only spanning entity between these two that Jacobi can find is the role played by the transcendental imagination, which we have already seen is set aside by Kant as "an art, hidden in the depths of the human soul." But according to Jacobi this is either no solution at all or it is the unexplored crux upon which the whole possibility of synthetic a priori judgments is based.[20] The mysteriousness that Kant maintains fuses our apprehension of the world plays into the hands of all those who search for the unlimited well of possibility in the Kantian view of the world. For Jacobi, whose whole polemical project was designed to demarcate a space for faith in the burgeoning modern world of rationalist and abstract thought, this "most wonderful of wonders" was the forgotten well that allowed his religious quest room to sigh relief in the cage of rationalism. Imagination is a cop-out for the mysterious working of faith, Jacobi's foundational stone for all other human endeavor. For those who do not share Jacobi's religious sentiments, however, they have sought in the imagination the no-man's-land of Kant's cultural project, for the role of the transcendental imagination in its generation of schemata is purely time-bound. As Eva Schaper observes, "When Kant calls the schemata pure time-determinations, and schematised categories 'temporalized' categories, he points to imagination not as a third level of mind, but as the joint function of mental activity in coping with experience."[21]

So schemata are Kantian categories animated by time from one angle; from the other is where images of order emanate from the temporal disorder of the manifold. Schemata are intimately linked with worlds of purely human construction—how humans deal, manage, and represent the world of their own making. Imagination is thus a historical entity that cannot find a home within the ahistorical world of Kantian epis-

20. Jacobi, *The Main Philosophical Writings and the Novel* "Allwill," translated with an introduction by George di Giovanni (Montreal and Kingston: McGill-Queen's University Press, 1994), 156.

21. Schaper, "Kant's Schematism Revisited," 283.

temology. Here Kant is giving a glimpse of his epistemological limitations—limitations, however, that must be disregarded when one is concerned with the human assembly of the world—i.e., culture, history, and its products. Schaper again illuminates: "To think of the human forms of experience as immutable, as being the same for all men and at all times, simply will not do. Kant's own completely unhistorical bias may be understandable from the standpoint of the age in which he lived. But it is made questionable from the very implications of his thought on time in Schematism, on imagination, and on judgement."[22]

Without schemata and their allegiance to the dark arts of creation and imagination, Kant would be caught in an endless philosophical game of grounding rules upon further rules, and those again with further rules, ad nauseam. Schemata are that ill-explained capacity that Kant has to assume people possess, that enables them to follow rules without falling back on a further rule to explain such compliance. Kant is fumbling for a capacity unburdened by rules, but that grounds following rules. Schemata are the blindness and spontaneity that thought requires to expunge endless regression. At some point judgment must be able to occur immediately. What we confront in this short chapter of Kant's is the paradox of "rule-determined spontaneity."[23] The fact that this human capacity resembles in many ways some type of aesthetic apprehension of reality is evidenced by the very similar paradoxes that Kant utilizes in the third critique of "purposiveness without purpose" and "free play of the faculties." That critique designed to bridge the gap of nature and freedom, taking up the challenge of our aesthetic and historical existence, takes its cue from this small meditation on schemata-bridging intuition and concepts. The implacability of Kant's dualisms can be clearly seen before the third critique in Kant's paradoxical view of imagination as both free and conformable to law. Foucault, who thought through science and knowledge in purely historical terms, and who approached the production of that knowledge with what resembles an aesthetic understanding, seems in every way to follow from the broad tradition that has yawned from this problem of time, imagination, and schematizing.

It is not what schematism has failed to say in epistemology, but rath-

22. Schaper, "Kant's Schematism Revisited," 289.
23. Bell, "The Art of Judgement," 222.

er what it implies about the subjective, imaginative, and experiencing individual, the building block of culture and history, that has made it the fount upon which much modern thought has fed. What is presupposed by schematism is the fact that man does not confront the world, but is in a thoroughgoing relation of comprehension and construction. As Eva Schaper astutely points out, the main thrust of the schematism chapter so unnecessarily obscured by Kant is that we do not confront the world as beings of mind, but as "beings in time."[24] The connection here between Kant and Heidegger is palpable. Here we are closer to understanding Stuart Elden's exploration of the "historicising of the Kantian question." Schaper also lists Ernst Cassirer and his concern with culture, Bergson, the philosopher of process, Sartre, the existential psychoanalyst, Husserl, the phenomenologist, and Claude Levi-Strauss, the structural anthropologist, as members of a club who took their cue from the question Kant poses about man's place in the world, his being in time. She lumps them together as the "phenomenological rag-bag."

A whole tradition of modern thought has grown from Kant's scant admittance of the possibility that we are not simply mental creatures shifting through datum, but that we are active, social, creative, cultural, historical, and shaping beings, beings crafting and understanding our world through a ruleless but ruling imagination. We are learning to cope with experience while guiding and fashioning it. Schematism is Kant's confused recognition that the apprehension of the world is not set in mental stone by the understanding, but that the articulation of our environments is continuously under construction. In schematism Kant expounds not the mental armory of man, but the endeavor of man, opening the way for the explosion of the sciences of man, such as psychology, sociology, and anthropology. If the majority of the *Critique of Pure Reason* is taken up with the metaphysics of science and knowledge, with delimiting the past strengths and weaknesses of knowledge, the slit of existential light that schematism represents is instead better understood as a metaphysics of experience or a conducting of the future movements of knowledge. Foucault is at once both a member of the club and one of its critics.

Before schematism can illuminate Foucauldian archaeological his-

24. Schaper, "Kant's Schematism Revisited," 281.

tory, one must understand Foucault's limited investment in this tradition, or what he rejects of its problems. Foucault is a toiler in the codes of culture, but takes this work so far that it obscures the bearer of culture, the imaginative individual, and replaces this character with imaginative discourse. As he says in the foreword to the English edition of *The Order of Things*, "If there is one approach that I do reject, however, it is that (one might call it, broadly speaking, the phenomenological approach) which gives absolute priority to the observing subject, which attributes a constituent role to an act, which places its own point of view at the origin of all historicity—which, in short, leads to a transcendental consciousness."[25] This is indeed the very paradoxical crux upon which Foucault's archaeological masterwork, *The Order of Things*, rests. A towering work that explores so many of the imaginative garden paths, patchwork plains, and overgrown horizons of man's social and cultural production and comprehension, yet at its heart lies a resolute conviction that man is just another of these dreamy productions/comprehensions, and cannot be trusted to ground the whole gamut of social sciences that are initiated by him. Man disappears in and takes on the characteristics of the various realms of finite knowledge that he created. If one thing can be said of Foucault, it is that he shows how man can become a victim to his own knowledge, both literally when it imprisons him and philosophically when it becomes bent on erasing him.

Foucault is a direct bearer of the phenomenological "rag-bag" that he maintains is an inadequate method of historical research. Foucault admits that Kant is the initiator of this modern episteme, because his look into the limits of knowledge makes possible the idea of man as both generator and purpose of knowledge, as both source and object. When Foucault talks of Kant establishing a "transcendental-empirical doublet," this is another way of saying what schematism presupposes—that man trapped in time, intuiting the dumb manifold and filling his empty and ordered understanding with it, means only that he is at once comprehending and constructing. This is a hopelessly circular task of finding our finitude in the infinite well of ourselves, or even searching for an erstwhile infinitude in our finite selves. This leads to the attempts to fuse together the empirical and the transcendent, an impossible choice

25. Foucault, *The Order of Things*, xiv.

that Foucault understands as providing us only with the alternate options of positivism and eschatology, which means the truth of man seems both "reduced and promised."[26] When Foucault talks of the modern episteme discovering man's finitude, yet at the same time striving for transcendence, all he means is that modern knowledge finds its grounds of research in our tangible reality, our body, society, and language, yet also assumes a reality beyond this ground in a nontangible reason or transcendent perspective that can adjudicate our finitude. Thus we are doomed to reduction and promise. Foucault sees Kant's three prime questions—what can I know? what must I do? what can I hope for?—contained in the umbrella question *was ist der Mensch?* This is precisely the question posed and left to flounder in the mystery of the imagination by schematism. Foucault writes, "This question, as we have seen, runs through thought from the early nineteenth century: this is because it produces, surreptitiously and in advance, the confusion of the empirical and the transcendental, even though Kant had demonstrated the division between them."[27]

How amusing it therefore seems that Foucault's archaeological history is likened to the operation of schematism. From schematism the whole history of what man is flows. Foucault is engaged in this enterprise, but wishes to avoid the temptations of uninspiring positivism and grandiose eschatology, and thus turns away from man, dismissing this ordering principle of knowledge as just a figure written in the historical sand. Thus the question redoubles upon itself as not what is man, but what is history, and the same confusions and operations abound in this new environment. This is why Foucault's archaeology is sensed to operate with "schemas," "idealist configurations," "historicized categories," all of which Foucault recognizes by the term "historical a priori." History simply becomes the recipient of humanity's imaginative ability to synthesize. Where man was the starting point and history poured from him, under Foucault history is the given and man is poured into it. It is by this move that the actions of men can be compartmentalized and spatialized by historical a priories, or epistemes. But perhaps to understand this crux of Foucault's philosophy we must retrace Foucault's compartmentalizing of epistemes, his divining of historical a priories, for the

26. Foucault, *The Order of Things*, 320.
27. Foucault, *The Order of Things*, 341.

whole vast historical survey of the human sciences is aimed at this point of the modern episteme. This is no disinterested history; it is a critical history, a history of the present, designed to strike at the gut of modern anthropological and historical appetites.

The three life-science epistemes with their corresponding master concepts have been exhaustively discussed and dissected by Foucault's commentators, and this study is not overtly concerned with rehearsing the praises and admonishments of the discussion. But to adequately show the spatialization and alienation of history achieved by Foucault and his maneuver around the issue of causality, a short look at what characterizes the three epistemes is needed. The first of these is the remote and arcane era of Renaissance knowledge, a paradigm that is personified by an ever-expanding maze of resemblances and similitudes. This network is centered on processes of analogy, sympathy, convenience, correspondence, and reflection. This worldview takes the world to be an open but mysterious book, "the prose of the world," written in code by God. The various similitudes and forms of resemblance are the tools used to recognize the "signature" or "sign" with which God marks everything on earth. Order is read into the universe, with a balanced web of near and remote attraction and resemblance. This order suddenly gives way with no explanation to the classical episteme.

The classical episteme remodels reality not upon the basis of analogy, but upon the basis of analysis. The effect of this shift, this rupture, is to move away from the attempt to entwine the world in a vast network of similarity, reflection, and attraction, but instead separate reality out from itself by analyzing the separate identities of things, tabulating their differences and distinctions. The classical episteme of representation has as its major weapons taxinomia, where observed surface effects and structures are charted and classified, and mathesis, a universal method of weight and measurement. Instead of trying to infinitely and definitively tie everything together as attached and kindred by extensive sequences of resemblance, the classical era attempts to catalogue the infinity of the world by isolating its endlessly finite variation. Trapped between the columns of innumerably observed and measured facts, the mystery that set apart the Renaissance prose of the world gives way to an evident and understandable representation of thought. Elaborate interpretation and divination of the signs embedded in the world are replaced by the simple but demanding work of collecting the clearly marked, evident, and arbitrary surface of the world. The oddity of this worldview is shown by Foucault in his discussion of the painting *Las Meninas,* by Velasquez, where the subject of the painting, a royal couple, are slyly represented by being reflected in a mirror in the background of the room. Foucault takes this painting as an allegory for the way representation operates in the classical episteme. The object of representation (like the subject of the painting) cannot itself be adequately conceptualized. For knowledge to operate in this classical order, the object that all this vast amassing of representation is aimed at must remain unknown and concealed. This is an overture for the next coming episteme—an episteme where the subject "man" will enter history and the multitude of surface representation will fall away from him like the emperor's clothes.

Foucault's third episteme ushers in not only man to history, but history into history, also. The classical age of measurement could not accommodate concepts like history, progression, genesis, production, purpose, and evolution, for its successions of identity and difference did not aim at the creative and active experience of humanity.

In biological thought, function overcame structure. The study of language fastened onto a welter of evolving roots. In economics, circulation of goods came to be explained as a visible outcome of protracted processes of production. Everywhere, deeper, darker forces were substituted for the surface regularities of classical knowledge; throughout different disciplines, modern thought imposed dynamic, historical categories of explanation.[28]

Nothing, therefore, would be more pleasant, or more inexact, than to conceive of this historical a priori as a formal a priori that is endowed with history: a great, unmoving, empty figure that irrupted one day on the surface of time, that exercised over men's thought a tyranny that none could escape, and that then suddenly disappeared in a totally unexpected, totally unprecedented eclipse.[29]

Yet Foucault then gives us no reason that this is an "inexact" description of the historical a priori, simply asserting that formal and historical a priories are of a different stripe altogether. This difficulty in adequately conceptualizing the historical a priori should not alarm us, as the very

28. Merquior, *Foucault,* 51.
29. Merquior, *Foucault,* 51.

paradoxical nature of the term is a monument to its philosophical obscurity. We encounter this philosophical to-and-fro with Kant's schematism when he describes schemata as temporalized categories or sensible concepts. Foucault's whole historical endeavor simply rehearses this deep, dark nexus point of human imagination, an existential quandary and quarry that he displaced in history. Graham Bird described the operation of human imagination as presupposed by schematism as a "clutch mechanism," a description apt enough to be applied to Foucault's historical a priori. He writes, "the two faculties are connected by imagination, as though the latter faculty worked like a clutch mechanism."[30]

The historical a priori is simply a clutch mechanism that synchronizes the world of historical contingency with a formal regularity and grouping. Because the operation of historical a priories is so reminiscent of the mediating role of the imagination in schematism, the historical a priori oscillates between empirical and transcendental perspectives. Foucault is an idealist historian, while at the same time being a thinker devoted to temporality and the contingent. Historical a priories can be seen as images of contingency, or anonymous regulatory discourses governing contingency. In other words, Foucault avoids none of the epistemological pitfalls of any dualism. By erasing man, he felt that he had avoided these difficulties, but they are deeply embedded in his idea of an archaeological history. Eventually he would have to reckon with the imagination of man, whose synthesizing properties he had dissolved in history; this reckoning will be looked at later. For now this chapter will conclude with a look at the spatial effect that the historical a priori gives to history, an effect well understood by Foucault's waning intellectual forebear and dismissed existential high priest, Sartre. Sartre concedes but also qualifies: "of course his perspective remains historical. He distinguishes between periods, a before and an after. But he replaces cinema with the magic lantern, motion with a succession of motionless moments."[31]

Because the historical a priori is an imaginative synthesis of empirical and categorical history, a mysterious conception designed to fuse the

30. Graham Bird, *Kant's Theory of Knowledge* (London: Routledge and Kegan Paul, 1962), 52.

31. Jean-Paul Sartre, quoted in *Michel Foucault,* by Didier Eribon, translated by Betsy Wing (Cambridge, Mass.: Harvard University Press, 1991), 163.

temporal disorder and chaos with a definite regularity, it never fully justifies itself on either account. It is empirical, but it omits things that can disprove the regularity, or it misreads others so that they fit into the episteme. Empirical reality is simply material to be bashed into a shape, a shape that will exclude or retool all those things that would give movement and development to an episteme. The historical a priori is also a categorical entity; it does utilize the formal a priori to such a degree that it makes Foucault a transcendental historian. And yet it is so determined by history that it can have no life without it. Thus it emerges without warning and passes without notice. Its only assent to temporality is found in the fixed points of its beginning and its end. Between these historical markers a categorical tyranny evacuates time and change from the episteme. Foucault says it himself best when he assumes the ironical tone of his critics.

Discourse is snatched from the law of development and established in a discontinuous atemporality. It is immobilized in fragments: precarious splinters of eternity. But there is nothing one can do about it, several eternities succeeding one another, a play of fixed images disappearing in turn, do not constitute either movement, time, or history.[32]

When time and causality are evacuated from history like this, history becomes a playground, a space, or a jigsaw puzzle. When history is detemporalized, it does not cease to be history; it loses none of its color and movement, it simply loses its direction. The color and movement become trapped in a shape that becomes separated and detached for all time from the other shapes of history. The ability of history to speak to itself becomes lost. Habermas has a striking image for the effect when he writes that "The transcendental historian looks as if into a kaleidoscope."[33] Archaeological history is an attempt to re-foot the critique of reason away from its transcendental dependence on man and turn it to a look at the radical limitation of our endeavors by historicizing the a priori. This unfortunately renders Foucault's historical outlook as preoccupied with discontinuities between monolithic epistemes. Monolithic epistemes mushroom and give way without explanation. Under their legislation individual's statements become disconnected from their au-

32. Foucault, *The Archaeology of Knowledge* (New York: Pantheon, 1972), 166–67.
33. Habermas, *The Philosophical Discourse of Modernity*, 253.

thorship, and like iron filings, they become arranged by the magnetic ordering of a historical a priori. Epistemes can be far more differentiated than the archaeologist may care to admit. The crystals of history can become ever more distinct and numerous or be grouped in ever widening and connected units. The episteme foists upon history an arbitrariness that may not be contained therein. The arbitrary nature of archaeological history is dependent upon the arbitrary critical and transcendent standpoint of the historian digging into the layers of history. Foucault's aim is to defamiliarize, alienate, or disperse history from our complacent comprehension, an effect he achieves by making history just as mysterious, ungraspable, and dark as the imagination he used to light it. This is not history proper; it is a critical history, a philosophical history, history carved to make a philosophical point. Foucault's archaeological history proves him to be a crypto-idealist. By removing man from the story, history becomes a zoological garden of different species of thought, caged and labeled—schematized imaginative images of history that are traced, bordered, and surveyed by an imaginative critical individual. Critical thought can never avoid the capricious and arbitrary judgments of its devotees, yet by replacing the judgments of the individual with the statements of history, Foucault seems to be attempting to circumvent his own membership in the venture "man."

11

Genealogy

The Menippean Character of History

The Undifferentiated Difference of Unreason

Let us approach the problem of history more from Foucault's direction. Perhaps his spatial history is no random illusion of it, but instead a kind of perverse heightening and intensification of history in order to provoke the carrier of its message. History is turned upside down and fragmented as though it is an accusation against those who made it. Like a disturbed self-mutilator who cuts himself to know of his existence, Foucault dissects history— cutting it up to know that it lives, to see the blood flow from its brittle skin of progress, succession, and continuity, and thus to source the deeper meaning of being human. This psychological metaphor of history is not so flippant if you consider how concerned Foucault was to show the role of madness in history's production. Foucault makes great gashes on history's surface not to throw doubt upon history, but to throw doubt upon man. Foucault approaches the venture of man from that which we deny, those monsters of reason's sleep that we keep manacled by the vigilant wakefulness of thought. He wishes to redirect Kant's formulation negatively. What we say about man is not true; it is what we deny of him, what we don't say, what we silence of man that is his truth. Where once the question, "What is man?" was the beginning of our definition, now the question, "What isn't man?" betrays who we really are. In this respect madness becomes the sounding board of reason, as how we treat it and how we relate ourselves to it become the dark foundation upon which reason builds itself. In the words of John D. Caputo, Foucault is exploring a "hermeneutics of not knowing who we are." Seen from here, Foucault's rejection of a transcendental consciousness is less a rejection than an accusation that such transcendence is just a panic-ridden and pompous flight away from our more murky and troubled consciousness. To say man does not exist is just an extreme way of saying that we do not truly know ourselves.

Foucault cut his earliest philosophical teeth by meditating on the relationship between reason and unreason. This pursuit of otherness, of ulterior history, places Foucault in a familiar and well-trodden firmament of thought. Foucault himself examines his precursors in *Madness and Civilisation.* He mentions the "earthbound spectators" of madness, Goya, Brueghel, and Bosch, whose dark, everyday, and immediate pictorial imaginings are snapshots of life suffused with mixtures of dangerous psychosis and thoughtless idiocy. The more objective, divine perspective of an Erasmus appears in his *In Praise of Folly,* where the world takes on a maddening hue, thanks to the humanistic, scholarly distance that eliminates participation in the lunacy of worldly machinations. There are the great Renaissance dramatists, Cervantes and Shakespeare, where madness becomes allied with death, a dark knowledge of having gone too far, seen too much, been exposed for too long. As a constant reminder of human fallacy and finitude, madness carries an entirely negative value, but it is still assigned the seminal role of a self in reckoning. Foucault sees madness as in some way fraternal with art, scholarship, and literature. Foucault also makes heroes of those more modern carriers of madness's message, heroes who are able to receive its faint transmissions in a world that had almost blocked out its fury. Succumbing to its power, becoming carriers of its extremes, and being able to leave literary artifacts of their experience, writers like Nietzsche, Artaud, and Holderlin skirted this knowledge. Yet Foucault's immediate precursor is his disgraced countryman Louis Ferdinand Céline, a writer who forced dreams through reality and traced the hallucinatory provocations of the world. Though Céline never succumbed individually to lunacy, he became a willing participator in the madness of his century via his involvement in Nazism and anti-Semitism. Among the madness, fevered observation, and pained pessimist polemic of his work *Journey to the End of the Night*, he has one of his characters, a disgruntled and cynical psychiatrist, proclaim a demented new world order. He begins by declaring the doomed fate of human reason, a delirious exercise more resembling madness that will amount to nothing. He then proposes a curative: "Ferdinand, is it not true that in the face of a truly modern intelligence, everything in the end assumes equal importance? Nothing's white ... nor black either.... It's all unravelled. That's the new system! It's the fashion! Then why not, for a start, go mad ourselves? Right now? And boast of it to boot?"[1]

From this quote on the tenor of the modern mind, I have isolated the two directives of Foucault's thought that will be explored in this chapter. The first deals with madness and Foucault's strangely revering, yet grotesque attitude toward it. The other deals with his theory of power as an omnipresent network of power relations and the corresponding unraveling of truth, in which "everything in the end assumes equal importance." It is the relationship between madness and power that animates Foucault's conception of genealogy, enabling him to trace the "descents" and "emergences" of power that turns the customary ways of the world upside down and inside out. Power moves history, madness inverts it. And moving inversions are the province of that carnivalesque view of the world so well encapsulated by the Menippea. But first I will examine Foucault's initial appraisal of the problem of psychology.

Foucault's first critique of the modern world of madness was a look at the "alienated" world of psychology, obviously a very Marxist-inspired scrutiny. The basic premise of his first major work, *Mental Illness and Psychology*, is that madness contains an unadulterated truth that the history of Western rationality has attempted in the last few hundred years to quash with captivity and moralization. Madness is transformed into the externally profiled and controllable object "mental illness," which can then submit itself to the "science" or institution of psychology to preside benevolently and condescendingly over it. Psychology is the alienated structure of madness—the pious halo that hangs over and masks our troubled core. What is worse, psychology attempts to convince that

1. Louis Ferdinand Céline, *Journey to the End of the Night* (New York: New Directions, 1960), 422–23.

it "understands" madness, when it is in fact madness that gives life to psychology. Psychology is madness once removed, a pseudo-science designed to shield reason from its meaning-laden relation and age-old confrontation with the insane. This is reason's tyranny over the experience of the mad, as an attempt to "cure" the moral waste seen to be inherent in extreme states of being. The mad can tell us something about ourselves, yet we choose to alienate them from the human condition rather than assimilate them into a greater understanding of our character. It is important to know that this early work of Foucault's was treated with a great deal of doubt and even embarrassment by the author, who wished to remove himself from the stigma of Marxist interpretation. And yet the preface of *Madness and Civilisation* clearly asserts what ostensibly equates with the same position as his Marxist foundations: "We must try to return, in history, to that zero point in the course of madness at which madness is an undifferentiated experience, a not yet divided experience of division itself."[2] Foucault's investment in the power of madness resembles in some very important ways the basic philosophical journeys of Rousseau and Marx, or to say it in alignment with the last chapter, Foucault is engaged in a perverse phenomenological pursuit. Underneath the moralizing hum of the human sciences, beyond the specters of the asylum, clinic, and prison, behind the institutional crust we have allowed to mature over our history, we can revive a purer existence, an undifferentiated experience that will bring us closer to ourselves. This, of course, was the dream of a Marx who posited a future realm of unalienated Communism, of a Rousseau who posited the past realm of socially unsullied nature, and now a Foucault who posits a realm of undifferentiated unreason that has always existed and can be accessed and communicated with at any moment. John D. Caputo observes, "Foucault suggests that we will find a pure 'Unsinn,' a kind of perfect, pure, free, natural, undistorted, prepredicative madness, beneath the categories of the prison or the asylum."[3]

This climate of sympathy with and fêting of folly is replete with po-

2. Michel Foucault, *Madness and Civilisation,* translated by Richard Howard (London: Tavistock, 1967), ix.

3. John D. Caputo, "On Not Knowing Who We Are: Madness, Hermeneutics and the Night of Truth," in *Michel Foucault and Theology,* edited by James Bernauer and Jeremy Carrette (Aldershot, UK: Ashgate, 2004), 123.

litical implications, and is in a strange sense a re-footing of critique, not upon the basis of the timeless will, but upon a prerational knowledge of the absolute margins of thought. Praising unreason is always going to be allied with a political position of institutional criticism.

Correlatively, madness became the paradigm for a subjectivity freed from the constraints of social adaptation, a kernel of authenticity that had to be preserved or rediscovered without making concessions to the established order. Praise of folly and criticism of systems of constraint thus appear as the major thrusts of a work whose utilization in the political struggle became, from that moment on, a matter of course.[4]

In much the same way as Marx's Communism and Rousseau's nature are institutional zero-grounds or empty templates for comparison with the institutional face of the world, Foucault's "Unreason" is a maddening silence or maniacal laughter at the "madness" of institutional reality. And in much the same way as Communism and nature are completely unadorned states of which little of substance could be, or was said by Marx and Rousseau respectively, Foucault's history of madness is rather a history of the institutional rendering of madness. He traces the Middle Ages and Renaissance's limited but brave communication with madness, its tragic, comic, and imaginative aspects, through to the Great Confinement, onward to the "human" and "moral" therapeutics of Pinel and Tuke, on to the birth of the asylum, and lastly toward Freud personifying the distance of the asylum in the figure of the psychiatrist. At all moments Foucault gives us not the essence of madness, but the reflections that reason gives us of madness. Foucault can say very little about the actual experience of madness when it is set up as a critical standpoint. Madness is the dark, meaningless void that gives Foucault the critical authority to wail upon the history of institutions. But unlike Marx and Rousseau, who both believed firmly in the ability of their institutional empty spaces to consecrate a new world, Foucault knows that madness is emptiness and silence, with no possibility of generating a world on its own.

Foucault still sees in madness a repository of truth, but it is simply a dark truth communicating with a truth of light. In reason and unreason, he simply rehearses the everlasting play of death and life, of extrem-

4. Robert Castel, "The Two Readings of 'Histoire de la Folie' in France," in *Rewriting the History of Madness*, edited by Arthur Still and Irving Velody (London: Routledge, 1992), 67.

ity and moderation. One cannot be understood without reference to the other. The distinction between Marx's and Rousseau's undifferentiated states of unity and harmony and Foucault's undifferentiated state of madness is that Foucault's is an "undifferentiated experience of difference." Foucault does not believe that the human essence is one of unity and wholeness, but one of radical difference and division; thus he can allow his institutional hollow of madness to pass judgment upon the institutional world while also knowing madness has no reality apart from that world. Madness only has reality as it connects, conflicts, disrupts, suspends, mingles, attacks, and speaks with reason. Caputo also sees that Foucault is cognizant of this: "So Foucault is aware that there is no access to a 'pure' madness or unreason, to a pure, ante-historical essence of madness, but only to the confrontation of reason and unreason in this or that concrete historical context."[5]

If Marx and Rousseau are searching for the new Adam, the great singular and authentic progenitor of humanity, Foucault sees the world as the brotherly tension of a Cain and Abel. It is at this philosophical point that the figure of Nietzsche looms so large in Foucault's project. Not only does his historical and personal example spell to Foucault this reality, but his philosophical example is the only avenue left to take when you accept this premise. That arcane belief of madness being the progenitor of a work of art, where an artwork emerges from the depths of some artistic mania or melancholy, is reversed in Foucault. He explores this reversal in an essay on Holderlin. He writes that "The trajectory that outlines the flight of the gods and that traces, in reverse, the return of men to their native land is indistinguishable from this cruel line that leads Holderlin to the absence of the father, that directs his language to the fundamental gap in the signifier, that transforms his lyricism to delirium, his work into the absence of a work."[6] Foucault is hinting at the annihilation that madness brings to both art and life, but that is accompanying it at all times. Madness engulfs the work of art in "dissolution" and consecrates the moment of its absence. Madness is not the well from which art springs, but the black hole that it is hypnotized to chase and

5. Caputo, "On Not Knowing Who We Are," 123.
6. Foucault, *Language, Counter-Memory, Practice: Selected Essays and Interviews,* edited and with an introduction by Donald F. Bouchard (Ithaca, N.Y.: Cornell University Press, 1980), 84.

be engulfed in. The point is even more explicit in Nietzsche's life. After years of writing, chasing a truth that he always maintained that mankind could never live with, he falls catatonically silent for the last decade of his life.[7] How could Foucault ever write a history of madness or even hint at a fraction of its experience when in its purest form it is nothing but silence, lack, and absence? Unreason cannot promise a shining world without alienated institutions, but a world that can always and at every moment question and challenge all our ideas about them. It is this point that signals when genealogy must enter as a rejuvenated form of critique, for madness being nothing in itself, it simply offers up mischievously to the world of reason the status of untruth. Foucault writes, "Truth is undoubtedly the sort of error that cannot be refuted because it was hardened into an unalterable form in the long baking process of history."[8] So the world of reason, of truth, just becomes a vast series of hardened mistakes. Madness then becomes a historical melting agent, exposing the confidence of truth to its extreme limits in the hope of unraveling some particular "truth" and beginning again. All of this unraveling of particular, concrete, historical truths simply means that another truth must rise upon the ashes of the former, and then be exposed to the critique of extremity and difference once again. This is the circularity of genealogy's guiding principle, derived from Nietzsche: the all-pervasiveness of the will to power.

Every counterpower already moves within the horizon of the power that it fights; and it is transformed, as soon as it is victorious, into a power complex that provokes a new counterpower.[9]

This regime-relativity of truth means that we cannot raise the banner of truth against our regime. There can be no such thing as a truth independent of its regime, unless it be that of another.[10]

Truth, regime, and power relativity are the Nietzschean philosophical antidote to a worldview where madness is accepted as not being able

7. See also the conclusion to Foucault, *Madness and Civilisation*, which is devoted to making this point.

8. Foucault, *Language, Counter-Memory, Practice*, 144.

9. Jurgen Habermas, *The Philosophical Discourse of Modernity* (Cambridge, Mass.: MIT Press, 1987), 281.

10. Charles Taylor, "Foucault on Freedom and Truth," in *Foucault: A Critical Reader*, edited by David Couzens Hoy (Oxford: Basil Blackwell, 1986), 94.

to rejuvenate the world wholesale without engaging with the world of reason and its ability to institute what it learns. This relegates the world to a continuous regime of critique and interpretation. Constant interpretation will drag down what it criticizes, just to build up another monument for a continuing, yet fresh jest. It seems that Foucault does not shy away from this conclusion. When Foucault delivered an early conference paper in which he labeled Marx, Nietzsche, and Freud the "masters of suspicion," he credited them with ushering in a new age of endless "interpretation."[11] While this may seem an unappealing and pointless activity to some, Foucault heralds it as a new age of skeptical possibility. True to his French intellectual roots, Foucault has no qualms with a way of life that so closely resembles what Camus labeled the life of the "Absurd Man." In *The Myth of Sisyphus,* his paen to the profundity and dignity of being engaged in illogical, pointless, interminable, but indeed passionate ways of life, Camus highlights three human types that lead lives of distinguished absurdity: the Don Juan, the Actor, and the Conqueror. All occupy themselves with pursuits that have no end or purpose beyond the simple pleasure, passion, and pride of the moment. They want for nothing everlasting.

What, in fact, is the absurd man? He who, without negating it, does nothing for the eternal. Not that nostalgia is foreign to him. But that he prefers his courage and his reasoning.... Assured of his temporally limited freedom, of his revolt devoid of future and of his mortal consciousness, he lives out his adventure within the span of his lifetime.... A greater life cannot mean for him another life.[12]

To this cast of "presentist" characters we can add Foucault's vision of the scholar, or as he would have called himself, the "intellectual." This personage endeavors in the land of limitless interpretation that guarantees that everything is radically limited. The modern world is bequeathed with an infinite task of analysis, a hermeneutics of depth. How far can we keep digging into the layers of history? How many times can we retrace the descent of something? What Camus sees in the personal tone of character types and individual lifestyles Foucault inculcates as a critical or genealogical "attitude." Both are kinds of present-centered

11. Michel Foucault, *Foucault: Aesthetics, Method, and Epistemology,* edited by James D. Faubion (New York: New Press, 1998), 269–78.

12. Albert Camus, *The Myth of Sisyphus* (London: Penguin, 2000), 64.

ethics, but whereas Camus's is focused more on individual modes of life, Foucault's is generalized into more of a political position toward institutional reality. But just as the absurd hero cannot fathom some other, greater life, the genealogical stance cannot fathom another greater alternative to the idea, institution, or science that it is "interpreting." This brings us to a closer understanding of the Célinean formulation between madness, modern intelligence, and "all things being equal." Unreason, genealogy, and the relativity of systems of power are Foucault's variations on this melody. But before I delve further into the philosophical tensions of genealogy and its status as a variation or reformulation of Kantian critique, I will further explore its primary character as a historical method with Menippean and carnivalesque undertones.

Carnival, Menippea, and the Buffoonery of History

So little is known of the historical figure of Menippus that all that remains of him is a mocking laughter that has reverberated through history. The author of supposedly thirteen books, all of which are lost, but that spawned a plethora of imitators from his own time to the recent day, his mordant cynical amusement at the world seems to shine brightest when old ways, philosophies, faiths, and forms are in dissolution. The author of a book entitled *Necromancy,* Menippus is depicted in Lucian's dialogues as a traveler among the dead. From the lowered perspective of the underworld, he manages to raise himself above life, as if the dark underbelly of life provides a subterranean platform for the ridicule and satirization of human stupidity. Equating him in the long history of cynicism, Donald R. Dudley observes that "Menippus is one of a long line of satirists who have taken a tour of the Underworld to describe how there, where a truer standard of values prevails, their enemies are faring very badly indeed."[13]

The existence of an otherworldly standard for judgment of life, a kind of reversed and rebellious moral equivalent to scientific objectivity, is one of the main pillars of the classical Menippean position. A tour of the underworld will furnish the bewildered tourist with dethroned kings, heroes of the earth declaimed as frauds, the rich transformed into

13. Donald R. Dudley, *A History of Cynicism* (London: Bristol Classical Press, 1998), 71.

slaves, previously firm and stout moralists floundering as castaways, pious religious believers undressed as superstitious dupes. From the perspective of the underworld, the earth looks as a vast madhouse. There is a kind of secret knowledge here that rouses a mixture of frivolity and condemnation because "Lucian refers to him as 'the secret dog who bites as he laughs.'"[14] Menippus's perspective affords him the ability to see the world of human affairs as an exercise in lunacy. This necessarily involves him in the twin and often contradictory modes of laughter and derision while also succumbing to a moralistic purpose, albeit one that seems doomed. The worthiness of literary history's imitation of him lies in this ability to flirt with these two positions in an uneasy tension. The purposes of Menippean satire can be both righteous and profane, noble truth seeking and farcical investigation. This is because "He is a fantastic experimenter … who goes to the edges of the world to see truth for himself, and discovers absurdity rather than truth, and who comes back not as a prophet or redeemer, but as an imposter."[15]

Menippus is the wizened impostor in refined society, who refuses to be either a prophet of a future way of life or prescribe a redemptive tonic for a mad society; a plumber of the troughs and depths of life, seeking the limits of human experience; a writer whose laughter is offset with a critical bark. Already the classical Menippus reads like a resume of the neo-cynic Foucault.

Of the most sophisticated modern expositions of the hallmarks of Menippean satire, Mikhail Bakhtin's studies of Dostoevsky and Rabelais rank supreme and lonely among the literature. Bakhtin couples his well-executed understanding of Menippean satire with what he describes as the "carnival sense of the world," where the two are in a relationship of everyday and literary symbiosis. Bakhtin lists some of the most salient features of Menippean satire. It is helpful to explore some, since so many coincide with Foucault's historical project of genealogy. The most impor-

---

14. Luis E. Navia, *Classical Cynicism: A Critical Study* (London: Greenwood Press, 1996), 156. The reference to Menippus as a "dog" of course alludes to his philosophical pedigree in classical cynicism, where the word "cynic" derives from the Greek word meaning "like a dog," with all its negative connotations of being a mangy, snarling, disgruntled beast and its positive characteristics of assiduity, mental agility, and determination.

15. Joel C. Relihan, "Menippus in Antiquity and the Renaissance," in *The Cynics: The Cynic Movement in Antiquity and Its Legacy,* edited by R. Bracht Branham and Marie-Odile Goulet-Caze (Berkeley: University of California Press, 1996), 277.

tant of these, despite the Menippea's farcical and fantastic nature, is that the fantastic and farce are always subordinated to "ultimate questions." Fantastic, extraordinary, and comical situations are constructed solely for the purpose of investigating and trialing a philosophical idea. It is a critical endeavor, because "we emphasize that the fantastic here serves not for the positive embodiment of truth, but as a mode for searching after truth, provoking it, and, most important, testing it."[16] Menippea is also characterized by an "extraordinary freedom of plot and philosophical invention," which Bakhtin attributes to it being free from the fetters of memoir and history.[17] While in saying this he was comparing the genre of Socratic dialogue (with its literary origins cemented in the attempt to faithfully reconstruct actual conversations with Socrates) with the Menippea, it is obvious that in a more general sense, as a "fantastical critique," Menippea is freed from the responsibility of historical faithfulness and the demands of memorial accuracy. The Menippea is also attracted to what Bakhtin describes as "slum naturalism," in which plots and characters take place in the detritus of life, in its most worldly and bodily forms. As a rule, Menippea presumes that truth does not live in isolation from the world, but resides, moves, mutates, and influences in "brothels," "prisons," "the marketplace," "the high road," "taverns," and "erotic orgies." As Bakhtin observes, "The idea here fears no slum, is not afraid of any of life's filth. The man of the idea—the wise man—collides with worldly evil, depravity, baseness, and vulgarity in their most extreme expression."[18]

Menippea is also attracted to the altered states of man: those psychological maladies, doubles, deliriums, hysterias, intoxications, and passions, anything that destroys the "finalised quality" of life.[19] In conjunction with this character experience is a plot experience of "abrupt transitions and shifts, ups and downs, rises and falls, unexpected comings together of distant and disunited things," anything that heightens the incidence of strange couplings and radical splits.[20] Last, and adding to the overall effect of multiplicity, heterogeneity, and agonistic tension

16. Mikhail Bakhtin, *Problems of Dostoevsky's Poetics* (Manchester: Manchester University Press, 1984), 114.
17. Bakhtin, *Problems of Dostoevsky's Poetics*, 114.
18. Bakhtin, *Problems of Dostoevsky's Poetics*, 115.
19. Bakhtin, *Problems of Dostoevsky's Poetics*, 116–17.
20. Bakhtin, *Problems of Dostoevsky's Poetics*, 118.

that seem to characterize the Menippea, the genre delights in the insertion and parodying of other genres such as "novellas, letters, oratorical speeches, symposia, and so on."[21] This patchwork of texts adds to the overall sense of dispersal and unfamiliarity with which the Menippea attempts to suffuse life.

Bakhtin couples with this literary view of the world a real-life everyday folkloric counterpart in the experience of the carnival. Bakhtin demonstrates how the medieval and Renaissance worlds were marked by a deep and unquestioned experience of carnival that functioned as a pageantry of laughter that cut across the stifled world of officialdom. The reality of carnival in the lives of medieval men and women was so strong that Bakhtin posits that they lived a kind of double life, one leashed by hierarchy, formality, regulation, and denial, the other unleashed by laughter, reversal, parody, and the sensual. Bakhtin writes of the myriad forms of the carnivalesque: "They offered a completely different, nonofficial, extraecclesiastical and extrapolitical aspect of the world, of man, and of human relations; they built a second world and a second life outside officialdom, a world in which all medieval people participated more or less, in which they lived during a given time of the year."[22] It is obvious from this that Bakhtin recognizes in the forms of the carnival and the carnivalesque sense of the world a spirit of all-inclusiveness, which is made possible by the temporary suspension of rules, roles, titles, and authority. It is the laughing breath of freedom, delighting in a jubilant relativity of things when they have been stripped of the absoluteness that institutions place upon them. And yet the suspension of one set of rules does not mean that the carnival experience is one of chaos, where anything and everything is permitted. Those under the spell of the carnivalesque gladly submit to a separate establishment of rules, rules that do not foster order, obedience, hierarchy, and tradition, but instead promote parody, profanation, replenishment, and intimate communion.

Yet more than simple "suspension" and "striping," the carnival has a positive content of "heightening." There is a freedom to be found in accentuating the grotesque aspects of a world's governing ideas, a purposeful and playful distortion that opens the world out to "present a

21. Bakhtin, *Problems of Dostoevsky's Poetics,* 118.
22. Bakhtin, *Rabelais and His World,* translated by Helene Iswolsky (Bloomington: Indiana University Press, 1984), 5–6.

contradictory and double-faced fullness of life."[23] When the abstract is met with the grotesque, both are able to meet in a strangely familiar embrace, as each takes on the character of the other. The abstract and official are seen as meaningless and random where they can gladly relinquish their fearful hold on responsibility and power, while the fantastic, farcical, and the everyday are playfully crowned as truth, relishing the opportunity to act out and send up the powers that in general hold sway over them. This, Bakhtin maintains, is the ironic accord, the fruitful tension that people of the Middle Ages and Renaissance lived under. This "world inside out" is at once seen as the power of death and decay to be the source of rebirth and renewal. What is obvious about the carnival nub of this culture is that there is also a strong relation between art and life. Bakhtin characterizes it thus: "It belongs to the borderline between art and life. In reality, it is life itself, but shaped according to a certain pattern of play."[24] Carnival is art without the stage, for the people are everywhere involved in the spectacle, rather than mere observers. Carnival is pageantry without conscious performance—simply the pomp and ceremony that emanate instinctively from life itself. Of course the prevalence of carnival culture, gesture, and belief in the Middle Ages brought forth its own works of art brimming with the carnivalesque spirit, but properly speaking, the carnival relation to art was one of a keen eye for the aesthetic veins of life rather than a life contemplated and formalized by the aesthetic. Life as a moving work of art, rather than art as representation of life, is the structure proper to the carnivalesque. Art and life live in "free and familiar" relation to one another in the carnivalistic act. Art and life are unmediated.

So what connection does this developed understanding of the Menippea and the carnivalesque have with Foucault's historical project of genealogy? Again, its usefulness is connected with illuminating Foucault's constant attempts to "defamiliarize" history. Where Foucault's archaeological position achieves defamiliarization through its carving up of history into spatially rendered categorizations, schematized chunks of epistemic history bordered and delineated by epistemic "breaks," "shifts," and sudden mutations, genealogy achieves this defamiliarity by the assumption of a satirical standpoint to history. The use of Menip-

23. Bakhtin, *Rabelais and His World*, 62.
24. Bakhtin, *Rabelais and His World*, 7.

pean and carnival structures, techniques, and assumptions by Foucault assists his quest to weave into history myriad levels of radical ambiguity. Where archaeological history alienates our clear view by breaking it up into pieces because of the removal of its anchor of continuity in the human subject, genealogical history alienates our view by constantly turning our understanding inside out by positing some "other" level of experience. If we look at the broad historical genealogies Foucault paints, we will see some of the most obvious of Menippean hallmarks and carnivalesque stances. Foucault very clearly states his intention to view history as a carnivalesque reveler of history, as a Menippean misfit inverting and dethroning the very serious business of what he understands as a vast historical subterfuge.

The new historian, the genealogist, will know what to make of this masquerade. He will not be too serious to enjoy it: on the contrary, he will push the masquerade to its limits and prepare the great carnival of time where masks are constantly reappearing.... Taking up these masks, revitalizing the buffoonery of history, we adopt an identity whose unreality surpasses that of God who started the charade.[25]

We recall that the Menippea is unafraid of the detritus of history, dwelling in the ugly receptacles of life's condemned, mischievous, and afflicted. Settings in brothels, taverns, back roads, dungeons, and other societal and moral cul-de-sacs are the proper space for the story to emanate. Foucault also does not shy from these febrile pools of social life. The presence of leprosy and its houses of relegation overwhelmingly haunt *Madness and Civilisation*. That biblical affliction that ushered in our juvenile experiments in the forces of confinement and banishment set the stage for the story of madness and its subjugation and codification by reason. *Discipline and Punish* is forever associated with its gruesome beginning: the startling chronicle of the grisly, protracted, and sadistic execution of the regicide Damiens, a criminal ritualistically tortured, quartered, and burned. Do not forget Foucault's publication of the memoirs of the French hermaphrodite Herculine Barbin (an accessory to his assault on Victorian sexual politics in his *History of Sexuality*). It represents a heart-wrenching, deeply felt autobiography culminating in suicide that concludes with the blunt, methodical autopsy report

25. Foucault, *Language, Counter-Memory, Practice*, 160–61.

of Barbin's death, integrated by Foucault, which listed her anatomical anomalies and finally concluded that she was a man.

Sex, disease, and violence are the borderlands of Foucault's search for truth. The ideas and truths that comprise our life do not live in isolation from the world, but instead find warm fertile hosts in the filth, decrepitude, and ambiguity that we both create and are constantly attempting to expel, control, and understand. That which we consciously avoid, the threatening, our enemies, and the extremes within ourselves, are believed to say more about us than our moderate tastes, accommodating friends, and everyday comings and goings. Truth burns brighter and is experienced more acutely in the insalubrious atmosphere of this "slum naturalism."

With this investment in the unsavory, nothing excites the Menippean leaning more than the juxtaposition of opposites. Strange couplings of distant and disunited things are the stock and trade of Menippean satire, and Foucault follows suit. Again, shocked by the opening to *Discipline and Punish,* we are then treated to a rendition of the sober and disciplined timetable drawn up to regiment a day in the lives of the "young prisoners of Paris." Foucault highlights the strangeness of this coupling by noting that "less than a century separates" these two contrary attitudes to punishment.[26] What makes this bringing together of the incongruent and distant so poignant is the fact that it is designed precisely to demonstrate the lack of distance between them, both temporally and in principle. That modern trick of the surrealists to unite unrelated images in order to effect a relation with new, radical meaning is ably put to use in Foucault's historical discovery of this disquieting disciplinary combination. In many respects Foucault owes more to this avant-garde tradition than he does to the Menippean or carnival. The surrealist's love of the happy accident as a way of dramatically intervening in the everyday and routine interpretation of reality is the modern expression of the carnival and Menippean routines of inappropriate coupling. Plague and leprosy as the manure that nourishes politically utopian dreams of efficiency and expulsion are certainly viewed by Foucault in a sarcastic way as "happy accidents."

In a drastically succinct summary, *Discipline and Punish* is a work

26. Foucault, *Discipline and Punish: The Birth of the Prison* (London: Penguin, 1991), 7.

devoted to the exploration of the space between the horrifically violated body and the disciplined *homo docilis* in order to make the point that between these two distant poles there is little temporal or moral space at all. Having replaced spectacular, despotic, and cruel displays of power with the lifeless impulse to rational instruction and official regulation, the observer is left to wonder at the progress of the journey. We are left weighing a dramatic grand politics of the here-ever-after or the subdued routine of ubiquitous micropolitics. The perceived progress between these two worldviews is eradicated when placed side by side like this. But Foucault would not have bargained with the significant force of strange couplings and conflicting images if he did not want this to be his over-arching point. Later in *Discipline and Punish,* Foucault provides us with a conspicuous variant to this Menippean procedure: the curious shift or the unexpected transition. He writes, "If it is true that the leper gave rise to rituals of exclusion, which to a certain extent provided the model for and the general form of the Great Confinement, then the plague gave rise to disciplinary projects."[27] The plague as a force of disorder awakens humanity's desire to police itself, as the leper and his lesions stimulate our desire to cleanse the body politic of the unwanted. In both cases, sickness, the harbinger of death, sadistically breathes life into the forces of ruthless subjugation and fastidious discipline, blanketing the voices of others that undermine a burgeoning truth regime. Foucault states that the rational reaction to both these infections spawns two separate political dreams: the dream of the pure community purged of its impurities and the dream of a disciplined society segmented, surveyed, analyzed, and controlled. This frightening alteration from sickly disorder to orderly hygiene is a sudden transition designed to make the reader question the benignity or even legitimacy of our efficient and regimented establishment—a governance that gave birth to itself by means of the lessons it learned in the face of death and chaos. Foucault turns our understanding of the authority over us upside down. Not only does he see in history a carnivalesque masquerade in the way we have been behaviorally dominated, he uses the same trick against the deception by chronicling the unexpected mutation and presenting it in its most disaffecting manner.

From spectacle to surveillance is the central passage of Foucault's

27. Foucault, *Discipline and Punish,* 198.

genealogical period, and it involves perhaps his most compelling and wide-ranging decrowning, the somatic reversal. Unafraid of the filth, Foucault's genealogies are centered on that which has traditionally received the scorn of history ... the body. In a religious West that treats the body as marked for death and the soul as our eternal and free element, Foucault reinvests the body with a concern that has been denied it, attempting to show that the body is the site of disciplinary projects and thus also our possible site of freedom. *Discipline and Punish* is a work centered on the pivot of the body, as the site that determines our soul. Foucault traces the modern world's insertion of individual's bodies into a "mechanics of power," which in turn effects a new "political anatomy."[28] In a clever Menippean reinterpretation of the old stalwart of the organic theory of the state, the "body politic" is translated as a "political anatomy." The body politic as an organic entity is transformed into a political anatomy with a purely mechanical function. Bodily political mechanics replace bodily political organics. With even more Menippean finesse, Foucault realigns this growth in a mechanical political anatomy with Marx's study of the accumulation of Capital.

In fact, the two processes—the accumulation of men and the accumulation of capital—cannot be separated; it would not have been possible to solve the problem of the accumulation of men without the growth of an apparatus of production capable of both sustaining them and using them; conversely, the techniques that made the cumulative multiplicity of men useful accelerated the accumulation of capital.[29]

This accumulation of men is the process of their disciplinary and mechanical organization in a factory-like bodily arrangement. This is the new body politic, its organic functions atrophied by the desire for the efficiency of mechanization. Foucault interestingly aligns this process with Marx's tracing of the process of capital growth. Here Foucault shows his radical political stripes, but with an important disclaimer to have avoided Marxist idealism and economic determinism. Marx traces the growth of capital as the extraction of man's "essence" converted into capital. In other words, Marx is telling the story of humanity's plundered and subjugated soul. Foucault provides a parallel story from the

28. Foucault, *Discipline and Punish*, 138.
29. Foucault, *Discipline and Punish*, 221.

opposite pole, saying this process is unthinkable without the "production" of humanity's soul so as to arrange and train their "docile" bodies. In Marx the body is used and engaged to imprison the soul in the form of capital; in Foucault, the soul is manufactured in order to imprison the body in disciplined obedience. While Foucault aligns these two processes as related, there is no question which one he believes takes precedence. The concern on the body opens up a far more fruitful schema of power for dissection than Marx's mere economically determined mining of the soul, not to mention the fact that it sidesteps Marx's idealism. Foucault does not presuppose the existence of an essence to humanity as Marx does. In Foucault's Menippean history the freedom of the body is sacrificed to the artificial manufacturing of souls. This inversion grants to Foucault a boon of radical interpretive resources to bring to bear in a world when the Marxist interpretive resource has become exhausted. Foucault is both claiming himself as the heir to and surpassing of the Marxist attack on society.

This leads us to the great Menippean and carnivalesque crux of Foucault's genealogical method, his omnipresent and "productive" conception of power. This is a method that makes use of the carnivalesque idea of "heightening." In much the same way as the carnival view of the world found a newfound freedom in heightening the grotesque aspects of the world, so Foucault finds a freedom in heightening the grotesque reality of power. Ironically, this newfound interpretative freedom is won at the expense of the freedom of the will. I will discuss this later. Foucault takes great issue with power being conceived as purely a repressive force. Foucault gradually sees power, a force that has traditionally been seen as one of negation, as a positive power of invention. "Production" is the paramount word here, for it denotes that power is not simply tyranny, but creation. Its omnipresence is manifest by the fact that it can dominate and generate. It becomes both a power of death and a giver of life. In fact Foucault heightens the grotesquery of power to such an extent that it offers up to it everything: "The carceral network does not cast the unassimilable into a confused hell; there is no outside. It takes back with one hand what it seems to exclude with the other. It saves everything, including what it punishes. It is unwilling to waste what it has decided to disqualify."[30]

30. Foucault, *Discipline and Punish,* 301.

Foucault is devising a theory of power that enables it to not only constrain and prohibit something out of existence, but also provoke and coax something into existence. What this has the effect of doing to individuals is to transform them from being points where power is exercised, or to which it is applied, to reinscribing them into the power matrix in which they become effects or epiphenomena of power. Individuals are power's products and thus become powerless. And one should not question Foucault's insistence of the "universality of the carceral."[31] Foucault gives to power the status of a monadology, a monadology every bit as omnipresent and involuntary as the one he constructed in the name of history via his archaeological method. Thus we should be able to observe in this genealogical phase the same philosophical procedure with regard to the subject, the timeless will, freedom, and agency that we observed in the archaeological phase.

Foucault's extreme subject phobia requires him to demonstrate to a society that has built its "free" institutions upon the subject's innate interest and agency, that in fact there is a level of coercion and domination they have missed. Foucault subverts these misguided believers of the subject, representing their supposed "freedom" as the precondition for their coercion and mechanical dominion. Disciplinary techniques work upon the subject that believes that it is free. Our enlightenment and our free societies are the precondition for a productive domination to which we blind ourselves. Our freedom enables us to dominate ourselves. This is by far the greatest of Foucault's carnivalesque inversion of the world. Effectively our freedom is being taken from us by Foucault and then offered to his concept of power. Yet in the same way that he invoked this procedure upon history, thereby rendering it unable to explain its actions or causes, Foucault's power becomes all-pervasive, yet powerless to comprehend itself.

Heightening power involves offering up to it the creative power that the freedom of the will commands in questioning it. Yet again Foucault sacrifices the power of the subject into the realm of power, a move that would not be troubling if Foucault did not allow the very subject itself to be swallowed by his all-consuming system of power. This not only makes power an omnipresent power that cannot be combated, it

31. Foucault, *Discipline and Punish*, 303.

also inseminates power with the ability to combat authority. Thus Foucault becomes the new messiah of the radical political imagination while alienating individuals from the locus of their "productive" power. Thus he champions the use of transgression in local and regional struggles against the network of universal power, but analyzes that power without the formative and causative functions of will, intention, and atemporal freedom. Foucault dissolves the timeless moral will of the German idealist tradition into his monolithic Nietzschean conception of relativity of power systems. By empowering power with our timeless freedom, he is unable to demonstrate how that power will be combated. Power also loses all of its explanatory strength because it is haunted by the ghost of the timeless will that Foucault eliminated in his assault on the subject.

Thus power can only ever be perceived as a perverse and extreme Menippeanism with regard to history. Remember that one of the first hallmarks of a successful Menippean satirical stance is the flirtation between the position of laughter and derision and the satire's involvement in a moralistic purpose. Remember that the fantastic of the Menippea is always subordinated to probing serious moral questions, but once the extreme satirical and cynical nature of that grotesque fantastic reality has been observed, it throws the moral rationale constantly into doubt. Foucault's genealogical history resembles so closely the Menippean satire because the theory of power that sustains and drives the genealogy partakes in precisely this type of doomed flirtation. The moralistic freedom of the individual will is melted unrecognizably into the monism of power, blunting its atemporality while still deigning various local sites of this ubiquitous power to be places of critical endeavor. Foucault destroys the dualism that sustains him as a critical thinker and descends into a Menippean playfulness.

This study is less concerned with the historical validity of Foucault's actual histories (that is, the work of professional historians) and more inclined to dig out the myriad levels of Menippean satire and carnival inversion that Foucault either sees or implants in history. The issue is not whether such pathological alterity exists in history itself or if it exists in Foucault's historical sense. I seek to probe the results of this genealogical approach applied to the instances of alteration existent in history. How far can the genealogy be pushed? How much Menippean and carnivalesque salt can be dissolved in the waters of history before it becomes undrinkable? To show the heights that this ironical glance toward history can achieve, we need only observe Foucault's own appraisal of the carnival and festive tradition, the tradition that his theory of power mimics so frankly. Foucault sabotages even this cherished convention: "A whole literary fiction of the festival grew up around the plague: suspended laws, lifted prohibitions, the frenzy of passing time, bodies mingling together without respect, individuals unmasked, abandoning their statutory identity and the figure under which they had been recognised, allowing a quite different truth to appear."[32] Foucault maintains that what gained ascendency from the plague was in fact the opposite (or reversal) of this state of affairs. No communal festival, but an individuated division; no legal contravention and freedom, but penetrative restriction and check. In other words Foucault is obsessive about "abandoning the statutory identity" behind history. He wishes to expose all power regime's camouflages and disguises or "the figure under which they had been recognised, allowing a quite different truth to appear." This obsession even extends as far as making festive and carnival principles suffer from an unmasking as a fiction. He dismisses as a fictive existence that which he wishes so earnestly to inculcate into the normalized modern world. Foucault's Nietzschean mutation or heightening of Menippean and carnival gestures into the intellectual war machinery of genealogy is so all-embracing that it attempts to destroy even its own precursors. We began the chapter on Foucault by asserting that he represented the movement of reason chasing and devouring its tail; here genealogy copies this circularity.

We have noted that Foucault, as first and foremost a radical French intellectual, is a direct bearer of and contributor to the avant-garde tradi-

---

32. Foucault, *Discipline and Punish,* 197. Despite the fact that Foucault is here undermining the very festive tradition by which so much of his work seems nourished, there is an earlier example to be found of Foucault's initial sympathy with the idea of the festival. In a lecture given in Japan in 1970 entitled "Madness and Society," Foucault talks again with some nostalgia about the Middle Age's wonderfully organic relation to madness, including as evidence of this fruitful union the spectacle of that "non-religious" festival, the "Festival of Folly," where things are reversed, inverted, mocked, and overturned. Foucault includes this state of affairs in his attempt to show how "the truth appears" to people in the Middle Ages in the form of madness. The fact that Foucault would only a few years later reverse the reverence with which he held this tradition says more about how highly he regarded it than any suggestion that he had abandoned it; see Foucault, *Aesthetics, Method, and Epistemology,* edited by James D. Faubion (New York: New Press, 1998), 2:340.

tion, giving him a taste for those developments made by the conspicuous leaders of Surrealism. Let us not forget that Foucault wrote an appraisal of the surrealist author Raymond Roussel, was an admirer of Georges Bataille, and most leadingly for this study, composed a short essay discussing René Magritte's famous painting *Ceci n'est pas une pipe*. It seems Foucault was a great admirer of that most gifted surrealist in the art of unlikely combination, of the disconcerting placement of objects within the painting frame. He represents a visual saboteur to Foucault's role as historical saboteur, placing as he did contradictory historical images side by side in the historical field. Foucault learned the defamiliarizing effect this technique enables: "I cannot dismiss the notion that the sorcery here lies in an operation rendered invisible by the simplicity of its result, but which can alone explain the vague uneasiness provoked."[33] A lover of the tautological correspondence, the paradoxical equivalence, Magritte signals to Foucault the possibilities this technique has for erecting a riposte to history. Irony redoubling in a destructive circuit provides the needed perspective to unravel history. It is no wonder then that in many ways Foucault would also rehearse the ironical perversities of the surrealist's precursors, the Dadaists, those proto-surrealists who consumed themselves in ironical self-destruction. If carnival and festive delight were thought to have grown up in the shadow of the plaque, it seems natural that its modern variant of Dadaist joyous ridicule was born in the heart of World War I and its plague of poisonous ideologies bringing wholesale death. Dada, like carnival, wished to turn the world upside down and suspend the customary laws of social production. But whereas carnival was an unprocessed, laughing celebration centered on the space of the town square, art without footlights, Dada was a determined and scornful celebration centered around the theatre, the footlights turned from the stage to illume the absurdity of life, the former life merging with art, the latter art seeking to redirect life. The difference is profound and tells us something of Foucault's odd use of carnival's ironic accord, mutating it into something more in line with Dada's ironic discord. Note some tenets of the Dada Manifesto of 1918.

33. Foucault, *This Is Not a Pipe,* translated and edited by James Harkness (Berkeley: University of California Press, 1983), 20.

DADA—this is a word that throws up ideas so that they can be shot down...

DADA DOES NOT MEAN ANYTHING

I am against systems; the most acceptable system is that of having none on no principle.[34]

Dada, a celebration of nothingness that flutters seemingly with every blink of the eye between joyous creation and scornful destruction, provides us with some template as to the heights that Foucault took his genealogical look at history. Those conscientious objectors to society as a whole pushed their protestation and critique of the world to such an extreme that they ended up circling and reveling furiously in their cul-de-sacs of contradiction and paradox, pushing this oppositional stance into absurdity and not shying from the results. Dada's short-lived burst of illogicality when confronted with a world gone mad could never reach the sophistication or nuance, or the variety of artistic techniques and procedures, that the Menippean and carnival attitudes to life could. This is partly because the fury and speed with which they jumped at life meant they reached their antinomies so quickly that they could not invent a modus operandi to sustain their view past the embrace they made with their contrary. The therapeutic finiteness of their reaction to life stumbled on the rapidity with which it sought an infinite expression. Thus it devolved into an embracing of an infinite principleless ethos. Foucault, however, shows too many of the signs of the genuine and advanced form of the Menippean and carnival stance to be branded wholesale as an academic Dadaist. But what is obvious in Foucault is a movement away from the restricted and fixed philosophical boundaries of these traditions toward a more infinite and universal installing of their values. Because of this tendency, Foucault's theory of power takes on many of the characteristics of Dada's ironical discord and principleless nothingness. The Dadaists sacrificed their oppositional prerogative to itself in an endless catatonic circuit. All this shows us is how strong that initial critical impulse was to have ended up devouring itself. In much the same way, Foucault's theory of power has this same inhibition of critical emancipative avenues for action and a negativism that can only suggest to us how robust and fierce his critical spirit is, even if it has been consumed by the

34. Tristan Tzara, *Seven Dada Manifestos and Lampisteries,* translated by Barbara Wright (London: John Calder, 1977), 4, 5, and 9.

power systems he analyzes. But I will discuss this later, as there is further to be observed in Foucault's Menippean history.

Part of the revitalized buffoonery of history involves a reworking of the Menippean motions of plot freedom and invention and its connection with release from the fetters of memoir and history. While uncomplicated for a storyteller, this is of course problematic for a historian and scholar whose art is founded exclusively upon memoir and history. The historian's only working material is the raw facts of history memorialized, and he is charged with the duty to tell the story of history faithfully, so how can Foucault deviate from this trust? As such he cannot. But he can forage among the raw facts for those that are not normally admitted into the main story. He can weave a new story by recasting the extras and minor players in the costumes of the heroes. Here Foucault's greatest (and archaeological) work, *The Order of Things,* is a case in point. The cast of characters that Foucault exhibits as representative of the various epistemes that he is channeling is at once humbling in its virtuoso staging and bewildering in its shunning of the normally crowned master thinkers of those ages. And it is not as if Foucault is discovering neglected thinkers that he views as worthy of renewed interest, having suffered an injustice at the hands of modern historians who could not see their greatness. Rather, he uses them as paltry and mediocre evidence of a plot arrangement he devises: insentient blind witnesses in a courtroom convened by Foucault himself. In the English preface to that work Foucault states that his story is coming from a differing angle and thus requires a recasting. He writes, "There are shifts of emphasis: the calendar of saints and heroes is somewhat altered (Linnaeus is given more space than Buffon, Destutt de Tracy than Rousseau: the Physiocrats are opposed singlehanded by Cantillon)."[35]

Foucault is able to recast the story so radically because of his differing perspective, which a few pages later he states as "to reveal a *positive unconscious* of knowledge: a level that eludes the consciousness of the scientist and yet is part of scientific discourse."[36] Minor and forgotten characters will willingly dance for the puppeteer who seeks to seize their consciousness from them in favor of an "unconscious" of the puppeteer's

35. Foucault, *The Order of Things* (London: Tavistock and Routledge, 1989), x.
36. Foucault, *The Order of Things,* xi.

own devising. Major characters are thus alienated from the proceedings. The mere belief in a "positive unconscious" that directs thought leaves to one side the problem of major historical causes embodied in the work of the major figures of scientific history. Foucault writes, "In this work, then, I left the problem of causes to one side; I chose instead to confine myself to describing the transformations themselves, thinking that this would be an indispensable step if, one day, a theory of scientific change and epistemological causality was to be constructed."[37] Does Foucault not recognize that the struggle for a theory of scientific change and epistemological causality had been raging in the precincts of the conscious subject? No wonder, then, that the positive unconscious resembles a herding pen for the minor characters of history's story. Foucault constructs houses for the mimics that systematically deny admittance to the heralds and originators. What manner of novel arrangements can then be afforded the Menippean historian who has been released from faithful plot and memoir? This state of affairs is brought about solely by the denial of the agency of the subject, or the question of the will. Plot invention and absent memory are the freedoms granted by ignorance of the timeless freedom of the will. The raising of the positive unconscious of knowledge, or the episteme, or the historical a priori, or madness, or Power/Knowledge as the essential level of knowledge is simply a smoke screen to usurp the progenitors of knowledge from their handiwork. Of course the standpoint of the archaeological "episteme" and the genealogical "darkness" are not simply two separate approaches for achieving the same historical outcome. At a more general level they are the same thing, grandly expressed as the haunting of man by his "other."

The unthought (whatever name we give it) is not lodged in man like a shrivelled-up nature or a stratified history; it is, in relation to man, the Other: the Other that is not only a brother but a twin, born not of man, nor in man, but beside him and at the same time, in an identical newness, in an unavoidable duality.[38]

To chronicle the life of madness in its fascination for and apprehension by reason, and to posit an unconscious epistemological ground that governs the dispersal of knowledge at a given time, allows both these

37. Foucault, *The Order of Things,* xiii.
38. Foucault, *The Order of Things,* 326.

enterprises to revolve around the idea of an unacknowledged double reality that surreptitiously accompanies our more conscious deeds. The connection between this philosophical assumption and the historical incidence of festive reversal has also been noticed by some of Foucault's more insightful commentators. William Connolly discusses such festivities while discussing Foucault's desire to "slacken" the power of order over our lives.

Seasonal festivals were enacted in which that which was forbidden was allowed and those who were normally subordinated (because their order necessitated it) were temporarily placed in a superior position. In these festivals, that which was officially circumscribed or denied was temporarily allowed and affirmed. The participants were able to glimpse the injustices implicit in their own necessities; they were encouraged to live these necessities with more humanity during normal periods of the year.[39]

Connolly's observation highlights Foucault's channeling of this carnival tradition, even going so far as to slyly mention in a footnote that Foucault's favorite role is to play that of the "modern fool."[40] But Connolly's recognition of this directive in Foucault's thought also highlights where Foucault diverges from this tradition and what is missing from his modern take upon it. Connolly is trying to bring Foucault back into the critical fray by circumscribing his work within the perennial problematic of political legitimacy. In other words, Foucault's dredging of the built-up blockages of unreason, the unthought, the Other, the extra-subjective, the unconscious is seen by Connolly as having the effect of "slackening" the political order and making it more aware and receptive of the "dirt" that it itself produces. A much more yielding and flexible political order ensues that constantly seeks to question the productions, rigidity, management, coercion, and suppression inherent to any imperatives of order. Order and legitimacy for that order are maintained by a provision of "slack" that is at once the "precondition of and limit to virtue in a modern polity."[41] Just like the carnival festivals that not only suspend but reverse the order of the day, Foucault's opening of the world of unreason to reason's glance encourages reason to "glimpse the

39. William E. Connolly, *Politics and Ambiguity* (Madison: The University of Wisconsin Press, 1987), 95.
40. Connolly, *Politics and Ambiguity*, 93.
41. Connolly, *Politics and Ambiguity*, 96.

injustices" of their order and "live these necessities with more human-ity." Like the political order, whose ferocity and uncompromising im-peratives he seeks to "tame or relax," Connolly also wishes to tame and relax the ferocity and uncompromising imperatives that Foucault throws at the ordered world from the underworld of unreason.

What Connolly is alluding to when he mentions the life of festival and carnival peoples is the therapeutic role this reality plays for the po-litical order. And for that matter Bakhtin, too, understands the stances of carnival life and the Menippean worldview to be therapeutic correc-tives to the stern life of order. Admitted into the circle of life, into the province of reason and order, the exchange between the two promotes a healthy fusion, one mitigating the other. Even if Foucault hopes for some kind of similar meeting of the worlds of reason and unreason, there is not a lot to suggest that Foucault has the remotest faith in this possibil-ity. Where the everyday and life-stemming world of carnival has a posi-tive content because of its being woven into the very sinews of society, Foucault's wholly theoretical construction of Menippean history and his scholarly standpoint of a carnivalesque thwarting of reality mean that he transforms these entities into providing only a negative standard. There is a certain pessimistic "turn" to Foucault's embracing of these tradi-tions. What Connolly, Bakhtin, and the medieval world see as a releas-ing valve for the pressure of overregulation Foucault transforms into a sovereign political position that can never be accommodated into the world. Unreason and the "Other" only make sense in their conjectural confrontation with the world, not their remedial cooperation. If mad-ness could be accommodated into society, Foucault would simply reject it as a new regime that would spawn a new world of unreason. On this issue Foucault is unequivocal: "'The Whole of Society' is precisely that which should not be considered except as something to be destroyed. And then, we can only hope it will never exist again."[42]

Where Connolly rightly points out that Foucault's position does not preclude a space for moral reasoning and judgment, indeed, where Fou-cault stops inquiring, a large and pressing question of legitimacy looms that Foucault simply ignores. Connolly does seek to overextend Fou-cault's project into places it is unwilling to go. In Foucault's ardent de-

---

42. Foucault, *Language, Counter-Memory, Practice,* 233.

sire to provide absolutely no justification for any system at all, Connolly simply asserts that we can leave him in this genealogical quandary, be receptive to his concerns, and take off where he refuses to go—just assimilate him into the conversation of consensus. What Connolly wishes to do is transfuse Foucault's genealogical uncovering of the Other in all its guises into the larger modern political exchange. In other words, he strives to bring the world of unreason into life's dialogue in the same way as festivals of reversal had a meaningful life-affirming exchange with the ordered world upon which they were designed to throw ambiguity. Connolly is of course free to do this, but does this inadvertently give to Foucault's genealogical position the status of positive content? It is my view that Foucault's appropriation of the carnivalesque and the Menippea is designed solely for the negative purpose of scrubbing off the historical, institutional, and subjectifying barnacles that accrue on man's surface. All those constructed selves, "Madman," "Prisoner," "Deviant," "Patient," are removed via genealogical analysis, but not to reach some core of man, or even contribute to the project of finding a wide and general enough consensus to bring all life's ambiguities to the fold, but rather to reveal that man has no essence whatsoever and proclaim that this fact will always haunt a society bent on constructing selves. Foucault removes our institutional clothing to reveal us as nonentities, and this is as far as he will go. All selves are socially and institutionally constructed, and as such, they will always do violence to man's potentialities, and will always subjugate some aspects of existence that throw doubt on the unity and order institutions produce. This is the pure purpose of genealogy, which seeks nothing outside fostering institutional instability and ambiguity. Dostoevsky formulates it best in *Crime and Punishment* when he talks about the role of untruth: "What is the most offensive aspect of all this? Not that what they say is untrue; it is always possible to forgive untruth; untruth is valuable because it leads to truth. No, what is vexatious is that they set up their falsehood and fall down and worship it!"[43]

The issue surrounds genealogy either being a curative, some constructive passage to truth, or merely the destructive urge to glorify untruth. Foucault wrangles with these two options in his *Nietzsche, Gene-*

43. Fyodor Dostoevsky, *Crime and Punishment* (Oxford: Oxford University Press, 1995), 129.

alogy and History. Foucault states that the task of genealogy is to become "a curative science."[44] Taking off from Nietzsche's preoccupation with all things physiological, history is seen as a body in which the genealogist searches for its minor cuts and bruises and its fatal conditions and attempts in some way to treat them. This is also carefully connected with Foucault's earlier insistence in *The Archaeology of Knowledge*— that archaeology is a similar procedure to "diagnosis." It is around these two terms that the problem coagulates, for the metaphor nicely explains the difference between archaeology and genealogy, yet it is also a mixed metaphor that obscures what Foucault is really doing. To say that archaeology is a diagnostic and genealogy curative does present us with a difference between the two, despite the fact that each term is presupposed by the next. Archaeology is a more disinterested operation that seeks only to diagnose a historical situation on an epistemological ground. This, of course, leads to the more political stance of genealogy that attempts to cure or alleviate a said situation whose epistemological (or discursive) grounding has found an institutional (or nondiscursive) expression. This is a very sound metaphorical explanation of the operative difference, and yet leading connection, between archaeology and genealogy.

Yet how much is Foucault precisely "curing" with genealogy? Foucault is always careful not to prescribe any remedy to the historical body he has diagnosed, so how can he in good faith call genealogy a curative science? Diagnosis always leads to the attempt to cure, and thus it is understandable that Foucault moves to this position. But the reality is that Foucault is rather the historical doctor who tells the patient that he is fatally ill, and there is no cure available. But again this dire prognosticator is made possible because of the extraordinary weight and freight that Foucault gives to the carnivalistic and Menippean aspects of genealogical research. He tellingly points out that "Genealogy is history in the form of a concerted carnival."[45] But the idea of history as a "concerted carnival" eradicates all of the therapeutic and curative powers that are the carnival's sole reason for being. These powers of the carnival are dependent upon carnival gestures and structures being limited in space and time so that their therapeutic effects can be felt in the non-carnival

44. Foucault, *Language, Counter-Memory, Practice*, 156.
45. Foucault, *Language, Counter-Memory, Practice*, 161.

times. If carnival is set up as an idea, and worse still, a "concerted" idea, no curative is forthcoming, because it can never find a non-carnivalistic place upon which to administer its benefits. Foucault translates the organic existence of the carnival into an abstract idea, a temporally limited experience into a timeless criterion. What this amounts to is the desire to raise to the level of revolution what is merely intended as sanctioned subversion and temporary liberation. What incites the chagrin of the radical political imagination is the reality that an "allowed fool" can bring no real libel against an order that can tolerate it, and that indeed fosters it. The fool must be crowned permanently, the masks always worn so that no authority can ever rise to give it legitimacy. The total revolution of Marxism becomes the Foucauldian absolute carnival or, as Umberto Eco dubbed this action when discussing Bakhtin's views on carnival, "The hyper-Bakhtinian ideology of carnival." He writes of Bakhtin something that can be far better applied to Foucault: "Therefore, there is something wrong with this theory of cosmic carnivalization as global liberation. There is some diabolic trick in the appeal to the great cosmic/comic carnival."[46]

Carnivalization is not permitted to be reabsorbed by authority, but must stand alone, timeless and boundless as a standard no one can touch; and herein lies the "diabolical trick." This desire to make transcendent the carnival aspect to the world and introduce a Menippean history is a direct result of the attempt to hide the foundational transcendent timeless will from one's critical labor. That timeless spirit must find repose somewhere in a radically critical philosophy, and if you deny it its proper place in the freedom of the will, it will settle elsewhere. Carnival that seeks the curative health of a society is an organic unity with the institutions of that society. It is rendered ridiculous and impotent if considered in isolation to the work it brings to bear on institutions. This brings the ire of radical thinkers, who then see it as just an extension of those institutions and attempt to rejuvenate it by divorcing it from them, raising it to a cosmic dimension and presenting it as the revolutionary reality of history. But as we have seen with the Dadaists, this universalization of the carnival only devolves into inaction. Foucauldian power,

46. Umberto Eco, V. V. Ivanov, and Monica Rector, *Carnival!* edited by Thomas A. Sebeok (Berlin and New York: Mouton, 1984), 3.

the by-product of Foucault's Menippean history and universalized carnival, is precisely that type of heightening that leaves it amorphous and everywhere, and leaves us lowly and unable to struggle against it. The trick as always is the diffusion of the timeless will into some other reality. The reason is the obedient flight of the radical imagination from the institutionalized face of the world. Foucault's archaeological and genealogical work is haunted by this timeless figure, which walks hand in hand with this oppositional conformity, and toward the end of his career he would obliquely observe his omission of this phantom.

12

Ethos and Attitude

The Return of the Phantom Self

In this concluding chapter on Foucault, I wish to examine the thinker's readmission of the free activity of the self into his imaginative rationale, where before it had been conspicuously absent. The term "imaginative rationale" is carefully chosen so as not to overplay the reemergence of this figure in Foucault's theoretical and conceptual edifice. The radically skeptical construction of history that Foucault had built throughout his archaeological and genealogical development is in no way conceptually crowned with the spire of the self. I will show that Foucault never gives the self a definitive form. In fact he characterizes it as an open wound of possibility that has no a priori content. The timeless will of the self is the ethereal phantom that Foucault now sees stalking the halls and corridors of his historical architectonic. This ghost in no way holds the structure together, but certainly constitutes the hidden personality of the building, a haunting presence that one feels wherever one is in the house. In this way, Foucault speaks more of the reactivation of an "ethos" or "attitude" with regard to the self, rather than definitively tracing what constitutes its scope and activities. This examination will thus be centered upon Foucault's posthumous volumes of the *History of Sexuality* and his seminal, but short text on Kant's essay on the Enlightenment. Despite its brevity, the generosity that the period (the Enlightenment) receives at the hands of the normally merciless Foucault and the two seminal figures it invokes makes this an important essay for dissection. From these texts one can isolate three bearings of Foucault's later work: a fascination with pagan lifestyles and values, a balancing of his relations with the intellectual monolith of the "Enlightenment," and a fusion of these awakenings with his historicizing of the present by the invocation of the literary figure of Baudelaire. These streams will constitute the fields of analysis for this concluding chapter, which by way of comparison will culminate in a look at Albert Camus's own formulation of the pagan mindset, his concern for revolt and the present, and his critique of the Enlightenment. The similarities of their slants on these subjects serve to highlight the obvious differences in their theoretical approaches to politics.

Greco-Roman Sexual Mo(re)deration

True to his traditional way of attacking a new subject for research, Foucault begins his multi-volume work on the history of sexuality by looking for the moral codes and ethical arrangements that determine the sexual subject. He seeks the configuration(s) of power/knowledge that work upon a passive, inactive self by coaxing a form agreeable to the dominant hand out of its ceaselessly impressionable nature. In other words, Foucault stays reasonably close to his determinist historical outlook, an outlook where the determining power/knowledge dyad produces selves. The research however fails to stay true to this time-tested modus operandi. Foucault delved further and further in his last days into the Greco/Roman world of classical and antiquity texts on sexual ethics and found a power relation that, until that time, he had not been able to recognize in his many other excursions into power relations. At the cradle of the Western experience and consciousness Foucault locates a power relation to which man subjects himself, a self-contained power over oneself. Before delving into this discovery of Foucault's later work, it will be helpful to succinctly observe what Foucault so drastically moved away from in the first volume of the *History of Sexuality*.

The first volume sets itself the task of furthering the claims of productive power by overturning the dominant view of the Victorian era as a prudish, repressed culture of dignified and socially austere sexual virtues. Taking aim at Freudian and other strands of psychoanalytical thought that confer upon themselves the mantle of liberators of our suppressed sexual drives, Foucault propels the wedge of his productive power into what he calls the "repressive hypothesis." The Victorian regime was not one that squashed into submission the happy frankness and lenient fluency that previous ages had with their sexual climate, but is instead the age that monstrously overproduced sexual experience into a "science of sex." Foucault notes, "Yet when one looks over these past three centuries with their continual transformations, things appear in a very different light: around and apropos of sex, one sees a veritable discursive explosion."[1]

It is not as though people slowly stopped talking about sex; indeed the opposite occurred as society multiplied the languages with which they could speak of it. Sex is removed from the purview of the personal and inscribed into the heavens of discourse, be they social, scientific, medical, educative, judicial, political, or psychological. In other words, like so much of Foucault's analysis, he is describing a historical passage from some supposed uncorrupted experience of sex, to an instituted experience of sex. And when raw experiential occurrences are codified, they are changed and produced into something that disfigures their purity. We are, as always, dealing with the radical political imagination, which has no patience with the human urge to institute what it learns. All radically anti-institutional positions boil down to this simple distaste. Of course, Foucault necessarily covers his tracks by maintaining that there is no "pure sexuality" that he is seeking, but is instead just showing another marriage of power and knowledge, another discursive formation. And yet his reason for uncovering this complex experience of sex is certainly to demonstrate to us that underneath these configurations of discourse lies something simple and unassaulted by order and institution. Foucault states that in this period, "Sex was driven out of hiding and constrained to lead a discursive existence. From the singular imperialism that compels everyone to transform his sexuality into a perpetual discourse ... an immense verbosity is what our civilisation has required and organised."[2]

1. Michel Foucault, *The Foucault Reader,* edited by Paul Rabinow (London: Penguin, 1984), 301.
2. Foucault, *The Foucault Reader,* 314.

Power does not constrain our sexual desires, but those desires give fuel to the urge to codify and institute, thus regulate, the menu of sexual pleasures. The desire to transform our simple and existential experience of the world is understood as a pernicious "imperialism" of the self, and our "immense verbosity" is nothing more than the institutional face of that desire. When it comes to institutions, Foucault is really not far removed from Rousseau and his hatred of the arts and sciences, those bouquets over our chains. And like Rousseau he seeks a purer, uninstituted life, a life where our passion to understand ourselves and our experience of the world does not get translated into moral and scientific codes. Most criticism of Foucault has come from those quarters that ask him to give voice to this pure, uninstituted, uncodified realm, because these critics know that it is here that they will find the silent, emancipatory lynchpin of Foucault's work, the theoretical zero-ground that enables humankind to lift itself from the imperious grounds of arbitrary power and discourse. Just because Foucault continuously and consistently denied such a possibility, we should not be fooled into thinking that he was doing something altogether different or working in a different imaginative landscape, for the sudden change in tone, texture, and subject matter of the last volumes of the *History of Sexuality* is the proof that this search was always innate to the project, from start to finish. This has been seen in his dissolving of the critical powers of the free subject endowed with will into the realms of history and power.

Many commentators have been puzzled by the sudden turn of Foucault's later work. Many favorable commentators dismiss the inconsistency as a case of enemies lying in wait who have inflated his newfound ethical concern, a position that can and should be assimilated into the greater scheme of his oeuvre. To these thinkers, just because Foucault never talked about the subject and agency did not mean that he had conclusively mislaid them; they simply were not part of the province of his earlier thought.[3] Others use the turn to dismiss him as a hopeless intel-

3. Preeminent among these favorable interpretations is that of Foucault's late-career interviewers Hubert L. Dreyfus and Paul Rabinow, who state, "However, as we will seek to show, the interpretation of Foucault as making normative but unjustified theoretical claims, as well as taking unargued-for political positions ... is not consistent with Foucault's general approach"; see Dreyfus and Rabinow, *Foucault: A Critical Reader,* edited by David Couzens Hoy (Oxford: Basil Blackwell, 1986), 113. This project to advance Foucault's standing as a grounded oppositional and transgressive thinker, while also admitting that Foucault does

lectual case whose inventiveness was based upon an omission, an error. His work on history, power, and madness is fundamentally flawed by this oversight.[4] The truth of the matter is somewhere in between. The new discoveries are entirely commensurate with his earlier work, and yet they were also deliberately hidden; he should not be apologized for, nor should he be set aside. This theoretical hide and seek is a necessary consequence of his rereading of the critical spirit initiated by Kant. As stated in the introduction, Foucault is simply exploring a particular temporal expression of the ahistorical world of Kantian critique. He is charting an important temporal direction of the timelessness of the radical political imagination. This privileged temporal direction is the present, and paradoxically, he finds a model for how to authentically live in an eternal present in the past of the pagan lifestyle.

Foucault fears the past and future so adamantly because he has realized that real (rather than fictive or utopian) past and future are only ever brought into being by institutions. Institutions are always the expression of an attempt to conquer time in the future, a future that is always open-ended and up for auction, or the reality of a time conquered in the past, a past that seems arbitrary and nameless and that the timeless imagination cannot accept. Not only this, but he has realized that the radical political imagination is only capable of seeing a past and future that are institutionless. These are the respective positions of the other radical theorists discussed: Rousseau and Marx. And while he cannot reconcile himself with the institutional reality of time and history management, he also cannot align himself with a radical past and future that can have no reality and that have also exhausted their critical and evaluative usefulness. Thus he turns to the eye of the present, a pure present that he finds beautifully encapsulated by the pagan ethical life.

It is then no surprise that the last two volumes of the *History of Sexuality* are dedicated to isolating the Greco/Roman ethos of life management away from any sort of institutional manifestation. Again, this

---

confuse this supposed grounding, is also the thrust of their major work on him: Dreyfus and Rabinow, *Michel Foucault: Beyond Structuralism and Hermeneutics* (Chicago: University of Chicago Press, 1983).

4. Jurgen Habermas's charge that Foucault's work lacks a normative benchmark is the prominent variety of this species. This position is found in many places, but is best expressed in Habermas, *The Philosophical Discourse of Modernity* (Cambridge, Mass.: MIT Press, 1987).

study is not concerned with the historical validity of the picture of antiquity that Foucault presents or the quality of his research on the matter. It is instead concerned with what his view on this period implies with regard to his approach to institutional reality. What is surprising about both of these tomes is the degree with which they attempt to isolate the pagan view of life from any kind of institutional, codified, or moralized representation. According to Foucault, the novelty of the pagan life is the degree to which it remains true to a morality that is self-imposed, rather than dictated from above by a standard that was greedily extracted from this enclosed circuit of the self regulating itself. Unfortunately, only lengthy quotes can demonstrate the prevalence of this concern in Foucault's later thought. The basic premise that underscores both the last two volumes is succinctly stated below:

Now, it seems clear, from a first approach at least, that moral conceptions in Greek and Greco-Roman antiquity were much more orientated toward practices of the self and the question of askesis than toward codifications of conducts and the strict definition of what is permitted and what is forbidden.[5]

The foregoing is only a rough sketch for preliminary purposes; a few general traits that characterized the way in which, in Classical Greek thought, sexual practice was conceptualised and made into an ethical domain. The elements of this Domain—the "ethical substance"—were formed by the "aphrodisia"; that is, by acts intended by nature, associated by nature with an intense pleasure, and naturally motivated by a force that was always liable to excess and rebellion. The principle according to which this activity was meant to be regulated, the "mode of subjection," was not defined by a universal legislation determining permitted and forbidden acts; but rather by a "savoir-faire," an art that prescribed the modalities of a use that depended on different variables (need, time, status).[6]

These lengthy quotes enlighten us about what Foucault finds so attractive about pagan ethical activity—namely, its ignorance of any obedience to universal strictures. By being so inscribed in the personalized operations of an individual caring and fashioning itself, it thus balks at any institutional, moral, or scientific systematization, as this would have passed on that individual power to something or someone else. There is

5. Foucault, *History of Sexuality,* vol 2, *The Use of Pleasure,* translated by Robert Hurley (London: Viking, 1986), 30.
6. Foucault, *The Use of Pleasure,* 91.

an alluring irony here. Greek free males (as Foucault constantly reminds us so as not to convey the picture that the classical world was a golden age where all luxuriously took part in this self-cultivation) encounter a world laden with *aphrodisia*, or "the works, the acts of Aphrodite."[7] This natural garden of sexual pleasures constitutes the ethical substance of antiquity by requiring a form of moderation in the face of this possibility of excess. The use of pleasure, the care of the self, and the aesthetics of the self are all predicated upon the need for moderation when confronted with objects of desire. Foucault has paradoxically found his institutionless heartland in a way of life that puts a premium upon moderation. In other words, the model that Foucault discovers and puts forward as a way out of the universalizing totalities of modernity, the attitude or ethos with which to burst free from the limits placed on our lives, is in reality a technique of the soul that makes a virtue of austere restraint and temperance. Obviously Foucault needs something more from this ethic of moderation. He needs to transform this ethos of self-restraint, this attitude of limitation, into a philosophic, critical, and ultimately political position that can destroy the limitation and restraint placed upon us by our institutional creations. But can this sober activity be resurrected in the service of a transgressive pushing of our limits? It is this question that this chapter attempts to answer.

It is important to qualify that Foucault ultimately links his discovery of the pagan relation of man to himself and of "technologies of the self" to a later time in the West's history, where Christianity has taken hold of this self-evaluating procedure. Paradoxically for Foucault, this pagan production of the self mutates into a Christian search or discovery of the self in order to better relinquish it. Thus the good work on the self achieved by the pagan way becomes codified into hard, frozen moral codes that ensnare the self and begin to mold and reconstitute it in its own estranged image. Christianity displaces the pagan concern with self-mastery and stylistic existence with subordination before God and a purged, desiccated selfhood.

In Christianity what one would be asked to attain is no longer the proud virility of a master; it is an inner purity of being. What incites one to transform oneself is no longer the choice of a noble existence glorified for posterity; it is

7. Foucault, *The Use of Pleasure*, 91.

the commandment or will of God. Sexuality is thought to be problematic not because of the dangers of excessive, unhealthy or dignified indulgence, but because the flesh is forever impure.[8]

This mutation from self-production freed from overt external control to self discovery and renouncement channeled by external doctrine and morality must have its attending institutional face, which Foucault finds in the idea of "confession." For Foucault this early church procedure of "confessing" is the highly effective institution that achieves the contradictory modes of discovery and abandonment. Confessing is at once an unearthing of the self's motivations and real essence and a moral purging of them into the cold furnace of a stern, regulated world. Discovery and desiccation of the self are achieved at the same time in the confessing moment. Foucault takes this technique to have been so successful for the church that it is taken up and used by the secular world that we moderns inhabit, becoming an integral part of what Foucault sees as the modern conceptions of "pastoral" power and "biopower." Foucault still views us moderns to be thoroughly "confessing" animals. And it is precisely this development that makes Foucault hold up the pagan ideal against it.

The historical development that Foucault traces shows us just how much he held up the pagan Greco-Roman ideal of ethical selfhood. It is important to qualify Foucault's historical study as no disinterested study of the period, but the deliberate following of a vein of gold in our history, one that can be mined for use in the present, an antidote to the instituted, regulated world we inhabit today. Foucault jettisons a degree of that Nietzschean skepticism that renders all things relative, hence equal, and hence fancifully devoid of preference (in truth, he never abandoned preference for certain ways of life, certain regimes and certain approaches; those preferences were just cloaked, hidden, and masked by a slavish adherence to his alienating of the freedom of the will from the self into other realms, a procedure we have observed is endemic to his work). He undoubtedly holds up the aesthetic self-fashioning of pagan times as an ethical/aesthetic beacon for critical moderns who have exhausted their prior critical resources of past and future illusory benchmarks. Despite this partial abandonment of his sweeping Nietzschean cynicism in em-

8. John Rajchman, *Truth and Eros: Foucault, Lacan and the Question of Ethics* (New York and London: Routledge, 1991), 91.

bracing the pagan, he finds enough of aesthetic, stylistic, and artistic attitudes to life and the self to assimilate the other great inheritance he received from his intellectual hero—the value of the creative life. Remember that Nietzsche also looked back to the Greeks for their unique artistic vision on life, the famous Dionysian/Apollonian fusion that gave birth to the Greek's great contribution to art, the tragedy. Let us also not forget what he says on the stylistics of life in *The Gay Science.*

One thing is needful.—To "give style" to one's character—a great and rare art! It is practised by those who survey all the strengths and weaknesses that their nature has to offer and then fit them into an artistic plan until each appears as art and reason and even weaknesses delight the eye. Here a great mass of second nature has been added; there a piece of first nature removed—both times through long practice and daily work at it.[9]

Or consider his glowing assessment of Socrates in *The Wanderer and His Shadow:*

In him converge the roads of the most different philosophic modes of life, which are in truth the modes of the different temperaments, crystallised by reason and habit and all ultimately directed towards the delight in life and in self.[10]

It can almost be maintained that Foucault is arbitrarily transfusing these very sentiments into his look at ancient Greek attitudes and ethos to the self, if it weren't for the plethora of texts he surveys to demonstrate the prevalence of these views. Both Nietzsche and Foucault deem philosophy to be a way of life rather than a purely theoretical exercise, devoid of contact with one's own life. And they both find in antiquity, at the birth of philosophy, its historical origins as concern with the "philosophic life," rather than philosophy as a life-wrung science. In this respect Foucault still remains a good Nietzschean, despite his gradual attraction to the mystique of the self's power over history. Indeed, in his later years he seems to be actively embarking on a project of fusing the Nietzschean and Kantian aspects of modernity into a meaningful union of critical and aesthetic reality. The remnants of this attempt are already seen in how he has characterized the Greco/Roman sensibility.

9. Friedrich Nietzsche, *The Gay Science* (Cambridge: Cambridge University Press, 2001), 163.
10. Friedrich Nietzsche, *Human, All-Too-Human,* part 2 (London: Allen and Unwin, 1924), 242.

So what is it that Foucault seemed to welcome about this period of ethical activity? Pathologically unable to see the self reflecting upon itself in our recent history, he is caused to be somewhat dumbfounded to find it in such ancient sources. It is no surprise, then, that he marvels at some other elements of the ancient approach to life. First, it is right to emphasize the radical individualism that is entailed in his look at this period. Foucault views the abundance of ancient activities concerning self-examination and self-construction as solely for the purpose of individual enhancement, and any benefits or detriments this activity brought to the community, state, or others was unintended. Moral and ethical acts were directed by and toward the individual, rather than those acts being precipitated by concerns outside the individual. The individual's activity on himself is useful to others as a model of autonomy, not as a source for foreign truths and dictates that they can appropriate and follow. This is an important point to make, considering Foucault had previously denied such a radical individualism.

The other marvel that Foucault detects in his review of the ancients is the procedure of truth telling, or *parrhesia*. This is again significant, considering he had dismissed the notion of any normative standard of truth whatsoever throughout the majority of his career. He discussed this concept rather thoroughly in lectures he gave in the last few years of his life, and traverses all the differing modes under which the ancients spoke of the truth.[11] The curious thing about Foucault's discussion of truth telling in the Hellenist and Roman world is how remote it is from any sense that there is a definable truth to which one has access. *Parrhesia* seems not to be a certain relation of an individual to the truth, but a courageous stance of speech regarding openness and frankness. Courage and speech seem to be more integral to *parrhesia* than the truth content of it. Also, the form of *parrhesia* that Foucault seems to hold up as a new development in the realm of truth is a type of private, Socratic style of courageous truthfulness with regard to oneself. Again here, it is placed in the service of the care of the self. It is not a desire to find the truth of one's self, but the courage of being truthful when dealing with one's self. The self has no defined truth, but an attitude of truthfulness is needed when speaking about the self. Alexander Nehamas, in his *The*

11. The content of these lectures has been complied in Foucault's *Fearless Speech*, edited by Joseph Pearson (Los Angeles: Semiotext(e) [distributed by MIT Press], 2001).

Art of Living, discusses these lectures at length and, discerning a curious empathetic mirroring of Socrates by Foucault, he quotes:

"If I attend to you," Foucault writes, uncannily identifying his own voice with that of Socrates as he does throughout these lectures, "it is not in order to transmit to you the knowledge that you lack, but so that, having realised that you know nothing, you will learn thereby to care for yourselves."[12]

The last and most important feature of the ancient Greek worldview that Foucault notices as fascinating, and one that we have already encountered previously, is the aesthetical inventing of the self. To demonstrate that this discovery is more than just a disinterested examination of a particular historical period by Foucault in the posthumous volumes of his *The History of Sexuality* (of which numerous examples can be referenced), it is far more enlightening to look at those interviews where in more candid moments he espouses this ancient life of the self to modern ears. From these interviews it is obvious that he has found some solution to the repressive political quandary that he had so meticulously set up throughout his career.

What strikes me is the fact that in our society, art has become something that is related only to objects and not to individuals, or to life. That art is something which is specialized or which is done by experts who are artists. But couldn't everyone's life become a work of art? Why should the lamp or the house be an art object, but not our life?[13]

This sentiment represents the first prescriptive statement that Foucault put his name to, and represents his way out of the skeptical, mechanistic institutional monolith to which he had condemned modern man. This also coincided with the public awakening of his homosexuality and the enlightening interviews that he gave on this subject. In general, his attitude to homosexuality is that, as a modern, burgeoning social consciousness, it should cultivate an attitude of inventiveness, creativity, and improvisation. Talking on the subject of homosexuality and its relation to the stylistics of the self, he is unequivocal on the benefits that this approach to life confers: "It can yield intense relations not resembling

12. Alexander Nehamas, *The Art of Living: Socratic Reflections from Plato to Foucault* (Chicago: University of Chicago Press, 1998), 166.
13. Foucault, "On the Genealogy of Ethics: An Overview of Work in Progress," in *The Foucault Reader,* edited by Paul Rabinow (New York: Pantheon Books, 1984), 350.

those that are institutionalised."[14] But even in displaying this benefit, he warns of the danger that can erode it. Here is his sagely advice to his interviewers: "But the idea of a program of proposals is dangerous. As soon as a program is presented, it becomes a law, and there's a prohibition against inventing."[15]

Ingenuity and creativity of the self become the tonic to the institutionalized world we inhabit. But this prerogative and possibility of the self are always endangered by the prohibition that they place upon themselves by institutionalizing their dictates. Thus Foucault needs desperately to demarcate the operations of the self. He must entomb it in its own operations so as to rein in its natural inclination to live and express itself beyond the limitations of the present and the limitations of itself. It seeks to extend itself beyond its temporal limits and limits of selfhood. This he can achieve only by a strict balance among the three inventive aspects of Hellenistic-Roman culture that he has divined: individualism, truthfulness, and creativity. All of these things are centered squarely upon the self, and they are designed purposively to trap the institutionalizing urge into that self, concerned only with its own life and thus its own present. A radical individuality about the self perpetrates a consensus that no one individual or group can ever dictate a proper style of life for anyone. The individual will only ever decree to himself, and thus he lives in an eternal present, unable or unwilling to receive directives from outside himself, from outside his own time, or indeed to prescribe any norm that may find currency outside of the individual experience of that self. His sense of truth extends only to himself, as there is no outside truth for him to obey. A truth that he has devised for himself only has value to others as an example of how he may be truthful to himself. It can never give him a truth to follow, because it can never extend itself beyond the present of itself.

Adding to the radical alignment to the present that a thorough individualism fosters is the severely neutered sense of truth that Foucault allies with this. Truth belongs not to the individual as a possession or discovery, but as a stance or adopted process or attitude. In many ways it resembles Foucault's idea of freedom not as a goal, destination, or pos-

14. Foucault, "Friendship as a Way of Life," in *Ethics: Subjectivity and Truth*, translated by John Johnson, edited by Paul Rabinow (New York: New Press, 1997), 138.

15. Foucault, interview, "Friendship as a Way of Life," in *Ethics*, 139.

session, but as an undefined work that that finds its worth and goal in own operation. Truth so conceived is only ever a contingency and a negotiable, finding no common ground upon which a consensus can intelligibly be translated. It is a kind of inverted truth whose sole aim is to unravel and throw doubt upon other concrete atemporal "truths" that find expression beyond the simple, present-centered ethos of "truthfulness." Paradoxically, this Foucauldian ethos of truthfulness is designed to guarantee the temporality of all truth claims by a resolute eternal sense of contingency.

This peculiar relation of truth to the individual is designed to guarantee in an instituted world the possibility of extending beyond the prohibitions and limitations by which this world is characterized. It holds tight to the belief that by assuring the self an endless scope for invention, artistic rendering, and improvisation, that unfettered individual can always balk at the social exclusions and embargos created by equally imaginative and resourceful individuals that find their creations powerful enough to find life and expression beyond themselves. The point is to allow the self every possibility of illustration, and another of his interviewers highlighted the problems of this approach to Foucault. In the interview entitled *Sexual Choice, Sexual Act,* the interviewer presents Foucault with some quotes from the American sociologist Philip Rieff on his thoughts about the cultural significance of Oscar Wilde. His position was that Oscar Wilde is a symbolic figurehead for a culture that places individuality and aestheticism at the center of its experience to such an extreme that the mad desire to allow everything to be expressed ends only in nothing being true. He writes, "A culture achieves the assault of sheer possibility against it only so far as the members of a culture learn, through their membership, how to narrow the range of choices otherwise open,"[16] and again, "Sociologically, a truth is whatever militates against the human capacity to express everything. Repression is truth."[17]

The interviewer goes on the remark how similar this position of "truth is repression" is to Foucault's own sentiment, expressed in numerous works that truth is simply the "product of a system of exclusions."[18] Yet Foucault's work is designed in its entire import to transgress against

16. Foucault, interview, "Sexual Choice, Sexual Act,"in *Ethics,* 147.
17. Foucault, interview, "Sexual Choice, Sexual Act," in *Ethics,* 147.
18. Foucault, interview, "Sexual Choice, Sexual Act," in *Ethics,* 147.

this grim state of affairs, rather than accept it, because the alternative of aesthetically preening individuals who condemn the world to a crisis of relativity and a shrunken present is equally difficult to accept. And herein lies the great problem of Foucault's turn to the self and aesthetics of life. Foucault is troubled and seeks a resolution to what he had seen as the inescapable fact that all truth is ultimately identical to repression. He thus seeks a pure nexus point that is devoid of that repression and that can provide an uninstituted way out of social exclusion, domination, fabrication, and production. The only site worthy enough to accept the mantle of self-exclusion, domination, fabrication, and production is the self itself. Thus the concept of asceticism is paramount to understanding this conclusion. For Foucault radically alters the traditional interpretation of asceticism. The strange espousal of moderation and restraint that Foucault detects in classical thought he sees as an antidote to the interpretation of *askesis,* or asceticism as a form of self-repression. Foucault writes, "Asceticism as the renunciation of pleasures has bad connotations. But ascesis is something else: it's the work that one performs on oneself in order to transform oneself or make the self appear which, happily, one never attains. Can that be our problem today? We've rid ourselves of asceticism."[19]

Foucault transforms the concept of asceticism as self-repression and limitation into an endless work on a self that never attains a whole, concrete, completed form. This endless work of the present provides the broadest canvas possible for an inventive aesthetic experimentation with an infinitely pliable self. While Foucault is a pedant for the limitation of history, a strict disciplinarian when it comes to radically proclaiming the historicity and temporality of all cultural products, he achieves this only by devising an unlimited, boundless, and bottomless present for the self to play in. As soon as that playful self attempts to create something that will live beyond that paltry timeless present and create something timely, it is ultimately always crowned with untruth. An eternal present is the site where we see Foucault's timeless imagination register itself.

In Foucault's discussion of Greco-Roman sexual mores we find an analogue to the way Foucault will eventually conceive the Enlightenment. It is to here that we now turn, with a look at his seminal text "What Is Enlightenment?"

19. Foucault, "Friendship as a Way of Life," in *Ethics,* 137.

A Reborn "Lumiere"?

"What Is Enlightenment?" is Foucault's statement of his reconciliation with the "Enlightenment" milieu that has encouraged his work and the positive declaration of his affiliation with modernity. The first thing to be said about Foucault's newborn take on modernity and the Enlightenment is that he is loath to conceive them as simply a defined period of history. As opposed to the time when he characterized these vague periodicities as a defined set of practices, disciplines, and discourses, he now wishes to add to this understanding the idea of the activation of an attitude or ethos: "And by 'attitude,' I mean a mode of relating to contemporary reality; a voluntary choice made by certain people; in the end, a way of thinking and feeling; a way, too, of acting and behaving that at one and the same time marks a relation of belonging and presents itself as a task. No doubt, a bit like what the Greeks called an 'ethos.'"[20] What can obviously be taken from this quote is the fact that Foucault at the very least finds association between the Greek thought he so painstakingly studied and a modern attitude that is discernable since Kant's philosophical revolution. This admission makes this an indispensable companion text to his works on pagan thought and its relation to modern thought. And while it may seem insubstantial for Foucault to have chosen one of Kant's slightest and most accessible (albeit famous) pieces of writing, Foucault has very astutely discerned in this text the fundamental dynamic that Kantian thought has bequeathed to the modern world. Foucault clearly aligns his interpretation of this small piece of writing to the work of the three critiques.[21] Foucault highlights this dynamic by focusing on one particular thought that Kant's text gives voice to: namely, the idea that we collectively feel that we both belong to a historical period of Enlightenment and know that enlightenment is a task for our continued devotion. This is an ambiguous double reality that Foucault identifies as at once the recognition that we are in history and the startling realization that we have power over it. He writes, "We must also note that this way out is

20. Foucault, "What Is Enlightenment?" in *Ethics,* 309.
21. Foucault, "What Is Enlightenment?" in *Ethics,* 308. Foucault deliberately asserts that Kant's discussion of the historical specificity of the Enlightenment cannot be divorced from his theoretical critiques, saying, "The critique is, in a sense, the handbook of reason that has grown up in the Enlightenment; and, conversely, the Enlightenment is the age of critique."

presented by Kant in a rather ambiguous manner. He characterizes it as a phenomenon, an ongoing process; but he also presents it as a task and an obligation."[22] Or formulated more blankly, "Men are at once elements and agents of a single process."[23]

What Foucault seems to be coming to terms with is the basic paradox upon which this study has built itself—namely, that Kant has presented us with a very interesting historical proposition, one that is very tempting but is very difficult to confirm as an actuality. The possibility of having the ability to transcend history as autonomous agents of change unfettered by time is forever thwarted by the reality that whatever process that transcendence brings about will always be corrupted by a history, indeed, by a world that is indifferent to the aims of our will. That is why we are both "agents" that direct and "elements" that are directed. It is a "phenomenon" that we may have caused, but that we cannot hope to control entirely, and from which we can never relinquish membership, because our dignity as free beings makes an "obligation" upon us. Yet what for many moderns would seem a trapped condition is for Foucault the ultimate guarantee of limitation and the inexhaustible. Just like his pagan archetype, who will forever prod, probe, improvise, invent, and test his self but will never come close to realizing its essence and truth, so Foucault embraces a modern, enlightened world that sets this unceasing unsatisfied yearning as not simply a personal prerogative, but a historical one, as well. Foucault lauds Kant as the first to have introduced into history a radical reflection upon its present and an indication of how that present represents at all times a possibility for a different way of being. Kant perceives enlightenment as at once a historical fact and a historical mission, as an "is" and an "ought." Foucault reflects on this curiosity he has missed throughout his career: "It is in the reflection on 'today' as difference in history and as motive for a particular philosophical task that the novelty of the text appears to me."[24]

It is between these two impossible positions that Foucault knows that difference, or the maximum allowance of possibility, will always be assured. For the present will always provide that slim province of truth for the "is" and the "ought" awkwardly combined. What looks to be the in-

22. Foucault, "What Is Enlightenment?" 305.
23. Foucault, "What Is Enlightenment?" 306.
24. Foucault, "What Is Enlightenment?" 309.

tractable, abstract, unconvincing, balancing act of the three critiques—a taut scramble between epistemological limitation, moral transcendence, and thorny historical expression—is rendered somewhat more supple and alluring, condensed as it is in this text. The text represents a whole philosophical task that is trying to come to terms with its contemporary reality. Foucault is obviously enthralled by this contemporary historical reflection of a hereto-unhistorical philosophy, and finds in this reflection by Kant a great ambiguity that fits nicely with his project of defamiliarizing history so as to leave it always unable to hold a total authority over its subjects. This entails moving Kantian critique away from its traditional provinces of universalism and totalitarian reason, or what Foucault descriptively calls the "blackmail of the Enlightenment."[25]

Kimberly Hutchings observes that Foucault detects an admission of historical reality in Kant's text: "In 'What Is Enlightenment?' Foucault argues that Kant's reflections on his time signify a departure in philosophical critique from preoccupation with universals to preoccupation with the specificities of the present."[26] What Foucault admires in this text is the way in which Kant seems to have planted a philosophic and historical seed in the present and presented the work of critique as a constant, unending planting. To perhaps vainly take this agricultural metaphor further, Foucault is uninterested in what from the past nourishes this seed, and is also uninterested in harvesting its future fruit. The point is always to allow the undeveloped seed of possibility to be propagated in the present social, political, and cultural earth. Only service to this present-centered goal will oblige traditional forms to be passed over in favor of contemporary energy and safeguard against that contemporary energy never maturing into future traditional forms. This is not to say that past and future social, political, and cultural forms won't be considered, but simply to say that the primary goal of Foucauldian selfhood is to keep the channels of possibility always open in the present. It is essentially a turning back to the original contemporaneous foundation of critical modernity as a "way out" of the institutional fruits that that tradition has nursed through to maturity. It is also the constant reactivation of contemporaneity in an effort to avoid dogmatic future ex-

25. Foucault, "What Is Enlightenment?" 312.
26. Kimberly Hutchings, *Kant, Critique and Politics* (London and New York: Routledge, 1996), 119.

pression. It is a devotion to the initial impetus of critique, situated in an eternal present, avoiding serious communion with any past and deigning the future as beyond its concern. Where Kant says, "Each moral act at the time it is done is, as it were, an absolutely new beginning, not determined by history, or by nature,"[27] Foucault affirms in his name, "thus we are always in the position of beginning again."[28]

Obviously Foucault is achieving a strange circumvention of the Kantian timeless will's urge to go out into history. Kant was obviously all too aware of the radically present-tensed nature of the timeless will, and thus turned to history and teleology in his third critique to lend some temporal balance and ballast to that knife-edged operation of his morality. Teleology and history are invoked to give some semblance to the free, timeless moral act. To be more than a pointlessly endless rejuvenating of the present, the moral will must be able to see a passage from the past confirming our collective ongoing enlightenment and freedom, and must be provided with a goal it can grasp and reasonably work for in the future. And this all along has been the difficulty that this book has maintained is an impossible project: the fleshing-out of the timeless moral will with illusory historical substance. It is this difficulty that both Rousseau before Kant and Marx after him failed to avoid because of their investment in some impression of future freedom. Foucault avoids this problem by not being obligated by this investment at all. He seeks no evidence of purpose in history and transmits no aspiration of progress into the future. He is happy with critique being inscribed in the contingency of the present, and only had to prise off the historical barnacles that had accrued on the pure critical act of a timeless will to reaffirm his faith in a species of thought, whose only real project he sees as the constant transgression of history. And Foucault places a guard on the gates of this recovered critical spirit and its true place in contingent reality. It is interesting that in criticizing a modern culture for opening as far and wide as achievable the gates of possibility, Philip Rieff would evoke the English dandy Oscar Wilde as the figurehead for this movement; for when defending it, Foucault presents as a hero his French counterpart, Charles Baudelaire. Baudelaire is his champion in the defense of Kant's critical

27. Lewis White Beck, "Introduction," in *Kant On History*, edited by Lewis White Beck (Indianapolis: Bobbs Merrill, 1963), xxvi.
28. Foucault, "What Is Enlightenment?" 317.

message as essentially present-tensed in nature. Having shorn the Kantian critical moment of its history and setting it in the blurring movement of the present, he sets the scene for a Baudelairean modernity as lying "in adopting a certain attitude with respect to this movement; and this deliberate, difficult attitude consists in capturing something eternal that is not beyond the present instant, nor behind it, but within it."[29]

Baudelaire is the obvious choice for Foucault, as he embodies personally the differing streams of his later thought: a modern critic/artist, life/art devotee who characterizes modern life as the plucking of the eternal out of the present. Baudelaire represents for Foucault the modern virtue of not discovering who one is, but developing who one is. Who else expresses better a culture that desires the greatest variety of possibility, who seeks to hemorrhage on all levels of opportunity, than the man who heroizes the modern aesthete as "a kaleidoscope gifted with consciousness"?[30] What we see here is an aesthetic-ethico trend that slowly developed in Foucault and a clear statement of his membership to the avant-garde spirit who had always sought to free art from its independent realm and transfuse its energy back into life.

Early twentieth century avant-garde movements, such as Dada and Surrealism, tried to overcome the very distinctions between art and life, aesthetics and ethics, firstly by undermining the traditional categories of art, and secondly by attempting to develop new forms of life based on artistic practice. Foucault's statement here would seem to be aligned with this particular attack upon the modern phenomenon of the autonomization of the aesthetic sphere.[31]

Foucault's invocation of Baudelaire (who sits right at the genesis of the avant-garde sentiment that enthralled Europe), is a clear statement of his intent to bring Kantian critique closer in line with a counter-modern strand of thought that Baudelaire can be seen to have been an eager and influential contributor. Baudelaire is the present loving tonic that Foucault prescribes to the universalizing and duty-bound conception of morality that he still smells in Kantian critique. We are given a clue as to how he perceives that tonic doing its work when he links the

29. Foucault, "What Is Enlightenment?" 310.

30. Charles Baudelaire, *The Painter of Modern Life and Other Essays*. (London: Phaidon, 1964), 9.

31. Timothy O'Leary, *Foucault and the Art of Ethics* (New York and London: Continuum, 2002), 122.

"ironic heroization" of the present and the "elaboration of the self" in an action that he calls the "transfiguring play of freedom with reality."[32] The fact that this phrase, the "transfiguring play of freedom with reality," resembles Kant's own thoughts on genius, aesthetics, and the "free play" of the faculties, shows us just how important Baudelaire is to Foucault's new vision of critique. Baudelaire is the real-world exemplar of Kant's thought that genius is the playful freedom of cognitive faculties, a play of unencumbered freedom with some given reality. What Baudelaire does with his own life mirrors what Foucault wants to fuse with Kantian critique. Hutchings elucidates this point when she says that "Kant's characterisation of the work of genius is recalled (by Foucault) in the way in which critical ontology exemplifies creative self-legislation without in any sense being able to lay down the law for others."[33]

We observed early on that an attempt was made to overcome the timelessness of the Kantian moral act via regulative ideas of history and teleology; to give morality a guarantee in time. We also saw how Foucault rejects this desire to give historical expression to the critical power of the will by aiming directly at the heart of the present. He now seeks to destroy even its universality. If Kant says, "make the maxim of your will hold as a universal legislation," Foucault significantly abridges this to, "make the maxim of your will." His fear that the universalizing of the timeless, ahistorical will may prescribe a foreign law for others means that he seeks a totally disinterested operation of the will that will prescribe only for itself. He needs a ruleless and unrestrained procedure that still retains some array of critical functions. He finds the template for this in the disinterested reflective judgment of taste and the original free play of cognitive powers utilized by the genius. Unlike those who have sought to unite the second critique with the teleological and historical aspects of the third critique, Foucault seeks to unite it with the artistic and aesthetic aspects of the third. The coupling of Kant with Baudelaire is simply Foucault's way of deuniversalizing Kant's critical project and making it a wholly individual creative self-legislation for the delight of that sole individual. Foucault's project is more the much easier attempt to magnify the freedom of our moral choices through the freedom of artistic expression than the attempt to magnify that moral

32. Foucault, "What Is Enlightenment?" 312.
33. Hutchings, *Kant, Critique and Politics*, 121.

freedom through history. The individual's own creative self-expression will be its own critical standard against instituted universalism. This has the significant effect of greatly expanding the individual's own scope for freedom, where a critical standpoint that had to universalize its maxims at least had to surrender a radical creative freedom to its fellow man.

We must be careful not to overstate the case for Foucault having appropriately limited the universalist pretensions of Kantian critique, and having rightfully dismissed its dangerous historical posturing, for he has simply replaced one arrangement of limitation and limitlessness with another. Where Foucault warns against participation in "projects that claim to be global or radical" and holds that the only legitimate critical activity can be a limited bringing to bear of the play of freedom upon "a material, an epoch, a body of determined practices and discourses," this in no way destroys the unlimited power of creative freedom that he has leased to the individual. Nor does this favoring of local and regional critical labor over a total and universal critical labor in any way destroy that labor's timeless foundation. In many respects Foucault seems to have misread the radical import of Kantian critique in the first place.

Criticism indeed consists of analysing and reflecting upon limits. But if the Kantian question was that of knowing [savoir] what limits knowledge [*connaissance*] must renounce exceeding, it seems to me that the critical question today must be turned back into a positive one: In what is given to us as universal, necessary, obligatory, what place is occupied by whatever is singular, contingent, and the product of arbitrary constraints? The point, in brief, is to transform the critique conducted in the form of a necessary limitation into a practical critique that takes the form of a possible crossing-over [*franchissement*].[34]

Indeed, the critical philosophy is certainly an analysis of the limits knowledge should not exceed, but this is precisely so as to stop it encroaching upon our ethical activity. And with respect to nature and history, Kantian ethical activity knows no limits and is always engaged in "crossing over" the limits of what is falsely given to us as universal and determined. Part of the Kantian procedure is certainly a negative look at the limits of knowledge, but so as to provide a positive space for practical critique. In many ways, Foucault's belief that he is turning the Kantian question "back into a positive one" is a Don Quixotesque philosophical

34. Foucault, "What Is Enlightenment?" 315.

chivalry. Kant himself says that he is simply circumscribing the limits of the phenomenal so as to explore the "wide and stormy ocean" of the noumenal, a world characterized by duty to a self-prescribed law. Foucault can always be dismissed as just another sailor on this ocean that Kant opened to discovery. There is nothing to suggest that Foucault is the savior of Kantian critique and every reason to suspect that this particular reworking or interpretation of critique was implicit in its project from the very beginning. After all, it keeps the timelessness of the project relatively unharmed, and it was only a matter of time before someone would read it as a narrowly present-based operation, centered upon individuals who self-legislate, and who will resign participation in any consensus building historical project.

What this critical gallantry on Foucault's part suggests is that he in some ways wishes to empower critique even further than Kant was willing to concede. While limiting it in certain directions, he greatly expands it in others. While he won't let that critical power roam unchecked across history in any shape, he will let it run rampant in the creative, self-fashioning individual, whose inventive action upon himself is seen by Foucault as constituting the constant calling into question of limits in an eternal present. Despite what it scorns of Kant's universalism, it simply rechannels it elsewhere, rather than excising it completely from the project of freedom. One must ask where the universal elements of Kantian critique are directed. We recall that Kant asks not that the will itself be universalized, but that the maxims or products of one's will be so treated. This means that the worldwide aims of critique go out into the world, a universal form being attached to those maxims that the will deigns as fitting for the whole world. The only reason those maxims make their way into the world is that they have been endowed with universal form, a kind of hardy apparel to be worn before entering the harsh realities of historical phenomena. Foucault, as we have seen, is loath to allow such universalism to seep out of this operation of the timeless will, having seen the disastrous historical projects that are built around these universal maxims. But there is everything to suggest that the universalism itself is not abandoned. The products of critique may not be able to be universally grounded, but the act or engine of critique itself, occurring in a self-legislating individual, can be a site of universalism if it is imprisoned in that individual and in the present. Foucault's recruitment of Baudelaire (and his project of finding the eternal within the present) to this critical adaptation is evidence of this turning of universality away from the world and into the individual. This is also a manifestation of an uncertainty that we saw in Foucault's appraisal of pagan sexual practices. We saw how Foucault takes the moderating concept of asceticism and transforms it into an approach to the self that enables it to expose and transgress limits, rather than apply them. This strange inversion of necessary limitation into consecrating a limitless self is seen in Foucault's attitude to critical thought. Christopher Norris described this movement in this fashion: "It is largely by means of this semantic slide, this elision of the differences between 'ascesis' and 'aesthesis,' that Foucault so adroitly negotiates the passage from Kant to Baudelaire."[35] It is this liberty-taking retranslation, this tampering with the texture of limitation and the limitless in ancient thought, that is mirrored in how Foucault conceives the modern will of critique. By combining the moderation of asceticism and the immoderate inventing of artistic practice, Foucault can also retranslate Kantian ethics. The operation of the individual's will itself is universalized, rather than its products. The mutation of Kant's austere and limited duty of oneself to a self-prescribed law becomes the more immoderate indulgence of a universal rulelessness when it comes to each individual's capacity to give himself his own law. What on the surface seems to be the limitation of a Kantian universalism that is transmitted into history is really the turning of the universality further in on itself, an intensification of the timelessness and lawlessness of the self.

I'll grant that it is a peculiar brand of critical endeavor in the face of institutional reality, but no more so than Marx's desire to place its results in the future, or Rousseau's belief that it had an original impetus from the past. All three, the past, present, and future expansion of critical thought, are radical historical variants of a timeless imagination. The fact that critical politics are inherently timeless makes all these positions possible as particular timeless illusions of history. Foucault of course sees our wills as being negotiated and normalized by institutions, but he holds out a hope that the nature of our radically amorphous selves are

35. Christopher Norris, "'What Is Enlightenment?': Kant According to Foucault," in *The Cambridge Companion to Foucault,* edited by Gary Gutting (New York: Cambridge University Press, 1994), 175.

capable of recognizing and questioning those limits. This places him in the halls of those thinkers whose prime concern is to "give new impetus, as far and as wide as possible, to the undefined work of freedom."[36] And so we are justified in joining Timothy O'Leary in viewing Foucault as a beholden to the Enlightenment project: "Foucault, we could say, is a 'lumiere' because his project is to defend and expand the freedom of the individual. When he summarizes the features of the Enlightenment attitude he wants to reactivate, his commitment to the expansion of autonomy is clear."[37]

It could be said that as a difficult, but convinced member of the form of thought given to us by the Enlightenment, Foucault sees the light of the freedom shine at its brightest at a certain time of the day. Rousseau saw its radical luminosity at dawn, at the birth of our history, while Marx saw it burn magnificently at sundown, when lowering into the horizon of history. Both fixed the timelessness of the sun at these points, points of history that call for meditation and dreaming. Foucault is no different, except that for him freedom burns brightest right overhead, when the midday sun beats down on the work of the day, and when there is no time to dream of the past or future, but time only to work at the tasks of the present.

Three Moments of the Sun: Playing with the Symbol of Enlightenment, or a Comparison of Camus's and Foucault's Awareness of Limits

No European writer was more obsessed with the sun than Albert Camus. For the Algerian-born writer it was no simple metaphor, but the source of life itself, and his characters delight in its presence. And yet Camus does take the sun seriously as an allegorical figure of importance in Greek thought, and in the way the Greeks wove this giver of life into the tapestry of their worldview. All of this he thinks is an interesting foil to the very different metaphorical status that the sun receives at the hands of modern Europeans. Camus quotes Heraclitus in his short essay on the wonders of Greek thought, "Helen's Exile," saying, "The sun will not overstep his measures; if he does, the Erinyes, the handmaids of jus-

36. Foucault, "What Is Enlightenment?" 316.
37. O'Leary, *Foucault and the Art of Ethics*, 168.

tice, will find him out."[38] This slight intimation needs its further mytho-
logical background to make sense of Greek thought as seen by Camus.

Helios, the Greek god of the sun, a charioteer who careens through
the sky in his fixed circuit, is also often given the full name of Helios
Panoptes, the all-seeing. If Helios wishes to "overstep his measures,"
to change the course of his run or overstay his welcome, he will be set
upon by the Erinyes (in Roman myth "the Furies"), those who have been
issued by Nyx, the night. Such a fate befell Helios's son Phaethon, the
Shining One, who commandeered his father's chariot and brought woe
on the world. The Erinyes are allied with Nemesis, the goddess of justice, who polices the rightful balance of the world, and they are said to
torment their victims with insanity. A sun that oversteps its measure is
beset by the children of night under the command of measure and justice; those who have traversed the limit will go insane. All this is very
interesting when thought about in conjunction with Camus's statement
about his most famous of characters, Meursault, in *The Outsider*. To understand how the sun operates in this novel, one must take Camus on
his word that Meursault is simply a man, "in love with a sun that leaves
no shadows."[39] But this love comes about only through trial, discomfort,
and an acceptance of limits.

In the heart of *The Outsider*, Camus's novel of exile and strangeness, lies a somnambulant Arab fifing on a pipe befitted with only three
notes. In an oasis spring nestled among rocks he aimlessly blows, re-
peating over and over the only notes the flute is authorized to play. This
absurd, tripartite, tuneless melody floats across the atmosphere of the
entire novel. It flows back to its beginning and on to its end. It is a dumb,
thoughtless fanfare that signals the presence of three deaths, these notes
lending their meaninglessness to them. In the vicinity of these deaths is
the presence of the sun, of a luminosity that brings into sharp relief the
nature of the world to this novel's detached protagonist, Meursault.

The first death is his mother's, a death that he is forced to confront
at the body's showing in a room of strange architectural design. Death
lies in a bright room "with whitewashed walls and a glass roof."[40] The

38. Albert Camus, *The Myth of Sisyphus* (London: Penguin, 2000), 168.
39. Albert Camus, *The Outsider,* translated by Joseph Laredo (Harmondsworth: Penguin, 1982), 119.
40. Camus, *The Outsider,* 12.

sensually sensitive Meursault finds himself discomforted by this room designed to capture the light of the sun in all its fierce glory. A sun leaves no shadows when it is directly above us, but this room is designed to artificially fix this shadowless light throughout the day. Sun always floods through its transparent roof at all times of sunlight, while the white walls reflect its watchfulness from every surface to every other. Even when night falls, Meursault is blinded when the light switch is turned on. Meursault asks if one of the lights can be turned off, as his eyes are sore, but the caretaker apologizes that "he couldn't. That was how they'd been installed: it was all or nothing."[41] Even with the sun taking leave from the earth, moderns seek to fix and replicate its omnipresence, which does nothing but remind us of the stark centrality of death.

We next meet a sun that leaves no shadows when Meursault has his first confrontation with the Arabs on the beach; this is the first of three confrontations. Meursault notices that "the sun was shining almost vertically onto the sand and the glare from the sea was unbearable."[42] The sun is fixed at midday and has found a reflective accomplice in the equally omnipresent sea. All Meursault thinks about from this moment on is his discomfort and anxiety. The next time we see the Arabs, Meursault observes "the sun was crashing down onto the sea and the sand and shattering in to little pieces."[43] The third time we see Meursault, around two hours has transpired, and yet "for two hours now the day had stood still, for two hours it had been anchored in an ocean of molten metal."[44] Dazed and in physical pain because the earth has stood still and left the sun and sea to drown him in light, a shot rings out, and death once more accompanies this sun that leaves no shadows. Meursault is not in love with the radical luminosity, for it brings nothing but death and a guilty distress that cannot be explained in the institutions of men. When Meursault pathetically defends his actions in court, saying, "It was the sun," the institution stands confounded.

Finally, Meursault reconciles himself with the sun, a sun that he has loved throughout, but that at its zenith, at the height of its power, when it leaves no shadows, seems only to deceive, doing nought but to bring death and painful clarity. Again this reconciliation with the sun that knows no limits comes in the frightful countdown to his own life.

41. Camus, *The Outsider*, 14.

42. Camus, *The Outsider*, 54.

43. Camus, *The Outsider*, 56.

44. Camus, *The Outsider*, 59.

Imprisoned and awaiting trial, Meursault muses on the limitation and restriction that imprisonment has beset upon him. Curiously he concludes that such restriction and limitation bring no shame to the life of a man. He says, "I often thought in those days that even if I'd been made to live in a hollow tree trunk, with nothing to do but look up at a bit of sky overhead, I'd gradually have got used to it."[45] He then testifies that he would simply look forward to the modest entertainments of his day: birds flying past, clouds wafting over, and while he never says it, one presumes he would equally look forward to that one moment of the day when the sun would align with the opening of his imaginary prison and fill that wooden shaft with its universal, but fleeting brilliance, only to then pass out of that hollow's narrow maw. The hollow of a tree, an image that recalls the allowance of a midday sun that leaves no shadows, but also a necessary limitation and constraint, gives us a wonderful illustration of Camus's philosophy of the acceptance of limits while also accepting the stark reality of absurdity and death.

The number three is so important to Camus's novel because the whole piece is predicated upon three deaths and the more surreptitious presence of three moments of radical luminosity that accompany these fatalities. But there is unevenness to these amalgams of death and light. The first two artificially magnify the omnipresence of the sun and fix it beyond its natural limits, while death is illumed starkly by its eternal eye, and this coupling is accompanied by uneasiness and anxiety. The last moment of death and light does not really exist as a fact in the text, but is more alluded to, more imagined. Meursault's death is a future event and is never actually situated factually in the text. He evokes the image of the hollow tree as a passageway that channels the shadowless sun, but only for a brief moment of the day, and yet he feels nothing but a sober comfort and reassurance from the thought. The last coupling is a strange, missing revelation.

It is hard not to observe this change from an interminable, overbearing sun and its attendant destructiveness to a limited and bounded sun with its mellowed reassurance without recalling Camus's thoughts on the Greek myth of Helios, Erinyes, Nyx, and Nemesis. Meursault's love of a sun that leaves no shadows comes only when he has been tested

---

45. Camus, *The Outsider,* 75.

twice by its ever-seeing and illegitimate extension across the whole land-scape. This is not so different from what Camus finds so terribly wrong with the European culture that was at its zenith in his own day. He off-sets that cultural predicament with the Greek's healthy acceptance of limits: "Greek thought always took refuge behind the conception of lim-its. It never carried anything to extremes, neither the sacred not reason, because it negated nothing, neither the sacred nor reason. It took every-thing into consideration, balancing shadow with light. Our Europe, on the other hand, off in the pursuit of totality, is the child of dispropor-tion."[46]

Under the expanded metaphor of a new sun, Enlightenment Europe marches headlong into the future totalitarian rule of reason. As such, the Europe of Camus's day had plunged itself into a lunacy of war, geno-cide, and extremism that suggests it had been beset by the madness-bearing Erinyes, punishing those who have illegitimately extended the sun of reason. The Erinyes association with Nemesis and Nyx suggest both what we have transgressed, our natural limits, and also what we have made of our supposed enlightened age, a dark night of the soul. Camus's novel of the detached Meursault is more than just a meditation on the absurdity of life; that is just a surface and cursory glance at the text. Beneath this general theme hides a meditation on the idea of the sun and the powerful metaphorical hold it has had on modern European thought. It is a beseeching for the reinstalling of lost limits. It seems in-evitable that this plea could only come from a European outsider. Born in Algeria, Camus lovingly evokes the constrained style of life endorsed by his country. He asks the question, "where can one find the solitude necessary to vigour, the deep breath in which the mind collects itself and courage gauges its strength?"[47] Only in limitation can such measured self-appraisal be accomplished. He demonstrates this in his evocation of the Algerian city of Oran: "Obliged to live facing a wonderful landscape, the people of Oran have overcome this fearful ordeal by covering their city with very ugly restrictions."[48]

Oran is a city sandwiched between a desert on one side and the sea on the other, with fierce heat from the sun a permanent fixture. It is a

46. Camus, *The Myth of Sisyphus*, 167.   47. Camus, *The Myth of Sisyphus*, 141.
48. Camus, *The Myth of Sisyphus*, 147.

walled town that turns in on itself as if avoiding the all-consuming nature of the landscape. It knows the oppression and strangeness that nature herself can inflict when unchecked. A more modern novelist, Cormac McCarthy, beautifully encapsulates the nature of landscapes that
are overwhelmingly afflicted by that which illuminates them. He has an
aimless group of warriors, heralds of death, wandering through a desert
taking in the strange precision of their surroundings.

In the neuter austerity of that terrain all phenomena were bequeathed a strange
equality and no one thing nor spider nor stone nor blade of grass could put
forth claim to precedence. The very clarity of these articles belied their familiarity, for the eye predicates the whole on some feature or part and here was
nothing more luminous than another and nothing more enshadowed and in
the optical democracy of such a landscapes all preference is made whimsical
and a man and a rock become endowed with unguessed kinships.[49]

When things appear bathed in perfect elucidation, thoroughly enlightened, this in no way increases the world's intelligibility. Things ensconced in the all-consuming light appear both unbearable and equivalent. A strange indifference and nonchalance calm the sense of dread
that attends all scenes of radical illumination. It is here that Camus and
Foucault seem to be traveling the same terrain. Camus embodies this
diffidence in the face of the all-consuming irrationality of the world in
his alarmingly unresponsive character of Meursault. Foucault has theorized on and artfully constructed this type of cool detachment to preference throughout his whole intellectual vocation. As if facing a mad world
where certainty is always just uncovered as historical untruth, Foucault
builds an aloof philosophy that mirrors Meursault's personality. And yet
both Foucault's detached skeptical thinking and Meursault's unmoved
behavioral extremism are simply philosophical preludes to ideas of how
one can meaningfully engage with this world. It is from this starting
point that their worldviews begin to mimic each other. Admittedly, Camus is more of an imaginative chronicler of the absurd and the social
and philosophical consequences of this underlying circumstance, while
Foucault is the animated, but patient theorist of discourse and its myriad
fluctuations in history. But between these two quite different styles of

49. Cormac McCarthy, *Blood Meridian: Or the Evening Redness in the West* (London:
Picador, 1990), 247.

thinker there is a wealth of correspondence, numerous overlaps of general attitude, and hidden kinships in their prescriptions to the modern world. Both devise a philosophical melody of at times astounding likeness, and much of their similarity comes from their shared acceptance of a kind of hopelessly incongruous condition that humanity finds itself thrown into.

Both approach the sense of disquiet that the illogical has cursed upon the modern world with the courage of one who wishes to live heroically in this blasted environment. Both look to the ancients, or have an investment in the pagan sensibility, as a remedy to the extremism they perceive besets their intellectual worlds. Both place their weight behind a way of life that sponsors the present as the only proper province of action. Both present the task of life as an endless, fruitless campaign that one must embrace as the meaning of one's life. Both proclaim the need for some form of limitation to the deification of history. Both demand the necessity of rebellion against the condition in which humanity finds itself to uphold its dignity. And last, both espouse some form of aesthetic formulation of life. But the similarities always serve to highlight the obvious difference between these thinkers, which is a difference that materializes upon the issue of limitation.

On the issue of art and creation, Camus also takes his lead from Nietzsche, whom he quotes as saying, "we have art in order not to die of the truth."[50] In Camus's beseeching of the world to endure its absurdity, like a good modernist, he places art and creation at the head of this crusade. He writes, "All existence for a man turned away from the eternal is but a vast mime under the mask of the absurd. Creation is the great mime."[51] In these short sentences, Camus encapsulates Foucault's twin concerns that history is a buffoonery, a taking up of masks, and that a form of playacting constitutes some type of escape from history's ridiculousness. The self is nothing but a naked mannequin that we are free to clothe with whatever character our lives' desire. Freedom is self-creation. But the difference here is that Camus is somewhat more qualified in his embracing of this supposed exit from absurdity. He recognizes that "creation follows indifference" and that it is not an "escape for the intellectual ail-

50. Camus, *The Myth of Sisyphus*, 86.
51. Camus, *The Myth of Sisyphus*, 87.

ment," but rather a "symptom" of that ailment's reflection through life.[52] He warns that it would be wrong to "see a symbol in it" and consider it as a sanctuary. This admission is missing from Foucault's approval of the aesthetic attitude to life, as he does conceive of this approach as a way out. Creative self-legislation is Foucault's sanctuary from the absurdities of the instituted world, where for Camus it resembles more of its necessary movement. It is almost as if Camus is predicting or prophesying the form that will be taken by those who embrace this creative departure from absurdity rather than recognizing it as a corollary of their complaint. What for Camus is merely the "description" of a related phenomenon is for Foucault the rash prescription for the phenomenon.

There are also certain similarities that expose the differences in Camus's look at the "absurd man" and his Sisyphean character and Foucault's depiction of the self's nature and operation. Camus famously portrayed the lamentable condition of man with reference to the Greek idea of hell, a constant aimless repetition, encapsulated in the futile rock-rolling figure of Sisyphus. But Camus sees the myth of Sisyphus as a laudable and life-affirming story, stating we must "imagine Sisyphus happy."[53] He uses this heroically hopeless template to list a further three modalities of life that imitate the "metaphysical honour" of unfulfilled striving; the Don Juan (or lover), the Actor, and the Conqueror. While certainly beyond the scope of this book to discuss in any depth these characters, what do interest us are the commonalities of their nature. They all seem to thrive on a certain giving of style to their lives through the passionate repetition of their chosen profession; they all do nothing for the eternal, as they wish for nothing beyond the "adventure" of their "lifespan." They revolt against the future, explore their "temporally limited freedom," and shield their behavior from "any judgement but their own."[54] This description of the absurd man reads similarly to how Foucault describes the self's governance of the self, or the aesthetic elaboration of the self. We recall all the hallmarks of that self-related procedure, its heroization of the present, its scorning of expression beyond its own life and in the future, its denial of legislation for others or itself, its temporally limited autonomy. All point toward Camus's formulation for the

---

52. Camus, *The Myth of Sisyphus*, 88.   53. Camus, *The Myth of Sisyphus*, 111.
54. Camus, *The Myth of Sisyphus*, 64.

absurd man. But most of all, the formulation traps the self in a goalless motivation; not having a defined nature it can seek, it is forever transforming and inventing a self that will never find consummate expression. It resembles the self, rolling itself up and down the hill with Sisyphus, and like him, taking whatever difficult pleasure it can obtain from it. But Camus, unlike Foucault, is careful not to present this state of affairs as constituting unchecked license and freedom. In fact the freedom is a controlled binding.

The absurd does not liberate, it binds. It does not authorise all actions. Everything is permitted does not mean that nothing is forbidden. The absurd merely confers an equivalence on the consequences of those actions. It does not recommend crime, for this would be childish, but it restores to remorse its futility. Likewise, if all experiences are indifferent, that of duty is as legitimate as any other.[55]

While it is not to say that Foucault cannot apply these important qualifications to the radically liberated self he has composed, or to say that at points he doesn't hint that a certain limitation of the free ethical self is necessary, it should be emphasized that he is far more concerned about keeping that essential free possibility as widely open as feasible. Camus too is dedicated to this, but deems it just as important to expose the energies of this unfettered activity to channeling and control. He just accepts that such containment is natural and has its own authority within the grain of freedom. Foucault begrudgingly accepts the reality of institutional limitation to freedom, but his conception of the self is constructed in such a way as to make it unable to embrace any form of limitation. Thus it always rails against institution or common consensus.

The theme repeats itself the further one pushes into the similarities. While they both in some way scorn the eternal, Camus does so "without negating it."[56] And this difference shows in their attitudes toward the present. Again they both accept it as the way of the modern world, but only Foucault has the drive to find the eternal within it. Finding the perpetual in the present would be anathema to Camus, for it would be an extension beyond the natural limits of its temporal province. They both also seem to applaud the ancient world, welcoming a new pagan sensibil-

55. Camus, *The Myth of Sisyphus*, 65.
56. Camus, *The Myth of Sisyphus*, 64.

ity to the excesses of modern times. But again, Camus seems dedicated to enforcing its lessons (rightly or wrongly) of a thoroughgoing moderation with regard to all things and a committed meditation upon limits. Foucault too looks toward the Greeks and finds a concern for modesty and temperance in their example, but then seeks to redirect those virtues against them. He does this by locating a pure moral space of the self within that period that can then be resurrected to combat any limitation that can be located at any historical impasse.

And thus I turn last to history. Camus's record against the absolutist historical philosophies of Hegel, Marx, and many other political extremists is passionately documented in his controversial work *The Rebel*. And Foucault's distrust of those who wield the name of history like tyrants is also well documented. But Foucault's only way of limiting this tyranny of the illegitimately extended past and future is by establishing another tyranny that can stand up against their reemergence. As we have seen, this is accomplished by crowning the present and endowing it with the same critical power that other directions of time have previously enjoyed. The force of this approach can only be explained with recourse to the timeless spirit that inhabits the attempt.

Of course an awareness of limits is inherent to Camus's primary foundation in the absurd, for the absurd is conceived not as something itself, but as the feeling accompanying an unequal relation. Camus likens the absurd to a man attacking a group of machine guns with a sword, the absurdity lying in the "disproportion between his intention and the reality he will encounter."[57] This is the fundament of the absurd: limited humanity's confrontation with the universe. It is a divorce and confrontation of intention and the world, and thus it always presupposes a radical limitation at its base. Foucault does not have this sense of unbearable restraint inherent in his project. In fact, our look at the different conceptual phases of his project shows us that in general he avoids the confrontation and divorce of reality at all costs, giving to whatever fundamental reality he presupposes an all-consuming power. This we saw in his giving of all strength, authority, and freedom to history in his archaeological period. He then gives this inheritance to the concept of power in his genealogical turn. We now observe him pass this mantle of the unlimited on to the

57. Camus, *The Myth of Sisyphus*, 33.

individual self, occupying the present. Where Camus adopts the present as a limiting force in the face of the all-consuming, Foucault formulates the present as just another all-consuming entity. Where Camus makes the important distinction between rebellion and revolution, favoring rebellion over revolution for the natural limitation that always attends it, Foucault seems to have the present represent itself as the revolutionary heart of history. He fails to adequately learn the lessons from his radical political forbears, and allows the timelessness of the will to christen an eternalized present as history. Foucault's turning to the present fails to annul history or time, but simply installs it anew in a position it should never hope to inhabit always. His history of the present is just another illusion of history, and once again the sun of reason is at an illegitimate standstill. Foucault is just another European "child of disproportion."

PART 4

Kant and Kafka

🜋 13

The Unstable Temporal Landscape
of Critique

The Political Nature of Critique

The argument of this book has from the outset viewed Kant as a thinker whose critical philosophy has opened a wide and complex space for political thought and endeavor. It takes seriously the claim that practical reason is the lynchpin to the whole enterprise, rising to primary importance over theoretical reason in Kant's own estimation of critiques and humanity's purpose. As such, this book has given crucial weight to the role of Rousseau in the formation of Kant's critical project as the founding moral and political spirit of his critical universe. The analytical tradition of concerning oneself with the epistemological and theoretical aspects of the first critique and discarding the philosophically vague aspects of the rest as unrelated is considered an unbalanced travesty of Kant's intentions. To ignore the overarching political drive of this philosophy is to misconstrue its ultimate directive and be blind to one of the major tensions to have nourished generations of political thinkers. We should never forget that Kant's desire to define the precincts of theoretical reason begins its life as a political choice to alienate dogmatists and enthusiasts from the discussion of knowledge and morality. Theoretical and practical reason are linked in a strange concoction of limitation and limitlessness. Their relationship surveys both critique's own province and the illegal provinces outside it. It also then adjudicates those instances where reason must transcend the provinces it has carefully mapped. In attempting to legislate for the margins and limits of the various faculties, critique is always at the same time defining itself. The question is always how critique can define itself within the same process of defining reason. Does reason exist prior to critique, or vice versa? As a twin process, the Kantian dualism is thus circumscribed within the elastic circularity of critique itself. As critique and reason are legislating for the world, they are at the same time discovering themselves, their rights, and their limits. It is within the confines of this circular activity of the critique of reason that a difficult and contradictory political universe can thrive.

Kant radically reformulated the dualistic problematic of nature and freedom, science and morality, phenomena and noumena. But one term of the dualism is never contemplated without the specter of the other haunting it. Theoretical reason is tempted at all times by the ideas and ideals of reason, empirically disqualified figments that nevertheless regulate the function of knowing. Knowing is directed and limited by the limitlessness that defines doing and hoping. It wishes to soar with its clipped wings. At the same time, doing and hoping struggle constantly to give knowledgeable form to their limitless origins. Moral law is a ground that cannot be understood; it is simply an imperative striving with no conclusive phenomenal evidence of its successful operation. Practical reason soars majestically without a place to land. Kantian critique is beset by this twin need to ruthlessly police the border between nature and reason and act as that frontier runner who morally traverses our limits in search of a better world. It must obdurately uphold the regulations in one instance and be a conscientious objector in the other. Kantian critique is the borderland of the modern political imagination, and its divided loyalties between its two homelands are the options upon which that imagination sways. Like a frontier town, Kantian critique can accommodate a wide range of differing characters in a lawless conversation. It is Kant's confusion with the competing demands of the real and the ideal that makes critique the fertile bed of political interpretation that it is. Critique will always be a frustrated, but striving entity, where its political logic is unstable, swinging between its triumphant ideality and its thwarted reality.

In asserting the innately uncertain nature of Kantian critique, this conclusion ostensibly agrees with the view and analysis put forward by Kimberly Hutchings in her book *Kant, Critique and Politics*. Hutchings surveys the unresolvable Kantian aporias that have sustained some of the twentieth century's leading political theorists, and in so doing reveals the ambiguous directions critique has taken as a potent political energy. This potency, Hutchings claims, is the result of the challenge that critique offers to its advocates in attempting to overcome critique's intrinsic divisions. Exponents of critique are ultimately driven to fuse the dualism that gives them their initial conviction and mandate. My argument goes further than this by investigating the particular way in which this has been attempted by three figureheads of radical politics, Rousseau, Marx, and Foucault, and the multiple ways that these theorists have used the agency of history for this purpose. But the lines of convergence between this study's starting point and Hutchings's argument on the political nature of critique warrant discussion and outline. To conclude on Rousseau, Marx, and Foucault's uses of history it is necessary to revisit the problematics of critique. Kimberly Hutchings points out the divergent political span of critical practice: "The practice of critique thus comes to veer between the political options of rigid order or absolute anarchy, with the critical philosopher embracing in turn the roles of legislator and warmonger in a never-ending, but always unavailing, effort to achieve a peaceful resolution to the conflicts of reason."[1]

Hutchings's inspection of the political commentaries of the Kantian project attests to the myriad and often perverse political fascinations Kant can inspire. She demonstrates how Kant can be accused, commended, suspected, and praised by his analysts. Kant can be criticized for, revealed to be, or even forced into molding his critical project into the wildly differing postures of a warmongering violent process or a peacemaking conversation between austere participants. Dictatorial, authoritarian, and foundationalist to some, others see an anti-rationalist, anarchic, and libertarian version of critique. The breadth of opinion seems to range between this desire to see critique as an infinite, unfolding, tolerant, and democratic task or an ethically rigid metaphysical machine generating unyielding and insoluble decrees. Hutchings examines three differing in-

1. Kimberly Hutchings, *Kant, Critique and Politics* (London and New York: Routledge, 1996), 12.

terpretations of Kant's thought. She cites Susan Meld Shell, who sees it as a theory of property and rights; Hans Saner, who sees critique as rule of law over metaphysical disputes; and finally Onora O'Neill, who conceives critique as a ruleless, foundationless debate or tribunal.

Shell's position holds that Kantian critique is designed to help us in the commandeering of properties and powers. "Both Kant's metaphysics and his jurisprudence are theories of property. Both knowing and having are ways of appropriating or securing a right to the use of a thing, be it a concept or an object in the world."[2] In putting forth her view that Kant understands reason as a theory of property and as a manifestation of humanity's desire for the appropriation of rights, Shell offers a strict and totalitarian reading of critique. This reading takes critique as suffused with the power to take possession of its wants. It assumes no difficulty in critique's power to carry out its aims practically, as it is thoroughly focused on the "rights" of reason. Critique assumes an authority that it possesses by the simple right of its power to appropriate—a very Hobbesian view of Kant. A view of critique presuming such raw power neuters the magnanimous and stridently moral aspects traditionally associated with critique. It is almost enough to say reason has a theoretical right, and that its duty is a secondary practical question. But Shell is careful to show the downside of this domineering side of critique's power. She writes, "For Kant, however, ownership implies only a will to benefit, not the actual ability to do so.... The rights of man do not include the right to happiness. Modern men who complacently join in the Kantian project should find in the melancholy indignation at its heart a reason for concern."[3] The view offered here is a strange aberration from the standard understanding of the rights of man, but this is not to say it is wholly inaccurate. Critique confers on man not rights that bring him freedom and hope, but the freedom and ability to appropriate rights that make him a prince. The unhappiness and isolation brought by acquisitiveness and seizure here attend the Kantian critic. The critic here resembles Machiavelli's prince more than he does Kant's fair and morally generous serf. Morality is held as his principality, rather than being his gift to the world. This does not prevent him from doing good, in much

2. Susan Meld Shell, *The Rights of Reason: A Study of Kant's Philosophy and Politics* (Toronto: University of Toronto Press, 1980), 179.
3. Shell, *The Rights of Reason*, 179.

the same fashion as Machiavelli's prince can still be a good, yet powerful prince, but this is quite a distance from critique genuinely guaranteeing the good. Critique is not a standard adopted in agreement because it pledges happiness, but an ethical entity up for ownership, appealing to the desires it was designed to mitigate. Critique interpreted as property dealing cuts a sad and lonely figure for the critic. This is the temptation of critique, as it supposes a critique that may profess to its limitations but knows in reality that all its individual owners are free to transgress them. Critique is just another commandeered tool in a battleground that is more appropriately comprehended via the Nietzschean metaphysic of the will to power.

Hans Saner offers a more passive vision of critique as the monitor and arbiter to the disputes of reason. This understanding of critique takes its starting point from Kant's own historical battleground: the warring factions of dogmatism and skepticism, rationalism and empiricism. Contrary to the idea of critique outlined above, Saner assumes that critique is designed to be the mediator in the brutish state of nature in which any participator of reason finds himself. Closer to Kant's initial vision for critique, it is here taken as a constitutionally limited governor of the battlefield of reason, judiciously separate and not enfolded in the controversies of reason. He writes, "reason needs an authority above it, one that will continually purify its use. Kant gives various names to this authority; he calls it now experimental reason, now judicial reason, now critical reason."[4]

Yet by giving it these variant names of "reason," Kant also implies that critique is not truthfully separate from reason, but a "self-related" operation of reason. Critique is set up as the permanent trial of reason, and as such becomes a permanent institutional feature of a reason that was once ensconced in a state of nature characterized by disagreement and dispute. Critique is a progressive development upon reason that establishes the rule of law where brute force once reigned. In one sense, a tranquility of law settles over the pitched metaphysical camps, but in another sense this tranquility is characterized by constant questioning and restless intellectual movement. Critique is not a powerful temptation, but a foil to the very temptations of unlimited power. Saner writes,

4. Hans Saner, *Kant's Political Thought: Its Origins and Development*, translated by E. B. Ashton (Chicago: University of Chicago Press, 1973), 254.

"Reason is the permanent judge, and at the same time the permanent defendant. The trial of reason is its own self-imposed, infinite task of self-enlightenment and self-purification. The peace of reason is thus not a state of trustful rest but one of vigilance and self-examination."[5]

It is not that the approaches of Shell and Saner must be evaluated as to which one is more correct, but that the amorphous, complex, ambitious, and frustrated reality of critique allows both to have currency, depending from which side the problem is approached. One coming from the direction of metaphysical controversy takes critique to be a savior of level-headed judgment; the other, coming from the direction of the unknown political promise and latent potential of critique, views it also as a savior, but one with its own attendant risks and temptations. One sees critique as an untarnished limiter of metaphysical disputes, the bringer of peace; the other as simply another stage for new metaphysical disputes, the indication of future tense standoffs and newly armed combatants. One is authority and the rule of law, the other a political vacuum for those seeking authority. The downside to Saner's vision is that the peace of reason is a restless and precarious peace, remaining ever vigilant against the possibility of its suspension and dissolution.

Onora O'Neill provides the most sustained effort to reveal the political and judicial structure of critique through a very sophisticated reading of the political metaphors of tribunal, debate, and community utilized by Kant. The attempt here is uncover the paradox of Kant's project as falling back on an anti-rationalist grounding for the legitimation of reason: "The image of reason's authority as analogous to that of a tribunal also has a certain merit in that it suggests immediately that reason is not algorithmic. To have a tribunal is not to have an algorithm that the tribunal follows."[6] Critique here understood is not meant to have solid foundations, but is said to be constantly in the process of building its foundations through the unanchored workings of tribunal justice. Critique is also forged in the crucible of public debate, where an eternal balancing act of viewpoints seeks a higher, yet ever-receding resolution. This presupposes a vigilant community where a base minimum of democratic process guarantees the opportunity for all to be involved.

5. Saner, *Kant's Political Thought*, 256.
6. Onora O'Neill, *Constructions of Reason: Explorations of Kant's Practical Philosophy* (Cambridge: Cambridge University Press, 1989), 18.

Algorithmic structures of thought emerge from the shifting sands of judgment and discussion; or said in another way, a plan emerges from a procedure with no antecedent plan. Reason is an entity that must

be devised and deployed by a plurality of agents who share a world, but who are short of principles for doing the sharing. This is why the basic task of constructing principles of discursive order is analogous to that of constructing principles of political order, and why politics provides metaphors for articulating the task, principles and limits of reason.[7]

The political metaphors of tribunal, debate, and community here provide us with very illuminating templates for the operation and working functions of critique, but cannot give us clues as to the outcomes of critique. Critique cannot give us bearings as to what it will achieve and what discursive order it will establish. It is for this reason that O'Neill can warn that "Babel remains a constant threat," as with no antecedent plan to direct it, the products of critique can take any arbitrary form.[8] The inner paradox of this political reading is that critique is still assumed to be devising principles for the world, but has no principles for its own working that we can commonly assent to.

These three wide-ranging political interpretations of critique all display an incurable tendency to hinder the benefits they are designed to confer on the world. Critique conceived as the power to appropriate the use and ownership of the objects and concepts that enter its field condemns it to the possibility of a dictatorial, agonistic existence. Critique conceived as a judicial arbiter and mediator bringing peace to the constant quarreling of reason simply places it in a restless, ever-striving, and never-ending distrust of itself, having become its own defendant, while critique seen as a free and democratic debate without terms of reference, foundation, or a precedent "algorithm" finds itself unable to construct lasting principles that will bind the plurality of agents it is designed to help include. As Kimberly Hutchings has correctly observed, critique is trapped between a terminal oscillation of limitation and limitlessness: "The dual determination of critique in the acknowledgement of reason's limitation and the assertion of its legislative power implies a set of dichotomies and a series of attempts to overcome them."[9]

7. O'Neill, *Constructions of Reason*, 20.   8. O'Neill, *Constructions of Reason*, 18.
9. Hutchings, *Kant, Critique and Politics*, 37.

The three interpretations we have briefly revealed are not practical uses of the Kantian philosophy, but direct elucidations of the philosophy; thus they have no need to alleviate this unavoidable fluctuation. They simply accept it as the necessary recognition by a commentator of the contrary directions to which critique is forced to submit. This is the benefit of interpretation over utilization. What they do demonstrate for my argument is the radically political nature of Kantian critique. Critique can accommodate a vast array of political positions and interpretations within its expansive fold. The aim here is to discern the scope and atmosphere of the critical universe in order to color the general fates of those who toil in the borderlands of Kantianism. And yet there is a far more supple and complex, unified yet contradictory extrapolation of the Kantian political universe of critique, provided not by one of his numerous commentators, but by the literary imaginings of Franz Kafka. Kafka provides us with a compellingly coherent universe where limitation and limitlessness reside together in an uneasy tension. Kafka's work seeks to reveal the coherent, yet doomed world of modern critique by showing how the provinces of transcendence and materialism can coexist upon the immanent plane of secularism.

Kafka's is the first imagination to seek an answer to the dissipation of modern life and a modern societal dissipation that follows the contours of Kant's dissipated philosophical legacy. How is it that a practical philosophy with its cornerstone so firmly laid down in a transcendent will and a categorical imperative can be interpreted as not being governed by a transcendent standard or unconditional command? That it can be characterized by such earthly and nontranscendental models as the brutish state of nature and the capricious, unpredictable logic of the community, debating, and tribunals, rather than the inscrutable steadiness of some eternal morality? The answer lies in the timelessness that besets both of these seemingly separate options. The idea of timelessness is the bridge that connects this dichotomy. The categorical imperative is a negative principle advising its participants what intellectual directions it should renounce, what strategies it needs to deny for the proper working of the tribunal, so it can receive a moral bounty that is not limited by the tribunal that guarantees it. In this cautiously negative understanding of critique, its lukewarm caution leaves critique open to the more forthright and stern accusations of empty formality and severe prescription. Kant's legacy is dissipated because his vision of critique allows all these varied interpretations to cohabit, one easily mutating into a stronger other, another easily moderated or reduced to a more lenient view, or two operating in tandem without them recognizing their obvious differences. Timelessness has many lives in the world of critique. Kafka chronicles all these varied interpretations cohabiting, mutating, differing, rising, and falling within an all-encompassing, imaginative worldly cosmos.

Critique begins life in the unhistorical womb of transcendental moral timelessness, but lives its historical life out in a world of timeless political belief that creates illusory historical notions. There is no obvious difference between the idea of a transcendental morality that purposefully blinds itself to time and the idea of a worldly tribunal with no antecedent orientation or firm directive for the future in the world of Kafka. Both ignore the fullness of time, or indeed any difference between a world of timeless morality and a timeless state of nature. These couplings are alarmingly similar and seem almost vitally linked. Our modern secular sense of the eternal can only have earthly representation in justice and its endlessly attendant courts, blindfolded to time and history, and a social animalistic existence, where a new timeless state of nature breeds within a landscape of morality, a moral nature, or rational instinct. Where regulative ideas of God and the immortality of the soul are tangled in the barbed-wire fences of Kant's epistemological and moral borderlands, the true source of the infinite and transcendent in Kant is the never-ending process of critique and surveying. This replaces the old sources of divinity for the modern world. Critique is our strange heaven, where we seek communion not with a higher power, but with and among ourselves. The exploration of this thwarted secular religiosity is the province of Kafka's fiction. What writer has understood this fact more innately than Kafka, with his grubbily legal world of judgment so afflicted with temporal unsteadiness, but at the same time so desolately and secularly transcendent? Kafka's literature is timeless, not in the clichéd sense attributed to great writers, but in the sense that he so mesmerizingly evokes the timeless age of critique. Kafka is the first writer to clearly see the very modern link between judgment encapsulated in worldly judicial forms, the historical emptiness of transcendental moral grounding, and the emanation of arbitrary prescription from this coupling. The fact of his obvious fascination with human beings made uncannily animal, an allusion to the equally timeless state of nature and its strange new relation to our human societies, also confirms Kafka's brilliant tuning to the modern world created by critique. We now move to a more detailed examination of his art to better understand the myriad avenues critique has carved in our modern worldview.

Kafka's Vision of Critical Modernity

The first and most obvious starting point that lends a fruitful comparison of Kafka's art to the art of critique is the sheer volume of literature that has been written on Kafka.[10] It seems as though Kafka's literary world is open to almost indefinite critique, an inexhaustible resource for interpretation. From the above discussion of Kantian critique it is assumed that these two thinkers share this level of boundless reading. It is an inevitable consequence of the way they set up their unstable, flexible, and atemporal understandings of the world. The comparisons are so resounding that one could go as far as to say that Kafka is the literary companion to the modern world's dependence and partiality for critique.

In Walter Benjamin's essay on Kafka, written to commemorate the tenth anniversary of Kafka's death, he makes note of a peculiar reoccurring figure in Kafka's fiction ... the assistants. These characters, says Benjamin, are without family, or at least not afflicted by the demands made by the family circle, the familial being the most common Kafkan affliction among his doomed protagonists.

In Indian mythology there are the gandharvus, celestial creatures, beings in an unfinished state. Kafka's assistants are of that kind: neither members of, nor strangers to, any other groups of figures, but, rather, messengers from one to the other.... They have not yet been completely released from the state of nature.... It is for them and their kind, the unfinished and the bunglers, that there is hope.[11]

This group constitutes the atmosphere that the condemned characters find themselves subjected to. None of these half-formed envoys have a fixed place or firm position, as they are constantly moving, growing,

10. Nina Pelikan Strauss notes in her essay "Transforming Franz Kafka's Metamorphosis" that by 1977 there were around ten thousand works on Kafka in print; in *The Metamorphosis,* translated and edited by Stanley Corngold (New York: W. W. Norton, 1996), 126.

11. Walter Benjamin, *Illuminations* (New York: Harcourt, Brace and World, 1968), 116–17.

or declining in authority. They give off the impression of order and allegiance when there is nothing of the sort. They exist in a permanent twilight of justice. Ancestry has almost no hold on them, and as such Kafka gives them the most negligent of characterization. Their utter formlessness is the brilliant literary expression of the formlessness of critique; mere functionaries of judgment, they provide no handrail for the hero burdened by history. Critique creates this historically neutered army—individuals no longer vitally linked to institutions, but nevertheless belonging to them, housing their own indifferent operation, and lubricating the indifferent operation of institutions. Those constrained by the family, by generational weight, the weight of history's demands find themselves entirely alienated in this environment of timeless, unfinished reality. The three "lodgers," those "sticklers for order," emerge in the crisis of Gregor Samsa's metamorphosis at the point when his family is slowly weaning themselves from him. The all-pervasiveness of this universe of assistants cannot even secure the family's guiding hand from relinquishing the hero into its ineffectual grasp. Josef K. is plunged deeper into this abyss by his own uncle as he tries to secure the services of a lawyer for him. In this environment there can be no hope for the man who still feels the call of the family, the pressure of a past propelling him into a future. Hope only belongs to those history-less half-breeds still searching for their place in the world. If the turn to human society is characterized by our awareness of history, of awareness of a duty from the past given for our future, then this reality of critical "assistants" is a new state of nature billowing in our societal achievement. A more apt description of the modern actuality of critique has rarely been seen.

In this world the example of the father becomes a curse, just as the relationship between father and son, one generation to the next, becomes corrupted. Tradition finds itself dueling an unassailable foe of "nebulous officialdom." Benjamin observes Kafka's historical hour informing his work: "Kafka's work is an ellipse with foci that are far apart and are determined, on the one hand, by mystical experience (in particular the experience of tradition) and, on the other, by the experience of the modern big-city dweller."[12] Living on the cusp of two ages, tradition and critique, Kafka was able to lament them both. Unusually sensitive

12. Benjamin, *Illuminations*, 145.

to the war they were waging against each other, he deflected their mutual animosity into himself to better understand their reason for being. But as the examples of *The Trial* and *The Castle* clearly show, the side of the bureaucracy, assistants, officials, and the encroaching, yet uninviting city were undoubtedly winning over the old world that haunted him like a burden from the past.

Among Gregor Samsa's first thoughts upon awaking in his monstrous state are the duties of his occupation, an occupation forced upon him by his family's past financial disgrace. We later find that the family's economic standing was never as dire as Gregor was led to believe, his father having saved away a little money unbeknownst to his hard-working son. The past that sustained Gregor's life, gave it its orientation and meaning, is shown to be a lie. The source of this lie, the father's violent and rash hurling of an apple at his son, will eventually and slowly become his son's killer, the apple of Gregor's fall festering in the wound of his back. The fact that his death sentence is lodged in his back beautifully demonstrates the direction of time that is seen as the death knell for the modern world. The eternal and everyday metamorphosis of forms and people that critique demands destroys the past that once sustained life. Gregor's past is cut off from him at the moment when the family intemperately and fearfully judges its future to be in jeopardy. Gregor, still attached to the outdated ways of direction from the past, suffers a blow from behind as he fails to come to terms with his new, metamorphosed reality. As tradition is replaced by critique, the past is destroyed wholesale of its familiarity and orienting power, turning instead to a dead weight perceived by the new order to be dangerous to its movement into the future.

The mythic order of fate where one's lot is determined behind one's back ... is displaced by a post-mythic in which the individual can no longer find his place in the texture of fate. This distance from the mythic force of fate, this interruption of the transference of a debt from generation to generation introduces into the world a new and more radical kind of guilt.[13]

In *The Metamorphosis,* the past is represented in its total destruction at the hands of critique, so destroyed because of its perceived ability for the total unraveling of the work of critique. The past undoubtedly

13. Eric Santer, "The Writing of Abjection," in *The Metamorphosis*, 200.

threatens critique, and so *The Metamorphosis* chronicles the past's violent and uncaring reception in the modern world. But Kafka also provides us with a more mystifying and disquieting vision of the past's relation to the modern world of critique. In *The Trial* we are confronted with a change of world equally as intense and as sudden as that seen in *The Metamorphosis*. Instead of finding oneself suddenly changed into vermin, Josef K. finds himself changed into an accused man; both changes are inexplicable, with no causal relation to the past. "Somebody must have made false accusation against Josef K., for he was arrested one morning without having done anything wrong."[14]

The past is cut off from both of these men, but Josef K. differs in that he has no knowledge of the past that led him to his present predicament. Gregor morphs into wretchedness and reminisces on the wretched conditions of his previous life as a struggling traveling salesman. He registers little astonishment at his change, almost acknowledging it as simply another manifestation of his verminous, lamentable past existence. Yet the hopes of his past, his hopes and sacrifices for his family, still keep him going. His past is not much, but it is capable of sustaining him in his state of animal existence. By comparison, Josef K.'s life is a life of stature, making the new, shameful conditions of his life unbearable and limitlessly confusing. Josef K. faces the difficulties of unwarranted accusation with a superior and arrogant air, bringing the constant ire and annoyance of the many assistants he meets on his path. But why does he react with such haughty indignation, rather than the good-natured, if naive concern of Gregor? This is because Josef's past is totally unknown; his preoccupation is with what is missing or eliminated from his past, rather than what was the firm bedrock of his past, as was Gregor's. The absence of a cause for his changed status is the only past that we can know of Josef. His past is a black hole of memory, forever the cause of his present pains and future demise, yet with absolutely no existence whatsoever. Where in *The Metamorphosis* the past exists as painful clash with the new world, by the time of *The Trial* the past has been excised from the body of the world; it no longer exists. Josef's world is determined by an event that never existed, where Gregor's world is determined by events that once existed, but that no longer provide passable roads of ac-

14. Franz Kafka, *The Trial*, translated by Idris Parry (London: Penguin, 2000), 1.

tion. These both seem very compelling analogies of the effect critique can have on the social body and the members of its existence. The one explores the condemned fate of a man with no past, the other the alienated lack of destiny for a man who does possess a past, but in a world that no longer recognizes it.

But what is the effect of this past that has been relegated to oblivion in *The Trial*? A past cannot be so easily erased; where would we find the traces of its existence? Again it is noted by Benjamin that the casual and knowing behavior of those whom Josef K. meets has a definite link to the past.

Whenever figures in the novels have anything to say to K., no matter how important or surprising it may be, they do so casually and with the implication that he must really have known it all along. It is as though nothing new is being imparted, as though the hero is being invited to recall to mind something that he has forgotten.[15]

It is as if Josef K. is expected to understand the rules of the game as if they had always existed. The phantom accusation leveled against him makes him a newborn child in the world, with everyone gently reminding this middle-aged infant of what everyone else knows almost innately. A past that is forgotten and cannot be recalled is constantly, alluringly, hazily, and frustratingly coaxed from K. by his mysterious co-cast. Yet K. remains always in the dark as to this expected familiarity with the machinery of judgment. Where Gregor's world knew his past but had moved beyond it, Josef's world has a past for everyone but himself, a past that he is destined to never know. If Gregor is the trailblazer of critique, still reminded of the ways of old, Josef is his progeny, a man after the conflict of ages where the old ways are denied him. It is as if Kafka is rehearsing the effects that critique will have upon humanity, both collectively in the figures of the formless assistants and individually in the forlorn and anxious figures of his heroes. The past is no longer real to any of them, but simply haunts them. Critique is a secular religion of anxiety, replacing the traditional religion of belief in the modern transition that Kafka chronicles.

---

15. Benjamin, *Illuminations*, 131.

"You probably don't believe that I'm a defendant?" K. asked. "Oh yes, of course," said the man and he stepped a little to one side, but in his answer there was no belief, only anxiety.[16]

The impoverishment and yet popularity of the theological explanation of Kafka that have flourished in Max Brod's interpretative wake are explained admirably by this Kantian approach to Kafka. He is of course composing parables, but only parables that are fit for our critical world, in the same way that Camus's outsider is the Christ we deserve. This religious approach hits its mark on far too many occasions for us to dismiss it as wholly inappropriate, yet it misses the mark in a way that makes it unsatisfying. Where its interpretative reach seems greatest is in its receptivity to the sense of infinitude that pervades the works and the accompanying sense of limitation and lowliness that afflicts itself upon the individual protagonist, in much the same way as the boundless God of old confines his creations. But despite the overbearing Judaism that is said to influence his output, Kafka lived in a world without God, and as such his sense of the limitless and the limited is of a different species. It is not God that gives us our tantalizing taste for the infinite and transcendent, but instead the unending critique of reason and its grounding in the noumenal transcendence of the will. It is no longer God that restricts and confounds us, but the critique of reason that borders our endeavors and puts us into existential uncertainty.

The past is not the only casualty in this critical universe; the future suffers its own corruption and absence. And again Kafka provides us with two negative visions of the legacy critique has left for time. Again we concentrate upon the twin texts of *Metamorphosis* and *Trial*. The *Trial*'s attitude to the future is simple and unequivocal, summed up by the word postponement. When K. visits the artist Titorelli he is famously confronted with three possible outcomes for his case: actual acquittal, apparent acquittal, and prolongation. Here K. finds the option of prolongation to his liking: "Prolongation means that the proceedings are kept permanently in their first stages. To achieve this the accused and his helper, but particularly his helper, must keep in uninterrupted personal contact with the court."[17] If acquittal is the end of a thing, the process

16. Kafka, *The Trial*, 51.
17. Kafka, *The Trial*, 125.

of prolongation is nothing more than the postponement of the future. Future is perpetually suspended from the reach of the critical laborer, for "the case can't stand still." Any desired goal, any satisfactory end to a process, any communion with an outcome, is purged from the possibilities of critique. A satisfactory ending is forever purged also from Kafka's characters and his writings themselves. Josef K. muses to himself before his demise, "Are they going to say when I am gone that I wanted to end the case at the beginning and that now, at the end, I want it to begin again?" The man denied a past and with a receding future is of course going to be utterly tangled with beginnings and endings. How can he order his life in such temporal confusion, a temporal confusion mirrored by critique? Where does critique begin and end? Does it precede reason or come after it; does it let reason begin its work, or does it end its tribulations? These questions are left hanging by both Kant and Kafka.

Kafka's own writing is also subject to this extreme entanglement of starts and stops. We know that his notebooks and diaries are littered with the beginnings of stories, left to flounder in their initial genesis. We also know that Kafka was always unhappy with the endings of his stories, never knowing how to adequately complete the momentum behind their inspirational beginnings. One recalls to mind Camus's famous assessment that Kafka's "endings, or lack of endings," require the reader to constantly reread, constantly begin again and reassess. The reader of Kafka finds himself in much the same position as the student of critique, forever forced to begin again, as the end must always be scrutinized. All of Kafka's novels were unfinished, not because they lacked endings, but because the journey from beginning to end traced by Kafka always seems unfinished. Edwin Muir noted this fact when he wrote, "We know the end he had in mind for all his stories; but the road to it could have gone on forever, for life as he saw it was endlessly ambiguous; so that there seems to be a necessity in the gaps that are left in his three stories; if he had filled up these gaps, others would have appeared."[18] Kafka's imagination succumbs to a kind historical and temporal watering down or dissipation, for the space between beginning and end can forever be filled. This is a similar fate that the radical political imagination suc-

18. Edwin Muir, "Introduction," in *America*, by Franz Kafka, translated by Willa Muir and Edwin Muir (London: Penguin, 1976), 9.

cumbs to because of its adoption of the powers of critique. The past can regress infinitely into nonexistence as the future pushes further into inexpressibility, while all the while the present endlessly propagates itself. This is the story that this book has attempted to trace.

Of all the endings Kafka was unhappy with, none was more unsatisfactory to him than that of *The Metamorphosis*. No doubt the ending leaves a bitter aftertaste. A new and disturbing sun rises from the curvature of Gregor's sister's back as she stands and stretches on the train traveling to the family's new life. This is the family's redemption, but certainly no redemption that calls to mind the traditional religious meaning of the term, as it has been won at the expense of their dead son. The true shifting of this sense of redemption is made clear if we examine the German word Kafka used to describe Gregor. "The exact sense of his intention is captured in the *Ungeziefer,* a word that cannot be expressed by the English words bug or vermin. *Ungeziefer* derives (as Kafka probably knew) from the late Middle High German word originally meaning, 'the unclean animal not suited for sacrifice.'"[19] Gregor Samsa, before his change, was sacrificing himself for his family. While this sacrifice may have been a source of abjection, it was in the old religious sense of the term a noble and dignified enterprise that gave meaning to his life. With his change Gregor is suddenly deemed unsuitable for such a purpose. The meaning of his life evaporates, while his memory still attempts to cling to this dutiful handrail from the past. Sacrifice is always determined by past duty. But in a world where sacrifice loses its meaning, where the past has become "unsuitable," what becomes of that religious term that conjures the future ... redemption? What redemption can the family have in this brave new world, a world where redemption isn't prefixed by sacrifice? The sister's outstretched body now resembles the body of a whore: "she had blossomed into a beautiful, full-bosomed girl ... they must start looking around for a nice husband for her."[20] Redemption in the world of critique is nothing more than a cheapened future, somewhere to sell, be sold, bid, and buy, and thus assign yourself to a second-rate meaning of life. The critical investment in the future is to

19. Stanley Corngold, "Kafka's 'The Metamorphosis': Metamorphosis of a Metaphor," in *The Metamorphosis,* translated and edited by Stanley Corngold (New York: W. W. Norton, 1996), 87.

20. Kafka, *Stories 1904–1924,* translated by J. A. Underwood (London: Abacus, 1981), 145.

be tinged with the never-acknowledged, constantly forgotten, but always present guilt of having excised the past. The future can never be dignified and gallant because of the severing action critique effects upon the past. Critique creates a marketplace of ideas with destroyed origins and thus a diminished capacity for authentic prospects.

Of course having discussed the twin pressures of the past and future, beginnings and endings in the modern critical world, Kafka also masterfully describes the effect this has on the present. The present is characterized in Kafka's world by strange images of stationary movement. The overall effect that Kafka seems to be presenting by the juxtaposition of these contradictory elements is the idea of aimless pursuit, of déjà vu on the move, of the stale and everyday become powerful. Here the words of that modern pessimistic prophet of dilapidated social forms, Louis Ferdinand Céline, become of particular use in framing what is at stake in this modern take on the contemporary and the present. He too saw in travel and constant movement the sad modern condition's impoverished relation to the present, but also sought in it an alleviation of and power over that condition. His masterwork *Journey to the End of the Night,* with its governing relationship between his aimless journey and his bearing witness to the decay of society, provides a message of movement entirely fitting with Kafka's. Celine writes, "That's what moving about, travelling is; it's this inexorable glimpse of existence as it really is during those few lucid hours, so exceptional in the span of human time, when you are leaving the customs of the last country behind you and the other new ones have not yet got their hold on you."[21]

Movement in modern life is characterized by suspension, a novel arrangement where movement of the individual mind arrests that individual's movement in history. It is an inexhaustible search for a lucid state where one isn't tugged from either direction by the customs of old and the future's need for new, worthwhile customs—suspension between two times that guarantees unlimited movement in the present. The modern world wants to instigate these rare and exceptional lucid moments unburdened by history as the permanent state of things. If the world of institutions and tradition was a world rich in a history that seemed

21. Louis Ferdinand Céline, *Journey to the End of the Night* (New York: New Directions, 1960), 213.

to shackle and hinder the free-thinking movement of individuals, the world of critique releases its participants of history's numerous burdens, but allows them movement only in the vapid contemporary, the historically empty day-to-day. In this world, traditions still exist, but have no common circulation; institutions still exist, but they are bewildering and have no rhyme or reason.

Kafka gives us some enduring images of this state of inert movement, of activity combined with stillness. Of the most striking is the statue of justice that is fused with the god of victory that appears in *The Trial*. A figure traditionally viewed as a statue has in this instance been painted, the stony immobility of the monotone statue mutated into the movement of color and line in paint. The figure in the painting is also uncompleted, adding to the impression of further change. Josef notices the inappropriateness of it being painted in pastels, as if the figure wishes to remain elusive, not pinned down with strong shades, but hazily rendered. The blindfold juxtaposed with the act of running, the precise scales juxtaposed with the furious flapping of wings, all give off the uneasy feeling of inapt combination, because "justice has to be motionless or the scales will waver and there's no possibility of correct judgement."[22]

Of course this is an ominous representation of the forces gathered against Josef K., but behind this obvious interpretation, K. is also asking a question of himself and his age. How can he fully appraise the situation he finds himself in when he is constantly on the move, traipsing the city in search of a court that is everywhere? Correct judgment is impaired by the constantly moving referee of critique, a critique that is unmoving in its admission of other referees. Contradictorily, critique is everywhere and it is on the move, and this is what characterizes the present. But the present that critique creates can be a world of power or a world of dejection, and Kafka is careful to show both sides.

What better symbol for the eternal present, the ceaseless movement of the everyday, than the image of the newspaper? Kafka uses this modern object to great effect, as in *The Metamorphosis*, "The person in power at any moment reads or manipulates the newspaper."[23] The baton of familial power is passed throughout the story of *The Metamorphosis* via the newspaper. Gregor's act upon returning to the family after a long

22. Kafka, *The Trial*, 114–15.
23. Kafka, *The Metamorphosis*, 88.

day of work is to relax and read the paper. After a brief period of despondency his father accepts this comfy ceremonial mantle, a crown to his newly acquired employment and his reinstating as the family head. As the family's plight becomes more grim, this most mundane of honors is passed to the obnoxious boarders. Power is contained in a vessel that represents the empty present, the vacuous contemporary. As Mark Twain said, nothing is as old as yesterday's paper. Power belongs only to those who can manage to situate themselves constantly on the knife-edge of the present. The image of the armchair-bound peruser, so somnambulant and snug while the speeding present careers over his sleepy eyes, is another subtle, yet grand expression of movement and stillness, of the type of present bequeathed to moderns by the ceaseless operation of critique. Yet Kafka does not leave the symbol there. Gregor's meal of rubbish and rotting food is served to him upon folded-out newspapers. This is another reminder of the fate of the man who lives in the past in a world obsessed with the present; he is forced to consume his shame as it is presented to him daily and draped upon the everyday. But this is also a biting statement upon the stature and worth of the present in this modern world. It is fit only for that which will be discarded, for garbage that will rot and have no longevity. It will be devoured, not savored, and ultimately forgotten.

But Kafka encapsulates the personal debilitation that follows the modern present best in the profession he confers on Gregor. It is of the utmost importance to Kafka's modern mythmaking that his saddest hero is a traveling salesman, that modern unfortunate depicted as even more weakened and wrecked in Arthur Miller's dagger into the heart of the twentieth century, *Death of a Salesman*. This archetypal figure is the most poignant indictment of modern man's relation to time. Though this character is always on the move, nothing about his life changes. The hotel rooms are a blur of horrible familiarity, each room seemingly identical, with only small touches of variation. That is until he awakes and his world becomes startlingly unfamiliar, bewildering, and disorientating as he waits for his eyes and mind to adjust. His life is planned to the scheduled timetable of trains and buses: tabulated numbers that resemble temporal prison bars. The traveling salesman lives in an eternal present of appointments among the flurry of travel and movement, and yet his life registers no momentous changes, just a hypnotic humdrum rhythm that steadfastly massages mundanity and servitude into his soul. The traveling salesman's experience of the present is a desiccated temporal and historical reality, as all the joy and intensity that the present is capable of bestowing are sucked from it by the thinning past and future. The experience of this creature is entirely analogous to the experience of time that afflicts those modern societies that submit to the pace of constant critical labor. One is loath to go as far as to say that the traveling salesman is reduced to an animalistic existence, yet this extreme extension is what provides all the psychological and existential force behind Kafka's inconceivable story. And animalism and the primitive have a pride of place in a great deal of Kafka's fiction.

"Like a dog" are the famous last words uttered from Josef's mouth. A sudden realization of the primal, brutish existence of the life he had been living and the primal, brutish punishment that has befallen him, until that moment not fully realized. Killed in an unjust manner and submitted to in martyred supplication. But this is a shameful martyrdom, tinged with the cry of a primitive, bestial existence. A beautiful and frightening present, "a decisive moment" that drags into its profundity his past and his future. The animalism that has been his unwitting stock and trade, and the realization that this "shame would outlive him."[24] His past, present, and future contracted into a dishonorable social animalism. This animalism spanning time and ages is a recurrent theme. Think of the animal Odradek, whose name has no fixed origin, no past. The story's hero fears that this seemingly harmless creature of "no fixed abode" will "spool" itself into the lives of his brethren.

Everything that dies has previously had some kind of goal, some kind of activity at which it has worn itself down; with Odradek this is not this case. Is he, for example, likely one day to go rolling down the stairs, trailing thread behind him, at the feet of my children and grandchildren? Clearly he does no harm to anyone; yet the idea of his outliving me ... is one I find almost painful to contemplate.[25]

Harmless, yet feared, the ageless animal will entwine itself surreptitiously among the future generations, the worried fathers of the past unable to prevent this influence upon their brood. The purposelessness of

24. Kafka, *The Trial*, 178.
25. Kafka, *Stories*, 207.

this animal that will not die echoes the aimless working of a critique that once begun will not cease. The fact that Kafka has an animal encapsulate this timelessness says much about how he sees the elimination of history affecting those under its directionless spell. But Kafka's animals are not always so benign, as he has some animals tempting men into horrific deeds. In *Jackals and Arabs,* a traveler from the north is confronted by a pack of jackals who have "been waiting for (him) for ages; my mother waited, and her mother—in fact all their mothers, right back to the mother of all jackals, believe me!"[26] They hand him a pair of scissors to cut the throats of his Arab companions, imploring that he will "end the feud that divides the world." Animals bearing a temptation that they have carried eternally through their ancient bloodlines exist to proffer this perpetual lure to all travelers. Traveling, animalism, temptation, nature made unnatural. This combination of themes reoccurs throughout Kafka's oeuvre, as if he is reading a timeless tendency that has emerged in the severed sinews of history. In this story Kafka also alludes to another theme intimately connected with his ideas of modern animalism: music. The howling of the jackals is said to sound "like a tune."

We recall that Gregor Samsa in his previous human life was saving money to send his sister to a music conservatory. He did this despite having no ear for music himself, admitting to not even possessing an understanding of music; it has no effect upon him. Yet late in the story, when his animal instincts have swamped his human reserve, he falls under the spell of his sister's violin playing. Unable to stop himself from crawling closer to the source of the music, he asks himself, "could he really be an animal, if music affected him so deeply"?

Consider also the "former dog" from *Investigations of a Dog.* A dog looks upon a pack of his kin, whose very movements produce a frightening music, even though they dance in complete silence. It is music that seems to characterize these animals; yet one of their kind (who is at once bewildered by them, but also wishes to study them scientifically) finds their silence "more significant."[27] The same confusion over musicality and animalism is seen in *Josephine the Singer, or The Mouse People.* This story is devoted to meditating upon music's place in a race of "mouse

26. Kafka, *Stories,* 196.
27. Kafka, *Description of a Struggle and The Great Wall of China* (London: Secker and Warburg, 1960), 288.

people," a species of animal lovingly described in human terms. This strange race of mice are "totally unmusical," "not fond of music," and yet there is "no one her singing does not enthrall." Singing is "mentioned in legend," yet "no one can sing them anymore." Josephine, this rare musical individual of "enormous influence," is also accepted by her audience as representing "nothing out of the ordinary." And when she dies she will be "a minor episode in the unending history of our people," a people who "do not go in for history." The first-person narrator of this story is simply rehearsing the issue of how a people can recognize music when it is not in their nature to do so. If music is connected to animality, then the question becomes, how can a people delight in its animality when it has been trained by history to shed this timeless affliction?

Music serves to complicate the issue of animality. Where it is only in animality that music is appreciated, its accompanying feeling and pathos provide the hope of continued humanity. It is in flirting with the confusion of music that Kafka seems to making a point about the modern confusion of the civilized and the uncivilized, the natural and the cultural, the historical and the atemporal. Kafka uses music to demonstrate that the modern world, a world largely prepared by critique and the historical overcoming of tradition, leaves us suspended between a human and an animal existence. We have created ourselves as social animals, not in the sense that we are animals who live together, but in the sense that our ahistorical culture creates for us a new type of timeless animality. We construct ourselves as autonomous beings through the use of critical reason, but in so doing we flirt with an analytical instinct that can only be fostered by a society that brings us closer to the timeless animal kingdom that we supposedly left behind when we codified our history in our societies.

Well aware that he toiled in the "high art" of literature, Kafka had a profound interest in the "low art" of music: with the art that made people move rather than think—civilization fascinated by the uncivilized. Let us not forget that the most musical of philosophers have been theorists of nature and the passionate and vital states that circumvent our civilized veneer. Rousseau, an opera composer and musicologist before a philosopher, is the famous idolizer of the state of nature. The fact that based on this imaginative animal state he sought to regenerate our society through the general will and reawaken our dependence on feeling and passion show clearly the connection between music, nature, and dissatisfaction with society. Nietzsche, the early friend of Wagner and an enthusiastic, yet limited composer, wished to reawaken the Dionysian beast, the "spirit of music," among our pallid societies.[28] Nietzsche's coupling of the rough and animal principle of the will to power with his concern for a robust, artistic, and noble culture is the perfect expression of the animal and its society. He wished to bring into being the new social animalism that Kafka worried about and mused over in his passionately restrained writing.

Kafka even questions whether this new state of nature, this new man created by the historically destructive omnipresence of critique, has helped us in any way progress from our animal origins ... with the verdict mixed and hallucinatory. A warped, overgrown thornbush of progress, animality, freedom, will, history, and enlightenment is weaved for us in Kafka's *A Report for an Academy*. In this story an ape describes his five-year journey from apehood to manhood after being captured: the history of burgeoning humanity writ small and turned on its head, or perhaps a displaced history of critique? The ape opens his report with the destruction of his will that was required for his achievement.

This achievement would have been impossible had I sought wilfully to cling to my origins and to the memories of my youth. Wholesale abdication of my own will was the very first requirement I had set myself; I, a free ape, bowed to that yoke. This in turn, however, had the effect of increasingly cutting me off from my memories.[29]

To become newly human, this ape must surrender his will, or that element that supposedly constitutes our humanity, according to the dictates of the critical universe. By this Kafka also shows us that by solidifying our wills outside of time and history we have in fact become more animal. A history that helped us shed our impertinent instincts is replaced by a civilized instinct for criticism and baseless formal evaluation. Yet the effect for both man and ape is the same. We secure our wills and turn animal, the ape relinquishes his and becomes human, yet we

28. Allan Bloom noticed the musicality of these philosophers and their corresponding ambivalence to civilization in Bloom, *The Closing of the American Mind* (Harmondsworth: Penguin, 1989), 73.

29. Kafka, *Stories*, 219.

both suffer detachment from our origins and memories, and we are both cut from our histories. The comic idea of an ape developing a taste to be human and delivering a speech on this development serves only to make his audience feel ridiculous and question whether they we simply humans who have developed a taste for pretending to be animal. The story implores us to think about our own warped development. And Kafka includes a withering account of our idea of freedom. The ape goes to great pains to say that it was a "way out," not freedom, that he sought in becoming human. He says, "As for me, I neither demanded freedom then nor do I so now. By the way: freedom is something that men all too often dupe themselves with. And as freedom is among the most sublime of feelings, so is the corresponding illusion amongst the most sublime."[30]

Perhaps the freedom allied to critique is no freedom at all, nothing more than a "way out"—a "way out" of the cage of history. In escaping history through a new freedom we may have gained a great many things, but perhaps we have also lost the ability to know and engage with that history. In many ways this examination has simply been a look at the illusory and counterfeit histories that philosophers have sought to replace the living history, and how the idols of critique and freedom are used to help evaporate that living history from our view. Kafka has a proud, yet melancholy talking ape suggest this to us, and makes us question this world of critique we have built around us. The freedom of critique is a burden for us, yet is all we can now invest in, in our ahistorical existence. The ape cries, "Freedom! Certainly such freedom as is possible today is a wretched business. But nevertheless freedom, nevertheless a possession."[31]

In conclusion, Kafka provides us with one last enduring image of critique. We began this chapter describing Kant, his philosophy, and his followers as "surveyors," traversers of borderlands in epistemology and morality, following rightful contours of thought and redirecting others, always tempted by and promised communion with the transcendent. Kafka's "K.," from his unfinished novel *The Castle*, is also one of these "land surveyors," summoned by the castle to ply his profession, yet never admitted into its confines. K.'s quest is one of transcendence and un-

---

30. Kafka, *Stories*, 222.
31. Kafka, *Description of a Struggle and The Great Wall of China*, 289.

reachability, seeking the ultimate vantage point of the castle's height and majesty to carry out his inspection of the lay of the land, yet a complete survey of the world will forever elude him. Instead he remains stalled in a facile world of bureaucracy, banality winning out over transcendence. Courts, land-surveyors, animals, and families: all are used to put forward the same eternal messages by Kafka, the destruction of time and history, and infinite quests taking place in the finitude of secularism. Kafka's world is populated by endless doorways, stairwells, windows, rooms, hallways—locked, open, barred, and beckoning. This labyrinthine, yet enclosed, limited, yet limitless reality is a perfect imaginative expression of worldly infinitude. This unfamiliar infinitude was recognized early in the modern world's movement to the secular and material. Early in the history of humanism, that first flush of secularism in a world dominated by religion, François Rabelais satirized the unnatural, infinite nature of courts long before Kafka despaired their omnipresence.

For the court has not fully sifted all the documents; and the judgement will be given at the next Greek Kalends, that is to say never, because as you know, they can outdo Nature and violate their own articles. For the articles of Paris proclaim that God alone can perform actions without end, and that Nature makes nothing immortal, for she puts a term and a period to all things by her produced; seeing that *all things that rise, set,* &c. But these swallowers of the morning mist make the suits pending before them both infinite and immortal; and by so doing have recalled and confirmed the saying of Chilon the Lacedaemonian, consecrated at Delphi, that misery is the companion of lawsuits, and that those who plead in them are wretched creatures, since they come to the end of their lives long before they attain the rights they lay claim to.[32]

Nature has not made this world we inhabit, its unending and unresolved character, a sign of its creation by a humanity that seeks an intellectual immortality in a material, mortal world. Critique is our modern milieu, our apparatus for this impossible purpose, a state that allows us to live our lives under the spell of rights that will never fully crown us the demigods these rights seem to suggest we are. Attempts to crown our world with these rights by the devotees of Kantian critique have in all instances had to do so with the help of history. History is the only

32. François Rabelais, *The Histories of Gargantua and Pantagruel,* translated by J. M. Cohen (London: Penguin, 1969), 80–81. Words in italic are translated from the Latin.

way to bridge the Kantian gap of finitude and infinitude, nature and culture, phenomena and noumena, knowledge and morality. Unfortunately the tensions of critique make these various attempts at history illusory. This book has been a look at three radical political imaginations that have befogged history in their attempts to come to terms with the mire of Kantianism. Evidence has shown that the attempts by the three figurehead radical theorists Rousseau, Marx, and Foucault to use history to overcome Kantian dichotomies have not been effective. In addition to this, the attempt itself results in the considerable impairment of their understanding of and prescription for history.

As Kafka lays the most significant claim to be the literary genius of the modern age, his work is most capable of uncovering those neuroses, complications, and confidences that are constitutive of our age. This chapter has sought to show that Kafka obliquely comments on the "age of critique" by fleshing out the temporal instabilities that critique necessarily inflicts upon the life of humanity. Undoubtedly, Rousseau, Marx, and Foucault have all attempted to solve the issues around the historical nature of humanity with their philosophically driven forays into the past, present, and future. But these thinkers have explored the unbroken trinity of time separately and abstractly. Because these attempts have been philosophically directed by the ahistorical and atemporal philosophy of Immanuel Kant, their attempts prove stillborn. Kafka consistently seeks to demonstrate the neutered past, present, and future of modern life, and how the psyche of humanity is broken and bent on this fractured and disjointed temporality, a thwarted historical understanding made monstrous by critical endeavor. It remains only to attempt a summary of the lessons from this journey and point toward a way out of the illusions of critical history.

⤳ Conclusion

The Positive and Negative Poles of Critical History

In this conclusion I wish to look back on what may be called the positive and negative poles to which the radical political imagination is attracted. As the philosophies of Rousseau, Marx, and Foucault are all in some significant form of dialogue with Kantianism (even if in all cases either unwitting, clouded, or complex), the positive and negative directions of their radical political theorizing all stem from the common twin sources of Kantian freedom and timelessness. We are concerned here with the effect that this freedom and its constitutional timelessness have upon the formation of historical vision, for what all these projects share is a conflicted desire to expand into history (positive), tempered by an equivalent desire to escape from it (negative). This tension reveals that the positive and negative poles of the radical political imagination sway from one to the other. For the obvious paradox that we have been attempting to uncover in this book is the fact that the radicals' desire to storm the gates of history is powered by an insistent philosophical aversion to temporal and history thinking. Thus they invariably overplay their hand and expand beyond reckoning one dimension of time over and against the others. Thus they also fail to make intelligible a historical reality that is only revealed to those who view time in its Trinitarian unity.

This investigation, as with the thinkers investigated, begins and ends in the midst of a historical reckoning with the Kantian critical philosophy. As the author of many of the political tensions that have been inherited by critical theorists and social radicals for many generations, Kant often figures as the impossible exemplar and herald of political progressives. He is a herald because he provides the foundation upon which modern critical political dispositions find a legitimacy and authority. Yet he is also an impossible exemplar, because after so assuring those thinkers of their purpose, that purpose quickly interns them in a grim philosophical framework. It is in this framework that the radical will find his maneuverings and orientations being thwarted. This great paradox becomes exacerbated in many features of the Kantian philosophy and is found to reside also in its positive and negative implications for critical followers. But the realm where this paradox most awkwardly resounds is in the realm of history.

The Kantian philosophy is a convoluted array of antinomies stemming from his resolute division between phenomena and noumena, the empirical and the ideal. Whichever direction one turns in this diverse dualism, the attempt is always frustrated, for each position holds within it the grounds for its own undermining. As we saw previously, theoretical reason is regulated by ideals that it is not permitted to pursue, while practical reason receives its direction and approval from ideals that divorce it from the world it hopes to transform. Any who are in any way affiliated with the critical enterprise find themselves devising philosophies that internally labor to integrate the warring claims intrinsic to this mode of thought.

The deputing to history for this task, along with all its attendant effects in major political theorists captured by the Kantian procedure, has been the theme of this book. This deferral to history to bridge the schismatic gap between timeless morality and the empirical world is one of the most incapable avenues that Kant employed for the task. This is not because history itself is not capable of resolving the tensions, but because the deferred and abstract way in which history is regarded only perpetuates those tensions. The issue revolves around the fact that the initial moral impulse, whether acknowledged or not, makes history a deferred entity rather than a principal entity; a derivative agent rather than an essential one. In moving out toward historical realm, the radical political imagination treats it in a totalitarian fashion. History must bend to its timeless will. The consequences of appointing history to a timeless undertaking, without inquiring into the primary reality of historical existence in advance, is that incomplete and distorted images of history are all that the undertaking is capable of. I call this movement "positive" because here at least the radical acknowledges the need to embrace history. But the embrace is more like a throttling, and so the breath of history is expired in his hands.

That the political thinkers analyzed in this work accentuate one aspect of time as history's proper sphere of influence is confirmation that such an impasse is being reached in their thought. To so severely reduce the fullness and coverage of history by making it occupy a temporally narrow field, Rousseau, Marx, and Foucault have demonstrated their membership in a politics of critique incapable of comprehensive and flexible historical awareness. To involve ourselves in only one modality of time is to have transacted in a false image of history. Their historical reductions based on the exclusivity of the past, present, or future are simply the necessary consequence of placing too great an emphasis upon the timeless. Because a moral timelessness is the essential feature of these thinkers' projects, history will never be treated as primary, let alone as an equivalent concern to morality. Thus history will forever be corrupted by that timelessness unless some measure, moderation, and mediation can be infused into the timelessness that animates these thinkers. But it is precisely this lack of moderation that constitutes the positive advance of the critical endeavor into history.

While real history is being reduced and impoverished by this procedure, it is being done so in the name of a grandly conceived image of freedom. There is a demonstrativeness with which these thinkers embrace history—a positive enthusiasm to recast history in an image to which history can only be mildly responsive. The timeless is a force that seeks at all times to remake history in its image, but is without the temporal means of historical expression. Thus it must by necessity raise one part of time into its eternal realm and magnify it back upon history. One dimension of the real is accentuated at the expense of the others, and then is grotesquely leveled onto history. Rousseau does this with the past, Marx with the future, and Foucault with the present. This is the overbearing force of the timeless, positively advancing into history and sculpting it with its domineering eternity.

But the radical political imagination also has a negative timeless feature, one that doesn't attempt to historically institute its beliefs or attempt to artificially channel the timeless into history intimidatingly. This negative side doesn't request the creation of a historical space for freedom to exist unfettered, whole, and genuine, but states that freedom can only exist in its pure state as an eternal entity designed to sit aloft from and assist us in the struggle against history. In its negative guise, critique sets itself up as a way of escaping from history. It insists that the operation of freedom be an absolutely undetermined, spontaneous act. Thus it scorns attempts to divine the scope of freedom historically. It requires freedom to remain within the timeless and eternally stand aloof from the machinations of historical processes that may alter and damage it. It is in this sense that it is the opposite of the positive reconstruction of history, because its role is not to reconstruct history, but to impose its impulses to create a breach in history. Critique in its negative guise wishes to be a source of a power that can disrupt history. Rather than commanding history on its own terms, it is responsive to history and provides an escape from its injustices. Freedom here is not a historical reality, but a historically severing instrument, able to bring about an absolutely new beginning, undetermined by the forces of time. Thus it works against the ingrained inertia and devolving of time and history. Rather than seeking consummation in these environments, freedom sets itself up as their supervising idea, with no accountability to or dependability on its claims.

This negative side of critique wishes not to sully itself with extended and overestimated contact with history, not because such endeavors will distort history, but because such contact will dull and dampen the immediate incisive workings of freedom with such historical overreach. But this seemingly more moderate negativity of critique effects its own peculiar and equally distorting move on history. By being so dedicated to rupturing history with its timelessness, it seeks to disrupt history's primary reality as continuity. Freedom as a radical disuniting breach denies history its proper status as overseer of the various correlations between the past, present, and future. It destroys creative and lasting timespans, just as it is involuntarily incapable of enacting its own lasting timespans. Whatever permanence history can confer on reality (and this is not to say that it always can or should) is fundamentally denied by the operation of critical reason. And critical reason abrogates any responsibility it has to institute and make lasting any of the changes it so earnestly wishes to impose.

While the problems of timelessness's positive pole relate to the different illusions of history that its practitioners have summoned, the problems of its negative pole revolve around the issue of institutional reality and the vision of man constructed to counter it. Ultimately the problems of this approach are teased out if one looks at the type of questions that Kantian critical freedom is able to ask of institutional reality. The questions that critical reason asks of reality are of the kind that put to one side the issue of the historical emergence and temporal functioning of the objects it inquires on. As such the forms that its questions take are inquiries into "what" certain phenomena are, "what" is the definition of an institution, "what" is the nature of alienation, and "what" is the constitution of the unalienated man. It seeks an essential unchanging definition to things so as its timeless logic can judge its chosen objects with stability. By conceiving its objects outside of their history, it will of necessity search for definitions that will neglect and deny certain aspects of the object or excessively emphasize one part of its existence. Freedom thus conceived is only ever capable of raising rigid questions about what institutions are, what alienation is, and what an individual may be. Invariably these questions end in dogmatic answers, which will resemble imprecise and abstract denials, affirmations, and anguishes.

In contrast, a historically institutionalist approach asks not a "what," but a "why" of its objects. This guarantees for their answers an open-ended productiveness that is receptive to the demands that time and history make upon reality. To ask a "what is" demands a formality of approach that seeks a definition deaf to the myriad demands made upon it by time. When a seemingly adequate definition is then constructed, it finds itself far too inflexible to perform within the evolutionary (and also revolutionary) flux of time and history. The definition finds itself incapable of the suppleness and engagement that reality demands of it. To ask "why is" is the method of the institutionalist, because this places his question directly into the stream of past, present, and future. By keeping this historical connection intact this approach avoids the timeless critic's problem of always having to break the historical chain of being.

An institutionalist approach understands that institutions encapsulate all four dimensions of time. The eternal is its reason for being, as the institution wishes to install some lesson or insight into history that will live beyond those who instituted it. From here it then seeks with its architecture to place the past, present, and future into a meaningful relationship. This may involve at a certain time and place emphasizing perhaps the past, or maybe the present or future, but never attempting to establish it as the timeless and unchanging reality of history's drift. And while the institutionalist can allow for the historical spontaneity of the atemporal free moral act, he cannot allow for freedom and morality to have no substantial historical and institutional veracity. It has not been my purpose in this study to examine the problematics, paradoxes, and aporias of the historical institutionalist method (where an equal amount of analysis would surely uncover them), but simply to position it in a dialogue with the timeless critique of the radical political imagination so as to explore the intricacies that it inherits from Kantianism. And a look at the positive and negative poles of timeless freedom and its effects on history return us to those diremptions that factor so strongly in the Kantian project.

Posing the question of freedom in isolation from history (negative), but in the same process of thought to triumphantly identify with its necessarily temporally simplified results when combined with history (positive), results in its practitioners excessively overlooking the complex and varied reality of institutional history. This is a conflicted oscillation that mimics the conflicted oscillations of Kant's dualism. Timelessness that seeks out historical expression and understanding ends in illusions of history by emphasizing one aspect of time to the detriment of others (the positive pole). Timelessness that sets itself in conflict with history ends by disrupting the necessary continuity between past, present, and future that is the first condition of real historical awareness (the negative pole). This is the radical political imagination's variant of Kant's difficult conception of a theoretical reason that is regulated by ideals that are barred from its purview and a practical reason that receives its direction and approval from ideals that it cannot adequately institute into the world. Wherever the Kantian timeless freedom turns, it is frustrated in its attempts both to adequately grasp the nature of history and to effectively institute its desire to transform it.

And so the remedy must remain with the historical institutionalist: the one who sees the dualisms of life fused in concrete historical activity; the one who is pushed forward by the past as much as oriented and tied to the future; the one who sees his present informed from both directions; the one who makes his abode in the streams of history, in the knowledge that his constant effort is required to feel at home there; the one who refuses to shelter himself from the gusts of time and the hostilities of history. And perhaps, with time and effort, he can become one of history's hosts, and perhaps be raised upon those gusts.

Appendixes

ROUSSEAU'S NARRATIVE OF HISTORY

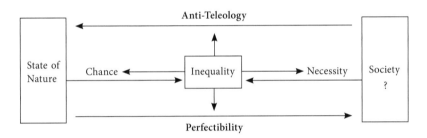

MARX'S ENGINE OF HISTORY

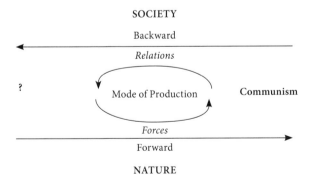

Bibliography

Primary Sources

Alighieri, Dante. *The Divine Comedy*. Part 1, *Hell*. Translated by Dorothy L. Sayers. Harmondsworth: Penguin, 1975.

Aristotle. *The Politics*. London: Penguin Books, 1969.

Baudelaire, Charles. *The Painter of Modern Life and Other Essays*. London: Phaidon, 1964.

Burke, Edmund. *Reflections of the Revolution in France*. London: Penguin, 1986.

Camus, Albert. *The Rebel*. Translated by Anthony Bower. Harmondsworth: Penguin, 1971.

———. *The Outsider*. Translated by Joseph Laredo. Harmondsworth: Penguin, 1982.

———. *The Myth of Sisyphus*. London: Penguin, 2000.

Céline, Louis Ferdinand. *Journey to the End of the Night*. New York: New Directions, 1960.

Diderot, Denis. *The Encyclopedia: Selections*. Edited and translated by Stephen J. Gendzier. New York: Harper and Row, 1967.

Dostoevsky, Fyodor. *Crime and Punishment*. Oxford: Oxford University Press, 1995.

Dreyfus, Hubert L., and Paul Rabinow. *Foucault: A Critical Reader*. Edited by David Couzens Hoy. Oxford: Basil Blackwell, 1986.

Engels, Friedrich. *Dialectic of Nature*. Translated by Clemens Dutt. Moscow: Progress Publishers, 1972.

———. *Karl Marx and Friedrich Engels Collected Works*. Vol. 27, *Engels: 1890–95*. London: Lawrence and Wishart, 1990.

Feuerbach, Ludwig. *The Essence of Christianity*. Translated by George Eliot. New York: Harper and Brothers, 1957.

———. "The Beginning of Philosophy." In *The Fiery Brook: Selected Writings of Ludwig Feuerbach,* translated by Zawar Hanfi. New York: Anchor, Doubleday, 1972.

Foucault, Michel. *Madness and Civilisation*. Translated by Richard Howard. London: Tavistock, 1967.

———. *The Archaeology of Knowledge*. New York: Pantheon, 1972.

———. *Language, Counter-Memory, Practice: Selected Essays and Interviews*.

Edited and with an introduction by Donald F. Bouchard. Ithaca, N.Y.: Cornell University Press, 1980.

———. *Power/Knowledge: Selected Interviews and Other Writings, 1972–1977.* Edited by Colin Gordon. Translated by Colin Gordon, et al. Brighton, Sussex: Harvester Press, 1980.

———. *This Is Not a Pipe.* Translated and edited by James Harkness. Berkeley: University of California Press, 1983.

———. *The Foucault Reader.* Edited by Paul Rabinow. New York: Pantheon Books, 1984.

———. *History of Sexuality.* Vol 2, *The Use of Pleasure.* Translated by Robert Hurley. London: Viking, 1986.

———. *The Order of Things.* London: Tavistock and Routledge, 1989.

———. *Discipline and Punish: The Birth of the Prison.* London: Penguin, 1991.

———. *Language, Counter Memory and Practice.* Ithaca, N.Y.: Cornell University Press, 1992.

———. "The Language of Space." In *Geography, History and the Social Sciences,* edited by Georges B. Benko and Ulf Strohmayer. Dordrecht and Boston: Kluwer, 1995.

———. "Friendship as a Way of Life." In *Ethics: Subjectivity and Truth,* translated by John Johnson, edited by Paul Rabinow. New York: New Press, 1997.

———. "Sexual Choice, Sexual Act." In *Ethics: Subjectivity and Truth,* translated by James O'Higgins, edited by Paul Rabinow. New York: New Press, 1997.

———. "What Is Enlightenment?" In *Ethics: Subjectivity and Truth,* translated by Catherine Porter, edited by Paul Rabinow. New York: New Press, 1997.

———. *Foucault: Aesthetics, Method, and Epistemology.* Edited by James D. Faubion. New York: New Press, 1998.

———. *Fearless Speech.* Edited by Joseph Pearson. Los Angeles: Semiotext(e) [distributed by MIT Press], 2001.

Hamann, Johann Georg. *Hamann: Writings on Philosophy and Language.* Translated and edited by Kenneth Haynes. Cambridge: Cambridge University Press, 2007.

Hegel, G. W. F. *The Philosophy of Right.* Oxford: Oxford University Press, 1979.

Jacobi, Friedrich Heinrich. "Concerning the Doctrine of Spinoza (1785)." In *The Main Philosophical Writings and the Novel* "Allwill." Montreal and Kingston: McGill-Queens University Press, 1994.

———. "David Hume on Faith (Preface, 1815)." In *The Main Philosophical Writings and the Novel* "Allwill." Montreal and Kingston: McGill-Queens University Press, 1994.

———. *The Main Philosophical Writings and the Novel* "Allwill." Translated and with an introduction by George di Giovanni. Montreal and Kingston: McGill-Queens University Press, 1994.

Kafka, Franz. *Description of a Struggle and The Great Wall of China.* London: Secker and Warburg, 1960.

———. *America.* Translated by Willa Muir and Edwin Muir. Introduction by Edwin Muir. London: Penguin, 1976.

———. *Stories 1904–1924.* Translated by J. A. Underwood. London: Abacus, 1981.

———. *The Metamorphosis.* Translated and edited by Stanley Corngold. New York: W. W. Norton, 1996.

———. *The Trial.* Translated by Idris Parry. London: Penguin, 2000.

Kant, Immanuel. *Perpetual Peace.* Translated by M. Campbell Smith. London: Allen and Unwin, 1915.

———. *Critique of Practical Reason.* Chicago: University of Chicago Press, 1949.

——. *Kant On History*. Edited by Lewis White Beck. Indianapolis: Bobbs Merrill, 1963.

——. *The Critique of Pure Reason*. Translated by J. M. D. Meiklejohn. London: Dent, 1986.

Marx, Karl. *Capital*. Vol 1. Moscow: Foreign Languages Publishing House, 1954.

——. *The Poverty of Philosophy*. New York: International Publishers, 1963.

——. *Grundrisse: Foundations of the Critique of Political Economy*. Translated by Martin Nicolaus. Harmondsworth: Penguin, 1973.

——. *Surveys From Exile: Political Writings*. Vol. 2. London: Allen Lane, 1973.

——. *Early Writings*. Translated by Rodney Livingstone and Gregor Bention. New York: Vintage, 1975.

——. "Economic and Philosophical Manuscripts." In *Early Writings,* translated by Rodney Livingstone and Gregor Bention. New York: Vintage, 1975.

Marx, Karl, and Friedrich Engels. *Marx and Engels on Malthus: Selections from the Writings of Marx and Engels Dealing with the Theories of Thomas Robert Malthus*. Edited, with an introduction by R. L. Meek. Translated by Dorothea L. Meek and Ronald L. Meek. London: Lawrence and Wishart, 1953.

——. *The Communist Manifesto*. Harmondsworth: Penguin, 1967.

——. *Collected Works*. Vol. 1. London: Lawrence and Wishart, 1975.

——. *The German Ideology*. Moscow: Progress Publishers, 1976.

Marx, Karl, Friedrich Engels, and Vladimir Lenin. *Marx, Engels, Lenin: On Historical Materialism*. Moscow: Progress, 1972.

McCarthy, Cormac. *Blood Meridian: Or the Evening Redness in the West*. London: Picador, 1990.

Montesquieu, Charles de Secondat. *The Spirit of the Laws*. Cambridge: Cambridge University Press, 1999.

Nietzsche, Friedrich. *Human, All-Too-Human*. Part 2. London: Allen and Unwin, 1924.

——. *The Gay Science*. Cambridge: Cambridge University Press, 2001.

Rabelais, François. *The Histories of Gargantua and Pantagruel*. Translated by J. M. Cohen. London: Penguin, 1969.

Rosenstock-Huessy, Eugen. "Heraclitus to Parmenides." In *I Am an Impure Thinker*. Norwich, Vt.: Argo, 1970.

——. *Speech and Reality*. Norwich, Vt.: Argo, 1970.

——. *The Multiformity of Man*. Norwich, Vt.: Argo, 1973.

——. *The Origin of Speech*. Norwich, Vt.: Argo, 1981.

——. *Rosenstock-Huessy Papers*. Norwich, Vt.: Argo, 1981.

——. *Lifelines: Quotations from the Work of Eugen Rosenstock-Huessy*. Edited by Clinton C. Gardner. Norwich, Vt.: Argo, 1988.

——. *Out of Revolution: Autobiography of Western Man*. Providence, R.I.: Berg, 1993.

Rousseau, Jean-Jacques. *The Political Writings of Jean-Jacques Rousseau*. Cambridge: Cambridge University Press, 1915.

——. *The Social Contract and Discourses*. London: J. M. Dent and Sons, 1938.

——. *Confessions*. Selected and translated with an introduction by J. M. Cohen. London: Penguin, 1953.

——. *Du Contrat Social*. Oxford : Oxford University Press, 1972.

——. *Emile*. Translated by Barbara Foxley. London : J. M. Dent and Sons, 1974.

——. *Reveries of the Solitary Walker*. Selected and translated, with an introduction by Peter France. London: Penguin, 1979.

————. *Rousseau, Judge of Jean-Jacques.* Hanover, N.H.: University Press of New England, 1990.

Rousseau, Jean-Jacques, and Johann Gottfried Herder. *On the Origin of Language.* Chicago: University of Chicago Press, 1966.

Spinoza, Benedict de. *Works of Spinoza.* Translated by R. H. M. Elwes. New York: Dover, 1951.

————. *Ethics.* London: Penguin, 1996.

Tzara, Tristan. *Seven Dada Manifestos and Lampisteries.* Translated by Barbara Wright.

London: John Calder, 1977.

Secondary Sources

Alexander, W. M. *Johann Georg Hamann: Philosophy and Faith.* The Hague: Martinus Nijhoff, 1966.

Alliez, Eric. *Capital Times.* Translated by Georges Van Den Abbeele. Minneapolis and London: University of Minnesota Press, 1996.

Arendt, Hannah. *The Human Condition.* Chicago: University of Chicago Press, 1969.

Arnold, N. Scott. *Marx's Radical Critique of Capitalist Society.* New York: Oxford University Press, 1990.

Avineri, Schlomo. *The Social and Political Thought of Karl Marx.* Cambridge: Cambridge University Press, 1970.

Bakhtin, Mikhail. *Problems of Dostoevsky's Poetics.* Manchester: Manchester University Press, 1984.

————. *Rabelais and His World.* Translated by Helene Iswolsky. Bloomington: Indiana University Press, 1984.

Beck, Lewis White. "Introduction." In *Kant On History.* Indianapolis: Bobbs Merril, 1963.

Beiser, Frederick C. *The Fate of Reason: German Philosophy from Kant to Fichte.* Cambridge, Mass.: Harvard University Press, 1987.

Bell, David. "The Art of Judgement." *Mind* 96, no. 382 (1987): 221–44.

Benjamin, Walter. *Illuminations.* New York: Harcourt, Brace and World, 1968.

Best, Steven. *The Politics of Historical Vision.* New York: Guilford, 1995.

Bird, Graham. *Kant's Theory of Knowledge.* London: Routledge and Kegan Paul, 1962.

Bloom, Allan. *The Closing of the American Mind.* Harmondsworth: Penguin, 1989.

Brazil, William J. *The Young Hegelians.* London: Yale University Press, 1970.

Breckman, Warren, *Marx, the Young Hegelians, and the Origins of Radical Social Theory.* Cambridge: Cambridge University Press, 1999.

Broome, J. H. *Rousseau: A Study of His Thought.* London: Edward Arnold, 1963.

Cameron, David. *The Social Thought of Rousseau and Burke.* London: Weidenfeld and Nicolson, 1973.

Caputo, John D. "On Not Knowing Who We Are: Madness, Hermeneutics and the Night of Truth." In *Michel Foucault and Theology,* edited by James Bernauer and Jeremy Carrette. Aldershot, UK: Ashgate, 2004.

Cartledge, Paul. *Agesilaos and the Crisis of Sparta.* Baltimore: Johns Hopkins University Press, 1987.

Cassirer, Ernst. *Philosophy of the Enlightenment.* Boston: Beacon Press, 1961.

Castel, Robert. "The Two Readings of 'Histoire de la Folie' in France." In *Rewriting the History of Madness,* edited by Arthur Still and Irving Velody. London: Routledge, 1992.

Catley, Robert, and Wayne Cristaudo. *This Great Beast: Progress and the Modern State.* Aldershot, UK, and Sydney: Ashgate, 1997.

Cohen, G. A. *Karl Marx's Theory of History: A Defence.* Oxford: Clarendon Press, 2000.

Coleman-Norton, P. R. "Socialism at Sparta." In *The Greek Political Experience: Studies in the Honor of William Kelly Prentice.* New York: Russell and Russell, 1969.

Colletti, Lucio. "Introduction." In *Early Writings,* translated by Rodney Livingstone and Gregor Benton. New York: Vintage, 1975.

Cone, Carl B. *Burke and the Nature of Politics: The Age of the French Revolution.* Lexington: The University of Kentucky Press, 1964.

Connolly, William E. *Politics and Ambiguity.* Madison: The University of Wisconsin Press, 1987.

Corngold, Stanley. "Kafka's 'The Metamorphosis': Metamorphosis of a Metaphor." In *The Metamorphosis,* translated and edited by Stanley Corngold. New York: W. W. Norton, 1996.

Cristaudo, Wayne. *The Metaphysics of Science and Freedom.* Aldershot, UK: Avebury; Brookfield, Vt.: Gower, 1991.

———. "Hegel, Marx and the Absolute Infinite." *International Studies in Philosophy* 24, no. 1 (1992): 1–16.

Cropsey, Joseph. "Karl Marx." In *History of Political Philosophy,* edited by Leo Strauss and Joseph Cropsey. 3rd ed. Chicago: University of Chicago Press, 1987.

Deleuze, Gilles. *Kant's Critical Philosophy: The Doctrine of the Faculties.* Minneapolis: University of Minnesota Press, 1984.

Dreyfus, Hubert L., and Paul Rabinow. *Michel Foucault: Beyond Structuralism and Hermeneutics.* Chicago: University of Chicago Press, 1983.

Dudley, Donald R. *A History of Cynicism.* London: Bristol Classical Press, 1998.

Eco, Umberto, V. V. Ivanov, and Monica Rector. *Carnival!* Edited by Thomas A. Sebeok. Berlin and New York: Mouton, 1984.

Elden, Stuart. *Mapping the Present.* London: Continuum, 2001.

Ellison, David. *Ethics and Aesthetics in European Modernist Literature.* Cambridge: Cambridge University Press, 2001.

Eribon, Didier. *Michel Foucault.* Translated by Betsy Wing. Cambridge, Mass.: Harvard University Press, 1991.

Flynn, Thomas. "Foucault's Mapping of History." In *The Cambridge Companion to Foucault,* edited by Gary Gutting. Cambridge: Cambridge University Press, 1994.

Fossen, Anthony van. "Globalisation." In *Everlasting Uncertainty: Interrogating the Communist Manifesto 1848–1998,* edited by Geoff Dow and George Lafferty. Annandale NSW: Pluto Press, 1998.

France, Peter. "Introduction." In *Reveries of the Solitary Walker,* by Jean-Jacques Rousseau. Selected and translated by Peter France. London: Penguin, 1979.

Gibbons, Sarah, L. *Kant's Theory of Imagination.* Oxford: Clarendon Press, 1994.

Goodman, Dena. *Criticism in Action: Enlightenment Experiments in Political Writing.* Ithaca: Cornell University Press, 1989.

Gordon, Colin. "Afterword." In *Power/Knowledge,* by Michel Foucault. Brighton, Sussex: Harvester Press, 1980.

Gossman, Lionel. "Time and History in Rousseau." *Studies on Voltaire* 30 (1964): 311–49.

Grandgent, C. H. *Companion to The Divine Comedy.* Edited by Charles S. Singleton. Cambridge, Mass.: Harvard University Press, 1975.

Grimsley, Ronald. "Introduction." In *Du Contrat Social* [The Social Contract]. Oxford: Oxford University Press, 1972.

Gutting, Gary. "Foucault and the History of Madness." In *The Cambridge Companion to Foucault*, edited by Gary Gutting. Cambridge: Cambridge University Press, 1994.

Habermas, Jurgen. *The Philosophical Discourse of Modernity*. Cambridge, Mass.: MIT Press, 1987.

Halle, Louis J. *The Ideological Imagination*. London: Chatto and Windus, 1972.

Hassner, Pierre. "Immanuel Kant." In *History of Political Philosophy*, edited by Leo Strauss and Joseph Cropsey. 3rd ed. Chicago: University of Chicago Press, 1987.

Hindess, B., and P. Hirst. *Mode of Production and Social Formation*. London: Macmillan, 1977.

Hook, Sidney. *From Hegel to Marx: Studies in the Intellectual Development of Karl Marx*. Ann Arbor: The University of Michigan Press, 1968.

Horowitz, Asher. *Rousseau, Nature, and History*. Toronto: University of Toronto Press, 1987.

Hutchings, Kimberly. *Kant, Critique and Politics*. London and New York: Routledge, 1996.

Israel, Jonathon I. *Radical Enlightenment: Philosophy and the Making of Modernity 1650–1750*. Oxford and New York: Oxford University Press, 2001.

Jones, James F. "The Argument as Hermeneutic Quest." In *Rousseau's Dialogues: An Interpretative Essay*. Geneva: Librairie Droz, 1991.

Kamenka, Eugene. *Marxism and Ethics*. London: Macmillan, 1970.

Kumar, Krishan. *Utopia and Anti-Utopia in Modern Times*. Oxford: Basil Blackwell, 1987.

Lowith, Karl. *From Hegel to Nietzsche*. Translated by David E. Green. London: Constable, 1965.

Mandel, Ernst. *The Formation of Economic Thought of Karl Marx*. London: Unwin Brothers, 1971.

Manuel, Frank E., and Fritzie P. Manuel. *Utopian Thought in the Western World*. Cambridge, Mass.: The Belknap Press of Harvard University Press, 1979.

Masters, Roger D. *The Political Philosophy of Rousseau*. Princeton, N.J.: Princeton University Press, 1968.

McLellan, David. "Introduction." *Capital*. Vol 1. Moscow: Foreign Languages Publishing House, 1954.

——. *The Young Hegelians and Karl Marx*. London: Macmillan, 1969.

Melzer, Arthur M. *The Natural Goodness of Man*. Chicago: University of Chicago Press, 1990.

Merquior, J. G. *Foucault*. Los Angeles: University of California Press, 1985.

Navia, Luis E. *Classical Cynicism: A Critical Study*. London: Greenwood Press, 1996.

Nehamas, Alexander. *The Art of Living: Socratic Reflections from Plato to Foucault*. Chicago: University of Chicago Press, 1998.

Nicolaus, Martin. "Foreword." In *Grundrisse: Foundations of the Critique of Political Economy*, by Karl Marx, translated by Martin Nicolaus. London: Allen Lane, 1973.

Norris, Christopher. "'What Is Enlightenment?' Kant According to Foucault." In *The Cambridge Companion to Foucault*, edited by Gary Gutting. New York: Cambridge University Press, 1994.

O'Flaherty, James C. *Unity and Language: A Study in the Philosophy of Johann Georg Hamann*. Chapel Hill: University of North Carolina Press, 1952.

O'Leary, Timothy. *Foucault and the Art of Ethics*. New York and London: Continuum, 2002.

Olney, James. *Memory and Narrative: The Weave of Lifewriting.* Chicago: University of Chicago Press, 1998.

O'Neill, Onora. *Constructions of Reason: Explorations of Kant's Practical Philosophy.* Cambridge: Cambridge University Press, 1989.

Plamenatz, John. *Karl Marx's Philosophy of Man.* Oxford: Clarendon Press, 1975.

Rajchman, John. *Foucault: The Freedom of Philosophy.* New York: Columbia University Press, 1985.

———. *Truth and Eros: Foucault, Lacan and the Question of Ethics.* New York and London: Routledge, 1991.

Rapaczynski, Andrzej. *Nature and Politics: Liberalism in the Philosophies of Hobbes, Locke and Rousseau.* Ithaca, N.Y.: Cornell University Press, 1987.

Relihan, Joel C. "Menippus in Antiquity and the Renaissance." In *The Cynics: The Cynic Movement in Antiquity and Its Legacy,* edited by R. Bracht Branham and Marie-Odile Goulet-Caze. Berkeley: University of California Press, 1996.

Saner, Hans. *Kant's Political Thought: Its Origins and Development.* Translated by E. B. Ashton. Chicago: University of Chicago Press, 1973.

Santer, Eric. "The Writing of Abjection." In *The Metamorphosis,* translated and edited by Stanley Corngold. New York: W. W. Norton, 1996.

Schaper, Eva. "Kant's Schematism Revisted." *Review of Metaphysics* 18, no. 2 (1964): 267–92.

Schmidt, Alfred. *The Concept of Nature in Marx.* London: NLB, 1973.

Shaw, William S. *Marx's Theory of History.* London: Hutchinson, 1978.

Shell, Susan Meld. *The Rights of Reason: A Study of Kant's Philosophy and Politics.* Toronto: University of Toronto Press, 1980.

Shklar, Judith. *Men and Citizens.* Cambridge: Cambridge University Press, 1969.

Stelzig, Eugene L. *The Romantic Subject in Autobiography.* Charlottesville: University Press of Virginia, 2000.

Strauss, Leo. *What Is Political Philosophy?* Glencoe, Ill.: Free Press, 1959.

———. *Natural Right and History.* Chicago: University of Chicago Press, 1963.

Strauss, Leo, and Joeseph Cropsey, eds. *History of Political Philosophy.* 3rd ed. Chicago: University of Chicago Press, 1987.

Strauss, Nina Pelikan. "Transforming Franz Kafka's Metamorphosis." In *The Metamorphosis,* translated and edited by Stanley Corngold. New York: W. W. Norton, 1996.

Talmon, J. L. *The Origins of Totalitarian Democracy.* London: Mercury, 1966.

Taylor, Charles. "Foucault on Freedom and Truth." In *Foucault: A Critical Reader,* edited by David Couzens Hoy. Oxford: Basil Blackwell, 1986.

Temper, Mark J. *Time in Rousseau and Kant.* Geneva: Librarie E. Droz, 1958.

Tucker, Robert C. *The Marxian Revolutionary Idea.* London: Allen and Unwin, 1970.

Vaughan, C. E. "Introduction." In *The Political Writings of Jean-Jacques Rousseau,* edited with notes by C. E. Vaughan. Cambridge: Cambridge University Press, 1915.

Williams, Huntington. *Rousseau and Romantic Autobiography.* Oxford: Oxford University Press, 1983.

Wokler, Robert. "Rousseau and Marx." In *The Nature of Political Theory,* edited by David Miller and Larry Siedentop. Oxford: Clarendon Press, 1983.

Yack, Bernard. *The Longing for Total Revolution.* Princeton: Princeton University Press, 1986.

Index